Zune Game Development Using XNA 3.0

Dan Waters

Zune Game Development Using XNA 3.0

Copyright © 2009 by Dan Waters

ISBN-13 (pbk): 978-1-4302-1861-6

ISBN-13 (electronic): 978-1-4302-1862-3

9 8 7 6 5 4 3 2 1

Lead Editor: Ewan Buckingham
Technical Reviewer: Shane DeSeranno
Editorial Board: Clay Andres, Steve Anglin, Mark Beckner, Ewan Buckingham, Tony Campbell,
    Gary Cornell, Jonathan Gennick, Michelle Lowman, Matthew Moodie, Jeffrey Pepper,
    Frank Pohlmann, Ben Renow-Clarke, Dominic Shakeshaft, Matt Wade, Tom Welsh
Project Manager: Beth Christmas
Copy Editor: Marilyn Smith
Associate Production Director: Kari Brooks-Copony
Production Editor: Ellie Fountain
Compositor: Dina Quan
Proofreader: Liz Welch
Indexer: Carol Burbo
Artist: Kinetic Publishing Services, LLC
Cover Designer: Kurt Krames
Manufacturing Director: Tom Debolski

Distributed to the book trade worldwide by Springer-Verlag New York, Inc., 233 Spring Street, 6th Floor, New York, NY 10013. Phone 1-800-SPRINGER, fax 201-348-4505, e-mail orders-ny@springer-sbm.com, or visit http://www.springeronline.com.

For information on translations, please contact Apress directly at 2855 Telegraph Avenue, Suite 600, Berkeley, CA 94705. Phone 510-549-5930, fax 510-549-5939, e-mail info@apress.com, or visit http://www.apress.com.

Apress and friends of ED books may be purchased in bulk for academic, corporate, or promotional use. eBook versions and licenses are also available for most titles. For more information, reference our Special Bulk Sales–eBook Licensing web page at http://www.apress.com/info/bulksales.

The source code for this book is available to readers at http://www.apress.com. You will need to answer questions pertaining to this book in order to successfully download the code.

This book is dedicated to my baby girl, Sydney. Sydney, when you are old enough to read, you will see that even while writing about all this technical stuff, I was still thinking of you first.

I also dedicate this book to my wife Jasmine, who has supported me through the months of very, very late nights (and a burgeoning energy drink habit) to make the most of this opportunity.

Finally, this book is dedicated to my grandmother Louise, who passed away in 2008. Rest in peace, Grams. We love and miss you very much.

Contents at a Glance

Contents

About the Author

DAN WATERS is an Academic Developer Evangelist at Microsoft, supporting students and educators in Florida, Georgia, Alabama, and Mississippi who use Microsoft technology in (and outside) the classroom. Prior to his work at Microsoft, Dan spent eight years as a developer designing and building business applications for companies in a wide range of vertical industries.

Dan is an avid musician and suffers from an addiction to guitars, which can be spotted in several rooms in his home. He produces electronic music in his spare time.

Dan also enjoys traveling, gaming, bacon (occasionally), and most important, being a proud papa.

About the Technical Reviewer

 **SHANE DESERANNO** is a software developer who has worked at Microsoft for about 10 years. Currently he is working on the Zune Services team. Shane lives in the beautiful town of Snohomish, Washington, with his wife and two children. His other interests include participating in the Society for Creative Anachronism, geocaching, and playing Dungeons & Dragons.

Acknowledgments

I'd like to start out by thanking my family, immediate and extended, for being always kind and understanding, and for encouraging me to develop any talent I may have ever demonstrated: my wife Jasmine for being by my side for the past 10 years unconditionally; my daughter Sydney for being as much a joy as she is an inspiration; my older brother Stephen for opening my eyes early to the potential of a career in technology; my mom Wendy for teaching me big words at a young age; and my dad F.A. for years and years of man-advice, delicious barbecue, guitars, college, and of course, risqué jokes.

I have been fortunate to have some outstanding career mentors over the years. At the University of Texas at Arlington, these included Tom Rethard (whose advice I finally starting to take) and Dr. Carter Tiernan, who took her job as an advisor beyond the requirements.

Early in my career, I was fortunate to work with individuals such as Max Friz, Jason Bentley, Mikael Livingston, and Rupen Sheth, who "broke me in" to the cold, desolate world of IT consulting after the dot-com bust. I still look very favorably upon those days. These guys are some of the smartest and most personable folks I have ever met.

I also want to thank some of my other technical mentors: Brent Lintz, Casey Kramer, and Leigh Sperberg from Software Architects; Anna Swinney, Glen Jones, Brent Wells, and James Patterson from Frito-Lay/PepsiCo, and Keith Brock of Motus Digital (who was and continues to be an incredible influence and role model).

To my colleagues at Microsoft: to all of the US ADE team, you are some of the best friends I've had in my career. Special thanks go to Gus Weber, who has always been a tremendous force on the team and epitomizes the word *execution*. Thanks to Philip DesAutels, who has a keen eye for opportunity and potential where others may see none, and has helped me and my family in so many ways since joining the company. Thanks to Jim Pinkelman, an incredible organizational leader who inspires and mobilizes a large group to get things done in such an affable way.

Of course, this book would not have been possible without an incredible team supporting me. Thanks to Shane DeSeranno for the time he dedicated to this book's correctness; Beth Christmas for keeping me on track; Marilyn Smith for her amazing eagle eyes during the copyedit stage; Dina Quan for the fantastic layout; Ellie Fountain for guiding the book through the production process; and Ewan Buckingham, Fabio-Claudio Ferrachiati, and Joohn Choe for getting the ball rolling.

And thanks to you, dear reader, for picking up this book.

Introduction

Welcome to Zune Game Development Using XNA 3.0, a book that was inspired by two of my lifelong passions: games and music. I was introduced to the wonder of PC games with ground-breaking titles such as Doom and Quake in the mid-1990s, and have been an avid gamer ever since. I was also brought up in a musical family. Over time, I have amassed a collection of guitars, drums, and other musical equipment that has ultimately failed in bringing my dreams of rock stardom to fruition.

I have also attempted to write my own games for different platforms with varying degrees of success. Since 1997, I have made efforts to wrap my head around technologies like DirectX and OpenGL to create a real game. I still have books on my shelf covering DirectX 3.1, game engine design, physics, and calculus. In my initial pursuits, I found it too difficult and time-consuming to learn such technologies with enough depth to be truly effective.

Rather than following my most heartfelt aspiration of making millions as a virtuoso guitar player, I opted for a computer science and engineering education, and became a software developer. I also tabled the idea of creating a real game due to the time investment, which I perceived as unrealistic.

My coding career eventually led me to work at Microsoft. Shortly after I started at Microsoft, XNA Game Studio 1.0 was released. I seized onto this glimmer of hope and made yet another attempt at creating my first real game.

Ten hours into working with XNA Game Studio, I had a rough version of Pong. Sure, Pong is not very impressive, but it has become the *de facto* "Hello World" application for new game developers. The best part was that I was able to see it running on my Xbox 360. At that moment, I was immersed in my own tangible accomplishment.

Microsoft has, in its own words, "democratized game development" to the level where you can build your own games. In the case of the Xbox 360, you can even distribute your games via Xbox Live Arcade Community Games. A new era of game development has dawned. Gone are the days of spending thousands of dollars on hardware and software just to be admitted into the inner circle of "serious" game developers. Microsoft has finally brought the joy of game development to the masses.

XNA Game Studio 3.0 adds support for creating games for the Zune portable media player. This concept is the focus of this book. Zune games bring several interesting concepts to the table. For example, you can listen to non-DRM music from your own library while playing a game, much as you can on the Xbox 360. Perhaps the most exciting element of Zune games is the ability to use the Zune's internal wireless hardware to create *ad hoc* game sessions with other Zunes.

To me, the true beauty of XNA lies in the fact that XNA games are based on the .NET Framework. This means that you can write satisfying, object-oriented code to implement cohesive objects and behaviors, without needing to worry about graphics. This makes your game a great candidate for automated tests, saving you a ton of time. Furthermore, it means that how you implement your game is entirely up to you. There is no right or wrong way to approach a particular problem; there is only the method that works for you and presents a satisfactory result.

The best way to learn XNA, regardless of your target platform, is to practice. Work through examples, try new things, and learn from your own mistakes. This book will help you develop a rich understanding of the XNA Framework and the Zune device, so that you can go on to produce games that are simply awesome.

What This Book Will Teach You

To understand Zune game development, you must first understand the XNA Framework. A good portion of this book is dedicated to the fundamental concepts involved in creating games with the framework.

You will first learn how to create a simple XNA game that you can run on your PC. This will demonstrate the basic concepts of XNA game development and set a course for success on the Zune. As you become more comfortable with XNA and its paradigms, you will learn how to translate those concepts to Zune development.

Not only will you learn about the technical side of game development specifically related to the .NET platform, but you will also get valuable information about tricks and techniques common to all games, including 2D space, trigonometry, sprites, animation, sound, and more.

You will learn all the requisites any eager reader looks for in a book such as this one. I will walk you through the creation of several different Zune games. You will see how to apply some advanced techniques. For example, you will master the music library and gain an understanding of network communications using packets. You will become familiar with the work flow of development and testing with the Zune device.

Developing for any mobile device requires cognizance of the device's limitations. You will need to think differently about input and control, as the Zune has very few physical buttons on it. Also, your personal coding style can greatly impact a device's memory and processor usage. You will learn good coding practices and habits to help you maximize your game's performance. You will develop an understanding of the currently available Zune devices, including their specifications and capabilities. To top things off, you will learn how to polish a Zune game, using graphics, effects, animation, transitions, and advanced input handling.

Zune Game Development Using XNA 3.0 is a comprehensive guide that will take you through the entire game development experience, teaching you important lessons along the way. Reading this book and following the examples will give you the experience and knowledge necessary to become successful in your endeavors with this burgeoning technology. My hope is to inspire you to take the ideas within and build on them to create something new and innovative.

Intended Audience

This book is intended for programmers with varying levels of experience in game development. You should have strong, practical experience with C# or a similar language (but note that C# is the only language currently supported by XNA Game Studio).

Whether you are an intermediate programmer aspiring to write your first game or a seasoned game development professional looking to branch out to a new platform, this book has something valuable to teach you. There is something here for individuals of every skill level, but I expect most readers to possess intermediate coding skills and a basic understanding of (or at least a passion for) games and game development.

The beginner will be introduced to many new programming concepts related to the .NET Framework, such as generic collections and highly structured object-oriented development practices. The beginner will benefit by starting with the first exercise of creating a game for your PC.

The intermediate student will feel sufficiently comfortable with most of the concepts and exercises in this book. Readers at an intermediate level will likely learn some useful new coding practices and will have little difficulty understanding the XNA Framework.

If you are an expert game developer experienced with other platforms such as C++, DirectX, Adobe Flash, or OpenGL, you will find the transition to XNA Game Studio to be a smooth and fulfilling one. You will be pleased to find that the required work to achieve most of your tasks is drastically reduced from what you might expect from your previous experiences with game development. You will be impressed by the consistency and speed with which managed code operates, even on the Zune. This book will serve as a guided reference to help you accomplish things you may have never thought possible in other software packages.

Regardless of your personal skill level or background, this book can help to take your programming and game development skills to the next level and open up new possibilities for single-player or social games.

How to Use This Book

Zune Game Development Using XNA 3.0 is much more than a reference manual. While you should be able to pick the book up at any time and find an example of what you are trying to accomplish, there is a clear path you can take through the book to master Zune game development in a well-rounded manner. This book has been structured in such a way that each concept builds upon the last, although you can jump in at almost any chapter using the downloadable example files.

In the information age, most of us use a search engine to find information on a particular technique. This can cause you to begin using an approach without fully understanding why you are using it; you only know that it works. Later down the road, you may find a bug or unintended behavior related to the usage of such a solution. To address this, I have made sure to highlight not only the how, but also the why.

As a programmer, you likely understand that there is no good substitute for hands-on experience. This book is full of such experiences that will help you make smart and informed decisions about the construction of a game. Rather than robotically enumerating the various methods and objects in the XNA Framework, this book frames the XNA development platform with real examples, real stories, real applications, and real games.

The exercises and knowledge checks provided throughout the chapters are intended to challenge your understanding of the concepts at hand. They are also intended to make you think about further applications in your own gaming goals.

Well-commented source code and documentation are available for every example. Having the code gives you the opportunity to explore and dig deeper. Some exercises suggest that you implement a particular game behavior in an existing project. This allows you to focus on a particular technique, without needing to write an entire game to demonstrate it.

Please feel free to play with and exploit the samples to meet your personal learning goals. By doing so, you may be able to hone your techniques, or even learn something brand new!

Chapter Overview

As I mentioned, you may feel inclined to dive directly into a specific area of interest. Here's what you need to know about how this book is organized and what you can expect to find in each chapter:

Chapter 1, Getting Started: This chapter shows you how to set up your computer for Zune game development. All the software you need is readily available for you to download and install, free of charge.

Chapter 2, Introduction to XNA Game Studio 3.0: In this chapter, you learn about how XNA games are organized from a programming perspective. This helps you gain the necessary context about the XNA platform to begin developing for the Zune.

Chapter 3, Game Content: This chapter covers the creation of assets for your game, including images and sound. It also explores the content pipeline, which is the system that loads and uses your content in the game. Near the end of the chapter, you build your own custom content pipeline extension to support a custom content type.

Chapter 4, Developing for the Zune: In this chapter, you learn about the development process using Zune devices, the Zune specifications, how to handle input and play sounds, and more. In this chapter, you build your first "real" Zune game, called OutBreak.

Chapter 5, XNA Fundamental Game Programming Concepts: This chapter explores some of the most common aspects of game programming, including 2D mathematics, collision detection, game state management and game component classes. At the end of this chapter, you build a more complicated, component-based game called Monkey Feeder.

Chapter 6, Advanced Techniques: This chapter covers some tips, tricks, and advanced techniques that you can apply to Zune games. These include querying device status such as the battery level, using touch gestures, landscape mode, using isolated storage, creating visualizers, and more.

Chapter 7, Final Exercise: Multiplayer Crazy Eights: This chapter brings together all the concepts from the previous chapters into one extended exercise. You will learn how to implement networking, game components, optimization, and advanced drawing techniques into one coherent game that you can play with other Zunes.

This book also has three appendices. Appendix A offers a list of online resources for more information about XNA game development. Appendix B is a quick reference for Zune game development techniques such as animation, input handling, and gesture support. Finally, Appendix C provides the answers to the "Check Your Knowledge" questions in Chapters 2 through 6.

Hardware and Software Considerations

Unlike some other game development platforms, the system requirements for XNA Game Studio 3.0 are easily met by most modern Windows-based systems. XNA Game Studio is actually an add-on to Visual Studio 2008, not a separate application. The system requirements for building games with XNA are mostly the same as the requirements for Visual Studio 2008. Running XNA games on the PC requires some specific hardware capabilities.

Both components of the development package can be obtained at no charge. XNA Game Studio 3.0 is a free product, as is Visual C# 2008 Express Edition (although any variant of Visual Studio 2008 with C# installed is supported).

Most systems running Windows XP (Service Pack 2 or 3) or Windows Vista should be able to develop, test, and deploy games to the Zune. If you are developing a parallel Windows game for faster testing, your video card must support Shader Model 1.1 (2.0 recommended) and DirectX 9.0c. If you plan to develop only for the Zune, you just need to meet the system requirements listed in the following sections. The faster your system is, the faster you'll be able to compile and debug. However, your computer's system configuration will not impact the speed at which your games run on the Zune device.

Visual Studio 2008 System Requirements

Supported architectures are x86 and x64 (WOW). You can use one of the following operating systems:

- Microsoft Windows XP, Service Pack 2 or Service Pack 3
  - Minimum of 192MB of RAM (384MB preferred)
  - At least a 1 GHz processor (1.6 GHz preferred)
- Microsoft Windows Vista or Windows Vista, Service Pack 1
  - Minimum of 768MB of RAM (1GB preferred)
  - At least a 1.6 GHz processor (2.2 GHz preferred)
- Microsoft Windows Server 2003, Service Pack 2
  - Minimum of 768MB of RAM (1GB preferred)
  - At least a 1.6 GHz processor (2.2 GHz preferred)

XNA Game Studio 3.0 System Requirements

Supported architectures are x86 and x64 (WOW). You can use one of the following operating systems:

- Microsoft Windows XP Home, Service Pack 2 or later
- Microsoft Windows XP Professional, Service Pack 2 or later
- Microsoft Windows XP Media Center Edition, Service Pack 2 or later
- Microsoft Windows XP Tablet Edition, Service Pack 2 or later
- Windows Vista Home Basic Edition
- Windows Vista Home Premium Edition
- Windows Vista Business Edition
- Windows Vista Enterprise Edition
- Windows Vista Ultimate Edition

Generally speaking, users running Windows XP Service Pack 2 or later or Windows Vista will have no problems installing or using XNA Game Studio, as long as their system meets the processor and RAM requirements.

Note that although XNA Game Studio may successfully install on Microsoft Windows Server 2003, it is not officially supported for this operating system, and the software may not work as expected.

Language Support

XNA Game Studio 3.0 itself is available only in English, but on Windows Vista, it is supported under any of the available language settings. On Windows XP, XNA Game Studio may fail to install under some language settings.

Administrator Permission Requirements

Administrative elevation is required to install, but not to run, XNA Game Studio.

Required Software

You'll need the following software:

- Visual Studio 2008 (any edition)
- Visual C# 2008 Express Edition

Video Card

To run XNA games on Windows, your video card must support Shader Model 1.1 (2.0 or greater recommended) and DirectX 9.0c.

Zune Requirements

XNA Game Studio 3.0 supports all currently available Zune devices, including first-generation Zunes. To enable gaming functionality on these devices, the firmware must be version 2.5 or later. Firmware updates can be initiated through the Zune PC software (see Chapter 4 for details).

Downloading the Source Code

All of the chapter exercises and examples, complete with all the sound and graphical assets required for the games, can be downloaded from the Apress web site (http://www.apress.com). You can access the source code from this book's details page or find the source code at the following URL (search for Zune): http://www.apress.com/book/sourcecode.

Moving Forward

As you work through this book, you will be armed with many professional-grade skills and techniques for not only mobile game development, but also game development in general. Should you feel inspired to explore more complicated examples or platforms such as the Xbox 360, you can reference the resources suggested throughout the book. Online and printed resources are available to help you achieve your wildest dreams with XNA Game Studio.

If you have questions or wish to start a dialogue, please feel free to contact me through my blog at http://www.danwaters.com. Another good place to get involved in the XNA community is through the official forums at http://creators.xna.com. If you create something that you think really stands out, send me a message through my blog to show it off, and you may even be featured in the XNA community spotlight!

On behalf of the XNA team at Microsoft and the publication team at Apress, I wish you a fun and fulfilling experience learning how to bring innovative new game ideas to life using XNA Game Studio 3.0 and the Zune. Let's get started!

CHAPTER 1

Getting Started

It's time to begin a fun and fulfilling journey into the world of game development! The road ahead is clear and straight, with a few interesting turns to keep you awake and engaged at the wheel. Regardless of your skill level with game development, I am confident that you will pick it up in no time.

Before we get started, think for a moment about how you might categorize yourself. Are you a novice coder, perhaps with some C++, C#, or Visual Basic experience? You will find that writing a game using XNA Game Studio is as challenging as writing any other application, and presents some new challenges of its own.

Are you an intermediate or expert coder who has never touched game programming because it seemed too difficult? Your experience designing and developing other programs will make your transition to XNA Game Studio very easy.

Perhaps you are a seasoned game developer with roots in the world of unmanaged code, such as OpenGL or DirectX. While XNA is not an appropriate platform for, say, Halo 3, you will experience the joy of using a product that allows you to work quickly and accurately, without needing to consult a compendium of formulas and functions.

Maybe you've been working with interpreted languages or scripting platforms to develop games, such as Dynamic HTML (DHTML), Silverlight, Flash, or Java. Developing games with XNA is a beautiful mix of power and practicality, and I know you'll come to love the work flow.

This chapter will get you started with your first XNA game. But first, you need to get the software.

Downloading and Installing the Software

Without question, the first tasks to undertake are downloading and installing the software tools you'll need to build games. The first application you should install is Visual Studio 2008. If you don't have the full Visual Studio 2008 suite, you can download Visual C# 2008 Express Edition.

Note Visual Studio 2005, which is required for a previous version of XNA Game Studio, will not work with XNA Game Studio 3.0. Any version of Visual Studio 2008, including Visual C# 2008 Express Edition, will happily run alongside your current Visual Studio 2005 installation.

If you already have Visual Studio 2008 or Visual C# 2008 Express Edition installed, skip ahead to the section on installing XNA Game Studio 3.0.

Installing Visual Studio 2008

As noted, you have two options for Visual Studio: install a retail copy of Visual Studio 2008 (make sure to install the C# language) or obtain Visual C# 2008 Express. The latter is a free version of Visual Studio 2008, intended for use by nonprofessional developers, enthusiasts, students, and others. Visual C# 2008 Express is just as full-featured as its bigger, more expensive cousins. Here, we'll walk through the steps to install Visual C# 2008 Express. (I'll assume that if you have the retail copy of Visual Studio 2008, it's already installed.)

■**Note** XNA Game Studio currently supports only the C# language. Be sure to download and install Visual C# Express, not Visual Basic Express.

---

1. Go to the Express download page at http://www.microsoft.com/express/download.

2. On the Express download page, navigate to the Visual C# Express download area, as shown in Figure 1-1, and click the Download button. This will begin an installation process that will download the latest version of the product for you. Alternatively, you can also use the Offline Install feature, shown in Figure 1-2, to download the entire Express suite of products at once, if you're interested in exploring other parts of Visual Studio.

Figure 1-1. *Downloading Visual C# 2008 Express Edition*

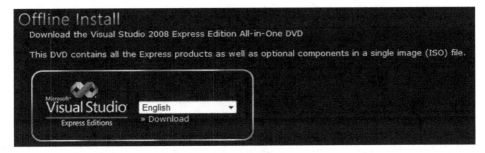

Figure 1-2. *Offline installation of the Visual Studio 2008 Express suite*

3. After the file vcsetup.exe has been successfully downloaded, double-click it to run the setup program.

4. Click Next on the initial screen (see Figure 1-3).

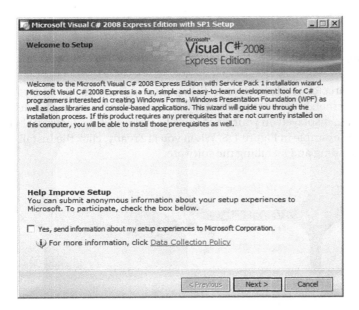

Figure 1-3. *Initial screen of the Visual C# 2008 Express setup application*

5. Read and accept the license terms, as shown in Figure 1-4. Checking the "Allow Visual Studio to receive and display online RSS content" check box means that you will see live news updates and information on the start screen of the application. No personal information is exchanged as a part of this process. Click Next to continue.

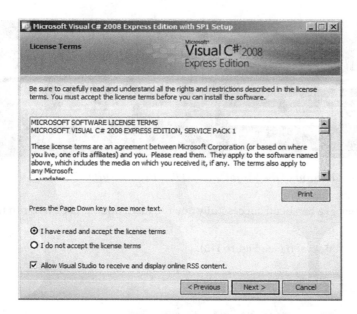

Figure 1-4. *Accepting the license terms of Visual C# 2008 Express*

6. Set the installation directory and check your disk space requirements. Be sure you are connected to the Internet, because the software you need will be downloaded at this time. The information displayed on your screen will likely be slightly different than what is shown in the example in Figure 1-5. When you are ready, click the Install button to begin downloading and installing the software.

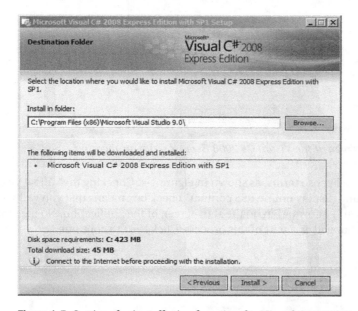

Figure 1-5. *Setting the installation location for Visual C# 2008 Express*

7. The software will begin downloading. If your system requires prerequisites such as the .NET Framework, those prerequisites will be shown in the list of downloads. Also, if you have elected to install SQL Server Express (optional), it will also be downloaded. You will be presented with a screen similar to Figure 1-6, displaying the download progress. After the required files are downloaded, the product will begin installing. In many cases, a reboot may be required after the installation of some prerequisites. Be sure to click the Reboot Now button so that setup can relaunch itself after the reboot.

Note SQL Server Express is not required for the exercises in this book and does not run on the Zune, but you may find it useful in the development of PC games.

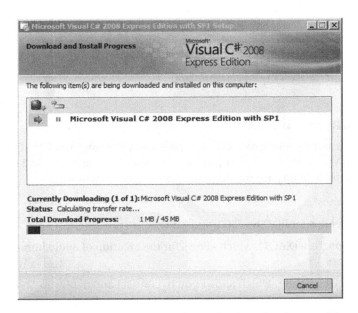

Figure 1-6. *The setup program shows the download status. The contents of this window will vary based on what needs to be installed for your system.*

8. At last, the installation procedure for Visual C# 2008 Express is complete. You'll see a summary screen, similar to Figure 1-7. Again, depending on prerequisites and any options you chose to install, your screen may have more entries. Note the request to register the product within 30 days. It's important to register the product (free of charge) to keep the software working. Click Exit to complete the installation of Visual C# 2008 Express.

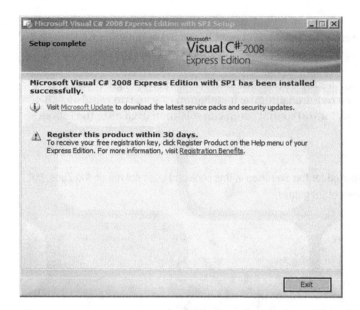

Figure 1-7. *Installation of Visual C# 2008 Express is complete.*

Installing XNA Game Studio 3.0

XNA Game Studio 3.0 is not a stand-alone product, but rather an add-on for Visual Studio 2008. You will be working in Visual Studio 2008 as you write games. XNA Game Studio 3.0 installs everything you need to develop games using XNA, including the following:

- XNA Framework libraries

- C# game project templates for PC, Xbox 360, and Zune

- DirectX Audio Creation Tool (XACT), which allows for the creation of audio libraries for Xbox 360 and PC games

- XNA Game Studio Device Center, which allows you to connect and deploy to Xbox 360 and Zune devices

Continuing in the tradition of other Microsoft nonprofessional developer tools, XNA Game Studio is available free of charge. Here are the steps for installing it:

1. Download the XNA Game Studio 3.0 setup executable from `http://creators.xna.com/en-US/downloads` and run it.

2. The Setup Wizard starts, as shown in Figure 1-8. Click Next to start the installation.

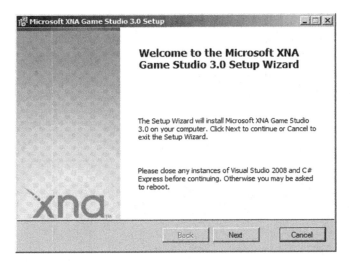

Figure 1-8. *The Microsoft XNA Game Studio 3.0 Setup Wizard walks you through the installation.*

3. The next screen presents the End-User License Agreement (EULA), as shown in Figure 1-9. Read it, accept it, and click Next.

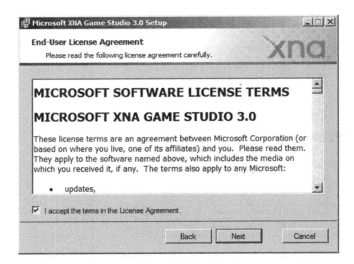

Figure 1-9. *Read and accept the EULA.*

4. On the next screen, you have the option to enable firewall rules to allow communication between other PCs and Xbox consoles running the XNA Framework, as shown in Figure 1-10. Enable these rules and continue.

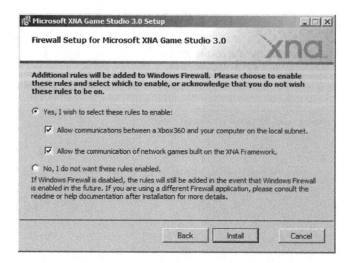

Figure 1-10. *Enable the firewall rules for XNA Game Studio.*

5. The setup program will continue through various phases of installing the software, displaying the status and a progress bar, as shown in Figure 1-11.

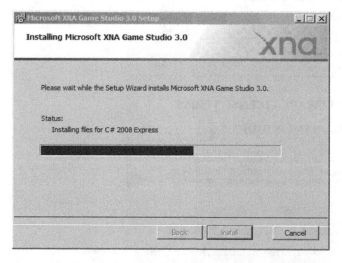

Figure 1-11. *The setup program shows the progress of the software installation.*

6. After a few minutes, the installation will complete, as shown in Figure 1-12. If you wish to visit the Creators Club web site, check the box, and you will be taken there when you click Finish.

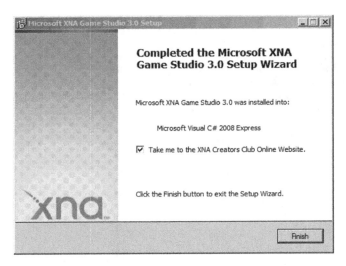

Figure 1-12. *Click Finish to complete XNA Game Studio 3.0 installation.*

XNA Game Studio 3.0 is now successfully installed!

Your First "Game"

Now that the required tools have been installed, it's time to make sure that everything works as expected.

Creating your first "game" in XNA Game Studio is an incredibly easy process. All it involves is selecting a couple of menu items and clicking Run. I'll take you through the very brief process of creating your first game, called Cornflower Blue.

1. Open Visual C# 2008 Express Edition or Visual Studio 2008. After installing XNA Game Studio 3.0, Visual C# 2008 Express can be found in the Programs list under Microsoft XNA Game Studio 3.0. You will be greeted with the program's initial screen as shown in Figure 1-13. If it's your first time running the tool, it will automatically configure the environment for first-time use.

2. Select File ➤ New Project to open the New Project dialog box.

3. Right now, you are just testing to make sure that your software installation works, so let's choose the fastest option for testing. In the Project Types list, make sure you have Visual C# ➤ XNA Game Studio 3.0 selected. Choose Windows Game (3.0) under Visual Studio Installed Templates, as shown in Figure 1-14. This will create a game that runs on your PC.

4. Choose a name for your test game, such as TestingGame.

5. Click OK to create the project.

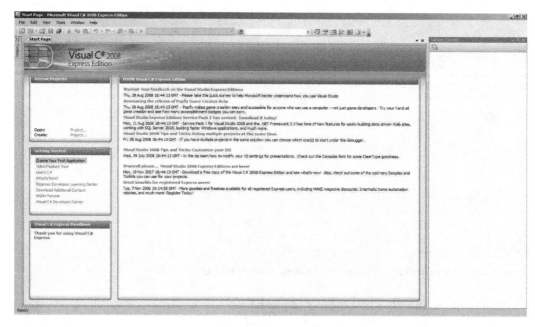

Figure 1-13. *Visual C# 2008 Express running for the first time*

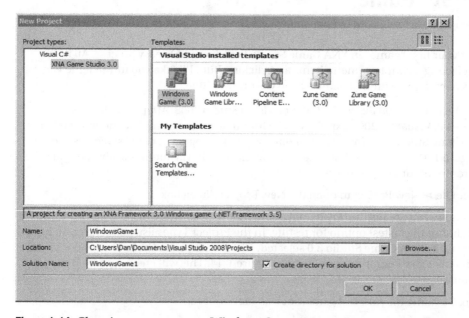

Figure 1-14. *Choosing to create a new Windows Game (3.0) project*

Note that a considerable amount of code already exists for your game. Every XNA game starts with a set of boilerplate code that drastically minimizes the work you need to do to arrive at a functioning game. If you have DirectX or OpenGL experience, perhaps you remember the amount of work required to put your own boilerplate code into a new C++ project: setting up the graphics device, viewports, game loop, and so on. It could be hours, days, or even weeks before you had the most basic outline of a game in an executable format. This is not the case with XNA Game Studio, which starts every project with a working game.

To see how easy XNA has made this process, press F5 to run your game with the debugger on.

Tip If you wish to run your game without debugging, press Ctrl+F5 instead of F5. This will build and run your game more quickly, but it will not load the debugging symbols. You will not be able to catch errors or use any debugging features. Still, it can be a handy tool to use if you don't need to debug.

After you press F5, the game is compiled and then run in debug mode. If your game does not run (meaning you have compile-time errors), address the errors and try again. You will see a window that looks like Figure 1-15, although it will appear in a bright blue color called Cornflower Blue, instead of the grayscale image shown in this book.

Figure 1-15. *Cornflower Blue in all of its glory*

I often demo this as a "next-generation game called Cornflower Blue." When I run through this process before an audience, I refer to Cornflower Blue as "the blue screen of life," a term I attribute to Microsoft XNA Most Valuable Professional (MVP) Bill Reiss.

Don't be fooled into thinking this isn't a real game. Admittedly, it does look like a rectangle painted blue. However, under the hood are the inner workings of a true game. Graphics device setup, clearing the screen to a color (Cornflower Blue, of course), and the game loop are all implemented for you, even in this simple example. Herein lies the inherent power of XNA: you can get started with everything you need in a heartbeat—literally, just a few clicks and keystrokes.

Summary

In this chapter, you learned how to install Visual Studio 2008 and XNA Game Studio 3.0 on your computer. You also learned how to create a very simple game—without writing even a single line of code.

XNA Game Studio 3.0 and Visual C# 2008 Express, both freely available tools, make game development accessible to everyone. Creating a new game is as simple as pointing and clicking, and from there, the sky is the limit. In the next chapter, you will learn more about writing games with the XNA Framework.

■ ■ ■

Introduction to XNA Game Studio 3.0

With Visual Studio 2008 and XNA Game Studio 3.0 installed on your machine, you are now ready to explore game development with a hands-on approach. However, before you begin focusing on Zune-specific programming techniques, you should understand how XNA games work. This chapter deals with the fundamental knowledge required to produce any XNA game, focusing on the major pieces of an XNA game and program flow. Of course, if you are already comfortable developing games with the XNA Framework, you may want to skip ahead to the next chapter.

In this chapter, you will be dealing with XNA in the context of a PC game, so we can concentrate on the basics. In many cases, the code you write will be portable across the PC, Xbox 360, and Zune platforms. One major difference on these platforms, aside from specific optimization concepts, is that XNA games written for the Xbox 360 and Zune run under the .NET Compact Framework, whereas PC games run under the full .NET Framework. This means that PC games can do almost anything a normal .NET application can do.

The Project Structure of an XNA Game

As you saw in the TestingGame project we created at the end of Chapter 1, plenty of boilerplate code comes with a brand-new XNA project. This code is generated automatically by Visual Studio 2008 code-generation tools and the XNA Game Studio game project template you selected. Figure 2-1 shows the Solution Explorer for a new XNA project, and Table 2-1 gives a brief description of each component of the project.

Tip You can bring up the Solution Explorer at any time by choosing View ➤ Solution Explorer. You can also dock the Solution Explorer window by double-clicking its title bar. This is a good idea, because the Solution Explorer is used very frequently.

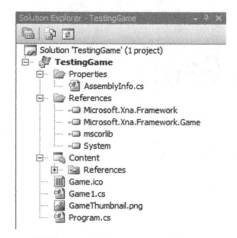

Figure 2-1. *The Solution Explorer view of a new XNA game project*

Table 2-1. *Components of a New XNA Game Project*

Project Component	Description
Properties folder	This folder contains a single file, AssemblyInfo.cs. This is a C# class file that defines some important properties, such as the title, description, author, and version.
References folder	This is a collection of the references to other .NET libraries (called *assemblies*) that your project needs to run. For example, if you are using a third-party physics library, you might add a reference to it here. You can also add references to other .NET projects.
Content folder	This folder is actually a subproject. It maintains its own list of references specific to the XNA content pipeline. It is customary to add your own folders to this project for content assets specific to your game. Content assets are noncode files, such as textures, models, fonts, and audio.
Game1.ico file	This is an icon file consisting of a bitmap image. As in any other Windows application, this icon will be displayed in Windows Explorer and in the upper-left corner of the application (by default).
Game1.cs file	This file contains the definition and implementation for the Game1 class, which inherits from Microsoft.Xna.Framework.Game. This class will be the focus of our first few examples.
GameThumbnail.png file	This graphic is used when your game is deployed to the Zune or Xbox 360. When you are viewing available games on the device, this thumbnail is displayed along with information from AssemblyInfo.cs.
Program.cs file	This file contains the entry point for the game. It creates an instance of the Game1 class and runs it. You also have an opportunity to process any arguments passed to the game, although it is uncommon and rarely necessary to do so.

Each of these files and folders represents a necessary component of any XNA game. You should avoid deleting them, although you can rename Game1.cs to something more meaningful if you like. You are also free to augment the solution in any way you choose, by adding more projects, classes, folders, and files.

Important Methods in an XNA Game

Every XNA game, by default, overrides a few select methods of its base class, Microsoft.Xna. Framework.Game. You should understand what each of these methods does, so that you can put code where it belongs.

OBJECT-ORIENTED PROGRAMMING CONCEPT CHECK: INHERITANCE

If you are new to C#, a *method* is analogous to a C++ or Visual Basic function. A method can take in values, perform calculations with them, and optionally output the results of its calculations. A method can also perform in the same way as a Visual Basic subroutine, in that it encapsulates frequently used code without returning a result.

You should already be familiar with the concept of *inheritance*. Inheritance represents an "is-a" relationship, whereby a parent class imparts fields and behaviors upon those classes that derive from it. A class that defines such overall behaviors is called a *base class*. Classes that inherit from the base class are called *derived* or *concrete* classes.

For example, suppose you are writing an application that draws shapes on the screen. For the application, you create a base class called Shape, as follows:

```
public abstract class Shape
{
    // Public fields
    public int XPosition;
    public int YPosition;
    public string ShapeName;

    // Public
    public abstract void Draw();
}
```

Your Shape class has a position associated with it and a method called Draw. Since your program doesn't know how to draw a generic shape without any information about its lines and points, the Shape class is marked as abstract. This means that you cannot create a new Shape class directly, and any classes derived from Shape must implement the Draw method specifically for that shape.

Continuing with the example, you add a derived class called Square:

```
public class Square : Shape
{
    // Public fields
    public int SideLength;
```

```
// Constructor
public Square(int sideLength, int x, int y)
{
    this.SideLength = sideLength;
    this.XPosition = x;
    this.YPosition = y;
}

// Implementation of the Shape class's Draw method
public override void Draw()
{
    int width = this.SideLength;
    int height = this.SideLength;

    // Draw a square using some real method, for example:
    //
    // DrawRectangle(this.XPosition, this.YPosition, width, height);
    //
    // where DrawRectangle might take top left, top right, width,
    // and height of the rectangle as arguments to the method.
}
}
```

Square derives from Shape and defines some of its own characteristics, such as a new field called SideLength. Square also implements Draw (using the override keyword), which is different from how Circle or Rectangle might go about drawing themselves. Also, Square is a concrete class that can be instantiated, so it must have a constructor.

When using your new Square class, you can instantiate it using the new keyword and the constructor you defined. Then you can call the Draw method directly on the concrete Square class to achieve Square-specific behavior.

The Square class illustrates the flexibility and power of inheritance, which is at the core of .NET development and the XNA Framework in particular. A code sample for this concept is provided with this book's downloadable code, in the Chapter 2 folder, entitled ShapeExample.

To bring this concept back to the subject at hand, let's turn to the Game1 class once again. Game1 inherits from Microsoft.Xna.Framework.Game. The XNA Framework's Game class implements a considerable chunk of game behavior. All you need to do is implement the few methods it asks you to, which are already implemented in your Game class by default.

If you don't already have a new XNA PC game project open, go ahead and create one so that you can follow along with the code. (This project won't be used for anything later in the chapter, so you can feel free to delete it after the method review.) Open the file Game1.cs and begin looking through it.

The only class in this file is the Game1 class, which inherits from Microsoft.Xna.Framework. Game. Accordingly, Game1 implements five important methods that descend from its parent class: Initialize, LoadContent, UnloadContent, Update, and Draw. For now, we'll ignore the two member variables and the constructor, and focus on at the methods that make up an XNA game.

Initialize Method

The Initialize method, shown in Listing 2-1, gives you a place to put any initialization logic that is unrelated to graphics content. It is the first method called by the XNA Framework after the game's constructor, and it is invoked only once during the game.

Listing 2-1. *The Initialize Method of the Game1 Class*

```
protected override void Initialize()
{
    // TODO: Add your initialization logic here
    base.Initialize();
}
```

The Initialize method is an appropriate place to set up objects that do not require content to be passed to them. For example, you could use this method to generate a large lookup table (such as degree-to-radian conversions) to speed up calculations in your game. You could check network availability, set up input mapping, and more. Here, you can also add XNA game components to the game. You will learn more about game components in Chapter 5.

The Initialize method is not appropriate for initializing objects or services that require assets from the content pipeline. This is because, at this point in the game's life cycle, no content has been initialized yet. Content will not be initialized until the LoadContent method, described next, has been called.

LoadContent Method

The LoadContent method, shown in Listing 2-2, is called directly after Initialize, and it occurs only once during the game's life cycle. This is where you load content assets from raw files directly into the content pipeline.

Listing 2-2. *The LoadContent Method of the Game1 Class*

```
protected override void LoadContent()
{
    // Create a new SpriteBatch, which can be used to draw textures.
    spriteBatch = new SpriteBatch(GraphicsDevice);
    // TODO: Use this.Content to load your game content here
}
```

This method will run before anything is drawn. Since any game will always have some startup delay—measurable or not—it is a good idea to load all of your content here to avoid making more work for yourself. Most players will understand if a game takes a little while to start up, but sometimes it can be egregious. In some rare cases, it might make sense for you to load game content in an on-demand fashion, outside this prescribed method.

If you are considering an on-demand loading model, where pieces of content are loaded at different times during the game's execution, you will need to be aware that loading content takes even longer when you do it during game play.

UnloadContent Method

The UnloadContent method, shown in Listing 2-3, is often underused, or not used at all. The XNA content manager class handles disposal of all content assets for you. In some cases, you may be required to allocate resources unrelated to the content manager.

To avoid memory leaks, improve performance, and help the .NET garbage collection process, you should use the UnloadContent method to dispose of any noncontent resources that you have allocated.

Listing 2-3. *The UnloadContent Method of the Game1 Class*

```
protected override void UnloadContent()
{
    // TODO: Unload any non ContentManager content here
}
```

Like the Initialize method, the UnloadContent method is provided as a place to perform a specific task (noncontent resource deallocation). For most simple games, UnloadContent will remain unmodified.

Next, we will explore the two most important methods in any XNA game: Update and Draw.

Update Method

The Update method, shown in Listing 2-4, is the appropriate method to implement the majority of your game logic. This method is called over and over again, at a default rate of 60 times per second, by the XNA Framework.

Nearly every update to the game world should be handled, or at least initiated, in the Update method. The following are some examples of common tasks you might implement here:

- Updating game objects
- Calculating the new positions of on-screen objects
- Playing sounds
- Handling input
- Detecting collisions
- Processing artificial intelligence (computer opponent logic)
- Detecting win conditions
- Managing the game's state
- Updating other objects, such as an audio engine or network session

These are just some examples of things you should do in the Update method. Technically, you are not provided with another place to handle game logic; the only remaining method is Draw.

It is considered good practice to off-load much of your game logic processing into custom classes and methods that you create yourself. You can then invoke these methods from the Update method, leaving Update itself looking fairly clean. The result of squeezing hundreds of lines of game logic into the Update method is not only unreadable, but it will present a veritable maintenance nightmare in short order.

Listing 2-4. *The Update Method of the Game1 Class*

```
protected override void Update(GameTime gameTime)
{
    // Allows the game to exit
    if (GamePad.GetState(PlayerIndex.One).Buttons.Back == ButtonState.Pressed)
        this.Exit();

    // TODO: Add your update logic here
    base.Update(gameTime);
}
```

In this method, the first chunk of code checks the value of the GamePadState returned by a connected Xbox 360 controller or Zune input pad. If the Back button is pressed on one of these devices, the game will exit. If you are writing a PC game, you will need to check the KeyboardState instead of the GamePadState. You will learn more about this in Chapter 4.

The other line of code, base.Update(gameTime), calls the Update method of the base class with a timestamp of the current game time. This allows the game to automatically update any components that have been added to the game.

The Update method also provides one argument of type Microsoft.Xna.Framework. GameTime. The gameTime variable is provided from up on high by the XNA Framework. You do not need to calculate it yourself, and it will always be populated and correct. The gameTime variable allows you to access the game information through its properties:

ElapsedGameTime: Provides the amount of time elapsed since the last call to Update. If you are using a variable-step game loop (explained shortly, in the "XNA Game Flow" section), you may need to access this value. In a fixed-step game loop, the ElapsedGameTime value will generally be equivalent to 1/60 second, unless you have specified it to be something else.

TotalGameTime: Provides the total amount of time that has elapsed since the game started. This property returns a TimeSpan object (part of the .NET Framework). The TimeSpan object is flexible and easily interoperable with other date and time functions within the .NET Framework. It is very easy to retrieve elements of time from years to ticks, whole and partial.

IsRunningSlowly: A Boolean property that you can use to display a message or take other actions if the Update method is overlapping its prescribed update intervals.

■**Note** The ElapsedRealTime and TotalRealTime properties retrieve the "wall-clock" time since the start of the game, although bugs have been reported with this feature in XNA 2.0. If you need to access the true current time, you may be better off using DateTime.Now instead.

Draw Method

The final method in a default XNA project is Draw, shown in Listing 2-5. This method is where you can clear the display and draw fonts, textures, and more. By default, Draw is called as often as possible. Draw may be called more than once before a single call to Update completes. This means that what you see on the screen always reflects the most current game state.

Listing 2-5. *The Draw Method of the Game1 Class*

```
protected override void Draw(GameTime gameTime)
{
    graphics.GraphicsDevice.Clear(Color.CornflowerBlue);

    // TODO: Add your drawing code here

    base.Draw(gameTime);
}
```

The first line of code in this method clears the graphics device to a solid color (Cornflower Blue):

```
graphics.GraphicsDevice.Clear(Color.CornflowerBlue);
```

The graphics device should be cleared every time Draw is called. Not clearing the graphics device means that every frame of the game will be rendered on top of the last. Imagine cutting up a reel of film and stacking each frame on top of the one before it.

The second line invokes the Draw method of the base class, thereby allowing the game to draw any drawable game components. Such components can be used to add postprocessing effects to certain objects.

Graphics, fonts, and other drawable assets are drawn to the graphics device using a SpriteBatch object. This object will be examined briefly over the next few chapters and in detail in Chapter 6.

Now that you know what each of these methods does, let's take a look at where they occur in a game's life cycle.

XNA Game Flow

In a default XNA game, the game flow is easy to understand. It consists of three main parts: startup, game loop, and shutdown. Figure 2-2 shows a simple view of the flow of an XNA game.

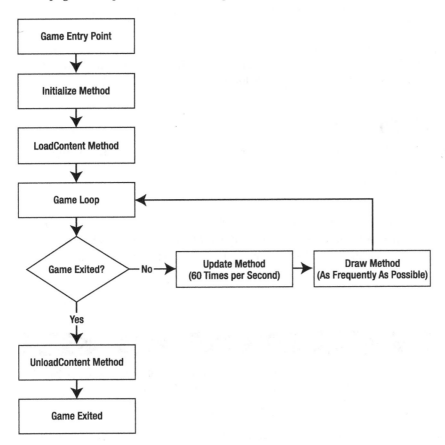

Figure 2-2. *XNA game flow*

The Game.IsFixedTimeStep property setting determines the type of game loop used for your game world. By default, this property is set to true, with an interval of 1/60 second. The frequency of Update and Draw calls is impacted by the value of this property, as follows:

Fixed-step game loop: If IsFixedTimeStep is true, Update will be called at the specified or default interval. This is called a *fixed-step game loop* because the game world is updated at a fixed interval. The Draw method will be called as often as possible. This is largely dependent on how long it takes your graphics device to execute the Draw method. If the Draw method finishes before it is time to call Update again, the game will idle until the next Update. A game idling for 1/60 second, however, is not noticeable to the eye and is nothing like a freeze or a lockup—it is only a means of conserving CPU cycles.

Variable-step game loop: If IsFixedTimeStep is set to false, Update will be called as often as possible instead of at a fixed interval. This is known as a *variable-step game loop* because the time between each update can change. It is entirely dependent on how fast Update completes with each cycle. Using this approach means that any time-sensitive calculations must use the elapsed time since the last Update, rather than relying on the more reliable timings of a fixed-step game loop.

In most cases, it is easiest to leave the IsFixedTimeStep property at its default value of true. Especially for simple games, the accuracy of more reliable timing is much preferred to any other perceived benefits of a variable-step game loop.

Putting It All Together

Now that you understand the crucial elements and flow of an XNA game, it's time to put it all together and create a functioning game.

Note From this point forward, I will refer to both Visual C# 2008 Express Edition and Visual Studio 2008 as *Visual Studio* or *Visual Studio 2008*. This book's examples are created using Visual C# 2008 Express Edition, although nearly all menu commands and other references will be identical for other versions of Visual Studio 2008.

EXERCISE 2-1. A SUPER SIMPLE GAME

In this very simple example, you'll see how to draw a graphic on the screen and animate it with respect to time. (If you want a preview of the game, you can take a peek at Figure 2-5, at the end of this exercise.)

1. In Visual Studio 2008, create a new project by selecting File ➤ New Project.

2. Select C# project types and the XNA Game Studio 3.0 subtype. Then enter SuperSimpleXNAGame as the name for your project, as shown in Figure 2-3. (Note that your location will most likely be different from what is shown in Figure 2-3, and if you are using a full version of Visual Studio, you may have more options available in the left pane.)

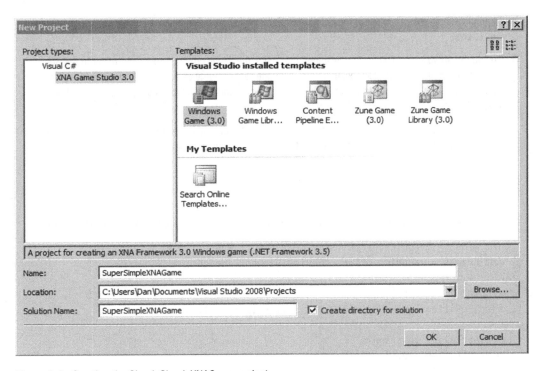

Figure 2-3. *Creating the SimpleSimpleXNAGame project*

3. Click OK to create the project. Visual Studio will churn for a short while, eventually leaving you in the default workspace view. Your Solution Explorer window, with all nodes expanded, should look like Figure 2-4.

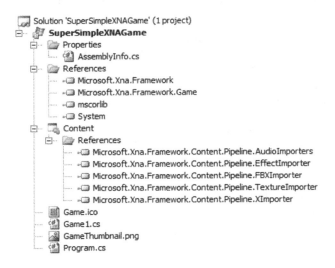

Figure 2-4. *The Solution Explorer window after creating the SuperSimpleXNAGame project*

4. Right-click the Content folder in the Solution Explorer and choose Add ➤ New Folder. Name this new folder Textures.

5. To add the artwork supplied for this example, right-click the newly created Textures folder in the Solution Explorer and choose Add ➤ Existing Item. Navigate to the source code folder Examples/Chapter 2/ Example 1/Artwork. Select the file Block.png and click the Add button. A copy of this file will be created in your Textures folder.

6. In Game1.cs, below the line that declares a new SpriteBatch and just before the constructor, add the following line of code. This code declares a new texture and a position variable.

```
Texture2D blockTexture;
Vector2 blockPosition;
float blockRotation;
```

7. In the Initialize method, replace the line beginning with // TODO: with the following lines of code.

```
int width = graphics.GraphicsDevice.Viewport.Width;
int height = graphics.GraphicsDevice.Viewport.Height;

// Center the block
blockPosition = new Vector2(width / 2, height / 2);

// Initialize rotation
blockRotation = 0.0f;
```

8. In the LoadContent method, replace the line beginning with // TODO: with the following line of code:

```
blockTexture = Content.Load<Texture2D>("Textures/block");
```

9. Rather than just display a cube on the screen, let's make things slightly more interesting by changing the position and rotation on a regular basis. In the Update method, replace the line beginning with // TODO: with the following lines of code:

```
blockPosition.X += (float)Math.Cos(gameTime.TotalRealTime.TotalSeconds);
blockPosition.Y += -(float)Math.Sin(gameTime.TotalRealTime.TotalSeconds);

// Move the object when keys on the keyboard are pressed
if (Keyboard.GetState().IsKeyDown(Keys.Left))
    blockPosition.X -= 1.0f;
if (Keyboard.GetState().IsKeyDown(Keys.Right))
    blockPosition.X += 1.0f;
if (Keyboard.GetState().IsKeyDown(Keys.Up))
    blockPosition.Y -= 1.0f;
if (Keyboard.GetState().IsKeyDown(Keys.Down))
    blockPosition.Y += 1.0f;

// Update rotation
blockRotation += -0.02f;
```

10. To draw the block on the screen, in the Draw method, replace the line beginning with // TODO: with the following lines of code:

```
spriteBatch.Begin();
spriteBatch.Draw(blockTexture, blockPosition, null, Color.White,
    blockRotation, Vector2.Zero, 1.0f, SpriteEffects.None, 0.5f);
spriteBatch.End();
```

11. In the Draw method, change the code Color.CornflowerBlue to another color of your choice, such as Color.Black. You can see a list of default colors by typing Color. (dot) and selecting one from the IntelliSense drop-down list.

12. Press F5 to run the game.

You should see a screen that looks something like Figure 2-5, with an animated block.

Figure 2-5. *SuperSimpleXNAGame running with a moving and rotating cube*

Notice how the block moves in a general path of a circle. You can see this more clearly by commenting out the line that increments the blockRotation variable in the Update method. This circular pattern is due to a mathematical formula, using trigonometry and the gameTime variable, which you have applied to the blockPosition variable. The rotation variable is simply incremented with each game update.

Check Your Knowledge

The following questions will help you apply what you've learned in this chapter to your own games. The answers are supplied in Appendix C.

1. Which object do you use to draw textures to the screen?

2. In which method do you set the initial state and values of objects and fields unrelated to content?

3. How do you change the background color of the game?

4. Which method do you use to change the state of your game on an ongoing basis?

5. The blockRotation variable in Exercise 2-1 is incremented by a scalar value of 0.02. The current time is not assessed or applied to this calculation. You might expect the rotation effect to slow down and speed up with regard to the load on the processor, but this effect is actually smooth. Why is that?

6. When you add an existing content item to the project, the file is not copied and the game references the file's original location. True or false?

7. Which object can you use to access the elapsed time in your game?

8. Which type represents a two-dimensional graphic?

9. Which method must you call to start drawing to a SpriteBatch object?

10. In which method do you initialize objects that hold references to content (such as textures)?

Summary

In this chapter, you learned about the fundamental concepts in the XNA Game Framework that compose any game written with it. You learned about the following:

- XNA game project structure
- The Initialize method
- The LoadContent method
- The UnloadContent method
- The Update method
- The Draw method
- How to create a simple XNA game for the PC

In the next chapter, you will learn about content in XNA. You will understand the XNA content pipeline, importers, processors, graphics, fonts, sounds, and everything in between, topped off with another hands-on example.

CHAPTER 3

∎∎∎

Game Content

The cornerstone of a good-looking game on any platform is the content. Sure, you could create an entirely text-based game for the Zune, but we're in the twenty-first century now! Of course, 30 years from now, when you pick up this book and read it for nostalgic reasons, you might have something to say about this formerly cutting-edge technology.

A game without interesting content in this day and age is like a song without music. The images your players see, the music they hear, the sound effects you play, and even the fonts they read can have an impact on their overall experience. Even if it's on a subconscious level, content can make a huge difference in a user's mental evaluation of your game.

Content is inextricably linked in many ways to the user interface. How many times have you played a game for the PC or a console and noticed that the game just didn't feel or look right? How did that impact your personal impression of the game?

In this chapter, you will learn about content—what it is, how to get it into your game, how to use it effectively, and more.

What Is Content?

The word *content* can mean a lot of things in different contexts. In the context of XNA, *content* refers to the artwork, music, sounds, fonts, textures, animations, models, effects, and other audio or visual elements that give your game that unique character.

These content elements are individually known as *assets*. Components and other dynamic elements, which are generally executed at runtime, are not commonly classified as assets. Therefore, they fall into a different category from content (usually effects). The exception to this is the effect type, which allows you to create a custom rendering effect for an object on the Xbox 360 and PC platforms. Such effects are imported to and processed by the XNA content pipeline (discussed in detail later in this chapter), as any other asset would be.

The following are some asset types that are commonly used in XNA games:

- Image files
- WAV and MP3 files (used primarily on the Zune)
- XACT audio packages (PC and Xbox 360 only)
- 3D models (PC and Xbox 360 only)
- Font files

- Effects files (PC and Xbox 360 only)

- XML files (sometimes used as a lightweight database or storage medium on the Zune)

Note On the Zune, only 2D graphical elements are supported. This means that Zune games cannot have 3D models or viewports in them.

These assets are really all you need to build a full-featured game for the Zune. It all comes down to manipulating pretty graphics on the screen and playing sounds, and these content types provide you with everything you need to do that.

Now let's take a closer look at each of these content types.

Types of Content

You can use many different kinds of content to spice up your game. Your choices on the Zune are only slightly limited by the Zune's hardware. Specifically, the Zune (at the time of this writing) does not have a graphics acceleration chip or advanced sound capabilities, meaning you cannot use 3D graphics or 3D sound.

Here, we'll look at adding images, audio, fonts, effects, and XML data to XNA games designed to play on the Zune.

Note The Zune does not support the rendering of 3D models, but they are an important part of XNA games on other platforms. File formats for models include X, FBX, XSI, and others. Many of these file formats are supported by default. 3D models are usually created by professional 3D modeling tools such as Autodesk 3ds Max, Autodesk AutoCAD, NewTek LightWave, Blender, Autodesk Softimage XSI, and the free Softimage XSI Mod Tool, which has built-in XNA integration for PC and Xbox 360 games.

Images

Images are perhaps the most common type of content asset that you will create (or have created for you) in the process of developing any game. Much of what you will see in this book is what I like to call "programmer art," which is a slightly derogatory term for art produced by people who are not artists. Individuals fitting the programmer archetype often hack out scrap art, which they intend to refine later, only to find that same scrap art living on in final versions of the game.

A truly successful game endeavor will have the programmer focused on programming, with an artist or two creating professional art assets. If you are one of the blessed few who have above-average art skills combined with well-refined programming acumen, consider yourself very lucky. Not only are you set up perfectly to produce your own XNA games largely by yourself, but a person with your skill set is in very high demand across the game industry!

What Images Are Used For

As previously mentioned, images really are the cornerstone of a player's interaction with your game. In your games, you can use images for the following applications:

- Game background
- Layering items in a user interface
- User interface elements (buttons, skins, and so on)
- Sprites (2D textures drawn on the screen to represent a game object)
- Animations

All images are really the same—a digital representation of some graphic—but how you use them in your game can vary greatly.

In Zune terms, you will almost always be working with the `Texture2D` object. `Texture2D` represents, well, a two-dimensional texture.

OF TEXTURES, SPRITES, AND IMAGES

You might be wondering why a texture is called what it is. The word *texture* conjures images of touching a surface—of having a tactile interaction with an object to learn what it feels like. A texture is usually used in the context of a 3D model. It's a graphic that is designed to give a particular appearance to a 3D shape. For example, in many shooter games, the world is "textured" with dirt, diamond-plated metal, crime scene tape, or other cool-looking industrial materials. Somewhere in the game is a 2D image file that is mapped onto that surface.

Due to the lack of 3D support in the Zune hardware, we will deal with only 2D surfaces. In a two-dimensional context, a 2D texture is drawn on a 2D surface, so in any case, you're just drawing an image on the screen. Accordingly, you can think of sprites, textures, and images as all being the same thing!

A *sprite* is commonly used to refer to an image as an active element in your game. Characters, projectiles, walls, enemies, and other game objects are drawn as sprites. While a static background texture is technically a sprite, that word is normally reserved for active game elements. A sprite always refers to a 2D graphics element.

In mythology, a sprite is a hyper and annoying little creature such as an elf, pixie, or imp. It makes sense that sprites usually have animations associated with them.

Supported Image File Types

The XNA Framework supports several different image file formats. Some are better than others for different purposes. Each of these file formats can be used to populate a `Texture2D` object. Generally speaking, the PNG format is preferred for new graphics. PNG graphics look nice, have excellent transparency support, and are easily created by most digital art programs.

The following image file types are supported:

PNG: The Portable Network Graphics (PNG) format has been around since the 1990s, and has lately become very popular for lossless graphics that require transparency. Many XNA game developers prefer PNG images because of their small file size, transparency features, and very efficient lossless compression. PNG graphics are still raster images, so scaling them up will lead to some pixelation. The graphics used in the examples in this book are in PNG or JPEG format.

JPG and JPEG: The JPEG Interchange Format, created by the Joint Photographic Experts Group in 1992, is most commonly used today to store photographs taken by digital cameras. JPEG images are compressed with some image quality loss, and transparency is not supported. If you have a JPEG image that you wish to use in your game as a background or similar graphic, the XNA content pipeline will have no problems importing it. However, this format is not preferred for sprites or other objects that may scale or require transparency.

BMP: Bitmap files are raw, uncompressed image files. The format has been around since the early days of Windows and OS/2. The color palettes in bitmap files are very limited, and the file sizes of most bitmaps are huge compared to other file formats. It's hard to make a bitmap image look good, so any bitmap assets you have should be converted to PNG and touched up before including them in your game.

DIB: A device-independent bitmap (DIB) is another extension for the BMP format.

DDS: The DirectDraw Surface (DDS) format is specific to DirectX technology and is commonly used in games that utilize DirectX. These files sport a transparency channel, just as PNG files do. If you are familiar with DirectX content types and know how to create DDS images, this format will work just fine for you in XNA.

HDR: The High Dynamic Range (HDR) file format is generally used by professional photographers to support a higher level of image contrast. High-end photo-editing programs such as Adobe Photoshop CS2 and CS3 support HDR images.

PFM: PFM files are portable bitmap files that can be created and read using Adobe's Creative Suite.

PPM: Portable Pixel Map (PPM) files are portable bitmap files used by tools such as Adobe Creative Suite and ULead PhotoImpact.

TGA: The TGA (or TARGA) file format, like DDS, has been used in many games throughout the years to store textures. TGA is rather antiquated compared to PNG. TGA does support transparency, but its color depth is limited compared to that of PNG. As with the DDS format, if you have assets in this format that you wish to use, the XNA content pipeline will process them for you without any problems.

How to Create Images

Many programs allow you to create graphical assets in the appropriate file formats. Most artists will use a tool like Adobe Illustrator or Adobe Photoshop to create PNG or TGA files requiring transparency. JPEG files can be created by just about any imaging program, including Microsoft Paint. The free tool Paint.NET, based on the .NET Framework, can also create most of these files, including transparent PNGs. DDS files are created exclusively by the DirectX libraries, by the DirectX Texture Tool.

We will be using Paint.NET in a few examples to create some low-grade "programmer art." Adobe Illustrator and Adobe Photoshop, while likely candidates for real-world use, are cost-prohibitive—we are trying to "keep it free" in this book!

A WORD ABOUT TRANSPARENCY

Before the glorious advent of alpha channels in graphics, the effect of transparency was achieved much like the green- and blue-screen effects of modern filmography. The transparent area of the graphic was filled with a specific color, such as pure green. Then, at runtime, pixels of that color were simply not drawn. Anything drawn to the graphics device before the "transparent" graphic appeared to be under it.

Thanks to file formats such as PNG and TGA, art can be conceived with transparency from the very beginning, eliminating the need to specify transparent areas or colors. Especially with PNG graphics, areas of an image can be fully transparent, slightly transparent, or opaque. This means that you can apply a drop-shadow effect in an image, for example, and see that effect seamlessly, regardless of what is behind it.

Let's look at some graphics that illustrate the concept of transparency (although since they are not in color, it may be difficult for you to discern some differences). First up is a sprite with no transparency drawn on a background. Notice the ugly white box surrounding the sprite.

The following shows the same sprite saved with an alpha channel as the background. Notice how smooth it is.

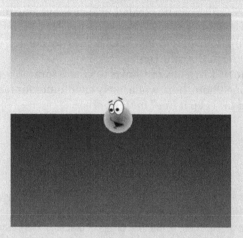

Finally, take a look at the same sprite with a drop shadow prerendered in the graphics program. Notice that the drop shadow is not baked onto any particular background color; the transparency gradient is accurate no matter what is beneath it.

Transparency is defined in the image-editing software used to create the asset. In order to ensure that all sprites in the sprite batch are blending together correctly using the textures' alpha channels, you need to modify but one line of code. Enabling alpha blending in XNA is easy. When you start drawing to a SpriteBatch object, you should use this overload of the Begin method:

```
spriteBatch.Begin(SpriteBlendMode.AlphaBlend);
```

This ensures that all the sprites drawn in this batch will have their alpha channels properly utilized, and transparency will work perfectly. Life is much easier thanks to these more advanced image file formats and the XNA Framework.

Animated Sprites

Animated sprites have a texture associated with them called a *sprite sheet* (also referred to as a *character sheet, animation sheet,* or other similar terms). Sprite sheets can be visually divided into a grid, usually one row with several columns. Each of these cells in the grid is one frame of a particular animation.

Figure 3-1 shows an example of a sprite sheet. This sprite sheet is a single image file that contains a simple "jump" animation for a stick figure.

Figure 3-1. *An example of a sprite sheet*

The image in Figure 3-1 can be logically divided into subimages, just by looking at it. This sprite sheet was created with the assumption that the stick figure occupies a space 40 pixels wide by 120 pixels high. Each of the visual columns, shown in Figure 3-2, is 40 by 120 pixels. As you can see, this sprite sheet has 13 frames in its animation. Of course, you wouldn't draw this entire texture to the screen at once, or you would see Figure 3-1 in your game.

Figure 3-2. *A sprite sheet visually divided into 13 frames*

When you draw a sprite, you have an option to specify a *source rectangle* and a *destination rectangle*. The source rectangle is the area of the sprite you would like to draw. The destination rectangle is the area of the screen to which you would like to draw.

In Figure 3-3, you see that the third frame is visually highlighted. If you were drawing the third frame of the animation, this is the portion of the texture that would be drawn.

Figure 3-3. *The third frame of the sprite sheet is shown.*

It's easy to develop a quick animation utility to loop through the frames of these sprites. This is done by determining which frame to draw, and then calculating the source rectangle to grab from the sprite. Since every frame is the same width and height, you can calculate the source rectangle easily using code similar to this:

```
Rectangle sourceRect = new Rectangle(
    frameIndex * width, 0, width, height);
```

I mentioned earlier that this particular sprite is composed of frames that are 40 pixels wide by 120 pixels high. The total image width is 13 frames × 40 pixels = 520 pixels wide. In the construction of a new rectangle, you must specify the x and y position of the top-left corner, the width, and the height of the rectangle.

The only variable in this case is the first argument: the x position of the top-left corner. The y position of the top-left corner will always be zero; the width of the rectangle will always be equal to `width`; the height of the rectangle will always be equal to `height`. Multiplying `frameIndex` by the width obtains the x position of the current frame. At frame 0, the x position will be 0. At frame 3, as shown in Figure 3-3, the x position would be 40 × 3, or 120. The resulting rectangle for frame 3 is drawn at (120, 0) and has the specified `width` and `height`.

These concepts lay the groundwork for creating animated sprites. There is currently no functionality built in to the XNA Framework for animated sprites, so you must write your own. In the example at the end of this chapter, we'll create a basic animated sprite class that you can use in your own games.

Image File Considerations for Zune

While, technically, you can use any supported image type in your Zune game, you should be aware of some best practices for using images on this platform:

Use a resolution of 240 by 320: The Zune display has a resolution of 240 pixels by 320 pixels. Therefore, to avoid unnatural scaling of backgrounds and other full-screen sprites, you should condense these to a resolution of 240 by 320. It's also extremely useful to draft out your user interface on a 240 by 320 canvas in your art program. That way, you can ensure that your game objects fit into this limited space in a visually appealing way.

Avoid large gradients: The Zune display supports up to 65,536 colors (16-bit color). If you are using images with 32-bit color, they will be properly loaded, but downsampled at runtime to 16 bits with an 8-bit alpha channel. It's a good idea to avoid using large gradients in your artwork, as the downsampling will probably produce some unsightly banding in the gradient. Figure 3-4 shows an example of a background you might create with 32-bit color. Figure 3-5 shows what this same image might look like when rendered in 16-bit color on the Zune device, illustrating the unsightly *banding* effect.

Figure 3-4. *A 32-bit color background image for the Zune*

Figure 3-5. *The background image in Figure 3-4 rendered on the Zune in 16-bit color*

Audio

Like graphics, audio can make a big difference in a player's gaming experience. Think about your favorite first-person shooter game, where hearing footsteps behind you is crucial to survival, or a game like Chess, where you need an auditory indication that time is running out. Audio augments and enhances the game-playing experience.

That said, you should understand an important insight into the role of audio in a Zune game. On PC and Xbox games, the likelihood of the player having muted audio or no audio at all is relatively inconsequential. It is expected that these gamers have speakers, and the majority of them expect to hear professional sound in the game. Playing a soundless game on the Xbox 360 can be eerily lonesome. The caveat with Zunes is that they have no internal speaker; everything is transmitted through the headphones or some external speaker connected to the headphone jack. Therefore, there could be many situations in which a player decides to play your game without audio, in a setting where headphone use may not be appropriate or possible. This means that the likelihood of Zune gamers playing with no sound is substantially higher than that of gamers using other devices. A possible work-around for this scenario is the inclusion of a "silent mode" in your game, where audio cues are instead delivered as more prominent visual cues.

The Zune is first and foremost a music player. In any case, audio is important and should not be ignored just because some users may not always wear their headphones. Consider all those folks on long flights who need all the sound they can get! The value of the environment that effective sound adds to a game is undeniable.

What Audio Is Used For

Audio is used for three basic purposes:

- Audio provides consistent sound during the game. This can be background music or ambient noise.

- Sound effects can and should be used to indicate actions that transpire in your game, such as a collision, an object spawning, the firing of a projectile, or as a supplement to an animation sequence.

- The use of audio can be effective to draw the user's attention to a specific activity or required input, such as the appearance of a window that demands confirmation, a change in turns, or the end of the game.

Supported Audio File Types

In PC and Xbox games, all of the audio used in the entire game is usually stored in one or more packages in the XACT Audio Project (XAP) format. An XAP file is created by the XACT program. XACT is included with XNA Game Studio and also in the DirectX Software Development Kit (SDK).

XACT is extremely powerful for managing nearly every aspect of a game's soundscape, but it is geared more toward the development of 3D audio and full-audio packages. XACT is also a very complicated tool to begin learning; it's really a full-fledged development environment for sounds.

The Zune device currently does not support the components of the DirectX audio subsystem required for an XACT project. This is good news for Zune developers who are more interested in putting together a working game than spending untold hours learning XACT and tweaking audio projects. For this reason, we'll leave XACT alone in this book (aside from the background information) and move on to things we can use.

On the Zune, you have three options for playing audio:

WAV: The good old-fashioned WAV file is the stalwart champion of the SoundEffect class. Any standard WAV file can be loaded and played on demand as a sound effect. Try to keep file size down when creating WAV files. Storage is limited on the Zune, so you don't want several hundred megabytes of WAV-formatted sound effects encroaching on your music library's territory. Keep sound effects short, and don't save them at unnecessarily high quality. The less data your game needs to load, the faster it will start.

■**Caution** WAV files can be very large. Loading them in an on-demand fashion can cause your game to run very slowly as it reads the file into memory.

MP3: MP3 files can be loaded into the content pipeline and played using the Song and MediaPlayer classes. If you are loading a file from memory, there will be a short delay before the MP3 sound is played for the first time (after that, it is cached and will play instantly). This makes the MP3 format ideal for your custom game music, and not so ideal for sound effects. If the MP3 is protected by Digital Rights Management (DRM), it cannot be played.

User's media library: Songs from the user's media library that are not protected by DRM can be played at any time during the game using the MediaLibrary, MediaPlayer, and Song classes provided by the XNA Framework.

How to Create Audio Files

Audio files can be created by all kinds of programs, such as the basic Windows Sound Recorder, the open source Audacity, and of course, more powerful tool sets such as Adobe Audition. You can create your own audio files and save them as WAV files (for sound effects) or create custom music.

■**Note** The creative process of making sound effects is called *foley* in the entertainment and gaming industries.

Fonts

Just about any game needs to display dynamic text on the screen at some point. You can avoid using fonts altogether by baking text into images, but having the ability to write a string to the screen is a useful and necessary tenet of game development.

In the first version of XNA Game Studio, there was no direct support for fonts. If you wanted to draw a string to the screen, you had to selectively draw areas of a large texture that had nearly every character of the font in it. The inclusion of rasterized fonts was such an obvious feature request that the XNA team implemented the SpriteFont object in the XNA Game Studio version 1.1 refresh release.

Any font that is installed on your development machine can be used in an XNA game. When the game is compiled, the font is converted to a packaged format that can be deployed to your destination platform (including the Zune). This means that any font you use will always be packaged with your game, eliminating the need for users to have specific fonts installed. In the case of the Zune, there is no real font infrastructure as there is on Windows, so this packaging is not only helpful, but necessary.

Adding font support to your game is as easy as adding a new sprite font item to your Content project. The name you specify when adding this item should map to the name of the font, such as Arial, Tahoma, or Gill Sans MT. The .spritefont file itself is actually an XML description of the font. This file includes the font name, font size, and the sets of characters to include in the packaged font.

If your game requires that the same font be drawn at drastically different sizes, it's a good practice to include two different sprite font items in the Content project. Text drawn with the font is eventually rasterized as a sprite (hence the name *sprite font*), so an 8-point font scaled up to 14 points will look pixelated and unpleasant. A difference of one or two points might not be noticeable to the eye, however.

Effects

The surfaces of 3D models usually have properties that define how the graphics card should shade them. These properties are applied by runtime effects called *shaders*. Shaders for DirectX are written in a language called High Level Shading Language (HLSL), usually in effects files with the .fx extension. Shaders define how the surface absorbs and reflects light from the surrounding light sources in the scene.

Because the Zune has no graphics hardware to support shaders of any kind, effects of this type won't work. Shaders also depend on lighting in a three-dimensional space, which the Zune cannot yet comprehend.

Instead of effect files written in a shader language like HLSL, effects applied to 2D sprites on the Zune are often accomplished using runtime components that are added to the game. Such components can give sprites particle systems, glows, shadows, and more. Components will be described in detail in Chapter 5.

XML Data

XML is a structured data format that is composed of text. XML is a powerful way of storing custom data. You can use this data to initialize strings, sprite positions, and other items that you would just feel bad about hard-coding. When used as content, XML is a one-way affair: you can only load it. If you need a solution to store data back to the Zune device, you should use XNA's storage capabilities, which you will learn about in Chapter 6.

When you add a new XML document to your Content folder, the default XML in that document looks like this:

```
<?xml version="1.0" encoding="utf-8" ?>
<XnaContent>
  <!-- TODO: replace this Asset with your own XML asset data. -->
  <Asset Type="System.String"></Asset>
</XnaContent>
```

The nodes in XnaContent allow you to define values that you can load into memory objects. The default asset, a String, is an example of a simple data type that you can initialize using XML.

In some cases, you may wish to use an XML document that is not formatted as shown in the previous example. The default XML format can be used directly in the XNA content pipeline. If you have XML that does not match this format, or schema, you need to write a custom importer and processor to parse the XML and populate your objects. Custom importers and processors are discussed later in this chapter.

The XNA Content Pipeline

When the XNA team members set out to develop an everyman's game development tool, they wanted to streamline as many of the aspects of game development as possible. They did this by creating a full-featured framework, including a lot of boilerplate code in project templates, and providing a powerful content engine that allows game developers to use their own content-creation tools. This section details the complex but crucial content pipeline.

What the Content Pipeline Provides

The content pipeline makes life easier for developers in a number of ways. It builds all of your game assets at compile time into an XNA-specific format, called XNB, without requiring you to do any extra work. The content pipeline is extensible; you can add to the wide number of supported asset types to handle proprietary file formats or data structures. It already supports quite a variety of commonly used file types, as discussed earlier in this chapter.

Possibly the most compelling aspect of the content pipeline is that it separates content creation from processing. Artists, sound designers and other asset creators can use the tools they are most comfortable with to create the assets. You, the developer, are responsible only for including these files in your project and loading them at runtime. No special processing is necessary on your part, unless you are dealing with a format that the content pipeline does not natively support.

While the underlying mechanism of the content pipeline is complex, the relationship that both developers and designers have with it is very simple. This simplicity makes it easy to bring content into your game and work with it freely, without the need to understand how it all works.

Content Pipeline Architecture

Due to the aforementioned simplicity of interacting with the content pipeline, you may never need to understand how the content pipeline works. However, if you want to support a new file format or create your own, it's useful to understand what goes on under the hood of the content pipeline.

In simple terms, the content pipeline imports content files, processes them, and outputs them as part of your game during compile time. When Visual Studio begins its build process, the content pipeline also builds its assets. The content pipeline's build process is fully integrated with Visual Studio, so any errors raised in the process of building content are output to the Errors window in the same way as any other solution build item. Content assets are integrated with the build system the moment they are added to your solution.

The content pipeline makes it possible for an asset to be converted from the format it was created in to part of the game's binary package. This transformation is shown in Figure 3-6.

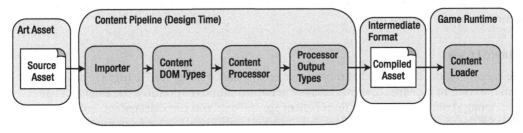

Figure 3-6. *The flow of the content pipeline's build process*

As you can see in Figure 3-6, the content pipeline takes an asset through several stages, from raw asset to XNA content object. In doing so, four main components are called upon by the content pipeline: the importer, processor, compiler, and loader.

Content Importer

An importer is used to bring an asset into the content pipeline at compile time before processing it. XNA Game Studio supplies importers for well-known file types. With a Zune, you will likely work the most with the WAV, MP3, Texture, and Sprite Font Description content importers. All of these content importers are supplied for you.

Content Processor

After the asset is imported by a content importer, it will be processed by a corresponding content processor. Content processors usually have the same name as their respective importers (such as Texture – XNA Framework). Most asset types, after being imported, can be found in the standard Content Document Object Model (DOM). The Content DOM makes processing imported assets very easy and generic, so it can support many different types without needing to change the high-level process. If you are working with a format not found in the Content DOM, you must write your own processor that includes functionality for reading and writing that format.

The job of the content processor is to take the imported asset and transform it to a managed object, such as `Texture2D`, `SpriteFont`, `SoundEffect`, and others.

Content Compiler

After the content processor converts your assets into managed objects, these objects are built into a binary format that is highly optimized for the XNA Framework. These binary content objects, which have the extension `.xnb`, are very specific to the XNA Framework and are not intended to be used by any other program.

The content compiler creates a ready-to-load game asset that has a specific name. Later, when calling `Content.Load`, you will notice that attempting to supply the file extension to the `Load` method will result in a runtime exception stating the asset could not be found. Because all assets are compiled down to the XNB format, you must load the asset by its name, which is not the same as its original file name.

At this point in the process, your game asset has been transformed from its original format to the compact binary format supported by the content pipeline. It is now ready to be loaded at runtime by the content loader.

Content Loader

The content loader is activated at runtime when you call `Content.Load` to bring in an asset from the content pipeline. `Content.Load` is a generic method that returns the asset as a specific managed data type, such as `Texture2D` or `SpriteFont`. You can call `Content.Load` multiple times for the same asset, but it will be truly "loaded" only once. For performance reasons, the content pipeline smartly avoids loading the same asset more than once, and will return the existing asset on subsequent attempts to load it.

The `Content.Load` method is usually called once per asset in the `LoadContent` method of your `Game` class. You can load content outside this method, but you need a reference to the game's `ContentManager` object. You may also experience a dip or halt in performance due to the hard disk activity associated with loading a brand-new asset into the `ContentManager`. When loading an asset, you should specify the original file name minus the file extension, including the relative path to the content project in which it resides.

Content Stages

As you've seen, the content pipeline takes an asset through several stages. As an example, let's look at the life of a typical content asset—a background image—as seen by the XNA Framework.

1. An artist creates an image in PNG format called `background.png`. The developer adds this file to the XNA game's `Content` project.

2. At compile time, `background.png` is imported into the content pipeline.

3. The image is processed by the Texture content processor as a supported type found in the Content DOM.

4. A managed object is created for the `background` asset, which is now known as `background`, not `background.png`.

5. The image is written to a binary format and saved as `background.xnb`.

6. At runtime, the background asset is loaded by the content loader and copied to a `Texture2D` variable using a line of code similar to this one:

```
myBackgroundTexture = Content.Load<Texture2D>("background");
```

7. The `Texture2D` object `myBackgroundTexture` is drawn by a `SpriteBatch` object in the game's `Draw` method.

Loading Content at Runtime

The easiest way to load content at runtime is by using `Content.Load` in the game's `LoadContent` method. `Content.Load` is a generic method, which means its return type can vary based on what you specify. A typical call to `Content.Load` looks like this:

```
objectType managedObject = Content.Load<objectType>("asset_path");
```

`managedObject` is an object of type `objectType`, and `asset_path` is the name of the asset, including the relative path to the `Content` project. Calling `Content.Load` not only loads the asset into the content pipeline, but also returns a reference to the loaded object for you to use.

Following are some examples of how to load commonly used asset types.

Images (Textures)

Textures are loaded using the following syntax:

```
Texture2D backgroundTexture = Content.Load<Texture2D>("Textures/background");
```

`Texture2D` is the type of the object (a managed type from the `Microsoft.Xna.Framework.Content` namespace) that provides access to the texture's width, height, and other texture-specific properties. This line of code will retrieve a `Texture2D` asset generated from the file at `Content/Textures/background.png` (or whatever the originating file format is).

Sprite Fonts

Sprite fonts are loaded using the following syntax:

```
SpriteFont tahomaFont = Content.Load<SpriteFont>("Fonts/tahoma");
```

The `SpriteFont` class gives you access to a few useful properties about the font, such as font spacing and line spacing, as well as a very useful method called `MeasureString`, which you can use to center text.

Sound Effects

Sound effects, new to XNA Framework 3.0, are loaded using the following syntax:

```
SoundEffect boomEffect = Content.Load<SoundEffect>("Sounds/boom");
```

The `SoundEffect` class gives you access to some useful properties about the sound effect, such as its name and duration, as well as the `Play` method, which you can call to play the sound effect.

In any case, all content that you can possibly load follows the same pattern. You need to specify only the asset type, the relative path to the content folder (without the file extension), and the object into which you want to load the asset. The extensibility of the content pipeline also makes it such that any custom content types you create, such as an animation, can be loaded into the pipeline in the same manner, as long as you have the content importer and processor readily available.

Now, it's time to try out the content pipeline for yourself and see how truly easy it is to get started building a game with custom content!

Custom Importers and Processors

To make your life easier or to support formats not already provided by the Content DOM, you can create custom importers and processors that plug in to the extensible content pipeline. *Parameterized processors* allow you to specify additional information to the content processor at design time, making the processor more flexible for your use in the game.

Writing a custom content pipeline object is something you probably won't need to do very often. Nonetheless, the ability to do so puts a very powerful tool at your disposal. This chapter's exercise takes you through the process of developing a custom, parameterized content type for a 2D animation based on a sprite sheet. This allows you to select any PNG file in your content folder and assign an animation interval and total number of horizontal frames to it using the Properties window. It saves a tremendous amount of time for using any animations that loop continuously. You can extend this code later to include play, stop, and pause functionality, if you wish.

Before getting into the actual step-by-step procedure, let's review the code that our custom content processor will use.

The Content Type Class

First, we will create the SimpleAnimation class, as shown in Listing 3-1. This is the top-level type you would use in your game, much like a Texture2D or SpriteFont. This class contains information about the animation, such as the number of frames, the animation speed, and a Texture2D object that is embedded into the class during the content processing phase. It also contains Update and Draw methods, which you can call from the main game loop to automatically advance the frames. In Chapter 5, you will learn how this class could be a DrawableGameComponent and draw itself automatically.

Listing 3-1 shows the SimpleAnimation class. Each method and public property is commented for your convenience, and the #region markers are used to allow for better readability while coding.

Listing 3-1. *The SimpleAnimation Class*

```
using System;
using Microsoft.Xna.Framework.Graphics;
using Microsoft.Xna.Framework;

namespace SimpleAnimationExtension
{
    /// <summary>
    /// This class represents an animated texture that plays continuously.
    /// </summary>
    public class SimpleAnimation
    {
        #region Private Fields

        private int _numFrames;
        private int _animationSpeed;
        private Texture2D _texture;
        private int _currentFrameIndex;
        private Rectangle _sourceRect;
        private TimeSpan _lastFrameUpdate;

        #endregion

        #region Public Properties

        /// <summary>
        /// Gets the number of frames in this animation.
        /// </summary>
        public int FrameCount
        {
            get
            {
                return _numFrames;
            }
        }
```

```csharp
/// <summary>
/// Gets the speed of the animation in milliseconds. This is the
/// rate at which the animation changes frames.
/// </summary>
public int AnimationSpeed
{
    get
    {
        return _animationSpeed;
    }
}

#endregion

#region Constructor(s)

/// <summary>
/// This method constructs a new SimpleAnimation object. It is
/// called by the content processor.
/// </summary>
/// <param name="texture">The Texture2D object to associate with
/// this animation.</param>
/// <param name="numFrames">The number of frames in the
/// animation.</param>
/// <param name="animationSpeed">The animation speed, in
/// milliseconds.</param>
public SimpleAnimation(Texture2D texture, int numFrames,
    int animationSpeed)
{
    _texture = texture;
    _numFrames = numFrames;
    _animationSpeed = animationSpeed;
    _currentFrameIndex = 0;
    _lastFrameUpdate = TimeSpan.Zero;

    _sourceRect = new Rectangle();
    UpdateSourceRect();
}

#endregion

#region Public Methods

/// <summary>
/// This method should be called with each game update. It
/// determines how much time has passed since the last update
/// and updates the frame accordingly.
```

```csharp
/// </summary>
/// <param name="gameTime"></param>
public void Update(GameTime gameTime)
{
    // Check to see if we need to advance the frame
    double timeDiff = gameTime.TotalGameTime.Subtract(
        _lastFrameUpdate).TotalMilliseconds;

    if (timeDiff >= (double)_animationSpeed)
    {
        _currentFrameIndex ++;
        if (_currentFrameIndex >= _numFrames) // loop back over
            _currentFrameIndex = 0;

        _lastFrameUpdate = gameTime.TotalGameTime;
    }
}

/// <summary>
/// This method draws the texture to a SpriteBatch object using
/// the current source rectangle.
/// </summary>
/// <param name="spriteBatch">The SpriteBatch object
/// to draw to.</param>
/// <param name="position">The position where you want to draw
/// the object.</param>
public void Draw(SpriteBatch spriteBatch, Vector2 position)
{
    UpdateSourceRect();
    spriteBatch.Draw(_texture, position, _sourceRect, Color.White);
}

#endregion

#region Private Methods

/// <summary>
/// Determines the source rectangle for the texture
/// based on the current frame.
/// </summary>
private void UpdateSourceRect()
{
    int width = _texture.Width / _numFrames;
    int height = _texture.Height;
    int frameOffset = _currentFrameIndex * width;
```

```
            _sourceRect.X = frameOffset;
            _sourceRect.Y = 0;
            _sourceRect.Width = width;
            _sourceRect.Height = height;
        }

        #endregion
    }
}
```

The SimpleAnimation class is quite straightforward. It has a constructor, a couple of public properties, two public methods, and a private helper method. The constructor initializes the class by setting the appropriate member variables equal to the arguments passed to it. The Texture2D object comes from the content processor. The animation speed and number of frames are passed from the designer to the processor and again to this constructor by the content loader. The constructor is also responsible for initializing the time the frame was last updated, as well as the source rectangle used to draw a fragment of the texture.

Of the private variables used in this class, only two are exposed as properties: AnimationSpeed and FrameCount. The current frame index is used to determine which frame is currently being displayed. The last update timestamp references the time of the last update (if the animation hasn't played yet, it's simply zero). The source rectangle is a simple rectangle that defines an area of the sprite sheet to draw based on the current frame index. Finally, the Texture2D object is a local copy of the asset generated by the content loader.

The Intermediate Content and Reader Classes

During the processing phase, a special class must be used to contain the intermediate data that the content processor needs. The TextureProcessor, for example, uses a type called TextureContent to process image files. Our content processor will hijack this data type and utilize the TextureProcessor to create our own SimpleAnimation type. This will be the SimpleAnimationContent class, shown in Listing 3-2.

Listing 3-2. *The SimpleAnimationContent Class, Along with Its Reader Type*

```
using System;
using Microsoft.Xna.Framework.Content.Pipeline;
using Microsoft.Xna.Framework.Content.Pipeline.Graphics;
using Microsoft.Xna.Framework.Content;
using Microsoft.Xna.Framework.Graphics;

namespace SimpleAnimationExtension
{
    /// <summary>
    /// Contains a texture object and custom properties.
    /// </summary>
    public class SimpleAnimationContent
    {
        public int FrameCount;
```

```
        public int AnimationInterval;
        public TextureContent TextureData;

        public SimpleAnimationContent(TextureContent data, int frameCount,
            int animationInterval)
        {
            TextureData = data;
            FrameCount = frameCount;
            AnimationInterval = animationInterval;
        }
    }

    /// <summary>
    /// Implements the reader for this content type.
    /// </summary>
    public class SimpleAnimationContentReader : ContentTypeReader
    {
        public SimpleAnimationContentReader()
            : base(typeof(SimpleAnimationContent))
        {

        }

        protected override object Read(ContentReader input,
            object existingInstance)
        {
            int animationInterval = input.ReadInt32();
            int frameCount = input.ReadInt32();
            Texture2D texture = input.ReadObject<Texture2D>();

            return new SimpleAnimation(texture, frameCount, animationInterval);
        }
    }
}
```

This file contains two classes. The first, SimpleAnimationContent, represents the intermediate type that the content processor deals with. It is unique and necessary because it contains a reference to the texture data—just as the usual Texture content processor would—plus, it attaches two custom properties to the binary file format. This class is serialized into the XNB format at compile time by the SimpleAnimationContentWriter class (shown next), cementing the texture data along with the custom properties we've defined.

The other class in this file, SimpleAnimationContentReader, reads an object of type SimpleAnimationContent at load time and returns a usable SimpleAnimation object. It does this by overriding the Read method and sequentially reading in certain data types. The order here is important, because it must match the order in which the values were written by the writer class.

The Writer Class

The writer class is invoked by the content processor to serialize the intermediate object, SimpleAnimationContent. Listing 3-3 shows the code for SimpleAnimationContentWriter.cs.

Listing 3-3. *The SimpleAnimationContentWriter Class*

```
using System;
using System.Collections.Generic;
using Microsoft.Xna.Framework;
using Microsoft.Xna.Framework.Graphics;
using Microsoft.Xna.Framework.Content.Pipeline;
using Microsoft.Xna.Framework.Content.Pipeline.Graphics;
using Microsoft.Xna.Framework.Content.Pipeline.Processors;
using Microsoft.Xna.Framework.Content.Pipeline.Serialization.Compiler;

namespace SimpleAnimationExtension
{
    /// <summary>
    /// This class will be instantiated by the XNA Framework Content Pipeline
    /// to write the specified data type into binary .xnb format.
    ///
    /// This should be part of a Content Pipeline Extension Library project.
    /// </summary>
    [ContentTypeWriter]
    public class SimpleAnimationContentWriter :
        ContentTypeWriter<SimpleAnimationContent>
    {
        protected override void Write(ContentWriter output,
            SimpleAnimationContent value)
        {
            output.Write(value.AnimationInterval);
            output.Write(value.FrameCount);
            output.WriteObject(value.TextureData);
        }

        public override string GetRuntimeReader(TargetPlatform targetPlatform)
        {
            // TODO: change this to the name of your ContentTypeReader
            // class which will be used to load this data.
            return typeof(SimpleAnimationContentReader).AssemblyQualifiedName;
        }
    }
}
```

By default, this class has only two methods. The first is the overridden Write method, which writes a SimpleAnimationContent object to a ContentWriter object. Again, note the order in which the properties are written to the content writer. The write order must match the read order in the Read method of the SimpleAnimationContentReader object in Listing 3-2. In this case, the animation interval is written first, followed by the frame count, and finally, the texture data. The order chosen is arbitrary, but it must be consistent between the reader and writer to avoid exceptions.

With the reader and writer in place, our next step will be to bring it all together using the final piece of the puzzle: the content processor itself.

The Content Processor Class

By default, your project will already contain a content processor class, called `ContentProcessor1.cs`. For our example, we will rename that file to `SimpleAnimationProcessor.cs`, as shown in Listing 3-4.

■**Note** You can also add a new content processor by right-clicking the project and choosing Add ➤ New Item ➤ Content Processor.

Listing 3-4. *The SimpleAnimationProcessor Class*

```
using System;
using System.ComponentModel;
using System.Collections.Generic;
using Microsoft.Xna.Framework;
using Microsoft.Xna.Framework.Graphics;
using Microsoft.Xna.Framework.Content.Pipeline;
using Microsoft.Xna.Framework.Content.Pipeline.Graphics;
using Microsoft.Xna.Framework.Content.Pipeline.Processors;

namespace SimpleAnimationExtension
{
    /// <summary>
    /// This class will be instantiated by the XNA Framework Content Pipeline
    /// to apply custom processing to content data, converting an object of
    /// type TInput to TOutput. The input and output types may be the same if
    /// the processor wishes to alter data without changing its type.
    ///
    /// This should be part of a Content Pipeline Extension Library project.
    ///
    /// </summary>
    [ContentProcessor(DisplayName = "Simple Animation Processor")]
    public class SimpleAnimationProcessor :
        ContentProcessor<TextureContent, SimpleAnimationContent>
    {
        private int _numFrames;
        private int _animationInterval;
```

```
        [DisplayName("Frame Count")]
        [Description("The number of animation frames in the texture.")]
        public int FrameCount
        {
            get { return _numFrames; }
            set { _numFrames = value; }
        }


        [DisplayName("Animation Speed")]
        [Description("The speed of the animation in milliseconds.")]
        [DefaultValue("100")]
        public int AnimationInterval
        {
            get { return _animationInterval; }
            set { _animationInterval = value; }
        }


        public override SimpleAnimationContent Process(TextureContent input,
            ContentProcessorContext context)
        {
            return new SimpleAnimationContent(input, _numFrames,
                animationInterval);
        }
    }
}
```

The first thing to notice is the using section. A reference to System.ComponentModel has been added. This is to add support for the items in square brackets above each public property. These attributes will show up in the Properties window at design time, allowing you to modify the values before they are passed to the content processor. This is what makes a content processor *parameterized*.

Aside from the properties (which have getters *and* setters), there is one method in this class, called Process. This method is overridden from the base class (ContentProcessor) and performs one simple task: it creates a new SimpleAnimationContent object using the TextureContent input and the parameters provided by the developer at design time.

Also notice the data types provided in the class declaration:

```
public class SimpleAnimationProcessor :
        ContentProcessor<TextureContent, SimpleAnimationContent>
```

This class inherits from the base ContentProcessor, which is a generic class. The first type is the input, and the second is the output. At this point, it becomes clear that this content processor's job is to turn TextureContent into SimpleAnimationContent by passing along the texture data, collecting parameters from the designer, and using all of this information to construct a SimpleAnimationContent class.

Also note that the class itself has an attribute in square brackets called DisplayName. This value will appear in the Properties window at design time to provide the developer with a friendly name for the content processor. Similarly, the attributes on the processor's properties (DisplayName and Description) are used to make life easier for the person using this processor.

The other attribute you see used is DefaultValue, which sets the default value of a particular parameter to something reasonable.

Now that you've seen the main classes that will make up our custom content processor, let's actually create it.

EXERCISE 3-1. A PARAMETERIZED CONTENT PROCESSOR FOR ANIMATIONS

In this example, you will learn how to create the components necessary to build a new content type called SimpleAnimation. SimpleAnimation contains all the logic needed to update and draw an animation based on the parameters you supply to it at design time, saving you from needing to build a custom animation class for animations that loop continuously.

This example shows you how to build a custom content processor that allows you to define any PNG file as a type that can be processed as a SimpleAnimation object. All you need to do is provide the animation speed (in milliseconds) and the number of frames in the animation at design time, and the class will take care of continuously animating itself.

This is a class that you can easily extend to add your own functionality, such as animations that stop, play partial frames, or anything you may require for your game's needs.

1. In Visual Studio 2008, create a new project by selecting File ➤ New Project.

2. From the XNA Game Studio project types, choose Content Pipeline Extension Library. Enter SimpleAnimationExtension for the name, as shown in Figure 3-7. Click OK.

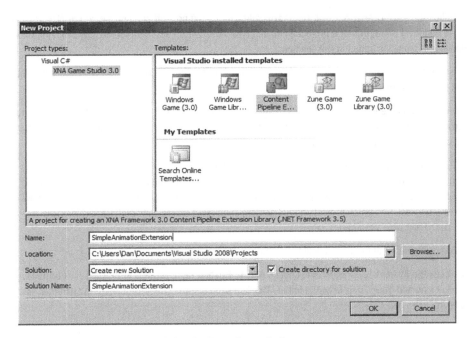

Figure 3-7. *Creating the SimpleAnimationExtension project*

3. Right-click the `SimpleAnimationExtension` project and choose Add ➤ Class. Name the class `SimpleAnimation.cs`, and then click OK.

4. Add the code for the `SimpleAnimation` class shown earlier in Listing 3-1.

5. Add a new file to the project by right-clicking the `SimpleAnimationExtension` project and choosing Add ➤ Class. Name the class `SimpleAnimationContent`, and then click OK.

6. Add the code for `SimpleAnimationContent.cs` shown earlier in Listing 3-2.

7. Right-click the `SimpleAnimationExtension` project and choose Add ➤ New Item. Choose the Content Type Writer file type and name it `SimpleAnimationContentWriter`. Click OK.

8. Add the code for `SimpleAnimationContentWriter.cs` shown earlier in Listing 3-3.

9. Right-click the `ContentProcessor1.cs` in the project and rename this file to `SimpleAnimationProcessor.cs`. This should automatically change the class name for you.

    Now, you should have a single project with four files: `SimpleAnimationContent.cs`, `SimpleAnimation.cs`, `SimpleAnimationContentWriter.cs`, and `SimpleAnimationProcessor.cs`. This is everything you need in the content pipeline extension project, so our work here is done. While I mentioned earlier that this is for PNG files, that restriction has not been explicitly placed on the processor. You could technically use any file type recognized by the standard texture importer.

10. Compile the project and correct any errors.

    Now, let's create a test project to see how it works. This is the part of the exercise where you see how all of the hard work of creating a custom content type really pays off.

11. Right-click the `SimpleAnimationExtension` solution (not the project) and choose Add ➤ New Project. Choose Windows Game from the project types and type `TestingAnimation` as the project name. Click OK. A new game project is added to the solution.

12. Right-click the `TestingAnimation` project and choose Set as Startup Project. This will ensure that this test game runs when you debug or run without debugging.

13. Right-click the References node in the `TestingAnimation` project and add a new project reference to `SimpleAnimationExtension`. This gives you access to the `SimpleAnimation` data type, which you will need when loading content.

14. Right-click the References node in the `Content` folder of the `TestingAnimation` project and add a new project reference to `SimpleAnimationExtension`. This gives you access to the content processor you created as part of the content pipeline extension. You will immediately have access to the new content processor. The game project and the content subproject should now both have references to `SimpleAnimationExtension`.

15. Create a subfolder in the `Content` folder called `Animations`.

16. Right-click the `Animations` folder and choose Add ➤ Existing Item. Browse to `Examples/Chapter 3/Artwork` and add `jump.png` from the folder. This is a simple sprite sheet for a jumping character, as shown in Figure 3-8.

Figure 3-8. *The sprite sheet for a jumping character, jump.png*

17. The project should look like Figure 3-9 in the Solution Explorer. Expand the `Animations` folder and select `jump.png`.

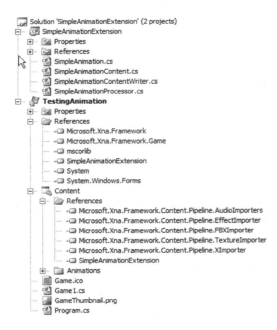

Figure 3-9. *The Solution Explorer view of the project*

18. In the Properties window, note that you can modify the content importer and processor. Leave the importer as the default (Texture – XNA Framework). Expand the Content Processor node and select Simple Animation Processor from the list.

19. Notice how the parameters you defined in the extension show up in the property sheet. For Animation Speed, type **50**. There are 13 frames in the sprite sheet, so type **13** for the Frame Count value. The properties for `jump.png` should look like Figure 3-10.

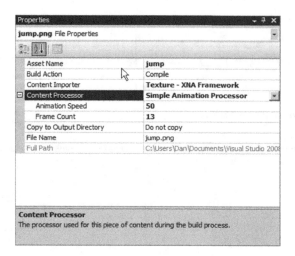

Figure 3-10. *Setting properties for the animation asset*

Let's write some code to utilize this animation. You'll be pleased with how simple this is.

20. Open Game1.cs, the file created for you in your new Windows Game project. Add the following line to the using statements:

```
using SimpleAnimationExtension;
```

21. Where the GraphicsDeviceManager and SpriteBatch variables are declared at the beginning of the class, declare a new SimpleAnimation object, like so:

```
SimpleAnimation _animation;
```

22. In the LoadContent method, add the following line after the sprite batch is instantiated:

```
_animation = Content.Load<SimpleAnimation>("Animations/jump");
```

23. In the Update method, add the following line before the call to base.Update:

```
_animation.Update(gameTime);
```

24. In the Draw method, add the following code after the graphics device is cleared and before the call to base.Draw:

```
spriteBatch.Begin();
_animation.Draw(spriteBatch, new Vector2(100, 100));
spriteBatch.End();
```

25. Press F5 to run the game with debugging. Observe the jumping character on your screen!

By creating a custom content type and implementing a new processor, you have a way to add custom behaviors and properties to a plain texture. In this example, all of the animation logic has been delegated to the SimpleAnimation class, and all you need to do is use your own content processor to take advantage of it! We added only seven lines of code to the stock XNA game to utilize simple sprite animation techniques. Now, you see the power of custom content types.

Check Your Knowledge

The following questions will help you apply what you've learned in this chapter to your own games. The answers are supplied in Appendix C.

1. What is the most practical file type for textures that make use of alpha blending?

2. Why are 3D asset types, such as 3D models, not supported on the Zune?

3. What does a `.spritefont` file contain?

4. The `SoundEffect` class can play both WAV and MP3 files. True or false?

5. Which component of the content pipeline transforms a compiled asset to a managed object at runtime?

6. What is the Zune's screen resolution?

7. What is the Zune display's color depth?

8. Which element of the content pipeline provides a model for commonly used asset types?

9. What type of asset can be used for configuration or special text-based data?

10. Why must you omit the file extension of an asset when loading it at runtime?

Summary

This chapter gave you an in-depth look into how content works in XNA games. You learned about the various types of content, restrictions and considerations specific to the Zune device, in-depth information about the content pipeline, and even built your own content type with a custom, parameterized content processor.

In the next chapter, you will learn how to develop for the Zune device, including some best practices for deployment and debugging. You'll get a quick primer in some often-used 2D trigonometry and math, and apply it to your very first Zune game: OutBreak.

CHAPTER 4

■■■

Developing for the Zune

In the previous chapters, you have learned a lot about the various aspects of developing games using XNA Game Studio. You have also learned about the content pipeline, which is a critical component of the XNA platform. Until now, all of the code examples have been for the PC. In this chapter, that changes. Now we will build games specifically for the Zune device.

If you don't have a Zune yet, don't worry! You will also learn how to create copies of your Zune project for the PC and arrange the project so that it compiles differently based on the target platform.

First, you need to understand the work flow of Zune game development. Because there is currently no emulator for the Zune device, you will need to get used to waiting a little longer each time you run or debug the application on the device. Other caveats exist, as you'll learn in this chapter.

In the course of mastering the work flow of development for the Zune, you will build a small test "game" that operates on both the Zune and the PC. At the end of the chapter, using those concepts, you will build a more complicated game called OutBreak, which will be your first Zune project worthy of being called a game!

Deploying to the Zune

The deployment process is very straightforward and simple. To deploy a Zune game project to the Zune device, the following conditions must be met:

- The firmware on the Zune must be up-to-date and compatible with the version of XNA Game Studio you are running.

- The Zune must be connected via USB to the computer.

- The connected Zune must be set as the default Zune in the XNA Game Studio Device Center tool.

- The Zune client software (for synchronizing movies, music, and so on) cannot be running, and no other processes can be synchronizing to the Zune.

Before continuing with this chapter, make sure you have set up your development environment, which includes Visual Studio 2008 or Visual C# 2008 Express or later and XNA Game Studio 3.0 or later. Chapter 1 covers downloading and installing Visual Studio and XNA Game Studio.

Note   You can download the latest version of XNA Game Studio from the XNA Creators Club web site (`http://creators.xna.com`). If you have a previous version of XNA Game Studio installed, including any community technology preview (CTP) versions, you must first uninstall those products before installing the new one.

Updating Your Zune's Firmware

The Zune firmware update process is done through the Zune client software, available at `http://www.zune.net`. At the time of this writing, the appropriate configuration is Zune firmware version 3.0 and XNA Game Studio 3.0.

Caution   XNA Game Studio 3.0 supports development on 64-bit platforms for the Zune. If you are running a 64-bit operating system, you must download the 64-bit version of the Zune software to install the proper drivers for the device.

To verify the Zune's firmware version and to update it if necessary, plug in your Zune device after installing the Zune client software and click the Settings button in the upper-right corner of the screen, as shown in Figure 4-1.

Figure 4-1. *Click the Settings button on the Zune screen to check your Zune's firmware version.*

From the Settings screen, click the Device tab. On the left side of that tab, click Device Update. If your firmware is up-to-date, you will see a screen similar to Figure 4-2. If your device firmware is not up-to-date, you will see an Update button, which you can click to start the firmware update process. When this process completes, your Zune will be ready for game development.

Figure 4-2. *The Device Update screen shows the status of your Zune's firmware.*

■Caution If you are using multiple Zunes, ensure that each of them has the latest firmware installed before attempting to use them in the development process.

Registering Your Zune with Visual Studio

To allow Visual Studio to deploy to your Zune, all you need to do is launch XNA Game Studio Device Center and add the device. This process is identical to that of adding an Xbox 360 console to Device Center.

XNA Game Studio Device Center is a utility that allows you to manage the devices to which you want to deploy. Zune development with XNA, unlike Xbox 360, does not require a Creators Club membership, so the procedure is straightforward.

To register your device with Device Center, follow these steps:

1. Select Tools ➤ Launch XNA Game Studio Device Center to launch the utility, as shown in Figure 4-3.

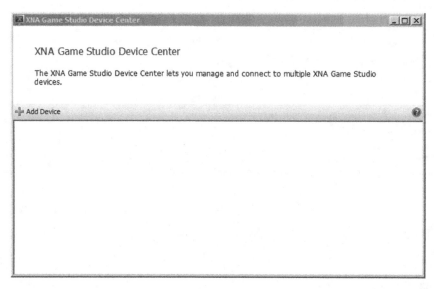

Figure 4-3. *XNA Game Studio Device Center*

2. Connect your device with the Zune USB cable.

■**Tip** You can connect multiple Zunes to different USB ports on your computer and add them to XNA Game Studio Device Center.

---

3. In the Device Center, click the Add Device button. The XNA Game Studio Devices dialog box appears, as shown in Figure 4-4.

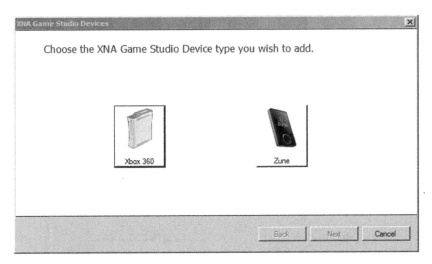

Figure 4-4. *The XNA Game Studio Devices dialog box*

4. Click the Zune icon. Your connected device should appear, as shown in Figure 4-5. If it does not, ensure that the device is not currently synchronizing or updating its firmware. You can try closing the Zune client to stop it from synchronizing.

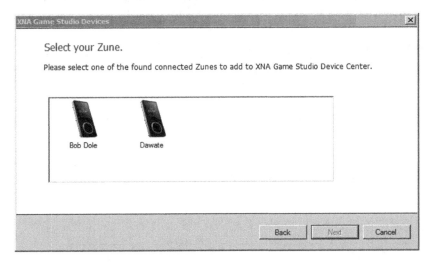

Figure 4-5. *The Select Your Zune dialog box when two Zunes are connected to the computer*

5. Select the Zune device you want to add and click Next. Visual Studio will now test its connectivity with the Zune, and you will briefly see the dialog box shown in Figure 4-6.

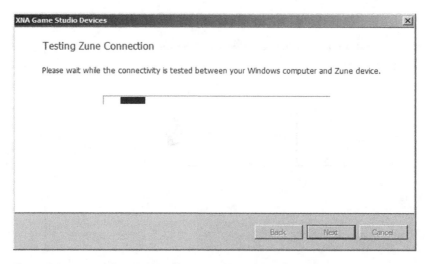

Figure 4-6. *Testing connectivity between Visual Studio and the Zune*

6. When the connectivity test completes, you will see a dialog box indicating that the connection was successful, as shown in Figure 4-7. If you have more than one Zune in Device Center, you will have the option to set the newly added one as the default device (the one to which Visual Studio will deploy your game). If this is the only device you've added, it will be set as the default device automatically.

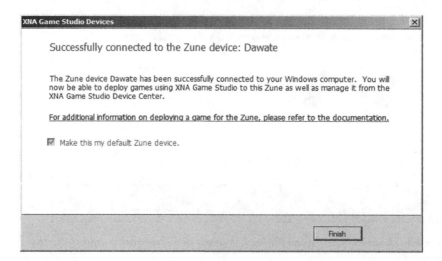

Figure 4-7. *The Zune device has been added successfully.*

7. Click Finish. You will see a list of devices in XNA Game Studio Device Center, as shown in Figure 4-8. The device with the green check mark icon is the one to which Visual Studio will deploy (the default device). There can be only one default device at a time, which means you cannot deploy to multiple Zunes at once.

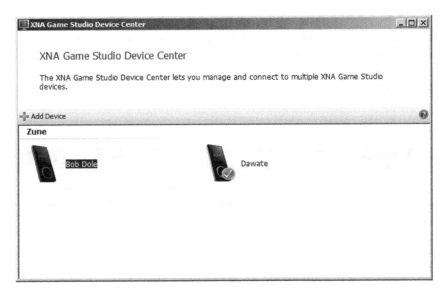

Figure 4-8. *XNA Game Studio Device Center with two Zunes added and one set as the default, which is where games will be deployed*

At this time, your Zune is registered with XNA Game Studio Device Center. When you plug it in next time, it will be available for you to use; you don't need to repeat this process.

If you later want to remove a Zune device from Device Center, all you need to do is right-click the device in Device Center and select Remove, as shown Figure 4-9. After confirmation, the Zune will be unregistered. You will need to add it again later if you wish to use it again.

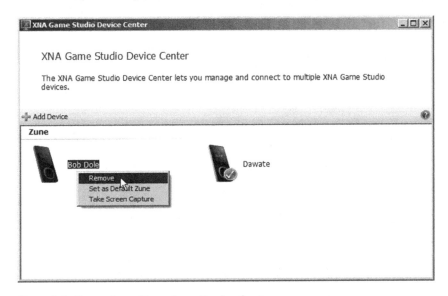

Figure 4-9. *Removing a Zune from Device Center*

■Tip A great feature that has been added in XNA Game Studio 3.0 is the ability to take a screen capture from a Zune that is running a game. While the game is running, simply right-click the Zune in XNA Game Studio Device Center and click Take Screen Capture. The result will be a PNG file at 240 by 320 pixels. See Figure 4-12, at the end of the following exercise, for an example.

EXERCISE 4-1. HELLO ZUNE

What's a programming book without the requisite Hello World example? In this short exercise, you will create a Zune game that displays some text on the screen. You will confirm that your configuration is ready to rock, and you will also see how to deploy a game to the Zune.

1. Connect your Zune to your computer and launch Visual Studio.

2. Launch Device Center by selecting Tools ➤ Launch XNA Game Studio Device Center. Check that the connected Zune is set as the default. (For an example, see Figure 4-8, shown earlier, where the Zune named Dawate is set to the default.) Then close Device Center.

3. In Visual Studio, create a new project by selecting File ➤ New Project.

4. In the left pane of the New Project dialog box, choose XNA Game Studio 3.0 from the Visual C# project types node. In the right pane, choose Zune Game (3.0). Choose a location for the project (or use the default), and type HelloZune as the project name, as shown in Figure 4-10. Click OK.

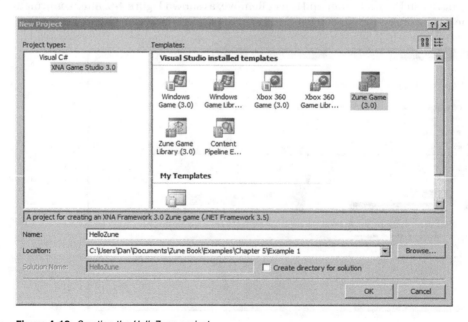

Figure 4-10. *Creating the HelloZune project*

5. To add a new sprite font to the project, right-click the Content node in the Solution Explorer and choose Add ➤ New Item. Select the Sprite Font template and name it Tahoma (or another font name that you know exists on your computer), as shown in Figure 4-11. You don't need to include the .spritefont extension; it will be added automatically. Click Add.

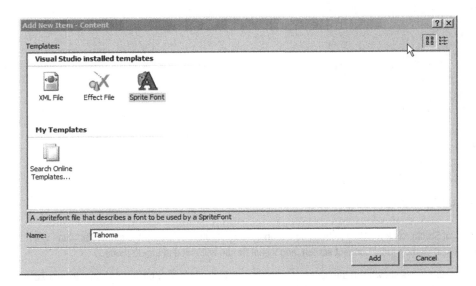

Figure 4-11. *Adding a sprite font*

6. Open Game1.cs. Immediately after the declaration of the spriteBatch variable and before the Game1 constructor, declare a SpriteFont variable to reference the font you just added, as follows:

```
SpriteFont tahomaFont;
```

7. In the LoadContent method, replace the // TODO: line with the code to load the font from the content pipeline:

```
tahomaFont = Content.Load<SpriteFont>("Tahoma");
```

8. In the Draw method, replace the // TODO: line with the code to draw some text on the screen using the default sprite batch. This code draws the text "Hello Zune" in black Tahoma at point (0, 0) (Vector2.Zero):

```
spriteBatch.Begin();
spriteBatch.DrawString(tahomaFont, "Hello Zune", Vector2.Zero, Color.Black);
spriteBatch.End();
```

9. Press F5 to run the game in debugging mode. This will catch any exceptions and allow the game to exit gracefully without a hard reboot of the device. If this is the first game you've deployed to your Zune, the XNA Framework components will be deployed first, followed by your game and its compiled assets. Look at your device during deployment to see which files are being copied.

10. When deployment is complete, the game will run, and you will see a static screen on the Zune, as shown in Figure 4-12. Congratulations! Your first Zune application is a success.

Figure 4-12. *The Hello Zune game in action*

11. In Visual Studio, click the Stop Debugging button (or press Shift+F5) to stop the game. The Zune will return to the XNA Game Studio Connect screen, and Visual Studio will exit debugging mode.

This simple "game" has shown you the basics of creating and deploying a very basic XNA game to your Zune device. Later in this chapter, in the "Your First Real Zune Game: OutBreak" section, you will create a slightly more complicated game with movement, game logic, input, and more.

Debugging, Running, and Rebooting

What is the practical difference between running with and without debugging, and why does the Zune reboot itself after your game exits?

The Zune reboot behavior is by design, and exists mainly to clean up resources and reload the firmware so that no leaks or possible exploits exist. You may notice that the games that come with the Zune 3.0 firmware do not reboot after exiting them. This is because they are signed by Microsoft and trusted by the firmware. There is currently no way to reproduce this behavior when creating your own game; the Zune will always reboot itself when your game exits.

Of course, a constantly rebooting Zune device can be a hindrance to the game-development process, when you are frequently testing code. Thankfully, when you run with debugging, the Zune will exit gracefully to the XNA Game Studio Connect screen, without rebooting fully.

Running with Debugging

As you've seen, when you are ready to deploy and test a game, or you can run it with debugging simply by pressing F5. You can also click the Debug icon in Visual Studio (it looks like a play icon).

For most purposes, running with debugging is preferred, because it is considerably more practical and provides more value to you during the development stage. Running with debugging has the following benefits:

- You can step into code that is executing on the Zune device itself.

- You can set breakpoints, watches, and use all the features of the Visual Studio debugger that you might use for any other application.

- When you stop debugging (by clicking the Stop Debugging button in Visual Studio or by pressing Shift+F5), the Zune does not reboot itself, so you can redeploy quickly and easily.

The drawbacks to running with debugging are as follows:

- Because debugging symbols are loaded and more information is being exchanged between the Zune and the PC, performance can be significantly slower.

- Problems related to networking can arise. If you are trying to test network connectivity, you should run without debugging so that all Zunes in the session run with relatively the same performance. Additionally, if you stop at a breakpoint, the program will block (wait for your input to the debugger), and it will stop receiving network packets.

- You may experience inconsistent program behavior. The game may run slower, faster, or just differently, depending on what the debugger is doing. To gauge your game's real performance, run without debugging.

Running Without Debugging

Depending on your needs at the time, you may prefer to run without the overhead of the debugger. Running without debugging has the advantage of providing truer, more consistent performance. Because there is no debugger overhead, you will have the maximum possible headroom available to run the game.

Running without debugging has the following drawbacks:

- You do not have the ability to step in and try to hunt down the source of erratic behavior.

- You lose control over the flow of execution.

- You cannot use watches, breakpoints, or other useful features of the debugger.

■**Tip** You can prevent the Zune software from launching when a device is initially plugged in by selecting Settings ➤ Device ➤ Sync Options in the Zune software and clearing the check box titled "Start the Zune software when I connect a device."

Creating Windows Versions of Zune Games

Suppose that you're developing a Zune game and make a minor change that doesn't really warrant a full deployment to the Zune—you know it will work, and you don't want to wait on the deployment process. For example, perhaps you want to test some new colors or change some text. You might wish there was a parallel Windows version of this game that you could use just to check that the game still runs after these minor changes. Thankfully, XNA Game Studio provides an automated way to do this.

The Create a Copy option, available from the project's context menu in the Solution Explorer, creates a new project file that references the same source code and content as the original project. This way, any changes you make are reflected in the output of either project. The next exercise demonstrates how to create a copy of a Zune game for Windows, using the Hello Zune game we created in Exercise 4-1.

■**Tip** The Create a Copy option can be used to create copies of your game to and from PC, Xbox, and Zune projects. This means that if you start with a Windows project, you can create a Zune copy of it later this way.

EXERCISE 4-2. A WINDOWS COPY OF HELLO ZUNE

Creating a Windows copy of a Zune game is easy. In this example, we'll use the HelloZune project we created in Exercise 4-1.

1. In Visual Studio, open the HelloZune project .

2. In the Solution Explorer, right-click the project (not the solution) and choose Create Copy of Project for Windows, as shown in Figure 4-13.

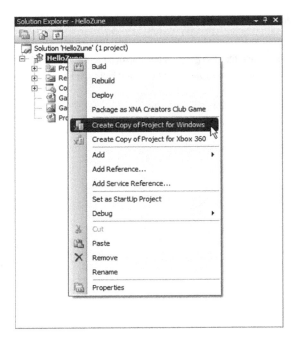

Figure 4-13. *Creating a copy of the project for Windows*

3. Notice the new project created in the Solution Explorer called `Windows Copy of HelloZune`, as shown in Figure 4-14. Open `Game1.cs`, and you will see that it contains the code we wrote in Exercise 4-1; this is the exact same file.

Figure 4-14. *The Zune project and the Windows copy in the Solution Explorer*

4. To run the PC version of the game, right-click the `Windows Copy of HelloZune` project in the Solution Explorer and select Set as Startup Project.

5. Press F5 to run the project with the debugger. Notice that the game is still deployed to the Zune, but it does not launch on the device. Instead, you see the game run on your PC. It looks like Figure 4-15.

Figure 4-15. *Hello Zune running on the PC*

CONSIDERATIONS FOR MULTIPLATFORM DEVELOPMENT

When you are working with a project that runs in more than one platform, as in Exercise 4-2, you will ultimately run into the problem of optimization. Code that runs excellently on the PC may not necessarily run well on the Zune, especially since the Zune's processor and memory capabilities are far less than that of a traditional desktop computer.

The approach of creating project copies is particularly useful for testing. However, if you plan to release a game on two or three different platforms, it is smarter to get the game in a working state first, and then make platform-specific optimizations later. This can be done using your own custom game libraries, multiple projects, source control, and other mechanisms. Do not assume that your game will run the same on one platform as it will on another, because it will not.

Furthermore, input is handled completely differently on the Zune, PC, and Xbox 360. PC games use keyboard and mouse input unless an Xbox 360 controller is detected. Zune controls map similarly to Xbox 360 controls, but they are not as intuitive as you might imagine (for example, a press of the middle button is the same as pressing A on the Xbox controller).

Aside from input, there are many other differences that distinguish these platforms. The Zune and Xbox 360 execute under the .NET Compact Framework common language runtime (CLR), whereas PC games execute under the full .NET Framework CLR, giving you access to more powerful tools. As another example, the `MediaPlayer` class is specific to the Zune, so attempting to access it in a PC game could lead to exceptions.

As you can imagine, it can be difficult to manage all of these caveats and nuances. Through tricks like compiler directives, however, you can achieve a fairly seamless experience for testing Zune games in PC projects. In this chapter, we will investigate the use of compilation directives to alter the output of a build based on the project type, allowing platform-specific code to run from the same codebase.

Zune Specifications and Optimization

Now that we have some simple elements of the game development work flow established, it's time to learn more about this very cool device and how to create games that perform well on it.

Reviewing the Core Zune Specifications

Current iterations of the Zune, both flash-based and hard-drive–based, share the following system specifications:

- 400 MHz processor
- 64MB of memory (16MB available for XNA games)
- 240 × 320 screen
- 16-bit color with 8-bit alpha channel
- Wi-Fi
- Touch-sensitive Zune pad input
- Windows Embedded operating system
- .NET Compact Framework

The two major areas of note in this list are the processor speed and RAM. While these specs appear to be limiting at first glance, the computing capability of the Zune is actually quite powerful compared to similar devices on the market at this time. The XNA Framework is incredibly efficient, although there is an inaccurate perception that managed code runs noticeably slower than unmanaged code.

Writing Performant Code for the Zune

Although the XNA Framework is great at optimizing and running complicated code, you should still make it part of your active mindset to write "performant" code (a term borrowed from a .NET architect friend of mine named Glen Jones).

Realistically, it is safe and perfectly fine to use things like generic collections and foreach loops, although these elements of programming have much faster alternatives. For example, working with arrays will always be faster than working with generic collections. Usually, for loops are faster than foreach loops.

Writing performant code is about balance. Don't be afraid to harness the power of the Zune; too much consideration for performance can end up costing you a lot of time. I suggest that you start with what you are comfortable coding. If a generic collection suits your needs, use one. Later, during the optimization stages of development, take a scalpel to your control flow and data types to determine where you are taking the biggest performance hit, and work backward in layers of abstraction.

Be careful not to pass enormous constant value types around all the time. I had one experience in mobile application development where the previous team had *megabytes* worth of constant values being passed around in nearly every function call. This would bring the application to its knees just a few layers into the call stack.

In general, you should write modular, cohesive code; use libraries; and adopt smart design patterns, which is a topic for another book. Optimization is important but not crucial in the opening phases of game development, so don't worry about it until it becomes a problem (especially since you are developing for the exact same hardware per user).

Here are a few pointers for improving performance on the Zune from the get-go:

Dereference frequently used variables: Let's say you are frequently accessing a game object's property in a block of code; for example, battleship.Guns[0].AmmunitionCount. You can dereference this easily into an integer like this:

```
int firstGunAmmo = battleship.Guns[0].AmmunitionCount;
```

Dereference this variable at the beginning of the code block, and use firstGunAmmo for the remaining calculations, instead of repeating the longer line of code. This makes your code more readable, and it also means that the property is retrieved only once. This reduces the number of calculations.

Use textures whose width and height are a power of 2: Most professional games use textures that have dimensions that are powers of 2, such as 4×4, 16×16, 32×16, and so on. Textures not fitting this format will still be drawn, of course, but it is computationally more expensive to rotate them due to anti-aliasing.

Be smart about content loading: Loading content on the Zune is one of the most computationally expensive operations you can perform. Loading all the content up-front, at the game's start, will eliminate the stalls and freezes associated with on-demand content loading. However, when done correctly, on-demand content loading can actually work in your favor. For example, if you have a level-based game where each level requires a substantial quantity of asset data to be loaded, adding the new assets between levels (and showing a loading screen at that time) could improve your game's overall performance, since assets will not be loaded until they are needed.

Handling Input on the Zune

Input handling on the Zune device can be slightly confusing. The part of the XNA Framework that allows you to access the state of the buttons and touchpad is the same that you would use for an Xbox 360 controller; there is currently no specific Zune input state class. The Zune controls are referenced in code by their analogs on the Xbox 360 controller.

Note On first-generation Zunes, there is no touch-sensitive pad. There is only a click wheel that works like a directional pad. This means that you should always support directional pad input, and support touch sensitivity as an added feature that can be disabled or enabled (if your game calls for it).

Accessing the Zune Pad

The Zune pad is a large, touch-sensitive area on the Zune. It operates exactly like a thumbstick on the Xbox 360 controller.

First, you should be aware of a couple of interesting caveats to the Zune pad's use that can cause frustration:

- Make sure the device is not locked when you try to use the input. On the upper-left area of the device is a sliding switch, which can be used to prevent any input on the device. If this switch is engaged, you may be wondering why your game isn't working.

- The Zune pad is not a multitouch device. It expects that only one finger is touching it at a given time. Trying to manipulate it with two fingers can result in strange behavior.

In code, the Zune pad is accessed like the Xbox 360's left thumbstick, and it outputs a 2D vector. The magnitude of this vector is always between zero and one, and the origin of the vector is in the center of the touchpad. Think of it as a simple 2D Cartesian coordinate plane, as illustrated in Figure 4-16.

In Figure 4-16, you see that the center of the Zune pad is at (0, 0). The x and y values can run anywhere from –1 to 1. The arrow shown in the figure is a vector representative of a touch at the absolute upper-right corner of the Zune pad, which translates in code to a Vector2 object equivalent to <1, 1>.

The value sent by the Zune pad changes based on where you touch it. Because the component values of a Vector2 object are of type float, the vector returned can look something like <-0.084, .587>. Because these values are always between –1 and 1, you can use the output of the Zune pad as ratios to modify other values using multiplication.

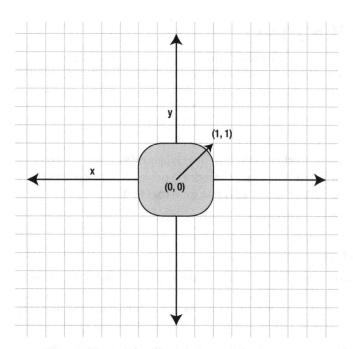

Figure 4-16. *How the Zune pad input control works*

For example, in the next exercise, we will add the following code to Game1.cs:

```
Texture2D characterTex;
SpriteFont normalFont;
Vector2 characterPosition = new Vector2(120, 160);
string displayText = "";
Vector2 displayTextPosition = new Vector2(5, 270);
const float sensitivity = 3.0f;
```

The characterPosition value will be updated in the Update method, based on the value of the Zune pad, and used later in the Draw method. It is initialized to a hard-coded Vector2 representing the center of the screen. Remember that the screen is 240 pixels wide by 320 pixels high. These values are simply those values divided by two.

The sensitivity variable is used to determine how far the character will move per unit on the Zune pad. You can modify this value to see the results. Increasing it causes the character to move more, while decreasing it causes the character to move less.

The Update method will include code to use the Zune pad input, as follows:

```
GamePadState inputState = GamePad.GetState(PlayerIndex.One);
Vector2 zunePadValue = inputState.ThumbSticks.Left;
zunePadValue.Y = -zunePadValue.Y;
characterPosition = characterPosition + (sensitivity * zunePadValue);
displayText = "Zune Pad:\r\n" + zunePadValue.ToString();
```

This code first gets the state of the Zune inputs using GamePad.GetState. (Note that, technically, only one player is active on the Zune at a time, so you should always use PlayerIndex.One). The value of the left thumbstick is then retrieved and stored in the zunePadValue variable. Remember that the Zune pad state is retrieved using the left thumbstick value, because that is how it is mapped in the framework.

Notice the line that negates the Y component of the zunePadValue variable. The XNA coordinate system has y increasing as it goes downward, whereas a positive y value from the Zune pad indicates that it was pressed upward. Failing to negate this value gives an "inverted y axis" kind of feel, and is less intuitive in 2D games than it might be in 3D games.

The code then updates the character position variable. It uses the current character position as a base, and adds to that the vector returned by the Zune pad state multiplied by the sensitivity variable. Thus, if the character is currently at (0, 0) and the Zune pad is pressed at (0.5, 0.5), the new value of the character position will be (0, 0) + 2.0(0.5, −0.5) = (0, 0) + (1, −1) = (1, −1). This works because the user is touching the Zune pad above and to the right of center. Intuitively, the user would expect the on-screen object to move up and to the right. You can see that this calculation fulfills that assumption by moving the character from (0, 0) to (1, −1). Remember that in XNA, when the y coordinate is negative, that means *up*, not down.

In the next exercise, you will gain some practical insight into how this works.

EXERCISE 4-3. ZUNE PAD INPUT HANDLING

In this example, you will see how the Zune pad can be used to control on-screen elements in a smooth, responsive manner. You will be modifying a position value and drawing a texture at that position. You can follow along with the source code provided in Chapter 4/Exercise 3/ZunePadExample. We'll be picking up the pace a bit in this exercise, because I assume you have followed the previous exercises and now have experience creating simple Zune Game projects in Visual Studio.

1. In Visual Studio, create a new Zune Game project called ZunePadExample.

2. In the Content project, add the asset character.png from the Chapter 4/Exercise 3/Artwork folder.

3. Add a new sprite font called Normal to the Content project. This is what we will use to view the value returned by the Zune pad. The default font face for XNA games is called Kootenay, which is a royalty-free font included with XNA Game Studio.

4. Open Game1.cs. Above the constructor, where the private variables are declared, add the following lines of code (which were discussed in the text preceding this exercise):

```
Texture2D characterTex;
SpriteFont normalFont;
Vector2 characterPosition = new Vector2(120, 160);
string displayText = "";
Vector2 displayTextPosition = new Vector2(5, 270);
const float sensitivity = 3.0f;
```

5. Locate the LoadContent method and add the following two lines in place of the TODO comment to initialize the game content:

```
characterTex = Content.Load<Texture2D>("character");
normalFont = Content.Load<SpriteFont>("Normal");
```

6. Locate the Update method and add the following lines that access the Zune pad, in place of the TODO comment (this code was also discussed in the text before this exercise):

```
GamePadState inputState = GamePad.GetState(PlayerIndex.One);
Vector2 zunePadValue = inputState.ThumbSticks.Left;
zunePadValue.Y = -zunePadValue.Y;
characterPosition = characterPosition + (sensitivity * zunePadValue);
displayText = "Zune Pad:\r\n" + zunePadValue.ToString();
```

7. Locate the Draw method and add the following lines that draw the character and the text on the screen, again, in place of the TODO comment:

```
spriteBatch.Begin();
spriteBatch.Draw(characterTex, characterPosition, Color.White);
spriteBatch.DrawString(normalFont, displayText, displayTextPosition,
    Color.Black);
spriteBatch.End();
```

8. Press F5 to run the game. You should see the character on the screen, as shown in Figure 4-17.

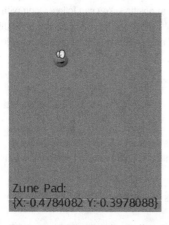

Figure 4-17. *The Zune pad example in action*

As you play around with your game, observe that the closer to the center of the pad you touch, the slower the character moves around the screen. The closer to the edge you press, the faster it moves. Be careful not to lose your character someplace off-screen, because there are no constraints in place to prevent it from going outside the play area. (Note that you could implement constraints easily by checking the position in an if statement before updating the character position in the Update method.)

Accessing the Directional Click Buttons

Older Zunes do not have a touchpad. They just have a four-directional click wheel with a center button. Newer Zunes with the touchpad are clickable as well. It is always a good idea to support the directional click buttons in case the end user doesn't have the touchpad. The games that come with the Zune 3.0 firmware, such as Hexic and Texas Hold 'em, have an option to disable touch. Disabling touch essentially causes the input subsystem to ignore touch and use only the directional click buttons.

The directional click buttons are used like normal controller buttons in XNA. They are accessed in code in the same way as the DPad collection of buttons for the Xbox 360. The following code snippet shows an example of how the DPad buttons are used:

```
GamePadState inputState = GamePad.GetState(PlayerIndex.One);
bool isUpPressed = inputState.DPad.Up == ButtonState.Pressed;
bool isDownPressed = inputState.DPad.Down == ButtonState.Pressed;
bool isLeftPressed = inputState.DPad.Left == ButtonState.Pressed;
bool isRightPressed = inputState.DPad.Right == ButtonState.Pressed;
```

The four Boolean variables defined here will indicate if the button is currently being pressed.

One thing to watch out for is the problem of multiple presses. Since the Update method is called many times per second (and this is usually where you handle input), you can't effectively compare the button state to ButtonState.Pressed as a trigger. Depending on how long the user holds down the button, you might have tens or hundreds of triggers, figuratively shooting far more bullets than you intend. After we take a look at accessing other buttons, we will build an input subsystem that checks for a new button press, rather than simply polling the button state.

Accessing Other Buttons

Because the Zune is a device with a very small form factor and an extremely limited number of inputs, we've already covered the majority of available input devices (the Zune pad and the directional click buttons). There are only three means of input left, and they are all buttons.

"But wait, I see only two other buttons," you say? Perhaps you forgot that you can actually press down the Zune pad. This is usually associated with the primary input activity for most games, covering actions such as fire, OK, select item, and so on. On the Xbox controller, the primary input (when it's not one of the triggers) is usually the A button, so naturally, pressing the Zune pad down is the same as pressing the A button (which is the same as pressing the middle button on first-generation Zunes).

The button marked with the play/pause icon is mapped to B, and the button marked with a back arrow is mapped to the Back button (which has a similar icon in the Xbox 360 controller).

All of these buttons can be accessed through the GamePadState's Buttons collection and compared to the ButtonState enumeration values to determine if they are being pressed.

Table 4-1 lists each of the available controls on the Zune, how they map to Xbox 360 controls, and how they are used in code in the XNA Framework.

Table 4-1. *Zune Control Mapping*

Zune Control	Xbox 360 Control	Associated GamePadState Property	Output Type
Zune pad	Left thumbstick	`ThumbSticks.Left`	`Vector2`
Click wheel	Directional pad	`DPad`	Group of `ButtonStates`
Center button	A	`Buttons.A`	`ButtonState`
Play/Pause	B	`Buttons.B`	`ButtonState`
Back	Back	`Buttons.Back`	`ButtonState`

Using an Input Handler Class for Zune and Windows Games

In this section, you will learn how to separate input handling from your main game logic in a way that both Windows and Zune games can use. This way, you can use the same input class library for Windows and Zune games, without needing to modify code for different versions of the same game.

The input handler class saves you a lot of time because it handles both keyboard and Zune pad input. If you are running the game on Windows, you can use either the keyboard or an attached Xbox 360 controller. If you are running the same code on the Zune, keyboard input will be ignored (since there is no keyboard on the Zune). The extraneous code does not present a problem, since the XNA Framework will safely ignore it, but you can use compiler directives to split out the platform-specific code if it really bothers you.

Another great feature of this input handler class is that it is extensible. You can always extend this class for a new game and add different properties suited to whatever game you are building. Additionally, this class provides support for "new" button presses. Earlier, I mentioned the problem of polling buttons for their pressed state and how that can result in many actions being triggered. Using this library, you can quickly and easily determine if a button was pressed, rather than checking to see if the button is down.

We'll look at two versions of the input handler: one that is specific to the Zune and does not include keyboard handling, and one that does handle keyboard input, so it can support Windows games as well as Zune games.

A Zune-Specific Input Handler

Listing 4-1 shows the Zune-specific version of the input handler, in which the implementation of `InputState` does not deal with keyboard input.

■**Note** This code is based on the input handler class included with most of the samples on the XNA Creators Club web site, including the Game State Management sample, which you can find at http:// creators.xna.com/en-us/samples/gamestatemanagement.

Listing 4-1. *Input State Handling, Centralized and Abstracted, for the Zune*

```
using System;
using System.Collections.Generic;
using System.Text;
using Microsoft.Xna.Framework;
using Microsoft.Xna.Framework.Input;

namespace InputHandler
{
    /// <summary>
    /// Helper for reading input from gamepad. This class tracks both
    /// the current and previous state of the Zune Pad and provides some
    /// properties to abstract specific presses.
    /// </summary>
    public class InputState
    {
        #region Fields

        public GamePadState CurrentGamePadState;
        public GamePadState LastGamePadState;

        #endregion

        #region Initialization


        /// <summary>
        /// Constructs a new input state.
        /// </summary>
        public InputState()
        {
            CurrentGamePadState = new GamePadState();
            LastGamePadState = new GamePadState();
        }


        #endregion

        #region Properties


        /// <summary>
        /// Checks for a Middle Button press (A by default)
        /// </summary>
        public bool MiddleButtonPressed
        {
            get
```

```csharp
        {
            return IsNewButtonPress(Buttons.A);
        }
    }


    /// <summary>
    /// Checks for a press of Up (DPadUp by default)
    /// </summary>
    public bool UpPressed
    {
        get
        {
            return IsNewButtonPress(Buttons.DPadUp);
        }
    }

    /// <summary>
    /// Checks for a press of Down (DPadDown by default)
    /// </summary>
    public bool DownPressed
    {
        get
        {
            return IsNewButtonPress(Buttons.DPadDown);
        }
    }

    /// <summary>
    /// Checks for a press of Right (DPadRight by default)
    /// </summary>
    public bool RightPressed
    {
        get
        {
            return IsNewButtonPress(Buttons.DPadRight);
        }
    }

    /// <summary>
    /// Checks for a press of Left (DPadLeft by default)
    /// </summary>
    public bool LeftPressed
    {
        get
        {
            return IsNewButtonPress(Buttons.DPadLeft);
```

```csharp
    }
}

/// <summary>
/// Checks for a press of the Play button (B by default)
/// </summary>
public bool PlayPressed
{
    get
    {
        return IsNewButtonPress(Buttons.B);
    }
}

/// <summary>
/// Checks for a press of the Back button
/// </summary>
public bool BackPressed
{
    get
    {
        return IsNewButtonPress(Buttons.Back);
    }
}

#endregion

#region Methods


/// <summary>
/// Reads the latest state of the gamepad.
/// </summary>
public void Update()
{
    LastGamePadState = CurrentGamePadState;
    CurrentGamePadState = GamePad.GetState(PlayerIndex.One);
}


/// <summary>
/// Checks if a button was newly pressed during this update.
/// </summary>
/// <param name="button">The button to check</param>
/// <returns>True if the button is down; false otherwise</returns>
public bool IsNewButtonPress(Buttons button)
{
```

```
        return (CurrentGamePadState.IsButtonDown(button) &&
                LastGamePadState.IsButtonUp(button));
    }

    /// <summary>
    /// Checks if a button is pressed down.
    /// </summary>
    /// <param name="button">The button to check</param>
    /// <returns>True if the button is down; false otherwise</returns>
    public bool IsButtonDown(Buttons button)
    {
        return CurrentGamePadState.IsButtonDown(button);
    }

    #endregion
    }
}
```

This input handler has three methods—IsButtonDown, IsNewButtonPress, and Update—which make up the most important part of this class. The method IsButtonDown is not directly used in determining button presses, but it is useful for whatever program may be consuming it.

The magic happens in the IsNewButtonPress method:

```
/// <summary>
/// Checks if a button was newly pressed during this update.
/// </summary>
/// <param name="button">The button to check</param>
/// <returns>True if the button is down; false otherwise</returns>
public bool IsNewButtonPress(Buttons button)
{
    return (CurrentGamePadState.IsButtonDown(button) &&
        LastGamePadState.IsButtonUp(button));
}
```

The InputState class maintains two copies of a GamePadState variable. The first copy, CurrentGamePadState, stores the state of the Zune's input. The current value stored here is updated every time the Update method of this class is called. The second, LastGamePadState, gives access to the buttons' state before the most recent update. By comparing the two game pad states, we can determine whether a button was pressed—that is to say, that the button was previously up and is now down. In the IsNewButtonPress method, you can see how this logic comes into play. The Boolean expression returned in this method gives a true or false indication of whether the button in question was previously up, but is now down. The IsNewButtonPress forms the foundation of the C# properties defined further up in the class, which are named according to specific controls. Let's take the MiddleButtonPressed property as an example:

```
/// <summary>
/// Checks for a Middle Button press (A by default)
/// </summary>
public bool MiddleButtonPressed
{
    get
    {
        return IsNewButtonPress(Buttons.A);
    }
}
```

This property has a simple getter that returns a call to `IsNewButtonPress` with the specified button. The power of this simplistic design lies in the fact that you can add as many properties as you like, and that you can change which buttons map to the named controls just by changing the button checked in the argument to `IsNewButtonPress`. You can extend this class and define your own properties, which enables you to reuse the class over and over. Imagine you have a game where the middle button should cause a projectile to fire. You might define a new property like this:

```
/// <summary>
/// Checks to see if the user pressed Fire.
/// </summary>
public bool Fire
.{
    get
    {
        return IsNewButtonPress(Buttons.A);
    }
}
```

This tells the game that a press of A means fire. Perhaps later you want to change `Fire` to mean the user pressed B. To do that, you would just change the code of this property to check `Buttons.B` instead.

Furthermore, since the same buttons are often used differently given other situations, you can add new properties that reference the same button to take advantage of this flexibility. Pressing the middle button could also indicate a selection of an on-screen element, but you wouldn't want to code this using the word `Fire`; that could become very unreadable. All you would need to do is add a new property:

```
/// <summary>
/// Checks for a menu selection.
/// </summary>
public bool Select
{
    get
    {
        return IsNewButtonPress(Buttons.A);
    }
}
```

To ensure that the `InputState` class always has the latest values, the `Update` method is employed. This method should be called as one of the first few line items of the game's `Update` method. This way, whenever the game is updated, the input state is updated also. The input state class's `Update` method performs only one major task: it sets the last input state to the current one, and then retrieves the current input state using `GamePad.GetState`.

How can this code be ported to support Windows as well? Technically, Windows games are supported by this code, but you would need to connect an Xbox 360 controller to deliver any input to the game. A better idea is to add keyboard support.

An Input Handler for Zune and Windows Games

Listing 4-2 shows a version of the input handler in Listing 4-1 that supports keyboard input. Note the emphasized lines, which have been added in this revision.

Listing 4-2. *An Input Handler Class That Handles Both Windows and Zune Input*

```
using System;
using System.Collections.Generic;
using System.Text;
using Microsoft.Xna.Framework;
using Microsoft.Xna.Framework.Input;

namespace InputHandler
{
    /// <summary>
    /// Helper for reading input from gamepad. This class tracks both
    /// the current and previous state of the Zune Pad and the keyboard,
    /// and provides some properties to abstract specific presses.
    /// </summary>
    public class InputState
    {
        #region Fields

        public GamePadState CurrentGamePadState;
        public GamePadState LastGamePadState;
        public KeyboardState CurrentKeyboardState;
        public KeyboardState LastKeyboardState;

        #endregion

        #region Initialization


        /// <summary>
        /// Constructs a new input state.
        /// </summary>
        public InputState()
        {
```

```csharp
        CurrentGamePadState = new GamePadState();
        LastGamePadState = new GamePadState();
        CurrentKeyboardState = new KeyboardState();
        LastKeyboardState = new KeyboardState();
    }


    #endregion

    #region Properties


    /// <summary>
    /// Checks for a Middle Button press (A by default)
    /// </summary>
    public bool MiddleButtonPressed
    {
        get
        {
            return IsNewButtonPress(Buttons.A) ||
                IsNewKeyPress(Keys.LeftControl);
        }
    }


    /// <summary>
    /// Checks for a press of Up (DPadUp by default)
    /// </summary>
    public bool UpPressed
    {
        get
        {
            return IsNewButtonPress(Buttons.DPadUp) ||
                IsNewKeyPress(Keys.Up);
        }
    }

    /// <summary>
    /// Checks for a press of Down (DPadDown by default)
    /// </summary>
    public bool DownPressed
    {
        get
        {
            return IsNewButtonPress(Buttons.DPadDown) ||
                IsNewKeyPress(Keys.Down);
        }
    }
```

```csharp
/// <summary>
/// Checks for a press of Right (DPadRight by default)
/// </summary>
public bool RightPressed
{
    get
    {
        return IsNewButtonPress(Buttons.DPadRight) ||
            IsNewKeyPress(Keys.Right);
    }
}

/// <summary>
/// Checks for a press of Left (DPadLeft by default)
/// </summary>
public bool LeftPressed
{
    get
    {
        return IsNewButtonPress(Buttons.DPadLeft) ||
            IsNewKeyPress(Keys.Left);
    }
}

/// <summary>
/// Checks for a press of the Play button (B by default)
/// </summary>
public bool PlayPressed
{
    get
    {
        return IsNewButtonPress(Buttons.B) ||
            IsNewKeyPress(Keys.LeftAlt);
    }
}

/// <summary>
/// Checks for a press of the Back button
/// </summary>
public bool BackPressed
{
    get
    {
        return IsNewButtonPress(Buttons.Back) ||
            IsNewKeyPress(Keys.Back);
    }
}
```

```csharp
#endregion

#region Methods


/// <summary>
/// Reads the latest state of the gamepad and the keyboard.
/// </summary>
public void Update()
{
    LastGamePadState = CurrentGamePadState;
    CurrentGamePadState = GamePad.GetState(PlayerIndex.One);
    LastKeyboardState = CurrentKeyboardState;
    CurrentKeyboardState = Keyboard.GetState();
}


/// <summary>
/// Checks if a button was newly pressed during this update.
/// </summary>
/// <param name="button">The button to check</param>
/// <returns>True if the button is down; false otherwise</returns>
public bool IsNewButtonPress(Buttons button)
{
    return (CurrentGamePadState.IsButtonDown(button) &&
        LastGamePadState.IsButtonUp(button));
}

/// <summary>
/// Checks if a key was newly pressed during this update.
/// </summary>
/// <param name="button">The key to check</param>
/// <returns>True if the key is down; false otherwise</returns>
public bool IsNewKeyPress(Keys key)
{
    return (CurrentKeyboardState.IsKeyDown(key) &&
        LastKeyboardState.IsKeyUp(key));
}

/// <summary>
/// Checks if a button is pressed down.
/// </summary>
/// <param name="button">The button to check</param>
/// <returns>True if the button is down; false otherwise</returns>
public bool IsButtonDown(Buttons button)
{
    return CurrentGamePadState.IsButtonDown(button);
}
```

```
        /// <summary>
        /// Checks if a key is pressed down.
        /// </summary>
        /// <param name="button">The key to check</param>
        /// <returns>True if the key is down; false otherwise</returns>
        public bool IsKeyDown(Keys key)
        {
            return CurrentKeyboardState.IsKeyDown(key);
        }

        #endregion
    }
}
```

Notice the addition of the IsNewKeyPress method. This does the same thing as IsNewButtonPress, except it works with keys instead of buttons. Two new KeyboardState variables have been added, and they are used in exactly the same way as their GamePadState counterparts.

Now turn your attention to the properties. In addition to checking for button presses, the code is also checking for the possibility of a key press. The OR (||) operator is used here, because the user could technically use one or the other. If AND (&&) were used, the Zune would never fire any inputs, because keys do not exist (therefore are never pressed) on the Zune device. However, at runtime, the Zune will operate happily even with the keyboard code in there. This is partly because both KeyboardState variables are initialized to a new KeyboardState and never change from that value.

You can take the code from Listing 4-2 and create a new game library project with it if you wish.

ENCAPSULATION, COHESION, AND THE OBSERVER PATTERN

A quick way to optimize your game code is to apply some well-founded object-oriented design principles. Encapsulation and cohesion go hand-in-hand.

Cohesion refers to the notion that a class or a method should do exactly what it says it will do—nothing more and nothing less—and that a class should contain only the methods pertinent to things the class should do. The InputState class is a good example of a cohesive class. It contains only properties and methods relevant to the input state. This makes the class very portable, in that you can move it to other game projects and avoid having to change, remove, or comment out code.

Encapsulation is more about choosing which properties and methods to expose publicly, as well as hiding the more mundane processing from any consumers of the class. In the InputState example, the only exposed properties and methods are the ones that are useful to external consumers of the class. Adding new properties to the InputState class to extend the functionality is also a good practice related to encapsulation.

The *Observer pattern* is a popular design pattern that allows objects to be notified by other objects. A similar approach is frequently used in XNA. A method, like Update, calls a similarly named method on another object in the program to notify it of some state change (or in the case of Update, to notify it that the game is updating). Check out this sample Update method:

```
protected override void Update(GameTime gameTime)
{
    // Allows the game to exit
    if (GamePad.GetState(PlayerIndex.One).Buttons.Back == ButtonState.Pressed)
        this.Exit();

    inputState.Update();
    audioEngine.Update(gameTime);
    networkSessionManager.Update(gameTime);

    HandleInput();

    base.Update(gameTime);
}
```

In this Update method, you see four calls to Update methods on other objects. Perhaps these are objects you have written yourself. The Update method is something you have written and exposed on these classes to accept update notification from the main XNA game loop.

Now you can see the purpose of the Update method in the original InputState class. When called from the game's Update method, the input state is automatically updated. The object is then ready to be queried by the HandleInput routine, which has the responsibility of actually doing something with the updated input state.

Through good design precepts, including cohesion and encapsulation, the Observer pattern comes to life. Notice how simplified the code in the Update method is now. There is no literal processing occurring in this method; instead, each major engine component in the game is notified that it should update itself. This approach lends itself well to reusability, readability, and tidiness of code. In the next chapter, you will learn about game components, which can be used to further abstract this pattern in a tidy, usable way.

Let's run through a quick exercise using the code from Listing 4-2 to handle input in a clean and efficient manner. In Exercise 4-4, you will use the InputState class in a simple game that runs on both the Zune and Windows.

EXERCISE 4-4. A ZUNE APP WITH WINDOWS COMPATIBILITY

In this exercise, you will learn to use the InputState class to build a simple game that changes colors of the screen based on which button is pressed (either on the Zune or Windows). In this application, we will change the game screen color like so: Down = black, Up = red, Right = green, and Left = blue.

1. In Visual Studio, create a new Zune game project called InputStateTestGame.

2. Add a new class called InputState to the project and add the code from Listing 4-2, except you don't need the statements to use System.Collections.Generic and System.Text, and the namespace should be InputStateTestGame. So, the class should begin as follows:

```
using System;
using Microsoft.Xna.Framework;
using Microsoft.Xna.Framework.Input;

namespace InputStateTestGame
{
    /// <summary>
...
```

3. Add a new sprite font to the class, called `Normal.spritefont`.

4. Add the following lines to the variable declarations section of `Game1.cs`, just after the declaration of the `spriteBatch` variable:

```
SpriteFont arialFont;
InputState inputState = new InputState();
Color backgroundColor = Color.DarkGray;
```

5. Find the `LoadContent` method and load the Arial sprite font:

```
arialFont = Content.Load<SpriteFont>("Normal");
```

6. Create a new private method called `HandleInput` in the `Game1.cs` file, below the `Draw` method. This class handles changing the background color based on which button was pressed. Note the effective utilization of the `InputState` class, and how easy it is to get input, regardless of whether it's a Zune or Windows implementation.

```
private void HandleInput()
{
    if (inputState.DownPressed)
        backgroundColor = Color.Black;

    if (inputState.UpPressed)
        backgroundColor = Color.DarkRed;

    if (inputState.RightPressed)
        backgroundColor = Color.DarkGreen;

    if (inputState.LeftPressed)
        backgroundColor = Color.DarkBlue;
}
```

7. Find the `Update` method in the `Game1.cs` file and add the following lines to update the input state class and handle the input. Add this code in place of the `TODO` comment.

```
inputState.Update();
HandleInput();
```

8. Find the `Draw` method in the `Game1.cs` file and locate the method that clears the device. Replace `Color.CornflowerBlue` with `backgroundColor`. The modified line should look like this:

```
graphics.GraphicsDevice.Clear(backgroundColor);
```

9. Add some helper text. In place of the TODO comment in the `Draw` method, add the following lines to draw the text:

```
string helperText = "Up: Red\r\n" +
    "Down: Black\r\n" +
    "Right: Green\r\n" +
    "Left: Blue\r\n";

spriteBatch.Begin();
spriteBatch.DrawString(normalFont, helperText, Vector2.Zero, Color.White);
spriteBatch.End();
```

The carriage return/new line sequence, `\r\n`, is used to create a multiline string. The helper text is drawn at (0, 0)—the top-left corner—in white.

10. Create a Windows copy of this Zune game by right-clicking the `InputStateTestGame` project in the Solution Explorer and choosing Create Copy of Project for Windows.

11. Test the game on both the Zune and in Windows by alternately setting the Zune and Windows projects as the startup project. On the Zune, the output looks like Figure 4-18. On Windows, the output looks like Figure 4-19.

Figure 4-18. *The color-changing application on the Zune after pressing Down to change the screen to black*

Figure 4-19. *The color-changing application on Windows after pressing the left arrow key to change the screen to blue (although the screenshot is in grayscale)*

As you've seen, handling input on the Zune and adding support for Windows is easy with our `InputState` class. It's a good idea to take this code and put it in a usable library of useful code for Zune games, which you can include in any other games you create. This is one example of many reusable components we will be creating throughout the course of the book.

SETTING WINDOWS GAME SIZE TO MATCH ZUNE DIMENSIONS

In developing Zune games with a Windows test version, you may find it useful to force the dimensions of the Windows version of the application to match those of the Zune. This can be done by setting the size of the preferred back buffer of the graphics device and applying the changes.

In gaming terminology, the *back buffer* is an area of memory on the graphics device where pixels are written before being drawn to the front buffer. The *front buffer* is the area of memory that contains the pixels currently being displayed. Separating the two buffers prevents the problem of concurrent reads and writes to and from a shared memory space.

Setting the preferred back buffer dimensions in XNA has the effect of automatically sizing the client boundary of the game. In Windows terms, this means the window displaying the game will be resized to match these dimensions. For the Zune, it just means that the back buffer's dimensions are explicitly set to be equal to the Zune's dimensions, which can lead to marginally increased performance. For either platform, setting these values explicitly is a win-win situation.

To set the preferred back buffer width and height, you must modify them, and then explicitly tell the graphics device to apply the changes. Find the Initialize method of your game and add these lines:

```
graphics.PreferredBackBufferHeight = 320;
graphics.PreferredBackBufferWidth = 240;
graphics.ApplyChanges();
```

Try it now using the application you created in Exercise 4-4. When you run the Windows version of the game, you will see that the window has been automatically resized to 240 × 320. You can test your Zune game with a touch more realism this way.

Playing Music in Zune Games

While we are slowly turning the Zune into a mobile gaming platform, that was not its original intent. The Zune is, and will remain, a music player. After all, that's what it was designed to be from the very beginning, and that's what it does best!

When a Zune game is launched, it executes under the .NET Framework in "developer mode." Your game and its actions exist only for the duration that it runs. Zune games have limited access to the local file system. They cannot access the firmware or do anything outside the protected bubble in which they execute. This protection is by design, and is what causes the Zune to reboot after a game exits. Rebooting the Zune causes it to reload its firmware and start anew, eliminating memory leaks, orphan threads, and other things that can create problems.

Developer mode exists mainly to protect the contents of the Zune from the crazy things developers can do. As a result, Zune games can play only those songs that are not restricted by a DRM system.

Let's take a look at some of the components involved in playing music in Zune games.

Using Media Player Component Classes

Three major components of the XNA Framework allow you to play music: the Song, MediaLibrary, and MediaPlayer classes. These classes reside in the Microsoft.Xna.Framework. Media namespace, so don't forget to add this namespace to your list of using directives.

The Song Class

The Song class gives you access to a lot of useful data for a particular song. You can access common song attributes, such as the album name, artist, track number, track name, duration, genre, and more. It also has an IsProtected attribute, which allows you to check for DRM protection before attempting to play a song.

Songs are usually acquired by indexing into the collection of songs available on an instance of the MediaLibrary class, like so:

```
Song firstSong = mediaLibrary.Songs[0];
```

The MediaLibrary Class

The MediaLibrary class gives you access to the library of music on the Zune. There are useful properties available on instances of the MediaLibrary class that allow you to get music by album, genre, artist, or even playlist. The Songs property gives you a collection of all the songs on the Zune.

Creating a new instance of the MediaLibrary class is very easy. The default constructor of this class takes no arguments, so all you need to do on the Zune is instantiate a simple variable like so:

```
MediaLibrary library = new MediaLibrary();
```

The other constructor takes a MediaSource argument, which is useful on PC or Xbox games where you want to use Windows Media Connect libraries or libraries on the local file system.

■**Note** To enumerate available media sources on other platforms (PC or Xbox 360), you can use MediaSource.GetAvailableMediaSources(). This method returns a list of available media sources on the device or computer.

The MediaLibrary class also allows you to access pictures on the device in an easy way. Instances of the MediaLibrary class have a property called Pictures. Indexing into this collection returns a Picture object, which in turn has a method called GetTexture. GetTexture returns a Texture2D object, which you can draw on the screen to create an interesting, personalized experience. Likewise, the Album object has a method called GetAlbumArt, which you can use to get a Texture2D object representing the album art.

The MediaLibrary class is very comprehensive, and these are just a few examples of the unique behaviors you can achieve with it.

The MediaPlayer Class

You cannot create your own instance of the static MediaPlayer class. You can use only a handful of static methods to control which song is playing. This actually saves you some code in the long run. The code to play a song (held in a Song object) is straightforward:

```
MediaPlayer.Play(song);
```

You can also use this method to play a SongCollection object, a special collection of songs that can be obtained in a number of ways. Usually, the Songs property of certain objects in a MediaLibrary is of type SongCollection, so you could also use code like this to play an entire artist catalog:

```
MediaPlayer.Play(mediaLibrary.Artists[artist_index].Songs);
```

Other useful static methods of the MediaPlayer class include Stop, Pause, Resume, MoveNext, MovePrevious, and GetVisualizationData. There are also some static properties that you can use to inquire about or alter the current state of the media player, such as Volume, PlayPosition, IsMuted, IsVisualizationEnabled, IsShuffled, IsRepeating, and State. The State property can be one of three values as defined in the MediaState enumeration: Playing, Paused, or Stopped.

Note By default, accessing MediaLibrary.Songs gives you a collection of all songs on the Zune sorted alphabetically by track name. You can achieve some randomization by telling MediaPlayer to play this entire collection and then setting MediaPlayer.IsShuffled to true. However, if you use MoveNext and MovePrevious, you must watch out for DRM-protected files.

You can set the volume of the media player by assigning a value between 0.0 and 1.0 to MediaPlayer.Volume. This value is logarithmic and represents a decibel value, so 0.5 is not really half as loud as 1.0; instead 0.5 is nearly inaudible. It's also important to note that the overall volume you hear is controlled by the Zune's master volume, which you cannot access through code unless you use the Guide class to show the built-in Zune menu, as described next. In effect, altering MediaPlayer.Volume will result in a volume less than or equal to the Zune master volume, so it's really useful only when you want to decrease (or reset) the volume.

Note Even when MediaPlayer.Volume is set to maximum (1.0f), it is still distinctly quieter than the maximum volume when the Zune is just playing songs. It is about half as loud.

Using the Guide

Another option for playing music is to use the built-in guide menu. On the Xbox 360, the guide is the menu that pops up when you press the Xbox logo button. That interface allows you to sign in to profiles, play music, and so on. Like the Xbox guide, the Zune guide can be hooked into via XNA. It brings up a Zune-specific menu for altering volume, playing music, and more. It's a very quick and convenient way to add music functionality to your game without needing to create a custom music browser.

The guide can be shown by calling Guide.Show(). Note that there is no guide interface for PC games, so you can't compile code for dual Windows/Zune projects unless you use conditional preprocessor directives, like this:

```
#if ZUNE
Guide.Show();
#endif
```

Your game will continue running its Update loop while the guide is shown. To prevent this, you can put your entire Update loop in an if statement that references the Guide.IsVisible property (which will not compile under Windows):

```
// in the Update method
if (Guide.IsVisible == false)
{
    // do all your updates
}
```

This is a quick and effective way to pause your game if the guide is shown.

There are some drawbacks to using the guide:

- The guide, being part of the Zune firmware, allows you to browse and attempt to play any and all music (including protected tracks). There is no API functionality (yet) in the XNA Framework to prevent a user from trying to play a protected track using the guide. If a user tries to play a protected track via the guide, no feedback will be given via the guide user interface to indicate that the track is protected and cannot be played. In the community technology preview (CTP) version, attempting to do this will throw an uncatchable exception.

- When the guide is displayed, it has a transparent background that can make it difficult to read, unless you black out your screen before showing the guide or use a preprocessor directive in the Draw method to clear to black when the guide is shown.

- When the guide is first shown, the track is automatically paused. You can see the play/pause icon in the lower right of the Zune when you bring up the guide, but it can be unclear to the user as to why the track stopped when the guide was shown. (This is unfortunate, but the overall convenience of the guide interface actually makes it quite an innocuous detail.)

Note The guide itself will not show up in screenshots taken from the XNA Game Studio Device Center.

If time allows, it is preferable to write and use your own audio/music engine, rather than use the guide.

Putting It Together

As an example of using these main components for playing music, we'll build a simple media player application for the Zune. In the exercise, we'll first declare some variables in the Game1 class to represent the core things we need for the music player:

- input: An instance of our InputState class, making it easier for us to capture input
- albumArtTex: A reference to the current album art
- noArtTex: The default texture when there is no album art or no song is playing
- albumArtPosition: A point on the screen where the album art will be drawn
- currentSongIndex: The index in the media library of the song currently being played
- regularText and boldText: Strings drawn on the screen in their respective fonts

- boldTextPosition and regularTextPosition: Points where these strings are drawn

- font and boldFont: Differently sized and styled versions of the Kootenay font

We'll add a RefreshAlbumArt method to handle drawing the album art on the Zune screen, as shown in Listing 4-3.

Listing 4-3. *The RefreshAlbumArt Method*

```
private void RefreshAlbumArt()
{
    if (MediaPlayer.State == MediaState.Playing ||
        MediaPlayer.State == MediaState.Paused)
    {
        Song currentSong = MediaPlayer.Queue.ActiveSong;
        if (currentSong.Album.HasArt)
        {
            albumArtTex = currentSong.Album.GetAlbumArt(this.Services);
        }
        else
            albumArtTex = noArtTex;
    }
    else
    {
        albumArtTex = noArtTex;
    }

    albumArtPosition = new Vector2(120 - albumArtTex.Width / 2, 100);
}
```

The RefreshAlbumArt method is responsible for setting the Texture2D object drawn on screen. If the currently playing song has album art, the Texture2D representing that art is extracted using the Album.GetAlbumArt method (passing in the Game class's Services property). Then, based on the art obtained, the position to draw the art is modified so that it is centered horizontally.

In the Update method, we'll add some input handling that advances tracks, updates the album art, and updates the status text for the currently playing song, as shown in Listing 4-4.

Listing 4-4. *Update Method for the Media Player Example*

```
protected override void Update(GameTime gameTime)
{
    // Allows the game to exit
    if (GamePad.GetState(PlayerIndex.One).Buttons.Back == ButtonState.Pressed)
        this.Exit();

    input.Update();
```

```
    if (input.PlayPressed)
    {
        switch (MediaPlayer.State)
        {
            case MediaState.Paused:
                MediaPlayer.Resume();
                break;
            case MediaState.Playing:
                MediaPlayer.Pause();
                break;
            case MediaState.Stopped:
                PlayNextSong();
                break;
        }
    }

    if (input.RightPressed)
    {
        PlayNextSong();
    }

    if (input.LeftPressed)
    {
        PlayPreviousSong();
    }

    switch (MediaPlayer.State)
    {
        case MediaState.Stopped:
            boldText = "Stopped";
            regularText = "Press Play to play a song.";
            break;
        case MediaState.Playing:
            Song currentSong = MediaPlayer.Queue.ActiveSong;

            boldText = "Artist: " + currentSong.Artist.Name +
                "\r\nAlbum: " + currentSong.Album.Name;

            regularText = currentSong.Name;
            break;
        case MediaState.Paused:
            boldText = "Paused";
            regularText = "";
            break;
    }

    base.Update(gameTime);
}
```

First, the input engine is updated. Without calling input.Update, the game will never know when any buttons are pressed. Then we check to see if Play, Right, or Left are pressed and act accordingly. The Play button behaves differently depending on the state of the media player. If no media is playing, it starts playing the current song. If media is currently playing, it pauses the media player. If the media player is paused, pressing Play will resume from the current track. Pressing Right causes the track to advance using the PlayNextSong method, shown in Listing 4-5. Pressing Left causes the track to move back using the PlayPreviousSong method, also shown in Listing 4-5.

After handling input, we must update the text displayed on the screen to match what is playing. Again, this is dependent on the state of the media player. If the player is stopped, we simply offer a directive to press Play. If media is playing, we set the bold text and regular text to the artist, album, and track name. If the media is paused, we simply display "Paused" on the screen.

Listing 4-5. *The PlayNextSong and PlayPreviousSong Methods*

```
private void PlayNextSong()
{
    for (int songIndex = currentSongIndex + 1; songIndex <=
        mediaLibrary.Songs.Count; songIndex++)
    {
        if (songIndex >= mediaLibrary.Songs.Count)
            songIndex = 0;

        if (mediaLibrary.Songs[songIndex].IsProtected == false)
        {
            currentSongIndex = songIndex;
            MediaPlayer.Play(mediaLibrary.Songs[currentSongIndex]);
            break;
        }
    }
    RefreshAlbumArt();
}

private void PlayPreviousSong()
{
    for (int songIndex = currentSongIndex - 1; songIndex >= -1; songIndex--)
    {
        if (songIndex < 0)
            songIndex = mediaLibrary.Songs.Count - 1;

        if (mediaLibrary.Songs[songIndex].IsProtected == false)
        {
            currentSongIndex = songIndex;
            MediaPlayer.Play(mediaLibrary.Songs[currentSongIndex]);
            break;
        }
    }
}
```

```
    RefreshAlbumArt();
}
```

The PlayNextSong and PlayPreviousSong methods are very similar in structure. The purpose of the for loops is to obtain the next available unprotected track; it will keep looking until it finds one. When an unprotected track is found, the MediaPlayer plays it. In both methods, the album art is automatically refreshed by the call to RefreshAlbumArt.

■**Note**   You can also use MediaPlayer.MoveNext() and MediaPlayer.MovePrevious() to advance the current track in the song collection. However, currently, if the next song in the queue is DRM-protected, this method will throw an exception. The purpose of the custom PlayNextSong and PlayPreviousSong methods is to provide checks for DRM protection so no attempt to play a protected song is made. It is safe to use the built-in methods if the MediaPlayer is playing a SongCollection that does not contain any protected tracks.

In the Draw method, we will clear the screen to black, draw the status text blocks, and draw the album art, as shown in Listing 4-6.

Listing 4-6. *Draw Method for the Media Player Example*

```
protected override void Draw(GameTime gameTime)
{
    graphics.GraphicsDevice.Clear(Color.Black);

    spriteBatch.Begin();
    try
    {
        spriteBatch.Draw(albumArtTex, albumArtPosition, Color.White);
        spriteBatch.DrawString(fontBold, boldText, boldTextPosition,
            Color.White);
        spriteBatch.DrawString(font, regularText, regularTextPosition,
            Color.White);
    }
    catch
    {

    }

    spriteBatch.End();

    base.Draw(gameTime);
}
```

The try-catch block is used because some track names, artist names, and album names may contain special characters that are not compiled by the content pipeline. The DrawString method draws a string of text character by character, so when an undrawable character is encountered, an exception will be thrown, and you will see a partial string of text. You can modify which characters are compiled into the sprite font by opening the .spritefont file and looking for the CharacterRegions tag. In that code, you can modify the Start and End elements to ensure all possible special characters are included in the sprite font. See if you can arrive at a more elegant solution than the try-catch approach.

Also notice that the albumArtTex object is drawn first. This ensures that the text will be displayed over the album art. If there is no album art, albumArtTex has been set to the default "no album art" texture by the RefreshAlbumArt method, so this is safe.

Now let's put this together into a media player.

EXERCISE 4-5. A SIMPLE MEDIA PLAYER

The Zune firmware sports a world-class music player with a lot of great features. So, why build another one? This exercise will help you understand how the main media components of the XNA Framework work together to make a basic music player. In turn, this understanding will prove valuable when you want to implement music in your games.

1. In Visual Studio, create a new Zune Game project called SimpleMusicPlayer. The sample code can be found in the Exercises/Chapter 4/Example 5 folder.

2. Add two new sprite fonts (use the royalty-free Kootenay font) to the Content project. Call one Kootenay and change its font size to 10. Call the other KootenayBold, change its font size to 10, and change its style to Bold. This can be done by editing the associated .spritefont files.

3. Add the NoArt.png file to the Content project from the Examples/Chapter 4/Exercise 5/Artwork folder.

4. Bring our old friend, the InputState class from earlier in the chapter (Listing 4-1), into the mix. You can do this by right-clicking the project, choosing Add Existing Item, and navigating to the Examples/Chapter 4/Exercise 4/InputHandler folder. Since you are copying code rather than using a game library, don't forget to change the namespace in InputState.cs to SimpleMusicPlayer. If you've created your own library for input handling already, then you are ahead of the game (in a good way). Just add a reference to your own library and be sure to include the namespace.

5. Declare the following variables (described earlier) in Game1.cs where the variables are declared:

```
MediaLibrary mediaLibrary;
InputState input;
Texture2D albumArtTex, noArtTex;
Vector2 albumArtPosition;
int currentSongIndex = -1;
string regularText, boldText;
Vector2 boldTextPosition, regularTextPosition;
SpriteFont font, fontBold;
```

6. In the `Initialize` method, initialize the media library and current song. The vectors are initialized to points on the screen that look good placement-wise. The volume is set to the maximum (`1.0f`).

```
protected override void Initialize()
{
    input = new InputState();
    mediaLibrary = new MediaLibrary();
    MediaPlayer.Volume = 1.0f;
    regularText = "";
    boldText = "";
    boldTextPosition = new Vector2(5, 5);
    regularTextPosition = new Vector2(5, 35);

    base.Initialize();
}
```

7. In the `LoadContent` method, load the two sprite fonts and the default "no album art" texture. Then call `RefreshAlbumArt()`.

```
protected override void LoadContent()
{
    // Create a new SpriteBatch, which can be used to draw textures.
    spriteBatch = new SpriteBatch(GraphicsDevice);

    font = Content.Load<SpriteFont>("Kootenay");
    fontBold = Content.Load<SpriteFont>("KootenayBold");
    noArtTex = Content.Load<Texture2D>("NoArt");
    albumArtTex = noArtTex;
    RefreshAlbumArt();
}
```

8. Add the `RefreshAlbumArt` private method shown in Listing 4-3.

9. Find the `UnloadContent` method and tell the `MediaPlayer` to stop playing. When the game exits, you want the audio to stop, especially if you are debugging and the Zune doesn't reboot.

```
protected override void UnloadContent()
{
    MediaPlayer.Stop();
}
```

10. Find the `Update` method and modify it so it looks like Listing 4-4.

11. Implement the `PlayNextSong` and `PlayPreviousSong` private methods shown in Listing 4-5.

12. Find the `Draw` method and modify it so it looks like Listing 4-6.

13. Ensure the connected Zune is set as the default in XNA Game Studio Device Center. Then press F5 to run with debugging.

14. Press the Play button to start playing tracks. You should see something similar to Figure 4-20.

Figure 4-20. *The SimpleMusicPlayer application running. The song in this screenshot harkens back to my college days. I played drums in a band called Morningside. We had no album art, and this song was called simply 7. I love it because it opens with a wicked drum solo.*

Your First Real Zune Game: OutBreak

We're going to shift gears a bit now and work on the very first full-fledged Zune game of the book, called OutBreak. OutBreak will roll together a lot of the techniques covered thus far, resulting in a game you will actually enjoy playing. You will learn a few new techniques to spice up your graphics as well.

In this example, you'll see the guide menu used to provide musical accompaniment. Simple game state management is also addressed, along with some other new concepts such as collision detection and text centering.

OutBreak is a paddle game, where the object is to clear the board of all the visible blocks. By *block*, I mean the object the player is trying to strike with the ball.

Before writing any code, let's take a look at some basic design elements that will lead us to implementing the game logic.

Designing OutBreak

During one interview a few years ago for a C# position, I was asked whether my coding style was *maverick* or *meticulous*. At the time, I wasn't sure what was meant by the question. Now I know that mavericks sit down and code, with little or no design planning, figuring things out as they go. Meticulous coders are structured almost to the point of refusing to write code until they have a signed-off design document. For the purposes of this example, we'll find some middle ground between the two and outline some basic rules that our game must follow.

The Rules

The general rules of this implementation of OutBreak are simple:

- A grid of blocks is displayed in some pattern at the top of the screen.
- The ball is initially traveling away from the paddle.
- The ball and paddle are recentered after each round.
- A score multiplier is used to reward knocking out multiple blocks with one paddle strike.
- The score multiplier increases with each block struck before hitting a wall or the paddle.
- The score multiplier resets to 1 when the ball hits the paddle or a wall.
- The player has a certain number of chances, or "lives," to clear all the blocks.

You could alter these rules a little to suit your wishes without changing too much code. No numbers are directly specified (for example, the maximum number of lives), because these are defined in code as constants.

Game States

The mechanism for dealing with game state is very simple: we use an enumeration to manipulate the state, and we check the game state at various times using a `switch` statement. We define four possible game states for the game:

- `Intro`: The first screen of the game appears, as shown in Figure 4-21.

Figure 4-21. *OutBreak in the Intro state*

- Ready: A countdown screen appears between rounds, as shown in Figure 4-22.

Figure 4-22. *OutBreak in the Ready state*

- Playing: The game is active, as shown in Figure 4-23.

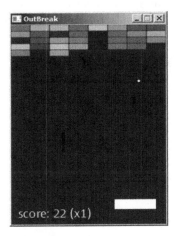

Figure 4-23. *OutBreak in the Playing state*

- GameOver: The game has ended, as shown in Figure 4-24.

Figure 4-24. *OutBreak in the GameOver state*

These four game states compose everything you'll see in the game. The next step is to figure out how to transition between these states. Figure 4-25 shows a traditional state diagram that will help you determine when to move between these game states. Each circle is a game state, and the arrows flowing between them represent the conditions that must be met for the game to transition to another state.

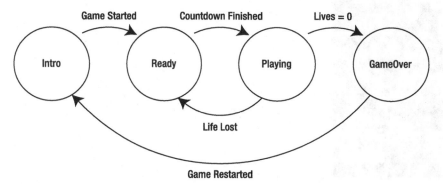

Figure 4-25. *States and transitions for the OutBreak game*

Figure 4-25 shows that the game state flow is very simple. The game displays the intro screen first. Then the game alternates between the countdown and playing screens, until the player has lost all her lives. When there are no lives left, the game moves to the GameOver state. The player can then restart the game by pressing a button, which changes the game state back to Intro, and the state flow resumes from the Intro state.

Creating OutBreak

Are you ready to write your very first real, playable Zune game? This example incorporates a lot of what you have already learned. Some important concepts demonstrated here are usage of the media player (via the guide), collision detection, drawing game objects, handling input, randomization, writing clean code using regions and classes, and maintaining a parallel copy of the game for Windows.

The structure of the Game1.cs file in this game has been modified slightly from the standard layout of what's included by default in an XNA game. I made extensive use of regions to separate code clearly, and I trimmed out some of the unused namespaces. Reading through this example should closely resemble your thought process while building the game, although you will likely see some code you don't understand yet. This is where the use of regions comes in handy. Regions are just ways of grouping code together; they aren't compiled, and are there for your convenience as a programmer. They provide easy reference to portions of code and help keep your code organized.

By the end of this chapter, you'll have a functioning game that runs on both Zune and Windows. If at any time you feel you are lost or don't have the correct code, check the supplied source code in the Examples/Chapter 4/Exercise 6/OutBreak folder.

Setting Up the Project

To get started, set up your project as follows:

1. In Visual Studio, create a new Zune Game project called OutBreak.

2. Right-click the OutBreak project in the Solution Explorer and choose Create Copy of Project for Windows. Make sure the Windows project is set as the default startup project.

3. Open Game1.cs and arrange it into regions. The rest of this example will refer to certain areas of the code by region name, so that you are adding and modifying code in the correct places. Create regions as follows:

   - Take the existing methods and enclose them in a region called XNA Methods.

   - Enclose the two private fields (spriteBatch and Graphics) in a region called Private Fields.

   - Enclose the Game1 constructor in a region called Constructor(s).

   - Collapse these new regions and add four new ones: Public Enumerations, Public Constants, Helper Methods, and Game State Transitions.

When collapsed, your code should look like Figure 4-26.

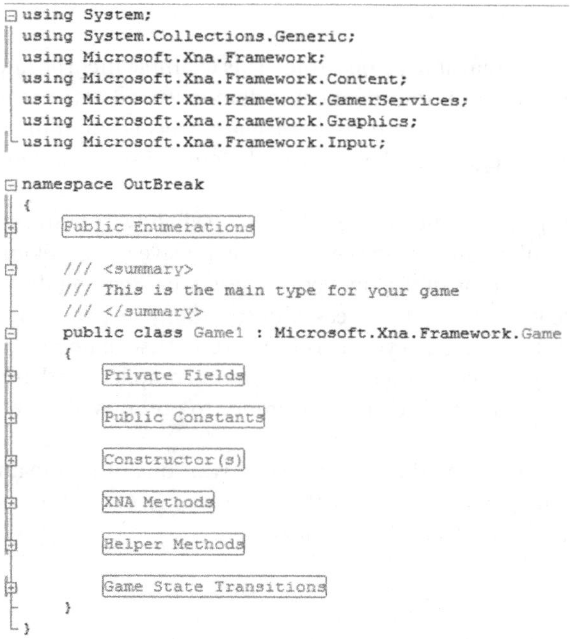

```
using System;
using System.Collections.Generic;
using Microsoft.Xna.Framework;
using Microsoft.Xna.Framework.Content;
using Microsoft.Xna.Framework.GamerServices;
using Microsoft.Xna.Framework.Graphics;
using Microsoft.Xna.Framework.Input;

namespace OutBreak
{
    Public Enumerations

    /// <summary>
    /// This is the main type for your game
    /// </summary>
    public class Game1 : Microsoft.Xna.Framework.Game
    {
        Private Fields

        Public Constants

        Constructor(s)

        XNA Methods

        Helper Methods

        Game State Transitions
    }
}
```

Figure 4-26. *The overall structure of the OutBreak Game1.cs file*

■**Tip** Use #region Region Name to mark the start of a region, and mark the end with #endregion. You can also select a block of code (of any size), right-click the selection, choose Surround With, then #region, which will automatically stick the selected code in a new region.

---

4. Refer to Figure 4-26 to make sure you are using all the namespaces needed for this example and nothing more:

```
using System;
using System.Collections.Generic;
using Microsoft.Xna.Framework;
using Microsoft.Xna.Framework.Content;
using Microsoft.Xna.Framework.GamerServices;
using Microsoft.Xna.Framework.Graphics;
using Microsoft.Xna.Framework.Input;
```

5. Add the required textures to the game's Content project by right-clicking it and choosing Add Existing Item. Navigate to the Examples/Chapter 4/Exercise 6/Artwork folder and add all six files in that folder: ball.png, paddle.png, block.png, gameover.png, outbreak_background.png, and outbreak_bg_dark.png.

6. Add a new sprite font to the Content project. Call it Normal.spritefont. This sprite font should be Kootenay, size 14. At this point, your Solution Explorer window should look like Figure 4-27.

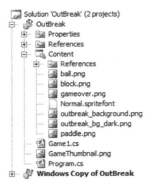

Figure 4-27. *The project structure of the OutBreak game*

Customizing the Input State Class

Once again, we'll use the InputState class we built earlier in the chapter. Add the InputState.cs file from Exercise 4-4 to the project. Change the namespace in this file to OutBreak. Add or modify the following properties to support our specific input actions in the InputState.cs file, as shown in Listing 4-7.

Listing 4-7. *Input Handler Class for OutBreak (InputState.cs)*

```
/// <summary>
/// Checks for a Middle Button press (A by default)
/// </summary>
public bool MiddleButtonPressed
{
    get
    {
        return IsNewButtonPress(Buttons.A) ||
            IsNewKeyPress(Keys.Space) || IsNewKeyPress(Keys.Enter);
    }
}


/// <summary>
/// Checks to see if Left is down.
/// </summary>
public bool LeftIsDown
{
    get
    {
```

```
            return IsButtonDown(Buttons.DPadLeft) ||
                IsKeyDown(Keys.Left);
        }
    }

    /// <summary>
    /// Checks to see if Right is down.
    /// </summary>
    public bool RightIsDown
    {
        get
        {
            return IsButtonDown(Buttons.DPadRight) ||
                IsKeyDown(Keys.Right);
        }
    }

    /// <summary>
    /// Checks for a press of the Play button (B by default)
    /// </summary>
    public bool PlayPressed
    {
        get
        {
            return IsNewButtonPress(Buttons.B) ||
                IsNewKeyPress(Keys.Enter) || IsNewKeyPress(Keys.Space);
        }
    }
}
```

These four properties support proper input from the Zune and the keyboard, providing a consistent and intuitive user experience, regardless of the platform. The Enter key or spacebar on the keyboard equate to pressing Play or the middle button on the Zune in this particular game. The left and right arrow keys will correspond to directional pad Left and Right. We added the two properties because we want to check the current state of the button so that the paddle moves smoothly, rather than just on a new key or button press.

Creating a Class for Block Objects

Next, we will create a game object class to represent a single block in the game. The block has only a few properties: color, position, and visibility. This class is more or less the same as a struct, as it just has some basic properties and a constructor to populate them. The next chapter will cover game component objects in great detail, but for now, let's keep it simple. Add a new class file to the project called Block.cs and fill it with the code shown in Listing 4-8.

Listing 4-8. *The Block Class for OutBreak (Block.cs)*

```
using System;
using Microsoft.Xna.Framework;
```

```
using Microsoft.Xna.Framework.Graphics;

namespace OutBreak
{
    public class Block
    {
        public Vector2 Position;
        public Color Color;
        public bool IsVisible;

        public Block(Vector2 position, Color color, bool visible)
        {
            Position = position;
            Color = color;
            IsVisible = visible;
        }
    }
}
```

Defining Enumerations

Enumerations are important and useful, because they are readable and easily accessible using IntelliSense. This game has two enumerations: one for the game state and one that you can use to determine which type of game element the ball struck last. Add the two enumerations shown in Listing 4-9 in the Enumerations region you defined earlier in the Game1.cs file, outside the Game1 class.

Listing 4-9. *Enumerations for OutBreak (in Game1.cs)*

```
public enum LastObjectBounced
{
    Paddle,
    Top,
    Wall,
    Right,
    Block,
    None
}

public enum GameState
{
    Intro,
    Ready,
    Playing,
    GameOver
}
```

The reason we have a LastObjectBounced enumeration is that sometimes, in paddle games, the ball can get "stuck" inside a paddle or other game object due to collision detection if it doesn't know what it hit last. Our collision detection logic, which you will see later, reverses the direction of the ball based on its collision status with some other object. Knowing that the ball hit a block last, for example, allows us to ensure the vector is reversed again if the ball still collides with the same object, even after having its direction changed.

The game uses a vector to indicate the direction of the ball. That vector is added to the ball's current position to update its location on the screen. As a result, the game logic moves the ball in increments of greater than 1 pixel, so the ball could feasibly land inside a block or paddle, rather than hitting its border precisely. Since we just flip the direction vector using the Vector2.Reflect method, the ball could still be inside that game object, and on the next update, it would reverse direction again because the collision is still true. The LastObjectBounced enumeration allows us to check for new collisions and ignore ones that could produce this behavior.

The GameState enumeration defines our four game states, outlined during the design phase of the game.

Defining Private Fields

We will use quite a few private fields to make this game work correctly. *Private fields* are member variables that are used to store shared data beyond the scope of method calls, such as the score, object positions, and more. Expand the Private Fields region in the Game1 class and modify its contents to look like Listing 4-10.

Listing 4-10. *Private Fields for OutBreak (in Game1.cs)*

```
// Default XNA fields
private GraphicsDeviceManager graphics;
private SpriteBatch spriteBatch;

// Game element textures
private Texture2D blockTex, paddleTex, ballTex;

// Background textures
private Texture2D introBackgroundTex, darkBackgroundTex, gameOverTex;

// Font
private SpriteFont normalFont;

// Gameplay objects
private List<Block> blocks;
private InputState input;
private GameState gameState;
private LastObjectBounced lastObjectBounced;
private TimeSpan screenTimer;

// Gameplay helper variables
private int paddleSpeed;
```

```
private int score;
private int numLives;
private int scoreMultiplier;
private bool isPaused;

// Game math objects
Vector2 initialBallDirection;
Vector2 ballDirection;
Vector2 ballPosition;
Vector2 paddlePosition;

// Text display position vectors
Vector2 textReadyLivesPosition;
Vector2 textCountdownPosition;
Vector2 textFinalScorePosition;
Vector2 textPlayingScorePosition;
```

The fields are organized by their general purpose. The default XNA fields are the ones provided by default. The Texture2D objects declare our drawable textures, and the SpriteFont object represents our font.

The game-play objects include a linear list of Block objects, the current game state, an instance of the input state class, the last collision object, and a TimeSpan object used to determine when the countdown screen (Ready state) is shown. The screenTimer object lets us count down on the countdown screen.

The game-play helper variables are value types that represent simple numbers and Boolean values, such as the score, the current number of lives, and whether the game is paused by invoking the guide menu.

The math objects are all Vector2 objects that we can use to calculate the current position and direction of moving game objects, such as the paddle and ball.

Finally, the Vector2 objects at the bottom are initialized to specific point locations where text is drawn on the screen. These variables are included to reduce hard-coding.

Setting Up Constant Values

Constant values are included to ensure that you have only one place to go to modify certain aspects of the game that should not change. That place is the Public Constants region. Expand that region and add the code shown in Listing 4-11.

Listing 4-11. *Constant Values for OutBreak (in Game1.cs)*

```
// Gameplay constants
public const int MAX_LIVES = 3;
public const int BASE_SCORE = 2;
public const int SCREEN_DISPLAY_TIME = 3;
public const int PADDLE_SPEED = 4;
public const int PADDLE_Y = 280;
public const int BALL_Y = 270;
public const int BLOCK_WIDTH = 30;
public const int BLOCK_HEIGHT = 10;
```

These constants can be changed at design time to modify the associated game-play elements. The suggested values here happen to work well for the game. SCREEN_DISPLAY_TIME is a value in seconds that determines how long the countdown screen is shown before moving into the Playing state.

Initializing the Game

The constructor doesn't need to change, so we can leave that region alone. Expand the XNA Methods region and find the Initialize method. As you learned early in the book, this is where you set up any values that need to be initialized before the game runs. Modify the Initialize method so it looks like Listing 4-12.

Listing 4-12. *Initialize Method for OutBreak (XNA Methods Region in Game1.cs)*

```
protected override void Initialize()
{
    // Set the screen and buffer size
    graphics.PreferredBackBufferWidth = 240;
    graphics.PreferredBackBufferHeight = 320;
    graphics.ApplyChanges();

    // Initialize game objects
    input = new InputState();
    screenTimer = new TimeSpan();
    blocks = new List<Block>();
    isPaused = false;
    initialBallDirection = new Vector2(0.5f, -7.0f);
    paddleSpeed = PADDLE_SPEED;

    // Initialize the screen element positions
    textReadyLivesPosition = new Vector2(10, 160);
    textCountdownPosition = new Vector2(10, 220);
    textFinalScorePosition = new Vector2(120, 250);
    textPlayingScorePosition = new Vector2(10, 295);

    base.Initialize();
}
```

The first three lines set the viewport width and height to the Zune screen dimensions of 240 by 320 and apply those changes. This forces the back buffer to these dimensions, and it also sets the Windows game's window size.

The next block of code instantiates the game objects. The initialBallDirection vector is copied to the ballDirection vector every time a new round starts; this is the default trajectory of the ball. With each update, it moves 0.5 pixel to the right and 7 pixels up, as we have defined it.

The final block of code sets up points that represent locations on the screen for text to be drawn.

Implementing Game State Transitions

The methods in Listing 4-13 are used by other methods in the game logic to transition the game correctly to other states. These methods do more than just altering the value of the gameState variable: they reset other values, rebuild collections, and so forth, depending on the state to which the game is transitioning. Near the bottom of the code, find the Game State Transitions region, expand it, and add the methods shown in Listing 4-13.

Listing 4-13. *Game State Transition Methods for OutBreak (in Game1.cs)*

```
private void MoveToIntroState()
{
    score = 0;
    scoreMultiplier = 1;
    numLives = MAX_LIVES;
    ballDirection = initialBallDirection;
    lastObjectBounced = LastObjectBounced.Paddle;
    ResetBlocks();
    ResetPositions();

    gameState = GameState.Intro;
}

private void MoveToReadyState(GameTime gameTime)
{
    screenTimer = gameTime.TotalGameTime;
    scoreMultiplier = 1;
    ResetPositions();
    gameState = GameState.Ready;
}

private void MoveToPlayingState()
{
    ResetPositions();
    gameState = GameState.Playing;
}

private void MoveToGameOverState()
{
    gameState = GameState.GameOver;
}

private void MoveToLevelComplete()
{
    gameState = GameState.GameOver;
}
```

These methods work as follows:

- MoveToIntroState: Resets the game entirely. The score, lives count, multiplier, directions, last collision object, game object positions, and collection of blocks are all reset to default values here. This method could theoretically be called at any time during the game to start completely afresh.

- MoveToReadyState: Accepts a GameTime argument because it is time-sensitive. It needs to know when it was invoked so that the countdown can begin from the current time. It also resets the game object positions and the score multiplier.

- MoveToPlayingState: Occurs between the countdown screen and the playing screen. To be safe, this method resets game object positions before transitioning.

- MoveToGameOverState: Changes the game state to GameOver.

- MoveToLevelComplete: Same as MoveToGameOverState, although it is really just a stub to provide future support for a game that has more than one level. This method is called when there are no more blocks on the screen.

Implementing Reset Helper Methods

In the game state transitions code, we called two methods that haven't appeared in our code yet: ResetBlocks and ResetPositions. These are helper methods that take care of resetting more complicated elements in the game. Find the Helper Methods region and add the two methods shown in Listing 4-14.

Listing 4-14. *Helper Methods for OutBreak (in Game1.cs)*

```
private void ResetBlocks()
{
    // Random RGB color values
    Random rnd = new Random();
    float red, green, blue;
    Color randomColor;

    int numRows = 5;
    int numColumns = 8;

    int x = 0;
    int y = 0;

    blocks.Clear();
    for (int row = 0; row < numRows; row++)
    {
        for (int col = 0; col < numColumns; col++)
        {
            red = (float)rnd.NextDouble();
            green = (float)rnd.NextDouble();
```

```
            blue = (float)rnd.NextDouble();
            randomColor = new Color(red, green, blue);

            blocks.Add(new Block(new Vector2(x, y), randomColor, true));

            x += BLOCK_WIDTH;
        }
        x = 0;
        y += BLOCK_HEIGHT;
    }
}

private void ResetPositions()
{
    try
    {
        // Put the paddle and ball in the middle of the screen.
        int screenWidth = GraphicsDevice.Viewport.Width;
        paddlePosition = new Vector2(screenWidth / 2 - paddleTex.Width / 2, ➥
            PADDLE_Y);
        ballPosition = new Vector2(screenWidth / 2 - ballTex.Width / 2, BALL_Y);
        ballDirection = initialBallDirection;
    }
    catch
    {
        throw new Exception("Don't call ResetPositions until after ➥
            the content is loaded.");
    }
}
```

The ResetBlocks method clears out the block list and runs a nested for loop for an 8 × 5 grid of blocks. In this loop, a brand-new color and position are assigned to the block. This is an example of a classic row/cell type of algorithm most people learn in introductory programming classes.

The ResetPositions method is interesting because it dynamically positions elements on the screen based on the size of the texture supplied. Centering objects is accomplished by taking half the screen width and subtracting half the texture width. This method affects only the position of the paddle and the ball. Because this method is dependent on the textures being loaded, the method cannot be used correctly until after LoadContent loads the textures. Speaking of the LoadContent method, let's take a look at that next.

Loading the Game Content

Expand the XNA Methods region and find the LoadContent method. Add the code shown in Listing 4-15 to initialize textures and fonts.

Listing 4-15. *LoadContent Method for OutBreak (XNA Methods Region in Game1.cs)*

```
protected override void LoadContent()
{
    // Create a new SpriteBatch, which can be used to draw textures.
    spriteBatch = new SpriteBatch(GraphicsDevice);

    blockTex = Content.Load<Texture2D>("block");
    paddleTex = Content.Load<Texture2D>("paddle");
    ballTex = Content.Load<Texture2D>("ball");
    introBackgroundTex = Content.Load<Texture2D>("outbreak_background");
    darkBackgroundTex = Content.Load<Texture2D>("outbreak_bg_dark");
    gameOverTex = Content.Load<Texture2D>("gameover");
    normalFont = Content.Load<SpriteFont>("Normal");

    // Move to the New Game state.
    // Requires that the textures be loaded so we can center objects.
    MoveToIntroState();
}
```

This is standard content loader code, with the addition of the call to `MoveToIntroState`. It would seem that we should call that method in the `Initialize` method, but it makes more sense (and is required) to call it here, because the textures must be loaded in order to dynamically position the ball and paddle based on their size. This is the last chance to call such methods before the game loop starts running.

Handling Input

Having the `InputState` class certainly reduces the amount of code we need to write, but we are creating a real game at this point. As such, it makes sense to have a method dedicated to handling the input. First of all, the `input` instance of the `InputState` class must be updated directly from the game's `Update` method. After that, we can call the `HandleInput` method. Find the `Helper Methods` region and add the method shown in Listing 4-16 to handle various types of input.

Listing 4-16. *HandleInput Method for OutBreak (Helper Methods Region in Game1.cs)*

```
private void HandleInput(GameTime gameTime)
{
    switch (gameState)
    {
        case GameState.Intro:
            // Wait for the play button to be pressed
            if (input.PlayPressed)
            {
                MoveToReadyState(gameTime);
            }
            break;
        case GameState.Playing:
```

```
            // Check Left
            if (input.LeftIsDown)
            {
                // Check boundary to the left
                if (paddlePosition.X > 0)
                    paddlePosition.X -= paddleSpeed;
            }

            // Check Right
            if (input.RightIsDown)
            {
                if (paddlePosition.X < GraphicsDevice.Viewport.Width -
                    paddleTex.Width)
                    paddlePosition.X += paddleSpeed;
            }

            // Bring up the Guide
            #if ZUNE
            if (input.PlayPressed)
            {
                Guide.Show();
            }
            #endif

            break;
        case GameState.GameOver:
            if (input.MiddleButtonPressed || input.PlayPressed)
                MoveToIntroState();
            break;
        default:
            break;

    }
}
```

This is your first real exposure to referencing the game state. Input should behave differently based on the current game state. For example, there's no point handling Left and Right input if the game is just sitting idly on the intro screen. To accomplish this, we have a switch statement that looks at the value of gameState.

On the intro screen, we only care if the user presses Play, which transitions the game to the Ready state.

When playing the game (in the Playing state), we want to handle three types of input: pressing Left, pressing Right, or pressing the Play button. When checking if Left is down, we move the paddle left only if it's not already all the way to the left, which we determine by comparing the paddle position's X component to the left boundary (zero). When checking if Right is down, we move the paddle to the right only if the current paddle's position (plus the entire width of the paddle) is less than the right boundary (the screen width). This keeps the paddle constrained equally on both sides of the playing area. When Play is pressed, the guide menu appears. Note the use of conditional preprocessor directives here. Guide.Show will not compile in the Windows version of the game, so we wrap this bit of code in #if ZUNE.

■**Note** The XNA, ZUNE, and WINDOWS build constants are predefined for you in XNA game projects.

Finally, in the GameOver state, pressing the middle button or Play will result in the game resetting to the Intro state. No other game states require input to be handled, but it's easy to support it by adding another case label.

Handling Collisions

In this game, we will use an incredibly simple method of checking for collisions. This method just checks to see if one rectangle intersects another. A *bounding box* is a rectangle around an object that represents its borders. The bounding boxes are set up and then checked to see if they intersect. If they do, some action is taken, depending on which objects are colliding.

Collision detection is really the meat of the game, as it drives most of the decisions made, such as win or lose, success or failure, life or death, and so on. As such, HandleCollisions is a rather beefy method. Find the Helper Methods region and add the HandleCollisions method shown in Listing 4-17.

Listing 4-17. *HandleCollisions Method for OutBreak (Helper Methods Region in Game1.cs)*

```
private void HandleCollisions(GameTime gameTime)
{
    Rectangle ballBoundingBox = new Rectangle((int)ballPosition.X,
        (int)ballPosition.Y, ballTex.Width, ballTex.Height);

    Rectangle blockBoundingBox = new Rectangle();

    Rectangle paddleBoundingBox = new Rectangle((int)paddlePosition.X,
        (int)paddlePosition.Y, paddleTex.Width, paddleTex.Height);

    float ballCenterX = 0.0f;
    float paddleCenterX = 0.0f;
    float distance = 0.0f;
    float ratio = 0.0f;

    // Check collisions with blocks
    foreach (Block block in blocks)
    {
        blockBoundingBox.X = (int)block.Position.X;
        blockBoundingBox.Y = (int)block.Position.Y;
        blockBoundingBox.Width = BLOCK_WIDTH;
        blockBoundingBox.Height = BLOCK_HEIGHT;
```

```
    if (block.IsVisible)
    {
        if (ballBoundingBox.Intersects(blockBoundingBox))
        {
            // The ball hit a block - increment score
            block.IsVisible = false;
            if (lastObjectBounced == LastObjectBounced.Block)
                scoreMultiplier *= 2;

            score += BASE_SCORE * scoreMultiplier;

            // Do a quick search to see if there are any blocks left
            bool allBlocksGone = true;
            foreach (Block b in blocks)
            {
                if (b.IsVisible)
                {
                    allBlocksGone = false;
                    break;
                }
            }

            if (allBlocksGone)
            {
                MoveToLevelComplete();
            }
            else
            {
                // Reflect in Y direction
                ballDirection = Vector2.Reflect(ballDirection,
                    Vector2.UnitY);
                lastObjectBounced = LastObjectBounced.Block;
            }
        }
    }
}

// Check collisions with the paddle
if (ballBoundingBox.Intersects(paddleBoundingBox))
{
    if (lastObjectBounced != LastObjectBounced.Paddle)
    {
        // Bounce the direction vector in the Y direction
        ballDirection = Vector2.Reflect(ballDirection, Vector2.UnitY);

        // Determine how far from the center of the paddle the ball hit
        ballCenterX = ballPosition.X + (float)(ballTex.Width / 2.0f);
```

```
                    paddleCenterX = paddlePosition.X + (float)(paddleTex.Width / 2.0f);
                    distance = ballCenterX - paddleCenterX;
                    ratio = distance / (paddleTex.Width / 2);

                    ballDirection.X = ballDirection.X + (ratio * 2);
                    scoreMultiplier = 1;

                    lastObjectBounced = LastObjectBounced.Paddle;
                }
            }


        // Check left & right collisions
        if (ballPosition.X <= 0 ||
            ballPosition.X >= GraphicsDevice.Viewport.Width - ballTex.Width)
        {
            if (lastObjectBounced != LastObjectBounced.Wall)
            {
                // Bounce the direction vector in the X direction
                ballDirection = Vector2.Reflect(ballDirection, Vector2.UnitX);
                lastObjectBounced = LastObjectBounced.Wall;
            }
        }


        // Check top collision (screen boundary)
        if (ballPosition.Y <= 0)
        {
            if (lastObjectBounced != LastObjectBounced.Top)
            {
                ballDirection = Vector2.Reflect(ballDirection, Vector2.UnitY);
                lastObjectBounced = LastObjectBounced.Top;
                scoreMultiplier = 1;
            }
        }


        // Check bottom collision (player loses a life)
        if (ballPosition.Y >= GraphicsDevice.Viewport.Height)
        {
            numLives--;
            if (numLives < 1)
                MoveToGameOverState();
            else
            {
                MoveToReadyState(gameTime);
            }
        }
    }
}
```

As you can see, this method is quite complicated, so we'll break it down so that it makes more sense. The next chapter will discuss collision detection in greater detail, so the explanation here is brief.

The first three lines of the method set up the bounding boxes for the objects we want to check for collisions: the ball, the paddle, and a block. The next four `float` variables are used when the ball hits the paddle to determine how far from the center of the paddle the ball hit. This allows the code to slightly alter the ball's direction based on where it struck the paddle.

Next is a `foreach` loop that loops through all the `Block` objects to determine which of them collide with the ball. This loop does a couple of things. If the ball collides with the current `Block`, that `Block` is made invisible and the score is updated. If no blocks are left, the level is completed. Otherwise, the ball's direction vector is flipped, and the `lastObjectBounced` variable is set to `LastObjectBounced.Block`. This `foreach` loop handles collisions between the ball and all `Block` objects.

After the `foreach` loop are four `if` statements that check other collisions:

- The first `if` statement checks for a collision between the paddle and the ball. If the ball and paddle collide, the ball direction vector is flipped in the y direction, and then has some modification applied to the vector's X component based on where the ball landed. Doing this adds a special dynamic to the game that is very intuitive for the player. If you want to "slow down" or "speed up" the ball, you can do this by positioning the paddle differently.

- The second `if` statement checks for left and right wall collisions. If the ball hits the left or right wall, the ball's direction vector is flipped in the x direction.

- The third `if` statement checks to see if the ball has hit the top of the screen. If so, the vector is flipped in the y direction without assigning any points.

- The final `if` statement checks to see if the ball has hit the bottom of the screen without touching the paddle. In this case, a life is lost and the game transitions to the `Ready` state. If there are no lives left, the game transitions to the `GameOver` state.

Putting It Together: The Update Method

All of the methods we need are in place to get the game updating correctly. Expand the XNA Methods region, find the `Update` method, and modify it to look like Listing 4-18.

Listing 4-18. *Update Method for OutBreak (XNA Methods Region in Game1.cs)*

```
protected override void Update(GameTime gameTime)
{
    // Allows the game to exit
    if (GamePad.GetState(PlayerIndex.One).Buttons.Back == ButtonState.Pressed)
        this.Exit();

#if ZUNE
    isPaused = Guide.IsVisible;
#endif
```

```
    if (!isPaused)
    {
        input.Update();
        HandleInput(gameTime);

        switch (gameState)
        {
            case GameState.Intro:
                // No processing for this game state
                break;
            case GameState.Ready:
                if (gameTime.TotalGameTime.Subtract(screenTimer).Seconds >=
                    SCREEN_DISPLAY_TIME)
                    gameState = GameState.Playing;
                break;
            case GameState.Playing:
                HandleCollisions(gameTime);
                ballPosition = Vector2.Add(ballPosition, ballDirection);
                break;
        }
    }

    base.Update(gameTime);
}
```

The first thing you notice here is another conditional preprocessor directive to update the value of the isPaused variable based on the visibility of the guide. The reason this depends on the platform is that the guide does not exist for Windows games. On Windows, isPaused will always be false, because there is no code to alter it. On the Zune, however, this value determines two things: whether the game updates during game play and what is drawn behind the guide in the Draw method.

Accordingly, the meat of the logic is wrapped in an if statement so that it executes only when the game is not paused. Without this bit of code, the game will continue to run in the background while the guide is displayed, which would not be a good thing.

If the game should be updating (meaning it's not paused), then the input engine is explicitly updated and the input is handled via a call to HandleInput. Then the game processing for each game state comes into play. In the Ready state, the timer is updated; if a number of seconds equal to SCREEN_DISPLAY_TIME has elapsed, the game transitions into the Playing state. During the Playing state, collisions are handled, and the ball's position is added to its direction vector to move it on the screen.

Notice how compact the Update method is. We extracted most of the core game logic into different methods so that this one stays neat and tidy, in case you need to add more game states or other engines to update.

Putting It Together: The Draw Method

The final piece of this exercise is the Draw method, which is responsible for drawing the game elements at their most recent locations. There is not, and there should not be, any game-play logic in this method. Expand the XNA Methods region, find the Draw method, and alter it to look like Listing 4-19.

Listing 4-19. *Draw Method for OutBreak (XNA Methods Region in Game1.cs)*

```
protected override void Draw(GameTime gameTime)
{
    graphics.GraphicsDevice.Clear(Color.Black);

    spriteBatch.Begin();

    switch (gameState)
    {
        case GameState.Intro:
            spriteBatch.Draw(introBackgroundTex, Vector2.Zero, Color.White);
            break;

        case GameState.Ready:
            spriteBatch.Draw(darkBackgroundTex, Vector2.Zero, Color.White);

            spriteBatch.DrawString(normalFont,
                "Lives: " + numLives + "\r\nScore: " + score,
                textReadyLivesPosition, Color.White);

            int remainingSeconds = SCREEN_DISPLAY_TIME -
                (gameTime.TotalGameTime.Seconds - screenTimer.Seconds) + 1;

            spriteBatch.DrawString(normalFont,
                "Get Ready... " + remainingSeconds,
                textCountdownPosition, Color.White);

            break;

        case GameState.Playing:
            if (!isPaused)
            {
                spriteBatch.Draw(paddleTex, paddlePosition, Color.White);
                spriteBatch.Draw(ballTex, ballPosition, Color.White);

                foreach (Block block in blocks)
                {
                    if (block.IsVisible)
                        spriteBatch.Draw(blockTex, block.Position, block.Color);
                }

                spriteBatch.DrawString(normalFont,
                    "score: " + score + " (x" + scoreMultiplier + ")",
                    textPlayingScorePosition, Color.White);
```

```
            }
            break;

        case GameState.GameOver:
            spriteBatch.Draw(gameOverTex, Vector2.Zero, Color.White);

            string scoreText = "Your Score: " + score;
            Vector2 textOrigin = normalFont.MeasureString(scoreText) / 2;

            spriteBatch.DrawString(normalFont, scoreText,
                textFinalScorePosition, Color.White, 0.0f, textOrigin, 1.0f,
                SpriteEffects.None, 0.5f);
            break;
    }

    spriteBatch.End();

    base.Draw(gameTime);
}
```

The Draw method is sensitive to the current game state. The game state determines exactly what is drawn on the screen. In any case, the screen is always cleared to black.

In the Intro state, the intro graphic is drawn—nothing too fancy is happening here.

In the Ready state, the darker background is drawn, followed by two text elements. The first element contains the current score and number of remaining lives. The second text element is the countdown text, which looks like "Get Ready . . . x," where x is the number of seconds remaining until the round starts.

In the Playing state, the paddle and ball are drawn. Then all of the blocks are drawn, but only if that block is visible. The score is displayed in real time at the bottom of the screen.

Finally, in the GameOver state, the "Game Over" graphic is drawn, along with the score. The score is centered using the MeasureString method, which we will discuss further in the next chapter. Notice that the code to draw the score text uses a different method signature for DrawString than you have seen so far. This allows us to specify the text origin as well as the position.

After the switch statement, the sprite batch is closed, and the entire screen is rendered to the device.

Testing OutBreak

Whew! All of the code is now in place for the game. You should have a good understanding of the design behind OutBreak and the purpose of each of the methods. Now, let's take it for a test drive.

First, test it on the PC. Right-click the Windows copy project and choose Set as Startup Project. It doesn't matter which Zune you have set for deployment; if deployment fails, the Windows game can still launch. Rebuild the solution and correct any compilation errors that arise. If you have trouble, compare your code with the complete sample code provided for this game. Press F5 to run the game.

The Enter and spacebar keys are used for play, as well as the middle button press, as we defined in the `InputState` class. Use the left and right arrow keys to move the paddle. Test the game play on your PC and enjoy.

Next, test it on your Zune. Right-click the Zune project and choose Set as Startup Project. Ensure you have the correct Zune set as the default device in XNA Game Studio Device Center. Press F5 to deploy and run the game. Use the Zune directional pad to move the paddle to the right and left. During game play, press the Play button to bring up the guide, and notice how the game pauses.

Congratulations—you have just built your first Zune game that also runs on Windows!

Check Your Knowledge

The following questions will help you apply what you've learned in this chapter to your own games. The answers are supplied in Appendix C.

1. How do you access XNA Game Studio Device Center?

2. How can you take a screenshot of a game running on the Zune?

3. Why would you want to run a Zune game without debugging?

4. What size textures are optimal for the Zune?

5. How does the Zune pad map to the `GamePadState` enumeration?

6. How do you ensure that Zune-specific code doesn't get compiled into the Windows version of the game assembly?

7. Which method do you need to call to force a Windows game to match the preferred back buffer width and height?

8. Which class is used to play, pause, and stop music and control the volume?

9. What is an alternative to writing your own music browser and player?

10. What kind of object does `GetAlbumArt` return?

Summary

By now, you should be feeling very confident about writing games for your Zune. This chapter took you through several different exercises that demonstrated how to handle input, play music, debug, and create Windows copies of Zune games. You were even introduced to collision detection, vector math, simple game state management, and more.

In the next chapter, you will learn how to make Zune game development an even easier experience using advanced game state management, game components, and different types of collision detection.

CHAPTER 5

■■■

XNA Fundamental Game Programming Concepts

In the previous chapter, you learned about all things Zune, from handling input to playing music. Now that you have a functional Zune game under your belt, it's time to address some of the fundamental concepts that underlie game programming in general.

There are at least two approaches to writing games in XNA. The first is the approach we followed in Chapter 4 to create the OutBreak game. This approach is also known as quick-and-dirty or maverick, and it generally works fine for a small project. However, if you are working on a larger-scale project, you will need to be more vigilant about writing good, solid, object-oriented code. By doing so, you will make less work for yourself in the long run. A game like OutBreak in its current state can quickly snowball into something nearly impossible to navigate and maintain, although it did serve its purpose as a final chapter example. This brings us to the other approach to game writing: the more traditional, structured method. This approach calls upon the great features of C#, XNA, and Visual Studio to factor code in an intelligent manner.

One of the surprising aspects about running XNA on the Zune is that it runs extremely fast for managed code. You have plenty of room to use your favorite things like generic collections, multilevel inheritance, and even .NET Language Integrated Query (LINQ) to get the job done faster.

Knowing that we have plenty of horsepower available to us in Zune games means we can further abstract and encapsulate various elements of the game. We can factor out the big pieces of the game architecturally, and work on them in a manner separate from the game itself, decoupling a lot of commonly used game features from specific game logic. Examples of such elements are game state management, game objects (or components), and stand-alone logic libraries (a physics engine, for example). Factoring these elements into their own cohesive units provides the added benefit of being able to unit test critical game logic without deployment, also covered in this chapter.

We begin this chapter with a primer on 2D mathematics and its application in XNA, which you must understand at a working level in order to be effective with your math-related game logic.

Math in Two Dimensions

I was one of those stubborn kids who always said that math, especially trigonometry, was useless and had no application in real life. Four-function calculators were all I would ever need to get by. However, in a world of interest rates, statistics, trends, and spreadsheets, having that extra knowledge never actually hurt me. Of course, I went on to minor in math in college to complement computer science. I'm quite glad I did, because the disappointing truth is that math is everywhere, and we simply have to deal with it. Whether you are a math *nut* or a math-*not*, this section should be read with the spirit of the conquest of knowledge. I promise, math really is important.

If you are reading this book with an eventual goal of entering into a professional role as a game developer, I must also assure you that any job in that field requires a solid understanding of math. Whether you're coding a game engine, artificial intelligence, game play, or designing levels, a certain level of math acumen is required in order to avoid months of on-the-job training.

With that said, let's take a look at how math operates in two dimensions. We'll start with the bare basics and move from there rather quickly.

The Cartesian Coordinate System

In 1637, French mathematician René Descartes published a treatise known as *Discourse on Method*, which outlined his idea for a system of axes that could be used to represent a point in space. Anyone who has taken middle-school geometry should be familiar with Figure 5-1.

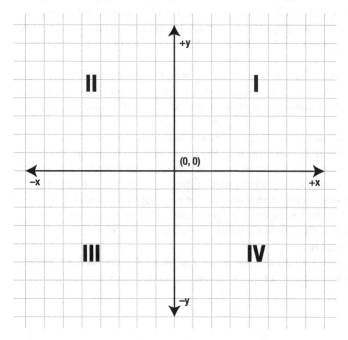

Figure 5-1. *An example of a Cartesian plane*

Figure 5-1 is an example of what came to be known as a *Cartesian plane*, named after Descartes. A *plane* is a conceptual area in space. A two-dimensional plane extends infinitely in two perpendicular directions (or *axes*) and has no depth.

The horizontal axis is called the *x axis*, and the vertical axis is called the *y axis*. The point at which the x and y axes intersect is known as the *origin*. Note that in the graphic, the x value is more positive to the right and more negative to the left. The y value is more positive downward and more negative upward. Any point on this plane is notated by its x and y components, such as (0, 1) or (–5, 12). The point at the origin is (0, 0).

The Roman numerals represent *quadrants* of the plane. In quadrant I, the x value is always greater than or equal to zero, and the y value is always less than or equal to zero. A bright student at one of my XNA sessions pointed out that developing games in XNA is like working in quadrant IV, which is a good way to think about it. However, in XNA, the y value is always positive (or zero) and increases downward. This is contrary to what you have probably learned in the past. If you were to draw an object at (1, 1), you would be naturally inclined to think "right one unit and up one unit." However, since the y axis is flipped, (1, 1) actually means "right one unit and down one unit." On the Zune, one unit is equivalent to one pixel. Figure 5-2 shows how the coordinate system of the Zune works.

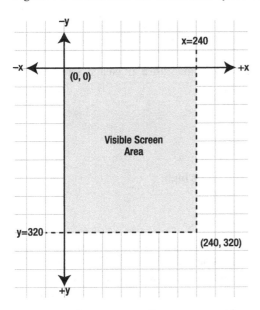

Figure 5-2. *The Zune coordinate system*

In Figure 5-2, the drawable game area ranges on the x axis from 0 to 240 and on the y axis from 0 to 320. (Remember that the Zune screen resolution is 240 × 320 pixels.) You could feasibly draw something at any 2D point in space, but it won't be visible unless it's within this range. If you have a 16 × 16 graphic that you draw at (0, –8), only half of the graphic will be drawn on the screen, because XNA positions the graphic by its upper-left corner. For example, if you were to draw a circle graphic halfway off the top of the screen, you would see something like Figure 5-3.

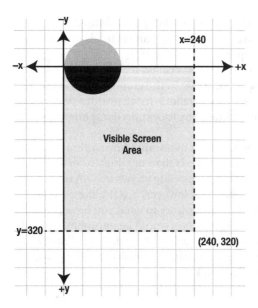

Figure 5-3. *A circle drawn slightly off-screen is still partially drawn.*

Understanding the coordinate system and how it works makes life a lot easier. The following are the main things to understand:

- The top left of the screen is (0, 0).
- X is the horizontal axis and increases to the right.
- Y is the vertical axis and increases downward.
- The drawable game area is 240 pixels wide by 320 pixels high.

Points and Vectors

A point is referred to by its x and y coordinates on a Cartesian plane. For example, (0, 0) is the point at the origin. On the Zune, the point (239, 319) would be the point at the bottom right of the screen. In code, however, the Point class is almost never used. This is because vectors provide the same functionality that you would seek in a point. You can store a point as a vector, which gives you the ability to add it to other "true" vectors.

A *vector* is a mathematical element that has an x value and a y value. These values are called *components*. The main thing that distinguishes a vector from a point is that a vector is generally used to indicate a direction. Vectors also have a property called *magnitude* (or *length*), which is a measure of how "big" the vector is. When you think of a vector in terms of a point's location relative to the origin, this is called a *bound vector*. When you are more concerned with the direction and magnitude of a vector (to denote direction or force, for example), this is called a *free vector*.

Vectors are denoted in the same way as points. For example, Figure 5-4 shows the vector $\vec{v} = (2, 3)$.

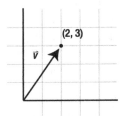

Figure 5-4. *A vector on a Cartesian plane*

Note A free vector can be translated anywhere on the plane without having its value change. The free vector (2, 3) is always the same vector, whether it starts at the origin or some other arbitrary point, and it is equivalent to the bound vector (2, 3), which refers specifically to the vector originating at (0, 0) and connecting (2, 3).

Vector Magnitude (Length)

In the case of Figure 5-4, $\vec{v}$ is a vector with x component 2 and y component 3. To figure out the magnitude of the vector, you can use the distance formula to find the distance between the point (2, 3) and the origin (0, 0). More concisely, the formula for the magnitude of a vector $\vec{v}$ is as follows:

$$\|\vec{v}\| = \sqrt{(x^2 + y^2)}$$

Specifically, our vector would have a length of about 3.6 units (the square root of 4 + 9). In code, however, you can access the magnitude in a much simpler way:

```
Vector2 myVector = new Vector2(2, 3);
int length = myVector.Length;
```

Unit Vectors

A *unit vector* is any vector with length 1. Unit vectors are frequently used to indicate direction only; they have no scale. The XNA Framework provides UnitX and UnitY properties statically on the Vector2 class, which you can use to get quick access to these vectors. Any vector can be converted to a unit vector by dividing it by its own length, a process called *normalization*. Normalized vectors are used in other, more advanced computations, such as vector reflection.

Adding Vectors

Vectors are also commonly added together. Remember that a vector can be moved anywhere on the plane without changing its value. This is because vectors indicate direction and magnitude, and have nothing to do with physical location. However, in XNA, points on the screen are also stored as vectors. It's convenient to do so because vectors have x and y components, and it becomes much easier to add other "true" vectors to these point vectors. In effect, adding a vector used as a direction to a vector just being used as a position will result in that object's position changing.

Adding two vectors is done by adding their components together. The result of this computation is a new vector called the *resultant* vector. (Really, any operation that results in a new vector calls the result of the operation the *resultant* vector). Let's assume you have two vectors: our original vector $\vec{v} = (2, 3)$ and a new vector $\vec{u} = (4, 2)$. Adding these vectors together results in a *resultant* vector $\overline{vu} = (6, 5)$. This is illustrated in Figure 5-5. Count the units of each vector to see how the lengths are added together.

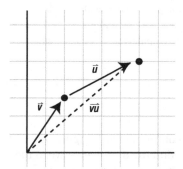

Figure 5-5. *Adding two vectors together*

In code, the Vector2 class provides a static method called Add that performs this computation for you. You saw this in the OutBreak game we created in Chapter 4, where the ball position was updated by adding the ball direction vector with each call to Update.

The length of a vector can be used to indicate strength, speed, or other terms that essentially resolve to the word *magnitude*. Imagine you have a tossing game where wind is a factor. You could have two vectors: the vector representing the current direction of the object you're tossing, and another vector representing the wind. When you add these two together in any Update iteration, you will have a new vector that you can apply to the object's current position. The longer the wind vector is, the stronger the effect. You'll see an implementation of this very concept in Exercise 5-1, coming up shortly.

Multiplication

Multiplication is not to be confused with the dot-product operation (discussed next). With regard to vectors, multiplication refers to multiplying each component of a vector by the same scalar value. An example of scalar multiplication is $2(x, y) = (2x, 2y)$. Scalar multiplication has the singular effect of increasing the magnitude of the vector without changing the direction, as shown in Figure 5-6.

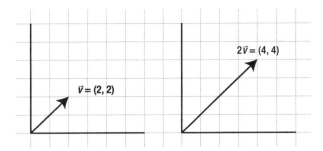

Figure 5-6. *A vector multiplied by a scalar value*

Dot Product

Unlike scalar multiplication, the dot product multiplies the components of two vectors together. For example, if you dotted (*a*, *b*) and (*c*, *d*) together, you would end up with a new vector (*ac*, *bd*).

The dot product is useful in many different vector operations, but probably the most familiar example that uses the dot-product operation is reflecting a vector about some other vector.

Reflection

In a game like Pong, or the OutBreak game from Chapter 4, you can accomplish reflection of a vector simply by negating one of the components. If the ball hits the paddle, multiply the x component of the vector by –1 to change its direction. But what if you could rotate those paddles? Would it still make sense for the ball to bounce as if the surface were straight? Not really.

XNA includes the Vector2.Reflect method, which takes an initial vector and a unit vector, and returns a new vector. This new vector is the initial vector reflected in the direction of the unit vector. Pong is a good example of when this is useful. If the ball hits the paddle, you use the UnitX vector in the operation to send it back to the other paddle (assuming your paddles are on the left and right of the screen).

So how does that math work? It's a little complicated. Let's put it in terms of a game object bouncing off some imaginary line represented as a vector.

Let *V* be the vector that represents the incoming object's direction.

Let *B* be the vector you're bouncing off.

Let *N* be the normalized version of *B* (length of 1).

Let *R* be the result of the reflection.

The formula for *R* is as follows: $R = 2 * (V \cdot N) - V$. Remember the order of the operators. This calculation can be achieved first by normalizing the bounce vector, and then dotting the result of that with *V*. Scalar multiply that result by 2, and then subtract *V* from the whole business once again. The result looks like Figure 5-7.

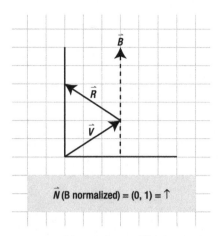

$\vec{N}$ (B normalized) = (0, 1) = ↑

Figure 5-7. *A vector V reflected off another vector B produces the result, R.*

In this case, the vector *V* has a value of (3, 2). The vector *B* is some vector with an x component of zero (this is a free vector, so its actual position does not matter). *N*, or *B* normalized, is equal to (0, 1).

To calculate the resultant vector *R*, we can use the formula $R = 2 * (V \cdot N) - V$. Let's start with the inner operation of *V* dot *N* $(V \cdot N) = (3, 2) \cdot (0, 1) = (3 \times (0, 2) \times 1) = (0, 2)$.

Next, we multiply (0, 2) by the scalar value 2, which gives us (0, 4).

Finally, we subtract the original vector *V* from this value to obtain *R*. $R = (0, 4) - (3, 2) = (0 - 3, 4 - 2) = (-3, 2)$.

You can see this is correct by looking at the graph. The free vector *R* moves left three units and up two units. This operation works with any vector.

This is much easier to accomplish in code than it is on paper, so here are some concrete examples of scenarios where you might need to use reflection:

- Reflecting in the x direction (about the y axis):

```
Vector2 newDirection = Vector2.Reflect(directionVector, Vector2.UnitX);
```

- Reflecting in the y direction (about the x axis):

```
Vector2 newDirection = Vector2.Reflect(directionVector, Vector2.UnitY);
```

- Reflecting in the direction of some other vector *V*:

```
Vector2 normal = Vector2.Normalize(V);
Vector2 result = Vector2.Reflect(directionVector, normal);
```

There are many other operations that the Vector2 class provides so that you don't need to dig deep into the math, but it's useful to know what's happening. It's particularly important to understand why vectors are used both as points (bound vectors) and to represent forces (free vectors). It's also important to be able to visualize them.

Besides the use of vectors, there are other math-related things that you will encounter in nearly every game regardless of the platform. One of those things is trigonometry.

Trigonometric Functions

Trigonometry is something we should have all learned in grade school. In case you missed out, here is a very fast crash course. If needed, more information and learning is just a search away on the Great Wide Internet.

Trigonometry refers to the measurement of triangles. If you take any point on the screen and draw a vector from it, the result can be expressed as a triangle. The direct line from the point to the end of the vector is called the *hypotenuse*. If you draw a line in the x direction equal to the x component of the vector, you get an imaginary side called the *adjacent* side. If you connect the remaining points, you get a side completely opposite of the initial point called the *opposite* side.

This imaginary triangle is also described by an angle, usually the angle between the hypotenuse and the adjacent side. This angle is normally described by the Greek letter theta (θ).

Three primary trig functions that you can use to find out more about any given triangle are sine, cosine, and tangent. These functions are defined as follows, using the length of the sides in the equations:

sin (θ) = *opposite/hypotenuse*

cos (θ) = *adjacent /hypotenuse*

tan (θ) = *opposite/adjacent*

You can also use the inverses of these functions to get the angle of the triangle in question. Each uses the same sides as the regular functions, but instead of calculating a ratio, they use that ratio to calculate the angle. For example, to find the angle of a triangle using inverse sine, you would use the inverse sine function:

$$sin^{-1}\left(\frac{opposite}{hypotenuse}\right) = \theta$$

The inverse trig functions become especially useful when you want to find the angle from one point to another. All you need to do is use the length of the vector and the vector's components. Usually, the opposite side is the vector's y component. The hypotenuse is the vector's magnitude. The adjacent side is the vector's x component.

In code, these inverse functions are referred to by their more formal names of arcsine, arccosine, and arctangent. The Math class in the .NET Framework provides Asin, Acos, and Atan methods to calculate angles given vector components. These methods return a double value that represents the angle in radians, and they also take a double as input. To determine an angle from a vector in code, you could use something like this:

```
double angleRadians = Math.Asin((double)(vector.Y / vector.Length));
```

Note Degrees are rarely, if ever, used in XNA. Radians are the preferred unit of measure for angles.

Finally, you may want to derive some vector based solely on an angle. In this case, the y component is represented by the sine of the angle, and the x component is equal to the cosine of the angle. In code, it looks like this:

```
Vector2 fromAngle = new Vector2((float)Math.Sin(angle), (float)Math.Cos(angleRadians));
```

Using Math in Your Games

With the general math review out of the way, let's go over some specific calculations that are commonly used in developing Zune games.

Positioning Screen Objects and Dividing by Two

When you draw a texture on the screen, using some bound vector *V* to represent a point, the top left of the graphic will be drawn at *V*. This is okay in some situations, but most modern games have quite a bit of centering and distribution that combine to create an aligned effect. Most of this is accomplished simply by dividing vector components by two. Division by two is used a lot in graphical applications to achieve centering. Here, you will learn why.

Centering Textures on the Screen

The approach for centering objects is really straightforward once you understand why you need to divide things in half. We'll start with the simplest example of centering an object in the middle of the screen.

If you were to use the zero vector to draw some object on the screen, it would appear with the top-left corner of the object at (0, 0). The code looks like this:

```
spriteBatch.Draw(texObject, Vector2.Zero, Color.White)
```

The result would look like Figure 5-8.

Figure 5-8. *Drawing an object at (0, 0)*

Now let's try to center this object. The first thing to do is to get the width and height of the screen. These can be dereferenced from the GraphicsDevice object:

```
int screenWidth = GraphicsDevice.Viewport.Width;
int screenHeight = GraphicsDevice.Viewport.Height;
```

In just about every case, on the Zune, screenWidth will be 240 and screenHeight will be 320. To get the position at the center of the screen, you must divide the width and height by 2. This will give you a point halfway across and halfway down the screen. A new vector representing the center of the screen can be defined like this:

```
Vector2 screenCenter = new Vector2(screenWidth / 2, screenHeight / 2);
```

If you were to draw the object at screenCenter instead of Vector2.Zero, it would look like Figure 5-9.

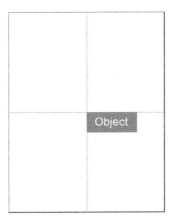

Figure 5-9. *Drawing an object at the screen center (120, 160)*

Okay, it's close to the center, but not quite. Because the texture is drawn from the upper-left corner and not the center of the object, you need to find the center of the object and take that into account. This is done in the same way that you found the center of the screen.

Looking at Figure 5-9, you can see that the object should be moved to the left by exactly half of the object's width, and moved up by exactly half of the object's height. What you are really doing is figuring out where the top-left corner of the object should be drawn so that the object appears centered. Arithmetically, you can figure this out in code:

```
int xPosition = screenCenter.X - (objectTexture.Width / 2);
int yPosition = screenCenter.Y - (objectTexture.Height / 2);
spriteBatch.Draw(objectTexture, new Vector2(xPosition, yPosition));
```

This code takes the absolute screen center and offsets it in the x and y directions dynamically based on the dimensions of the graphic itself. The result is shown in Figure 5-10.

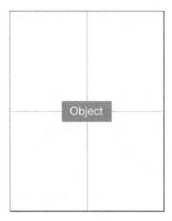

Figure 5-10. *An object perfectly centered in the middle of the screen*

The same code can be used to center an object with respect to any point on the screen. You would just replace screenCenter with the Vector2 object that you want to use as the new center of the object to draw. Listing 5-1 shows a small method you can use to obtain a new Vector2 for any texture object you want to draw at a given point.

Listing 5-1. *A Utility Method for Centering Texture Objects*

```
public Vector2 GetCenterOffset(Texture2D graphic, Vector2 centerPoint)
{
    int x = centerPoint.X - (graphic.Width / 2);
    int y = centerPoint.Y - (graphic.Height / 2);
    return new Vector2(x, y);
}
```

The recommended option for centering objects on the screen is to use an overload of the Draw method that includes an *origin* parameter. Specifying the origin is essentially the same thing as moving the reference point of the object from the top left to some new position. The only problem is that this overload of Draw contains a lot of other stuff you might not ordinarily need to use. Listing 5-2 uses this overload and draws an object centered at (100, 100).

Listing 5-2. *Using an Overload of the Draw Method with an Origin Parameter*

```
int originX = objectTexture.Width / 2;
int originY = objectTexture.Height / 2;
Vector2 objectOrigin = new Vector2(originX, originY);
Vector2 drawPosition = new Vector2(100, 100);

spriteBatch.Draw(objectTexture, drawPosition, Color.White,
    0.0f, objectOrigin, 1.0f, SpriteEffects.None, 0.5f);
```

The first three arguments of this version of Draw are the same as the most simple overload, setting a texture, position, and color. The second line of the method contains arguments for other drawing options:

- 0.0f: The rotation, which you can use to rotate the object as it is drawn.

- objectOrigin: The object origin vector that you calculated to find the center of the object.

- 1.0f: A scale factor of type float, which you can use to enlarge or shrink the texture (1.0f means no change; it is multiplicative).

- SpriteEffects.None: The SpriteEffects enumeration allows you to flip the texture horizontally or vertically.

- 0.5f: The layer depth, which is useful when you are trying to force objects to appear below or above other objects drawn in the same SpriteBatch. This is a float value between 0.0f and 1.0f, with 1.0f being the topmost layer.

Determining whether to precalculate the new position with the object center or use the extended overload of Draw with the origin is a matter of style. In any case, you will likely still need to perform some calculations, unless you calculate and store all of your object origins beforehand and reuse them.

Of course, a shorter way to accomplish the same thing while eliminating all those extra arguments would be to just subtract the object origin vector from the vector where the object is drawn. This results in a new vector at the correct point, like this:

```
spriteBatch.Draw(objectTexture, drawPosition - objectOrigin, Color.White);
```

Again, we subtract the origin because, to center the object, we need to reduce x by half the width and reduce y by half the height. Since the origin vector is computed as *(half the width, half the height)*, we can simply subtract the origin vector from the draw position to center the object.

Centering Text

Similar to textures, text drawn at a specific point starts with the upper-left corner of the text at that point. Centering text is a common requirement, and the MeasureString method of the SpriteFont class helps you accomplish this task. MeasureString returns a Vector2 object with x and y components that indicate the width and height of a block of specified text. You can divide this vector by two to get its center point, and then use it as the origin in DrawString.

Caution When working with multiple lines of text (with carriage return/new line sequences in them), the method shown in Listing 5-3 will result in the text being left-justified. The entire left-justified block of text will be centered. You need to center lines individually if you want each line to appear centered.

Listing 5-3 contains code that will allow you to draw text centered at some point, textPosition. This code would run in the Draw method with an active SpriteBatch.

Listing 5-3. *Centering Text Using a Longer DrawString Overload*

```
string sampleText = "Centered Text";
Vector2 textOrigin = myFont.MeasureString(sampleText) / 2;
spriteBatch.DrawString(myFont, sampleText, textPosition, Color.White,
    0.0f, textOrigin, 1.0f, SpriteEffects.None, 0.5f);
```

The mystery arguments are the same as the ones for the Draw method in Listing 5-2, described in the previous section. This is an easy way to center text using the origin, although the shorter way to do it is using the inline vector subtraction method shown after Listing 5-2:

```
spriteBatch.DrawString(myFont, sampleText, textPosition - textOrigin, Color.White);
```

In some cases, you might not want to center the text vertically. You might want to have the top of the text aligned with a certain point. This is especially useful when you are looking at a user interface mockup that says "draw the text here." You know you want to center it horizontally, but you want the top of the text to be aligned with some point. In that case, don't halve the entire vector returned by MeasureString; halve only the x component. Listing 5-4 shows how to center text horizontally, but have the top of the text starting at the point provided.

Listing 5-4. *Centering Text Horizontally, but Aligning the Top Where the Text Will Be Drawn*

```
Vector2 textOrigin = myFont.MeasureString(sampleText);
textOrigin.X /= 2;
```

Note In C#, the /= operator divides the left side of the expression by the right side and assigns the result back to the left side. This is the same as writing textOrigin.X = textOrigin.X / 2. Other similar operators exist, such as *=, +=, and -=.

Locating Sides of Objects

If you know the position and size of an object, you can use those properties to determine where the sides of the objects are. While there may be transparent areas of any given texture, it is most computationally efficient to consider the sides of the object to be equal to the rectangular texture size.

Finding these sides results in a *bounding box*, which represents the boundaries of the image. A bounding box is illustrated in Figure 5-11.

Figure 5-11. *A transparent object with an imaginary bounding box surrounding it*

The bounding box is always the same width and height of the texture itself. Since Texture2D objects expose these properties, you can use them to calculate a bounding box very easily given the coordinate of the top-left corner (also the object's on-screen position).

Creating a bounding box is a simple way to get access to all four sides of the object. However, sometimes you want to conserve resources by looking at only one side. For example, in the OutBreak game, we constrain the movement of the paddle so that it cannot move beyond the visible area of the screen. To do this, we use if statements with simple Boolean expressions such as these:

```
if (paddlePosition.X > 0)
{
    // Move the paddle left
    paddlePosition.X -= paddleSpeed;
}

if (paddlePosition.X + paddleTexture.Width < screenWidth)
{
    // Move the paddle right
    paddlePosition.X += paddleSpeed;
}
```

These statements are checking that a certain point is not out of bounds of the screen. The left side is easy, since the paddlePosition vector references the top-left corner. If the top-left corner has an x coordinate of greater than zero, it's okay to move it farther to the left until it butts up to the wall.

Checking the right side of the paddle is only slightly more complicated. Again, since the paddlePosition vector references the top left, you need to add the entire width of the object to figure out where the right side is. Look at that line again:

```
if (paddlePosition.X + paddleTexture.Width < screenWidth)
```

That Boolean expression adds the width of the object to its current position to determine the x coordinate of the right side. If the right side's x coordinate is less than the screen's width, there is still room to move it to the right.

Determining the boundaries of an object is also useful for the most basic form of collision detection. This form of collision detection uses bounding box rectangles.

Creating Bounding Boxes

Creating a bounding box for an object is very simple and has several applications. You need to know only three things to create a bounding box:

- The object's position

- The object's width

- The object's height

Bounding boxes are used to determine an imaginary rectangle around the object as it is currently displayed on the screen. The Microsoft.Xna.Framework.Rectangle class is most commonly used to store a bounding box.

To create a bounding box given an object's position and the `Texture2D` object for that object, you can use the following code:

```
Rectangle boundingBox = new Rectangle(position.X, position.Y,
    texture.Width, texture.Height);
```

■**Tip** It's more efficient to only instantiate one bounding box (for each object needed) and update its properties as they change, rather than instantiating a new one with every tick of the `Update` method.

Detecting Collisions with Bounding Boxes

The easiest way to figure out if two objects collide is to create two bounding boxes and use the `Intersect` method of the `Rectangle` class. If `Intersect` returns `true`, the objects collide. Otherwise, they do not. Let's see what this looks like in code:

```
Rectangle projectileBox;
Rectangle enemyBox;

projectileBox = new Rectangle(projectile.X, projectile.Y,
    projectileTex.Width, projectileTex.Height);

enemyBox = new Rectangle(enemy.X, enemy.Y, enemyTex.Width, enemyTex.Height);

if (enemyBox.Intersects(projectileBox))
{
    // The projectile hit the enemy
    // decrement enemy health, etc.
}
```

This is the simplest form of collision detection and performs the best (unless you are checking only one dimension, such as only the x axis, which can be done in one line of code using Boolean expressions). We'll cover more complicated forms of collision detection later in the chapter.

Emulating Physics

On the Zune, it's best to keep complex calculations to a minimum. Most commercially available physics engines eat a ton of processing, although there are a few available specifically for XNA games. If your game requires advanced physics, you will probably want to reuse an available physics engine, rather than undertake the daunting task of creating your own.

There are quite a few things you can do to achieve the look and feel of physics while implementing only one simple concept: acceleration. *Acceleration*, mathematically speaking, is the rate at which an object's velocity (or speed) changes. The gravitational constant, *G*, is defined as –9.8 meters per second per second, or –9.8 m/s^2. This means that an object falling towards the earth falls 9.8 seconds faster each second than it did the previous second.

Using Acceleration

Acceleration can be applied not only to gravity, but also to the concept of *easing*. Easing means that an object gradually moves from one speed to another. This is a visually pleasing effect. For example, if you wanted a button or other user interface element to move smoothly into place, you would use a formula with acceleration to achieve the effect of easing.

Easing in means that the object starts very slow and speeds up as it nears its destination. *Easing out* means that the object starts very quickly and slows down as it reaches its final point. Mathematically, the difference between these two is just acceleration versus deceleration.

Consider this simple formula to make an object fall at a constant speed. Such logic might appear in the Update method:

```
object.Y = object.Y + fixedFallDistance;
```

If you wanted to make the object accelerate or decelerate, however, you would need to maintain separate variables to hold these values. In code, you can update an object's velocity by adding the product of the acceleration value and the elapsed time:

```
velocity += acceleration * time;
```

Likewise, you can then use the velocity to update the position:

```
position += velocity * time;
```

In practice, the data types of position, acceleration, and velocity are all Vector2. An object can accelerate in either direction. An object can also move in either direction. Pragmatically speaking, it's much easier to do the math with all vector objects.

In addition, the time variable here is retrieved using gameTime.ElapsedGameTime. TotalSeconds and casting that value to a float. Doing so allows you the convenience of working in terms of seconds, as well as the ability to draw smoothly even if the game is not running in a fixed-step game loop.

Using Interpolation

Interpolation allows you to specify two vectors and a weighted value to calculate a new vector that lies somewhere in between those two vectors. This is extremely useful when building fly-in type animations for user interfaces, because by design, you know where the animation should start and end and how much time it should take.

The XNA Framework provides two methods for interpolation. The first is called *lerp*, which is short for linear interpolation. The code to perform a linear interpolation between two vectors looks like this:

```
Vector2 result = Vector2.Lerp(vector1, vector2, weight);
```

If you were to graph the response of the Lerp function, you would get a straight line between the two points. Assume you have two vectors, A and B, which are 10 pixels apart. Let $A = (0, 0)$ and $B = (10, 0)$. If you were to call Lerp with a weight value of 0.7f, you would get a new vector $R = (7, 0)$. This example would look like this in code:

```
Vector2 a = new Vector2(0, 0);
Vector2 b = new Vector2(10, 0);
Vector2 result = Vector2.Lerp(a, b, 0.7f); // will return a new Vector2 (7, 0)
```

The other option the XNA Framework provides for interpolation is called *smooth step*. Smooth step behaves the same as the Lerp function, but it uses a cubic equation instead of a linear equation. The result is a function you can use to create an animation that eases in and eases out.

EXERCISE 5-1. AN ACCELERATING BALL

In this quick example, you will see how to use the current elapsed game time to cause an object to move with acceleration. We'll build a PC game so that you can see the results quickly. The code for this example can be found in the Examples/Chapter 5/Exercise 1 folder.

1. In Visual Studio, create a new Windows Game project called AccelerationSample.

2. Add the file greenball.png to the Content project from the Chapter 5/Artwork folder.

3. Declare the following private member variables to the Game1 class in Game1.cs:

```
Texture2D greenBallTex;
bool ballIsFalling;

Vector2 acceleration;
Vector2 velocity;
Vector2 initialPosition;
Vector2 ballPosition;
```

4. Add the following code to the game's Initialize method. This code initializes the position, initial velocity, initial position, and acceleration values.

```
protected override void Initialize()
{
    acceleration = new Vector2(0f, 15f);
    velocity = Vector2.Zero;
    initialPosition = Vector2.Zero;
    ballPosition = initialPosition;
    ballIsFalling = false;

    base.Initialize();
}
```

5. Load the greenball.png file into its corresponding Texture2D object in the LoadContent method:

```
protected override void LoadContent()
{
    // Create a new SpriteBatch, which can be used to draw textures.
    spriteBatch = new SpriteBatch(GraphicsDevice);

    greenBallTex = Content.Load<Texture2D>("greenball");
}
```

6. Add the following code to the game's Update method. This code starts the acceleration or resets the position, depending on which key you press. If the ball is falling, it updates the ball's position using the acceleration formula shown earlier in the chapter. Note that acceleration is defined as "pixels per second per second," since we are normalizing our time variable to be in seconds.

```
protected override void Update(GameTime gameTime)
{
    float time;
    KeyboardState kbState = Keyboard.GetState();

    // Check for 'Enter'. This makes the ball start falling.
    if (kbState.IsKeyDown(Keys.Enter) && ballIsFalling == false)
    {
        ballIsFalling = true;
    }

    // Check for 'R' (for Reset). Resets the ball position
    if (kbState.IsKeyDown(Keys.R) && ballIsFalling == true)
    {
        ballIsFalling = false;
        ballPosition = Vector2.Zero;
        velocity = Vector2.Zero;
    }

    // Calculate the falling ball's position.
    if (ballIsFalling)
    {
        time = (float)gameTime.TotalGameTime.TotalSeconds;
        velocity += acceleration * time;
        ballPosition += velocity * time;
    }

    base.Update(gameTime);
}
```

Note the bolded code in this listing. This is the code that updates the velocity and position based on the elapsed time.

7. Draw the ball on the screen, using the following code in the Draw method.

```
protected override void Draw(GameTime gameTime)
{
    GraphicsDevice.Clear(Color.White);

    spriteBatch.Begin();
    spriteBatch.Draw(greenBallTex, ballPosition, Color.White);
    spriteBatch.End();

    base.Draw(gameTime);
}
```

8. Test the code by pressing F5. Press Enter on the keyboard to make the ball fall. Press R to reset the ball to its original position. Note the smooth movement as the ball gradually increases speed. You should see something similar to Figure 5-12.

Figure 5-12. *Exercise 5-1 in action, with an accelerating ball*

This concludes Exercise 5-1. Keep this code handy to modify in the next example.

Using Other Time-Dependent Functions

Using the elapsed time in your variables lends itself nicely to the use of other built-in functions that take a time variable. Oscillating functions such as sine and cosine are good examples. Even as the value of time increases infinitely, the result of sine and cosine passing in time is always between –1 and 1. An interesting use of the sine function would be to create a pulsating effect, where text or a sprite is drawn with a scale factor that is calculated with the sine function.

The result of sine and cosine can be altered in two ways:

Amplitude: You multiply the result of the sine wave by some scalar value to increase (or decrease) the final result. This effectively increases the range. If you have an amplitude of 2.0, the range will widen from –2.0 to +2.0.

Period: The *period* specifies how frequently the function oscillates. The shorter the period, the faster the oscillations. You can specify a period by multiplying the value passed to the function by some scalar value, such as `sin(2.0 * time)`. In this function, the period would be doubled.

The only difference between sine and cosine is that `sin(0)` is 0, whereas `cos(0)` is 1. In other words, the sine function starts at zero and the cosine function starts at its maximum amplitude. Both functions oscillate in the same pattern from there on.

A generic sine (or cosine) function looks like this: $y = A sin(pt) + b$. In this equation, A represents the amplitude, p represents the period, and b represents some vertical shift value. If you set b to zero, the sine function will oscillate around the center point zero. If you change the value of b, all of the outputs are shifted by that value. In some cases, you may want to ensure that you always have a positive value, so you could add two to any basic sine wave to shift the range of the function from (–1, 1) to (1, 3). You can also constrain the output of sine and cosine to only positive (or zero) values by using the `Math.Abs` (absolute value) function.

Let's implement a simple pulsing effect using a sine wave. This example uses the code from Example 5-1. In this example, we'll use a longer overload of the `spriteBatch.Draw` method than we have used in previous examples:

```
spriteBatch.Draw(greenBallTex, pulsingBallPosition, null, glowColor,
    1.0f, pulsingBallOrigin, pulseScale, SpriteEffects.None, 0.5f);
```

The following parameters are passed in:

- `greenBallTex`: The `Texture2D` object to draw.

- `pulsingBallPosition`: The `Vector2` object defined earlier; the middle of the screen.

- `null`: An optional parameter used to specify a source rectangle. Specifying `null` draws the entire texture.

- `glowColor`: The color defined in the `Update` method, which changes in an oscillating manner with time.

- `1.0f`: The rotation, which we are not modifying.

- `pulsingBallOrigin`: The origin `Vector2` calculated earlier. This centers the ball on the `pulsingBallPosition` point.

- `pulseScale`: The scale factor calculated using the sine function in the `Update` method.

- `SpriteEffects.None`: The sprite is not flipped horizontally or vertically.

- `0.5f`: The layer depth of the sprite. It can be used to alter the z-order (or layering) of sprites. Any value between 0 and 1 will work.

EXERCISE 5-2. A PULSATING EFFECT USING THE SINE FUNCTION

We'll keep the acceleration code in place from Exercise 5-1, since this example shows a minor addition to the math. In this example, we'll draw another ball right in the middle of the screen and have it pulsate.

The pulsating effect combines two elements. The first is the size; we will use the sine function to generate a scale factor, which we will use in the Draw method. The second is a color value, which we use to tint the sprite.

When a sprite is drawn without any tint, it is passed the color Color.White, which is 100% red, green, and blue. To tint a sprite red, we keep the 100% red element of the color and decrease both blue and green by the same factor.

Much of the math code works only with some specific data type, such as double. These values must be cast to work properly with our float variables.

1. Start with the code for Exercise 5-1 (found in Examples/Chapter 5/Exercise 1). Add the following private member variables:

```
Vector2 pulsingBallPosition;
Vector2 pulsingBallOrigin;
float pulseScale;
float redGlowAmount;
Color glowColor;
```

2. Add the following code to the Initialize method to set up these new variables:

```
pulseScale = 1.0f;
glowColor = Color.White;
```

3. Because some of the position variables depend on the ball's texture object being loaded, we must initialize some of these values after that object has been loaded in LoadContent. This code finds the center of the screen and the center of the ball object (to be used as the texture origin). Add the following lines to initialize other variables in the LoadContent method (after greenBallTex has been loaded):

```
pulsingBallPosition = new Vector2(
    GraphicsDevice.Viewport.Width / 2,
    GraphicsDevice.Viewport.Height / 2);

pulsingBallOrigin = new Vector2(
    greenBallTex.Width / 2,
    greenBallTex.Height / 2);
```

4. In the Update method, find the if statement that checks if the ball is falling. Modify that block with the bold code in the following snippet:

```
// Calculate the falling ball's position.
if (ballIsFalling)
{
    time = (float)gameTime.TotalGameTime.Subtract(fallStartTime).➥
TotalMilliseconds;
    time /= 1000.0f;
```

```
        ballPosition.Y = (initialVelocity * time) +
            initialPosition.Y +
            (0.5f * acceleration * time * time);

        // Update the pulse scale
        pulseScale = (float)Math.Abs(Math.Sin(5.0f * time)) + 1.0f;

        // Get the pulse color
        redGlowAmount = 1.0f - (float)Math.Abs(Math.Sin(5.0f * time));
        glowColor = new Color(1.0f, redGlowAmount, redGlowAmount);
}
```

The added code uses sine functions with a period of 5.0. Because absolute value is used, the pulse scale varies from 0 to 1. The value 1.0 is added, so the effective range of the pulse scale is from 1.0 to 2.0. The redGlowAmount variable is used to determine how much of the other colors should be mixed in with red to create the red glow effect. The value of the sine wave (with the same period of 5) is subtracted from 1, and this new value is passed in to a new Color constructor with full red and some equal fraction of the other colors. The result is a color that increases in red intensity as the sine function reaches a peak (because the other colors are closer to 0) and is closer to white when the sine function is close to 0 (because all colors are 100%).

5. Add the code in the Draw method to draw another ball in the middle of the screen with the current scale factor and glow color:

```
protected override void Draw(GameTime gameTime)
{
    GraphicsDevice.Clear(Color.White);

    spriteBatch.Begin();
    spriteBatch.Draw(greenBallTex, ballPosition, Color.White);
    spriteBatch.Draw(greenBallTex, pulsingBallPosition, null, glowColor,
        1.0f, pulsingBallOrigin, pulseScale, SpriteEffects.None, 0.5f);
    spriteBatch.End();

    base.Draw(gameTime);
}
```

The bolded call to spriteBatch.Draw is the longer overload of the method, as explained in the text preceding this exercise.

6. Press F5 to run the game. Use the same controls as in Exercise 5-1. Press Enter to make the ball fall and cause the center ball to start pulsating. Press R to reset. When the ball is falling, you should see something similar to Figure 5-13.

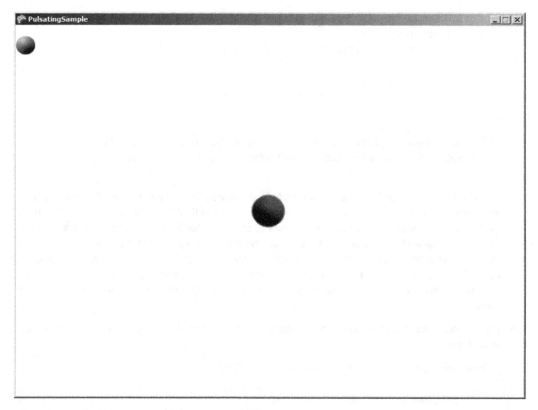

Figure 5-13. *Using periodic functions to create a pulsing effect*

Understanding a bit of trigonometry and physics is important to creating a game that behaves somewhat naturally. You could take this knowledge and apply it to your games, either by using some of the built-in XNA helper functions (check the MathHelper class) or by rolling some of it into a special library for your games.

Next, you will learn about some different ways of achieving collision detection and when to use each of the described methods.

Collision Detection Revisited

Earlier in the chapter, you learned that the most basic form of collision detection is performed by testing whether two bounding boxes intersect. This type of collision detection is called *simple collision detection.* In some cases, you may find that simple collision detection creates too many false positives, depending on the complexity of your sprite. In such cases, you could look at the more processor-intensive *per-pixel collision detection* method.

Simple Collision Detection

As described earlier in the chapter, simple collision detection involves drawing imaginary rectangles around screen objects and determining if they intersect. If they intersect, a collision has occurred. In code, such collision detection looks like Listing 5-5.

Listing 5-5. *Simple Rectangle-Based Collision Detection*

```
private bool CollisionDetected(Vector2 aPosition, Texture2D aTexture, Vector2
    bPosition, Texture2D bTexture)
{
    Rectangle boundingBoxA = new Rectangle(aPosition.X, aPosition.Y, aTexture.Width,
        aTexture.Height);

    Rectangle boundingBoxB = new Rectangle(bPosition.X, bPosition.Y, bTexture.Width,
        bTexture.Height);

    return boundingBoxA.Intersects(boundingBoxB);
}
```

This code creates two rectangles: one for each object. The box has the size of the object and is positioned at the same place as the object. With this logic, a collision would look like Figure 5-14.

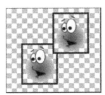

Figure 5-14. *A collision as identified by simple collision detection*

Note that because the object has a transparent background, the interesting parts of the graphics are not actually colliding. This is one example where simple collision detection can give you false positives. However, it remains the most computationally efficient way of detecting collisions from any angle.

Per-Pixel Collision Detection

A more accurate way to detect collisions is to compare each nontransparent pixel of both objects and determine whether any of these pixels exist at the same location. Per-pixel collision detection requires a more complicated algorithm, and using this method will likely slow down your game substantially. The smaller the textures are, the better it works, because smaller textures result in smaller iterations of each loop.

■**Caution** The use of per-pixel collision detection is extremely expensive, especially on a device with limited processor bandwidth, like the Zune. It will likely slow down your game. In most cases, simple rectangle-based collision detection is preferred. You can support both by checking for a bounding box collision first. If the simple collision is true, then you can perform per-pixel collision detection to gain a more precise result. This frees up processor cycles when there is no simple collision.

In (mostly) plain English, per-pixel collision detection works like this:

1. Construct one-dimensional arrays of colors that represent the texture data.

   ```
   Color[] greenBallData = new Color[greenBallTex.Width * greenBallTex.Height];
   ```

2. After the textures are loaded, populate the color arrays using the GetData method of the appropriate Texture2D object.

   ```
   greenBallTex.GetData(greenBallData);
   ```

3. With each update, create bounding boxes for each of the objects you want to check. Determine the area in which these objects intersect, which can be done using the static Rectangle.Intersect method. Then loop through every pixel in the intersection area and get each object's color value at that point. Check the alpha value. If both pixels here are not completely invisible, then a collision has happened.

Listing 5-6 shows an example of a collision detection algorithm that works with prepopulated texture data for two different objects: a green ball and a more graphical ball called "other ball." Some variables here are defined out of scope, such as the position variables, but they are included in this snippet because they are self-describing.

Listing 5-6. *A Simple Per-Pixel Collision Detection Algorithm*

```
private bool CheckPerPixelCollision()
{
    // Get bounding rectangles for each object
    Rectangle greenBoundingBox = new Rectangle((int)greenBallPos.X,
        (int)greenBallPos.Y, greenBallTex.Width, greenBallTex.Height);

    Rectangle otherBoundingBox = new Rectangle((int)otherBallPos.X,
        (int)otherBallPos.Y, otherBallTex.Width, otherBallTex.Height);

    // Determine the rectangle of intersection and
    // dereference its properties for performance.
    Rectangle collisionRegion = Rectangle.Intersect(greenBoundingBox,
        otherBoundingBox);

    int left = collisionRegion.Left;
    int right = collisionRegion.Right;
```

```
    int top = collisionRegion.Top;
    int bottom = collisionRegion.Bottom;

    Color greenBallCurrentColor, otherBallCurrentColor;
    int greenBallColorIndex, otherBallColorIndex;

    // Loop horizontally through the collision region.
    for (int row = top; row < bottom; row++)
    {
        for (int column = left; column < right; column++)
        {
            greenBallColorIndex = GetColorIndex(greenBoundingBox, row, column);
            otherBallColorIndex = GetColorIndex(otherBoundingBox, row, column);

            greenBallCurrentColor = greenBallColorData[greenBallColorIndex];
            otherBallCurrentColor = otherBallColorData[otherBallColorIndex];

            if (greenBallCurrentColor.A != 0 && otherBallCurrentColor.A != 0)
                return true;
        }
    }

    return false;
}
```

To see how this algorithm works in a game, let's run through a quick example.

EXERCISE 5-3. PER-PIXEL COLLISION DETECTION

This exercise has two goals. The first is to demonstrate how to implement per-pixel collision detection between two predefined objects. The second is to show you how poorly this algorithm, even in a modestly optimized state, runs on the Zune, so that you are discouraged from attempting to use it unless it is absolutely necessary. The code for this example can be found in the Examples/Chapter 5/Exercise 3 folder.

1. In Visual Studio, create a new Windows Game project (I called mine PerPixelCollisionSample).

2. Create a Zune copy of the game.

3. Add greenball.png and otherball.png from the Chapter 5/Artwork folder to the Content project.

4. Add a new sprite font to the Content project, and call it Normal.spritefont.

5. Add the InputState class from Chapter 4 to the project. Change the namespace to that of your project. I added some properties to the class to determine if a particular direction button is pressed down (not a new button press). These properties are LeftIsDown, RightIsDown, DownIsDown, and UpIsDown. Those last two names are slightly confusing, but these properties refer to the current button or key state for those directions.

6. Declare the following private variables in the `Game1` class in `Game1.cs`. The `Color` arrays will hold all of the color data for a given texture in a one-dimensional fashion.

```
Texture2D greenBallTex, otherBallTex;
SpriteFont normalFont;
InputState input;

string statusText = "";

Vector2 greenBallPos, otherBallPos;
Color[] greenBallColorData;
Color[] otherBallColorData;
```

7. Add the following code to the `Initialize` method to set up positioning and set the screen size:

```
protected override void Initialize()
{
    greenBallPos = new Vector2(100, 100);
    otherBallPos = new Vector2(150, 150);
    input = new InputState();

    graphics.PreferredBackBufferWidth = 240;
    graphics.PreferredBackBufferHeight = 320;
    graphics.ApplyChanges();

    base.Initialize();
}
```

8. In the `LoadContent` method, load the textures and font, and populate the `Color` arrays:

```
protected override void LoadContent()
{
    // Create a new SpriteBatch, which can be used to draw textures.
    spriteBatch = new SpriteBatch(GraphicsDevice);

    // Load graphical assets
    greenBallTex = Content.Load<Texture2D>("greenball");
    otherBallTex = Content.Load<Texture2D>("otherball");
    normalFont = Content.Load <SpriteFont>("Normal");

    // Allocate memory for the color data arrays
    greenBallColorData = new Color[greenBallTex.Width * greenBallTex.Height];
    otherBallColorData = new Color[otherBallTex.Width * otherBallTex.Height];

    // Populate the color data arrays
    greenBallTex.GetData(greenBallColorData);
    otherBallTex.GetData(otherBallColorData);
}
```

9. Add a new private method to the class called GetColorIndex. This method takes in a rectangle that represents the collision region, a row, and a column. The method uses this information generate an index value that is used in the Color array. For example, if you have a 3 × 3 intersection region, and you want the pixel in the second row, third column, this code would return an index of 5 (remember we are working with zero-based arrays).

```
/// <summary>
/// Takes a bounding box, row, and column and creates a one-dimensional index.
/// </summary>
private int GetColorIndex(Rectangle boundingBox, int row, int column)
{
    int index = 0;

    // How many rows down is the pixel?
    index += (row - boundingBox.Top) * boundingBox.Width;

    // How far from the left is the pixel?
    index += column - boundingBox.Left;

    return index;
}
```

This method is used directly by the collision detection algorithm. You don't need to worry about this method returning a negative index; even if it does, the for loop in which it is used is structured in such a way that only positive index values will be used.

10. Copy the code from Listing 5-6 and add that private method (CheckPerPixelCollision) to your class. (The code in Listing 5-6 is meant specifically for this exercise.)

11. In the Update method, update the input state object and check for input to move the "other ball" object around on the screen. Also update the status text based on the result of the collision detection algorithm.

```
protected override void Update(GameTime gameTime)
{
    input.Update();
    if (input.BackPressed)
        this.Exit();

    // Move the Other ball (face) based on user input.
    if (input.LeftIsDown)
        otherBallPos.X -= 2.0f;
    if (input.RightIsDown)
        otherBallPos.X += 2.0f;
    if (input.UpIsDown)
        otherBallPos.Y -= 2.0f;
    if (input.DownIsDown)
        otherBallPos.Y += 2.0f;
```

```
    if (CheckPerPixelCollision() == true)
        statusText = "<YES> Collision detected!";
    else
        statusText = "<NO> No collision detected.";

    base.Update(gameTime);
}
```

12. In the Draw method, draw the two ball objects and the status text:

```
protected override void Draw(GameTime gameTime)
{
    GraphicsDevice.Clear(Color.CornflowerBlue);

    spriteBatch.Begin();
    spriteBatch.Draw(greenBallTex, greenBallPos, Color.White);
    spriteBatch.Draw(otherBallTex, otherBallPos, Color.White);
    spriteBatch.DrawString(normalFont, statusText, Vector2.Zero, Color.White);
    spriteBatch.End();

    base.Draw(gameTime);
}
```

13. Test the Windows version of the game. Move the ball around with the arrow keys. Pay special attention to the fact that this likely runs on your computer without any performance hit (it certainly does on my quad-core Intel machine). Notice what happens to the status text when a direct collision is detected. Even though the bounding boxes technically intersect, a collision is not made unless it's supposed to look that way. Figure 5-15 illustrates the objects in such proximity that would cause a collision using simple collision detection. Figure 5-16 illustrates the objects in an actual collision.

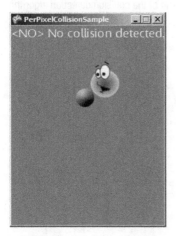

Figure 5-15. *Two objects positioned very closely, but not a true collision. This would register as a collision using simple bounding box collision detection.*

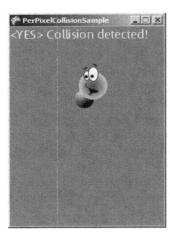

Figure 5-16. *Per-pixel collision detection in action*

14. Deploy this same code to a Zune device. Use the directional pad buttons to move the character around the screen. Note the slight lag in the movement. This is due to the complexity of the algorithm. Now imagine this algorithm checking more than two predefined textures, or trying to operate peacefully with other, equally complex game logic!

This exercise showed you how to implement per-pixel collision detection, but it also probably dissuaded you from trying to use it on the Zune, due to the incredible performance hit. It's rare that you want to check collision detection between only two objects. Consider the OutBreak game we built in the previous chapter. It checks collisions with up to 40 different objects. Imagine running the same code in a `foreach` loop!

Per-pixel collision detection is powerful, and it can be tempting to use it for some limited situations. However, for most applications, simple collision detection is far more practical and performs better. It's also unlikely that the user will notice you're not using per-pixel collision detection, especially on a small screen like that of the Zune. Unless you absolutely need this type of collision detection, save those CPU cycles for more interesting game logic.

Simple Game State Management

Before we delve into the magical world of components, I will briefly cover what I like to call "simple" game state management. For games that have only two or three game states, this is the easiest way to identify and manage what state your game is in. More advanced game and screen management is discussed in the next chapter.

Game state generally refers to what your game is doing at any given time, described by one word. Example game states are Start, Playing, and GameOver. The easiest way to use such game states is to create an enumeration in the same class file as your main game, outside the class, like so:

```
public enum GameState
{
    Start,
```

```
        Playing,
        GameOver
}
```

This enumeration is checked mainly in the game's Update and Draw methods. Normally, switch statements are used to determine the current game state, and that causes Update and Draw to behave differently for each case. For example, the only message a game in the Start state would watch for is a button press to start the game. When the game is in the Playing state, the more complex game logic is run instead. Likewise, in the Draw method, a game in the Start or GameOver states would likely draw some different background graphic on screen. Perhaps the GameOver state would also require a score to be drawn.

In any case, a GameState object is usually created and accessed throughout the game, whether to check the game state or to transition it to a new state. In the game's private member variable section, you would create a variable to represent the game state:

```
GameState gameState;
```

The initial game state would be set in the game's Initialize method:

```
protected override void Initialize()
{
    gameState = GameState.Start;
    base.Initialize();
}
```

In the game's Update method, the code behaves differently for each game state by way of a simple switch statement (this is sample code, not part of a larger game):

```
protected override void Update(GameTime gameTime)
{
    switch (this.gameState)
    {
        case GameState.Start:
            if (input.MiddleButtonPressed)
            {
                gameState = GameState.Playing;
            }
            break;

        case GameState.Playing:
            // All of the main game's update logic goes here, e.g...
            HandleInput();
            CheckCollisions();
            UpdateSounds();
            break;

        case GameState.GameOver:
            finalScoreText = score;
            if (input.MiddleButtonPressed) // start over
            {
```

```
                gameState = GameState.Start;
            }
            break;
    }

    base.Update(gameTime);
}
```

Likewise, the Draw method will behave differently for each game state, as in the following example:

```
protected override void Draw(GameTime gameTime)
{
    GraphicsDevice.Clear(Color.Black);
    spriteBatch.Begin();

    switch (this.gameState)
    {
        case GameState.Start:
            spriteBatch.Draw(startBackground, Vector2.Zero, Color.White);
            break;

        case GameState.Playing:
            // Draw all the game objects, text, etc.
            spriteBatch.Draw(playingBackground, Vector2.Zero, Color.White);
            spriteBatch.Draw(ballTexture, ballPosition, Color.White);
            spriteBatch.Draw(paddleTexture, leftPaddlePos, Color.White);
            spriteBatch.Draw(paddleTexture, rightPaddlePs, Color.White);
            spriteBatch.DrawString(font, scoreString, Vector2.Zero, Color.White);
            break;

        case GameState.GameOver:
            spriteBatch.Draw(gameOverBackground, Vector2.Zero, Color.White);
            break;
    }

    spriteBatch.End();

    base.Draw(gameTime);
}
```

This simple form of game state management is fairly easy to read and understand. You'll see a more detailed example of simple game state management in the Monkey Feeder game we will build at the end of this chapter.

However, with the addition of more game states and more advanced requirements, such as screen transitions and complex state transfer logic, a more robust system is needed. You'll learn about advanced game state management techniques in the next chapter.

Using Components

With all of this chapter's math studies under your belt, I feel it's time to lead you toward things that can reduce your development time. Game *components* fit that description. They allow you to apply good object-oriented design principles to entities in your game. You can take advantage of the XNA Framework's ability to automatically update and draw components that you add to your game.

The beauty of components lies in the fact that you can create an entirely separate class with update and draw logic, removing the need to put everything in Game1.cs (or whatever you name your main game class file). Components allow you to think of objects as whole entities, rather than a loosely coupled collection of textures, positions, speeds, states, and so on.

Components can be of two types:

Drawable: These game components are generally used for single objects, like a gun, tank, ball, projectile, and so on. Drawable game components inherit from the DrawableGameComponent class, which provides overridable methods such as LoadContent, Initialize, Update, and Draw. Drawable game components expose everything nondrawable GameComponent instances do, with the added feature of being able to draw themselves and load their own content independently of the main game's LoadContent method. To specify whether a drawable game component should be drawn, you can set its IsVisible property to true or false.

Nondrawable: These game components are often used to encapsulate specific logic, such as input handling, collision detection, and so on. Nondrawable game components are useful for any scenario where you need game logic that is constantly updated and tied to the main game loop. They are automatically initialized and updated at the appropriate times when you add them to the main game's Components property. Nondrawable game components inherit from the GameComponent class and provide the same overridable methods as drawable components, with the exception of Draw.

Game components are manually instantiated and added to the game's Components property. When added to this collection, each object is automatically notified when the object needs to be updated and drawn (and also when the object should be initialized, or when content should be loaded). This allows you to leverage all of the XNA Framework capabilities for individual objects, affording you the luxury of having a "mini-game" within each component.

■**Note** The game is told to notify its components via the base calls in the game's standard XNA methods, such as base.Update(gameTime). If you remove these calls, your components will not be notified by the main game loop, so be sure to leave those default lines in the game code.

Since these components are automatically drawn and updated, you may want to restrict whether an object should be updated or drawn. Components also expose properties such as Visible and Enabled, which allow you to control when a game component should draw or update itself.

Using components is a smart way to start writing your games. It keeps most of the hairy logic out of the main game and allows you to write relevant, cohesive code on a per-object basis. It also helps you to think in practical, object-oriented terms—each object is a game entity that operates independently of the rest of the game. This allows you to keep all of your true game logic in the Game class.

Furthermore, since drawable game components expose a LoadContent method, you can avoid having to use the main game's LoadContent to load all of your game's content at once. This lets you keep references to Texture2D objects in the entity class, rather than in the main game—again, leading to cleaner code.

Once you begin developing with game components, you'll see that this is the best path to take.

In the next exercise, we will make a component out of our InputState class. This time, we'll also implement the touchpad, with comparable behavior on Windows using the mouse cursor.

EXERCISE 5-4. THE INPUTSTATE CLASS AS A GAME COMPONENT

In this example, you will learn how to use a nondrawable game component to make game development a lot simpler. This exercise uses a modified version of the InputState class, which we will now componentize for future use in other games.

The input handler object does not need to be drawable. This component will inherit from GameComponent, which provides an Update method we will use to get the new game pad state.

The code for this exercise can be found in the Examples/Chapter 5/Exercise 4 folder. Note that in the text here, the method and class header comments have been removed from the listings to conserve space, but the downloadable code is fully commented.

This is a componentized, reusable version of the InputState class we have been working with. It's been substantially refactored throughout the course of this book, so that you can apply your new understanding of components in a way that makes sense. Going forward, this is probably the best version of the class to use.

This version of InputState also supports the touchpad. On Windows, the touchpad behavior is activated by holding the left mouse button and using the mouse to move. The result is a Vector2D that mirrors the behavior of the touchpad on the Zune (which is mapped to the LeftThumbstick control in the GamePadState class). The resulting vector is between -1.0f and 1.0f, and starts at the center of the window in Windows games. On the Zune, the vector represents the touch distance from the center of the pad.

1. In Visual Studio, create a new Windows Game Library project by selecting File ➤ New Project. Call it InputHandler.

2. Rename Class1.cs to InputState.cs.

3. Open InputState.cs. Remove the generated code and replace all of it with this stub:

```
using System;
using Microsoft.Xna.Framework;
using Microsoft.Xna.Framework.Input;
using Microsoft.Xna.Framework.Graphics;

namespace InputHandler
{
```

```
public class InputState : GameComponent
{

}
}
```

Note the inheritance from GameComponent. This gives us access to all of the nondrawable game component methods, including Initialize and Update.

4. Add the following private members to the class. These variables hold the previous and current states for both the keyboard and the Zune.

```
#region Private Fields

private GamePadState CurrentGamePadState;
private GamePadState LastGamePadState;
private KeyboardState CurrentKeyboardState;
private KeyboardState LastKeyboardState;

// Touch vector fields, and Windows support
private MouseState mouseState;
private Vector2 windowCenter;
private Vector2 windowSize;
private Vector2 touchVector;

#endregion
```

5. Add a constructor to the class, and initialize the input states declared earlier as shown. Note that the constructor must take a Game argument. This is so the component knows which Game class it is assigned to and can access that game's properties. The mouseState variable is ignored on the Zune.

```
#region Constructor(s)

public InputState(Game game)
    : base(game)
{
    currentGamePadState = new GamePadState();
    lastGamePadState = new GamePadState();
    currentKeyboardState = new KeyboardState();
    lastKeyboardState = new KeyboardState();
    mouseState = new MouseState();
}

#endregion
```

6. Create some public utility methods. These determine the status of various buttons and will work whether the game is running on Zune or Windows. There are four methods in total: two for the Zune and two for the keyboard. For each input device, there is one method that checks to see if a button or key is a new press, or if the button is currently down.

```
#region Public Utility Methods

public bool IsNewButtonPress(Buttons button)
{
    return (currentGamePadState.IsButtonDown(button) &&
        lastGamePadState.IsButtonUp(button));
}

public bool IsNewKeyPress(Keys key)
{
    return (currentKeyboardState.IsKeyDown(key) &&
        lastKeyboardState.IsKeyUp(key));
}

public bool IsButtonDown(Buttons button)
{
    return currentGamePadState.IsButtonDown(button);
}

public bool IsKeyDown(Keys key)
{
    return currentKeyboardState.IsKeyDown(key);
}

#endregion
```

7. Create a section for overridden methods. These methods are implementations of the GameComponent base class methods. We will be overriding Initialize and Update.

8. Add the code for Initialize. The only reason this method needs to be called is for the Windows emulation of the touchpad, which requires knowledge of the screen size (accessed via the game's Viewport class). The contained code must execute in Initialize rather than the component's constructor, because the component will have no knowledge of the graphics device until the parent game's Initialize method has been called. This method will then be called once automatically by the game loop.

```
public override void Initialize()
{
    Viewport windowViewport = Game.GraphicsDevice.Viewport;
    windowSize = new Vector2(windowViewport.Width, windowViewport.Height);
    windowCenter = windowSize / 2;
    touchVector = Vector2.Zero;

    base.Initialize();
}
```

9. Add the following code for Update, which updates the state of the mouse, keyboard, and Zune pad simulta- neously (remember that mouse and keyboard are ignored on the Zune). The game loop will call this method automatically when the component is added to the game. This method also calculates the mouse's distance from the center of the screen and divides it by the center coordinates. This converts the mouse position to

a vector identical to what would be returned by the Zune's touchpad, where each coordinate is between −1.0 and 1.0. Note how the y coordinate is negated. This is because the LeftThumbstick vector has a y component that is negative in the up direction and positive downward. The negation is done for consistency between the two platforms. Also note that touch emulation for Windows is active only when the left mouse button is down.

```
public override void Update(GameTime gameTime)
{
    // Set the previous input states to the current state.
    lastGamePadState = currentGamePadState;
    lastKeyboardState = currentKeyboardState;

    // Retrieve the current input states.
    currentGamePadState = GamePad.GetState(PlayerIndex.One);
    currentKeyboardState = Keyboard.GetState();
    mouseState = Mouse.GetState();

    // If the mouse button is down, activate "touch" on windows
    if (mouseState.LeftButton == ButtonState.Pressed)
    {
        touchVector.X = (mouseState.X - windowCenter.X) / windowCenter.X;
        touchVector.Y = -(mouseState.Y - windowCenter.Y) / windowCenter.Y;
    }
    else
        touchVector = Vector2.Zero;

    base.Update(gameTime);
}
```

10. Add a Properties region. These properties mainly serve to give you a shortcut. You can name these properties by the actions they represent. For example. NewDownPress should mean that the user either pressed Down on the Zune directional pad or the Down arrow key. You can create as many properties as you like and name them how you wish. This is where the class offers flexibility. Alternatively, you can create a new class that inherits from this one and define more properties specific to the game at hand.

11. Add the properties, as follows. The first property returns either the touchpad vector (LeftThumbstick) on the Zune or the touch vector as calculated by the mouse position if on Windows. This is the only place where we need to differentiate platforms, so this property uses conditional preprocessor directives. The other properties check for a combination of the Zune buttons and the keyboard.

```
#region Properties

public Vector2 TouchVector
{
    get
    {
        #if ZUNE

        return currentGamePadState.ThumbSticks.Left;
```

```
        #endif

        #if WINDOWS

        return touchVector;

        #endif
    }
}


public bool MiddleButtonPressed
{
    get
    {
        return IsNewButtonPress(Buttons.A) ||
            IsNewKeyPress(Keys.Enter);
    }
}

public bool NewPlayPress
{
    get
    {
        return IsNewButtonPress(Buttons.B) ||
            IsNewKeyPress(Keys.Space);
    }
}

public bool NewBackPress
{
    get
    {
        return IsNewButtonPress(Buttons.Back)
            IsNewKeyPress(Keys.Escape);
    }
}

public bool NewUpPress
{
    get
    {
        return IsNewButtonPress(Buttons.DPadUp) ||
            IsNewKeyPress(Keys.Up);
    }
}
```

```csharp
        public bool NewDownPress
        {
            get
            {
                return IsNewButtonPress(Buttons.DPadDown) ||
                    IsNewKeyPress(Keys.Down);
            }
        }

        public bool NewRightPress
        {
            get
            {
                return IsNewButtonPress(Buttons.DPadRight) ||
                    IsNewKeyPress(Keys.Right);
            }
        }

        public bool NewLeftPress
        {
            get
            {
                return IsNewButtonPress(Buttons.DPadLeft) ||
                    IsNewKeyPress(Keys.Left);
            }
        }

        public bool UpPressed
        {
            get
            {
                return IsButtonDown(Buttons.DPadUp) ||
                    IsKeyDown(Keys.Up);
            }
        }


        public bool DownPressed
        {
            get
            {
                return IsButtonDown(Buttons.DPadDown) ||
                    IsKeyDown(Keys.Down);
            }
        }
```

```
public bool RightPressed
{
    get
    {
        return IsButtonDown(Buttons.DPadRight) ||
            IsKeyDown(Keys.Right);
    }
}

public bool LeftPressed
{
    get
    {
        return IsButtonDown(Buttons.DPadLeft) ||
            IsKeyDown(Keys.Left);
    }
}

#endregion
```

12. Compile the code and correct any typographical errors. Now you can reference this full-featured, componentized library in other projects.

There are a couple of ways to reuse this class. The first is to build the project and reference the dynamic link library (DLL) output from the Debug or Release folder. The second is to keep the project somewhere safe and add it as a project reference to any future projects. You'll see how to reuse this in the Monkey Feeder game example.

You may be wondering how to disable a GameComponent, in the event that its logic is useless for the current game state (or some similar condition). As you will see in the next example, local instances to these components are usually kept in the game class itself. Since objects deriving from GameComponent take on several inherited properties, your component will have a few things available that you didn't code yourself. In particular, your new component has a property called Enabled, which you can set to false to prevent it from running its Update method.

Tip To stop a custom game component from updating, set its Enabled property to false.

Bringing It All Together with Monkey Feeder

The final example in this chapter brings together nearly of the concepts explored up to this point. The game we will build uses simple game state management, animation, simple collision detection, trig functions, texture scaling and rotation, touchpad input, and realistic (though simple) 2D vector physics. How can we possibly cram all of this into one game without it becoming bloated and unmanageable? By using game components, of course! This game uses both drawable and nondrawable game components.

Years ago, there was a highly addictive game on the Web (built in Flash) whose main objective was simply to toss wads of paper into a trash can. Though the game took place indoors, there was a wind factor, which added quite a bit of difficulty, because you had to estimate the angle at which to toss the paper to compensate for the wind force. The object of the game was to sink as many paper wads consecutively as possible.

In our rendition of the game, we'll be throwing bananas to a monkey on the beach. The touchpad can be used to put "spin" on the banana mid-flight to slightly alter the path. This brings me to the (ingenious) name of the game: Monkey Feeder. To give you an idea of what we're building, Figure 5-17 shows Monkey Feeder's game over screen.

Figure 5-17. *The Monkey Feeder game*

Note This example creates a unique sprite batch per component and draws it. This is certainly not the most optimal approach, but advanced sprite batch techniques have not yet been covered (they are covered in Chapter 6). To avoid confusing you any more than is necessary, we will keep it very simple in this game by using one sprite batch per component. In games where you have only a handful of sprite batches going, you will likely not notice a performance hit, but it is *far* more acceptable to use a shared sprite batch solution, as discussed in Chapter 6. Consolidating draw operations into one sprite batch object is one of the first things you can do to improve performance, and should really be done as a best practice rather than as an optimization.

Configuring the Solution, Projects, Folders, and Assets

As usual, our first steps are to create and set up the project.

1. In Visual Studio. create a new Zune Game project. Call it MonkeyFeeder.

2. Add an existing project to the solution. Browse to the InputHandler project we made in Exercise 5-4.

3. Create a copy of this project for Zune.

4. Add a reference to the MonkeyFeeder project. Choose the Zune copy of the InputHandler project from the Projects tab.

5. Create a copy of the MonkeyFeeder game for Windows.

6. Add a reference to the original InputHandler project to the Windows version of the game.

7. Working in the Zune MonkeyFeeder project, create two subfolders under Content: Textures and Fonts.

8. Right-click the Textures folder and add the following files from the Examples/ Chapter 5/Artwork folder:

   - arrow.png
   - banana.png
   - beachbg.png
   - gameover.png
   - monkeysheet.png
   - startscreen.png
   - water.png

9. Right-click the Fonts folder and add a new sprite font called Small.spritefont to this new folder. Change the properties so that it is 10pt Bold Kootenay.

10. Copy the file GameThumbnail.png from the Examples/Chapter 5/Artwork folder. Paste it into the MonkeyFeeder folder to overwrite the default one.

11. Right-click the MonkeyFeeder project and add a new folder. Call it Components. This is where we will store our future game components.

12. Rename Game1.cs to MonkeyFeederGame.cs. Your Solution Explorer window should look like Figure 5-18.

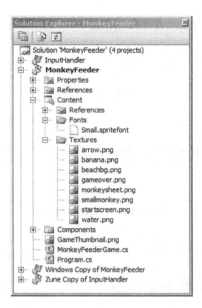

Figure 5-18. *The MonkeyFeeder solution, properly configured to begin coding*

Creating the Components

The game contains five drawable game components and one nondrawable game component (input handler). We will build the drawable components next so they can be used in the game. The five components are as follows:

- *Water*: This component draws a moving waterline on the right side of the beach.

- *Toss Arrow*: This is the visual component that is used to determine the angle at which bananas are thrown.

- *Wind Needle*: This component indicates a random wind speed and direction and exposes those values.

- *Monkey*: This is an animated monkey that runs through a sprite sheet animation and exposes a bounding box to make collision detection easier. The bounding box is shrunk to make the game more challenging.

- *Banana*: This is a projectile object whose direction is impacted by other factors in the game, including touch input (which turns the banana green).

Let's begin with the Water component.

Creating the Water Component

I decided that because this game is set on the beach outside a lush jungle, I wanted to create an effect of water lapping up on the shore. Not being artistically inclined, I did what anyone would do: I used a periodic trig function to dynamically position a transparent graphic, which gives the illusion of moving water!

This component implements the Math.Sin function, as described earlier in the chapter.

1. Right-click the Components folder in the solution and add a new class. Call it Water.cs.

Note For future reference, you can also choose Add New Item from the context menu and select Game Component, but it defaults to a nondrawable game component. The approach we use here is easier to explain.

---

2. Modify the namespaces being used (you only need three):

```
using System;
using Microsoft.Xna.Framework;
using Microsoft.Xna.Framework.Graphics;
```

3. Make the Water component inherit from the DrawableGameComponent class:

```
public class Water : DrawableGameComponent
```

4. Add a new region for Fields and add the following fields to that region:

```
#region Fields

private SpriteBatch spriteBatch;
private Vector2 position;
private Texture2D waterTex;

#endregion
```

5. Add a new region for the constructor (Constructor(s)) and add the default constructor, which uses an instance of the game.

```
#region Constructor(s)

public Water(Game game)
    : base(game)
{

}

#endregion
```

6. Add a new region called Overridden GameComponent Methods.

7. You can use IntelliSense to automatically implement various methods. If you just type the word over, a list of overridable methods pops up. Use the arrow keys to select the Initialize method, and implement it within the Overridden GameComponent Methods region:

```
public override void Initialize()
{
    position = Vector2.Zero;
    base.Initialize();
}
```

8. Override the Update method next. This method alters the position of the water texture based on a sine function with an amplitude of 10 and a period of 1/1000. An absolute value is used so that negative values from the sine function are converted to positive ones.

```
public override void Update(GameTime gameTime)
{
    // Use a sine wave with an amplitude of 10
    position.X = 10.0f * (float)Math.Abs(
        Math.Sin(gameTime.TotalGameTime.TotalSeconds));

    base.Update(gameTime);
}
```

9. Override the LoadContent method, which initializes the sprite batch and the texture for the component.

```
protected override void LoadContent()
{
    spriteBatch = new SpriteBatch(GraphicsDevice);
    waterTex = Game.Content.Load<Texture2D>("Textures/water");
    base.LoadContent();
}
```

10. Finally, override the Draw method.

```
public override void Draw(GameTime gameTime)
{
    spriteBatch.Begin();
    spriteBatch.Draw(waterTex, position, Color.White);
    spriteBatch.End();
    base.Draw(gameTime);
}
```

11. When this component is added to the game (and is enabled and visible), the water texture will be drawn according to the game time.

Creating the Toss Arrow Component

The next component to implement is a needle that bounces back and forth and is used to visually define a launch direction for bananas. We'll call it the Toss Arrow component.

1. Follow the same steps taken for the Water component: add a new class to the Components folder, use the same three namespaces, and inherit from DrawableGameComponent.

2. Add a `Fields` region to the new component and add the following fields:

```
#region Fields

// Graphics
private SpriteBatch spriteBatch;
private Texture2D arrowTex;

// Position and rotation
private float rotation;
private Vector2 position;
private Vector2 origin;
private int rotationDirection = 1;

private bool isMoving = true;

#endregion
```

3. Add a region called `Constants`. These values can be changed to tweak the response of the needle. Add the following constants to the region:

```
#region Constants

const float rotationSpeed = 0.05f;
const float maxRotation = 1.0f;
const float minRotation = -1.0f;

#endregion
```

4. Add a region called `Properties`. In this region is a single property that calculates a vector (with correct y orientation) that represents the direction the needle is pointing. This uses the sine and cosine formula mentioned earlier in the chapter to create a new vector object from rotation.

```
#region Properties

public Vector2 Vector
{
    get
    {
        double angle = (double)rotation;
        return new Vector2(
            (float)Math.Sin(angle),
            -(float)Math.Cos(angle)
            );
    }
}

#endregion
```

5. Add a region for the constructor and add the default component constructor that uses a Game instance:

```
#region Constructor(s)

public TossArrow(Game game)
    : base(game)
{

}

#endregion
```

6. Create a region called `Public Methods`. These methods allow the component to be controlled from other classes (namely the main game class). These methods are used to reset and pause the movement of the arrow.

```
#region Public Methods

public void Reset()
{
    isMoving = true;
    rotation = 0.0f;
    rotationDirection = 1;
}

public void Pause()
{
    isMoving = false;
}

#endregion
```

7. Create a region for `Overridden GameComponent Methods` and add the code for our four standard game loop methods. See the comments in the code for more information.

```
#region Overridden GameComponent Methods

public override void Initialize()
{
    // Initialize the default position (as calculated by
    // looking at the graphic in a graphics program)
    position = new Vector2(120, 320);
    rotation = 0.0f;

    base.Initialize();
}

protected override void LoadContent()
{
```

```
    // Create sprite batch, load texture, calculate origin
    spriteBatch = new SpriteBatch(GraphicsDevice);
    arrowTex = Game.Content.Load<Texture2D>("Textures/arrow");
    origin = new Vector2(arrowTex.Width / 2, arrowTex.Height / 2);

    base.LoadContent();
}

public override void Update(GameTime gameTime)
{
    if (isMoving)
    {
        // Flip the direction of the rotation if it's at either extreme
        if (rotation >= maxRotation)
            rotationDirection = -1;

        if (rotation <= minRotation)
            rotationDirection = 1;

        // Update rotation
        rotation += (rotationSpeed * rotationDirection);
    }

    base.Update(gameTime);
}

public override void Draw(GameTime gameTime)
{
    spriteBatch.Begin();
    spriteBatch.Draw(arrowTex, position, null, Color.White,
        rotation, origin, 0.2f, SpriteEffects.None, 0.5f);
    spriteBatch.End();

    base.Draw(gameTime);
}
#endregion
```

8. When enabled and visible, this component draws a needle and provides access to the direction that vector is pointing via its Vector property.

Creating the Wind Needle Component

The Wind Needle component uses the same texture (although scaled down by a constant factor) and most of the same logic as the Toss Arrow component, but this component is randomized with each turn and does not move. It also has a wind speed property, which affects how strong the force of the wind is on the path of the banana.

1. Follow the same steps for the previous components: add a new class called `WindNeedle`. `cs` to the `Components` folder, add the same three namespaces, and inherit from `DrawableGameComponent`.

2. Add a `Fields` region and add the following fields:

```
#region Fields

// Graphics
private SpriteFont smallFont;
private Texture2D needleTex;
private SpriteBatch spriteBatch;

// Position and rotation
private float rotation;
private Vector2 direction;
private Vector2 position;
private Vector2 origin;

// Wind speed
private int windStrength;
private string windStrengthText;

// Wind speed text position and origin
private Vector2 strengthTextPos;
private Vector2 strengthTextOrigin;

Random rnd;

#endregion
```

3. Add a `Constants` region for the minimum and maximum wind speed, and a scale factor for the needle texture:

```
#region Constants

const int windMax = 16;
const int windMin = 0;
const float windFactor = 0.03f;
const float drawScale = 0.1f;

#endregion
```

4. Add the empty constructor for the class.

```
#region Constructor(s)

public WindNeedle(Game game)
    : base(game)
{
```

```
}

#endregion
```

5. Add a `Properties` region. The `Vector` property returns a scaled-out vector in the direction of the arrow. The `WindStrength` property just exposes the internal variable.

```
#region Properties

public Vector2 Vector
{
    get
    {
        // Gets a scaled ratio of the wind strength to its maximum strength
        float windScale = windFactor * ((float)windStrength / (float)windMax);
        return Vector2.Multiply(direction, windScale);
    }
}

public int WindStrength
{
    get
    {
        return windStrength;
    }
}

#endregion
```

6. Add a region for `Public Methods`. In this region is a method called `Randomize`, which is used to randomize the wind's speed and direction. The direction is limited to a 180-degree (pi) range from 0 to pi. Because of the orientation of the needle (rotated 90 degrees counterclockwise), we need to subtract 90 degrees (pi / 2) to obtain the correct direction. The direction vector is calculated from the rotation in the same way that the Toss Arrow component does it, using sine for the x component and negative cosine for the y component. The wind direction is then normalized.

```
#region Public Methods

public void Randomize()
{
    // Randomize 180 degrees (pi) and shift
    // 90 degrees counterclockwise (pi/2)
    rotation = ((float)rnd.NextDouble() * MathHelper.Pi) -
        MathHelper.PiOver2;

    // Calculate the vector direction using sin/cos and normalize
    // to get a unit vector of length 1
    direction.X = (float)Math.Sin(rotation);
```

```
        direction.Y = -(float)Math.Cos(rotation);
        direction.Normalize();

        // Randomize wind strength
        windStrength = rnd.Next(windMin, windMax);
        windStrengthText = windStrength + " MPH";
    }


    #endregion
```

7. Create a region for Overridden GameComponent Methods and implement logic for the four basic XNA game loop methods. See the comments in the code for more information about what's happening in this component.

```
#region Overridden GameComponent Methods

public override void Initialize()
{
    // I found these coordinates manually in graphics editor
    position = new Vector2(31, 289);
    strengthTextPos = new Vector2(31, 300);
    rnd = new Random();
    Randomize();

    base.Initialize();
}

protected override void LoadContent()
{
    // Create sprite batch, load content, calculate origin
    spriteBatch = new SpriteBatch(GraphicsDevice);

    needleTex = Game.Content.Load<Texture2D>("Textures/arrow");
    smallFont = Game.Content.Load<SpriteFont>("Fonts/Small");

    origin = new Vector2(needleTex.Width / 2, needleTex.Height / 2);

    base.LoadContent();
}

public override void Update(GameTime gameTime)
{
    // Update the text origin for centering horizontally
    strengthTextOrigin.X = smallFont.MeasureString(windStrengthText).X / 2;
    base.Update(gameTime);
}
```

```
public override void Draw(GameTime gameTime)
{
    spriteBatch.Begin();

    // Draw the needle with a red tint
    spriteBatch.Draw(needleTex, position, null, Color.Red,
        rotation, origin, drawScale, SpriteEffects.None, 0.5f);

    // Draw the strength text (e.g. "10 MPH")
    spriteBatch.DrawString(smallFont, windStrengthText, strengthTextPos,
        Color.Black, 0.0f, strengthTextOrigin, 1.0f, SpriteEffects.None,
0.5f);

    spriteBatch.End();
    base.Draw(gameTime);
}

#endregion
```

When enabled and visible, this component displays a needle indicating a random wind direction and speed, and provides access to those values in a vector form that we can use in other parts of the game.

Creating the Monkey Component

There is nothing particularly special about the Monkey component. It runs a simple animation and exposes a bounding box for collision detection logic (which is slightly smaller than the actual bounds of the monkey graphic).

1. As for all the previous components, add a new class called Monkey to the Components directory, add the same three namespaces, and inherit from DrawableGameComponent.

2. Add the Fields region:

```
#region Fields

// Sprite batch and texture
SpriteBatch spriteBatch;
Texture2D monkeyTex;

// Position/bounding box
Vector2 position;
Vector2 origin;
Rectangle boundingBox;

// Animation specific fields
Rectangle sourceRectangle;
int currentFrame;
const int numFrames = 5;
```

```
const double animIntervalSeconds = 0.05f;
double currentInterval = 0.0f;

#endregion
```

3. Add the blank constructor:

```
#region Constructor(s)

public Monkey(Game game)
    : base(game)
{

}

#endregion
```

4. Expose the bounding box as a property in the Properties region:

```
#region Properties

public Rectangle BoundingBox
{
    get
    {
        return boundingBox;
    }
}

#endregion
```

5. Add a region called Utility Methods. This region contains one method,
   UpdateSourceRect, which is used to update the source rectangle for the animation
   based on the current frame.

```
#region Utility Methods

private void UpdateSourceRectangle()
{
    // Offset X by frame size * frame number
    sourceRectangle.X = currentFrame * (monkeyTex.Width / numFrames);

    sourceRectangle.Y = 0;
    sourceRectangle.Width = monkeyTex.Width / numFrames;
    sourceRectangle.Height = monkeyTex.Height;
}

#endregion
```

6. Add a region called Overridden GameComponent Methods. We'll walk through these methods step by step, since they are slightly more complicated.

7. Override the Initialize method. This sets up the bounding box and the animation variables.

```
public override void Initialize()
{
    // Initialize variables
    boundingBox = new Rectangle();
        sourceRectangle = new Rectangle();
    currentFrame = 0;
    base.Initialize();
}
```

8. Override the LoadContent method. This loads the content for the monkey, calculates its position and origin, creates (and shrinks) the bounding box, and updates the source rectangle (since we know the texture size now).

```
protected override void LoadContent()
{
    // Create sprite batch and load textures
    spriteBatch = new SpriteBatch(GraphicsDevice);
    monkeyTex = Game.Content.Load<Texture2D>("Textures/monkeysheet");

    // Calculate origin and position (Dependent on texture size)
    origin = new Vector2((monkeyTex.Width / numFrames) / 2,
        monkeyTex.Height / 2);

    // Move the monkey down 5 pixels so he's not right at the top of the
    // screen.
    position = new Vector2(120, monkeyTex.Height / 2 + 5);

    UpdateSourceRectangle();

    // Set up bounding box
    boundingBox.X = (int)(position.X);
    boundingBox.Y = (int)(position.Y);
    boundingBox.Width = monkeyTex.Width / numFrames;
    boundingBox.Height = monkeyTex.Height;

    // Shrink the targetable area (bounding box) of the
    // monkey by 20px on each side
    // This makes hitting the monkey more challenging.
    boundingBox.Inflate(-20, -20);

    base.LoadContent();
}
```

9. Override the Update method. This is used only to animate the monkey.

```
public override void Update(GameTime gameTime)
{
    // Check to see if the frame needs to be advanced.
    currentInterval += gameTime.TotalGameTime.TotalSeconds;
    if (currentInterval > animIntervalSeconds)
    {
        currentFrame++;

        // Loop if last frame
        if (currentFrame > numFrames - 1)
            currentFrame = 0;

        UpdateSourceRectangle();
        currentInterval = 0.0f;
    }

    base.Update(gameTime);
}
```

10. Finally, override the Draw method. This draws the monkey using the current source rectangle to get the current frame, with no rotation and a scale factor of 1.0 (original size).

```
public override void Draw(GameTime gameTime)
{
    spriteBatch.Begin();

    // Draw using current source rectangle.
    spriteBatch.Draw(monkeyTex, position, sourceRectangle, Color.White,
        0.0f, origin, 1.0f, SpriteEffects.None, 0.5f);

    spriteBatch.End();
    base.Draw(gameTime);
}
```

When enabled and visible, the Monkey component will draw an animated monkey and expose a bounding box property that can be used for collision detection.

Creating the Banana Component

The Banana component is by far the most influential component in the game play for Monkey Feeder. It draws a banana on screen, but also exposes methods so that it can be told to throw itself given a certain initial direction and wind speed. The banana's trajectory can also be adjusted in mid-flight using the touch capabilities of the Zune. When the touchpad is in use, the banana is tinted green so the users know they are affecting the input.

1. As with all the other components, add a new class to the Components folder called MonkeyProjectile.cs. Add the same three namespaces and inherit from DrawableGameComponent.

2. Add a region called Fields, and add the following fields to the class:

```
#region Private Fields

// Graphics
private SpriteBatch spriteBatch;
private Texture2D bananaTex;

// Position, direction, bounding box and origin
private Vector2 tossDirection;
private Vector2 windDirection;
private Vector2 initialPosition;
private Vector2 position;
private Vector2 origin;
private Vector2 adjustmentVector;
private Rectangle boundingBox;

// Rotation and scale factors for the texture
private float rotation;
private float scale;

// Used to tell if the banana's been thrown
private bool isThrown;

#endregion
```

3. Add a region called Constants with the following constant definitions. Again, these can be tweaked to alter game play in whatever way you wish.

```
#region Constants

// How fast the banana rotates.
const float rotationSpeed = 0.5f;

// How much of an impact use of the touch pad
// has on the direction of the banana.
const float touchFactor = 0.03f;

// How quickly the banana scales down.
const float scaleRate = -0.005f;

// How quickly the banana moves.
const float bananaSpeed = 5.0f;

#endregion
```

4. Add the blank constructor in its own region.

```
#region Constructor(s)

public BananaProjectile(Game game)
    : base(game)
{

}

#endregion
```

5. Add a region for `Properties` and add the following two properties. The first gives you access to the bounding box that surrounds the object. The second allows the program to know whether the banana is in flight.

```
#region Properties

public Rectangle BoundingBox
{
    get
    {
        return boundingBox;
    }
}

public bool Thrown
{
    get
    {
        return isThrown;
    }
}

#endregion
```

6. Add a region called `Public Methods` and add the following three methods to that region. These allow other classes to control the banana externally. The `Toss` method accepts an initial direction (from the toss arrow) and a wind vector (from the wind meter). The `Reset` method returns the banana to its initial position at the bottom of the screen and resets its rotation and scale. The `Adjust` method is used when touch input is engaged, and modifies the adjustment vector.

```
#region Public Methods

public void Toss(Vector2 toss, Vector2 wind)
{
    tossDirection = toss;
    windDirection = wind;
    position = initialPosition;
```

```
    isThrown = true;
    rotation = 0.0f;
}

public void Reset()
{
    position = initialPosition;
    isThrown = false;
    rotation = 0.0f;
    scale = 1.0f;
}

public void Adjust(Vector2 touchVector)
{
    adjustmentVector = touchVector;
}

#endregion
```

7. Add a region for Overridden GameComponent Methods. Because these methods are a little more complex, we'll walk through each of them.

8. Override the Initialize method with the method shown. It sets up the initial position for the banana and instantiates or assigns values to the other private variables.

```
public override void Initialize()
{
    initialPosition = new Vector2(120, 300);
    boundingBox = new Rectangle();
    adjustmentVector = Vector2.Zero;

    Reset();

    base.Initialize();
}
```

9. Override the LoadContent method with the following method. This method loads the banana texture and calculates the bounding box and origin for the banana.

```
protected override void LoadContent()
{
    // Create the sprite batch & load content
    spriteBatch = new SpriteBatch(GraphicsDevice);
    bananaTex = Game.Content.Load<Texture2D>("Textures/banana");

    // Set up the bounding box, now that we know the
    // texture size.
    boundingBox.X = (int)position.X;
    boundingBox.Y = (int)position.Y;
```

```
    boundingBox.Width = bananaTex.Width;
    boundingBox.Height = bananaTex.Height;

    // Set the origin for the texture.
    origin = new Vector2(bananaTex.Width / 2, bananaTex.Height / 2);

    base.LoadContent();
}
```

10. Override the Update method. This method modifies the current direction of the banana, taking into account its base (initial) direction plus the effects of the wind and adjustment vectors. It also modifies the bounding box to reflect the banana's current position on the screen.

```
public override void Update(GameTime gameTime)
{
    if (isThrown)
    {
        // Update the direction of the banana with the wind factor
        tossDirection += windDirection;

        // Adjust with touch, if any
        tossDirection.X += adjustmentVector.X * touchFactor;

        // Multiply by the scalar speed value
        position += tossDirection * bananaSpeed;

        // Rotate & scale
        rotation += rotationSpeed;
        scale += scaleRate;
    }

    // Update bounding box position. Width and height
    // do not need to be updated.
    boundingBox.X = (int)(position.X);
    boundingBox.Y = (int)(position.Y);

    base.Update(gameTime);
}
```

11. Lastly, override the Draw method. This method determines whether touch is activated and modifies the tint color to green if so. Then it draws the banana at its current position using the current rotation and scale factors.

```
public override void Draw(GameTime gameTime)
{
    // Tint the banana green if touch is being used.
    Color tintColor = Color.White;
```

```
            if (adjustmentVector != Vector2.Zero && isThrown == true)
                tintColor = Color.Green;

            spriteBatch.Begin();
            spriteBatch.Draw(bananaTex, position, null, tintColor,
                rotation, origin, scale, SpriteEffects.None, 0.5f);
            spriteBatch.End();
            base.Draw(gameTime);
        }
```

At this point, all of your components are built! You should have five drawable components in the Components folder, as shown in Figure 5-19. Compile the code and correct any typos or other errors.

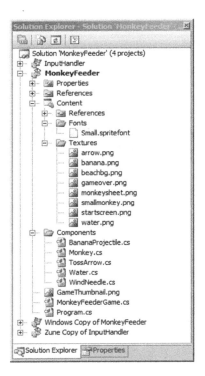

Figure 5-19. *Monkey Feeder is almost done! All the game's components are ready to go.*

The last step is to bring all these components together with a little simple game state management. In this game, there is still a small amount of game logic in place in the main code file, which serves as the "driver" for the game (changing game states, checking collisions, and handling input).

Putting the Components Together

At this point, all of your components should compile together happily. If you had issues compiling them, be sure to check out the Chapter 5/Exercise 5 source code.

Now we'll begin integrating all of these components with some simple game state management.

1. Open the main game's class file, MonkeyFeederGame.cs.

2. Add the following two using directives to the bottom of the existing list so that you can use the input handler and all the components you just built:

```
using InputHandler;
using MonkeyFeeder.Components;
```

3. Directly above where the MonkeyFeederGame class begins (within the MonkeyFeeder namespace), add the following game state enumeration, which defines the available game states for this game:

```
public enum GameState
{
    Start,
    Playing,
    GameOver
}
```

4. Move down to the MonkeyFeederGame class. Find the declared sprite batch and graphics device variables and move them into a new region called Fields. Add the remaining fields to this region:

```
#region Fields

// Default fields
GraphicsDeviceManager graphics;
SpriteBatch spriteBatch;

// Content
Texture2D startTex;
Texture2D beachTex;
Texture2D gameOverTex;
SpriteFont smallFont;

// Game components
InputState input;
Water waterComponent;
TossArrow tossArrow;
WindNeedle windNeedle;
Monkey monkey;
BananaProjectile banana;

GameState gameState;

// Score related variables
private int score;
string finalScoreText;
```

```
private Vector2 scoreTextPosition;
private Vector2 gameOverScorePos;
```

```
#endregion
```

5. Put the constructor in its own region and add the code following the line where `TargetElapsedTime` is assigned. This code instantiates the game components and then adds them to the game's `Components` collection so they will be automatically notified of game events.

```
#region Constructor(s)

/// <summary>
/// Creates a new instance of the MonkeyFeederGame class and
/// adds game components to it.
/// </summary>
public MonkeyFeederGame()
{
    graphics = new GraphicsDeviceManager(this);
    Content.RootDirectory = "Content";

    // Frame rate is 30 fps by default for Zune.
    TargetElapsedTime = TimeSpan.FromSeconds(1 / 30.0);

    // Add components
    input = new InputState(this);
    waterComponent = new Water(this);
    tossArrow = new TossArrow(this);
    windNeedle = new WindNeedle(this);
    monkey = new Monkey(this);
    banana = new BananaProjectile(this);

    // Make sure to add drawable components
    // in the order you want them drawn.
    Components.Add(input);
    Components.Add(waterComponent);
    Components.Add(tossArrow);
    Components.Add(windNeedle);
    Components.Add(monkey);
    Components.Add(banana);
}

#endregion
```

6. Put `Initialize`, `LoadContent`, `Update`, and `Draw` in a new region called `Overridden XNA Methods`. You can also delete the overridden `UnloadContent` method, which is not used in this game. We'll come back to the methods in this region in a moment.

7. Add a new region called Utility Methods. This region contains a single method, SetGameState, which causes the game to transition to the specified state. The local variable enableComponents is used to enable or disable all game components at once in this method, which is useful since two game states require that the components be invisible. The switch statement at the top of the method also gives you an opportunity to reset any values or perform other pretransition logic. Add this method:

```
#region Utility Methods

private void SetGameState(GameState state)
{
    // Enable or disable all the drawable components
    // using this variable.
    bool enableComponents = false;

    switch (state)
    {
        case GameState.Start:
            enableComponents = false;
            break;
        case GameState.Playing:
            enableComponents = true;
            score = 0;
            banana.Reset();
            tossArrow.Reset();
            windNeedle.Randomize();
            break;
        case GameState.GameOver:
            enableComponents = false;
            break;
    }

    // Apply enable/disable to the Enabled and Visible properties
    // of all the DrawableGameComponents in the game.
    waterComponent.Enabled = waterComponent.Visible = enableComponents;
    windNeedle.Enabled = windNeedle.Visible = enableComponents;
    tossArrow.Enabled = tossArrow.Visible = enableComponents;
    monkey.Enabled = monkey.Visible = enableComponents;
    banana.Enabled = banana.Visible = enableComponents;

    // Set the game state.
    gameState = state;
}

#endregion
```

8. Now, working within the Overridden XNA Methods region, change the code in the Initialize method to the following method. This sets up the back buffer and screen size, and also adds some extra compatibility for the Windows version of this game by forcing the window size to match the buffer and showing the mouse cursor. This is also where most of the local variables are initialized.

```
protected override void Initialize()
{
    // Set up graphics device, show mouse cursor on Windows
    graphics.PreferredBackBufferWidth = 240;
    graphics.PreferredBackBufferHeight = 320;
    graphics.ApplyChanges();
#if WINDOWS
    IsMouseVisible = true;
#endif
    // Initialize game state to Start
    SetGameState(GameState.Start);

    // Set up placement vectors
    scoreTextPosition = new Vector2(10, 10);
    gameOverScorePos = new Vector2(10, 100);

    // Init remaining fields
    score = 0;
    finalScoreText = "";

    base.Initialize();
}
```

9. Modify the LoadContent method next. This method just loads the content required for the game to run without adding any of its components, like the screen backgrounds and the font.

```
protected override void LoadContent()
{
    // Create a new SpriteBatch, which can be used to draw textures.
    spriteBatch = new SpriteBatch(GraphicsDevice);

    // Load in textures and fonts used in the main game loop.
    beachTex = Content.Load<Texture2D>("Textures/beachbg");
    startTex = Content.Load<Texture2D>("Textures/startscreen");
    gameOverTex = Content.Load<Texture2D>("Textures/gameover");
    smallFont = Content.Load<SpriteFont>("Fonts/Small");
}
```

Note When loading the same asset in multiple places, such as component-based games where the font is needed in more than one place, the asset is not actually reloaded. The XNA content loader just returns the reference to the existing asset.

10. The Update method is to be modified next. This is probably the longest method you've seen so far in the book, but remember that it is broken up by game state. I'll explain how the logic works after the listing.

```
protected override void Update(GameTime gameTime)
{
    // Allows the game to exit
    if (input.NewBackPress)
        this.Exit();

    // Determine what to do based on the game state
    switch (gameState)
    {
        case GameState.Start:
            // Wait for a button press to transition to Playing
            if (input.NewPlayPress || input.MiddleButtonPressed)
            {
                SetGameState(GameState.Playing);
            }
            break;
        case GameState.GameOver:
            // Display some cheeky text
            finalScoreText = "You fed the monkey " + score + " time";
            finalScoreText += score != 1 ? "s." : ".";

            if (score == 0)
                finalScoreText += "\r\nMonkey still hungry.";
            else if (score < 5)
                finalScoreText += "\r\nWhy tease monkey?";
            else if (score < 15)
                finalScoreText += "\r\nMmm, thank you.";
            else if (score < 25)
                finalScoreText += "\r\nYou do good!";
            else if (score < 50)
                finalScoreText += "\r\nWow! Monkey stuffed!";
            else if (score < 75)
                finalScoreText += "\r\nWicked Sick!";
            else
                finalScoreText += "\r\nNO MORE! I BEG!";
```

```
                // Wait for a button press to transition back to Start
                if (input.NewPlayPress || input.MiddleButtonPressed)
                {
                    SetGameState(GameState.Start);
                }
                break;


        case GameState.Playing:
            // Apply touch pad to banana's trajectory and check collisions
            if (banana.Thrown)
            {
                banana.Adjust(input.TouchVector);

                // Monkey fed
                if (banana.BoundingBox.Intersects(monkey.BoundingBox))
                {
                    score++;
                    banana.Reset();
                    tossArrow.Reset();
                    windNeedle.Randomize();
                }

                // Banana completely missed - game over!
                if (banana.BoundingBox.Right < 0
                    || banana.BoundingBox.Left > 320
                    || banana.BoundingBox.Bottom < 0)
                {
                    SetGameState(GameState.GameOver);
                }
            }

            else
            {
                // Toss the banana
                if (input.NewPlayPress)
                {
                    tossArrow.Pause();
                    banana.Toss(tossArrow.Vector, windNeedle.Vector);
                }
            }
            break;
    }

    base.Update(gameTime);
}
```

In the Start state, the game just waits for the Play button to be pressed. In the GameOver state, the score message (with some cheeky commentary added) is updated and the game waits for input to transition back to Start.

The core of the game is in the Playing state. If the banana is thrown, the banana's direction is modified with the touch vector. Then any collisions are detected (note how easy collision detection is when components expose bounding boxes). If the banana hits the monkey, the score is incremented and the game board is reset. If the banana hits some other boundary, the game transitions to the GameOver state. If the banana is not yet thrown, the game waits for user input to throw it and calls the Toss method on the banana to pass in the applicable vectors.

11. Like the Update method, the Draw method behaves differently depending on the current game state. Its code is a little bit simpler. Change the Draw method as shown, adding the required code:

```
protected override void Draw(GameTime gameTime)
{
    GraphicsDevice.Clear(Color.Black);

    spriteBatch.Begin();

    // Determine what to draw based on the game state.
    switch (gameState)
    {
        case GameState.Start:
            // Just draw the background
            spriteBatch.Draw(startTex, Vector2.Zero, Color.White);
            break;
        case GameState.Playing:
            // Draw the background and the score text.
            // The components draw themselves.
            spriteBatch.Draw(beachTex, Vector2.Zero, Color.White);
            spriteBatch.DrawString(smallFont, "Score: " + score.ToString(),
                scoreTextPosition, Color.Black);
            break;
        case GameState.GameOver:
            // Draw the background and score text.
            spriteBatch.Draw(gameOverTex, Vector2.Zero, Color.White);
            spriteBatch.DrawString(smallFont, finalScoreText,
                gameOverScorePos, Color.White);
            break;
    }

    spriteBatch.End();

    base.Draw(gameTime);
}
```

And, believe it or not, *we're finished*! Well, almost. There is one last thing to do to ensure the game is nice and tidy.

Setting Game Properties to Appear More Professional

Up until now, if you browse games on your Zune and find yours, it has the same name as your solution file and offers no description. This is not cool.

To fix this, expand the Properties node under the MonkeyFeeder project in the Solution Explorer, and open AssemblyInfo.cs. Change each of those assembly properties (aside from the GUID, of course) to better describe the product. Spaces are allowed.

Finally, make sure that you have replaced GameThumbnail.png with something a little more interesting, such as the graphic provided in the Examples/Chapter 5/Artwork folder.

Build, Run, Copious Celebration

Now is the time to reap the fruits of your labor. We'll test the game both on the Zune and Windows, with Windows being the first up to the plate.

1. Set the Windows copy of MonkeyFeeder as the startup project, and press F5 to run it, as shown in Figure 5-20.

Figure 5-20. *Monkey Feeder starting up on the PC*

2. Use Enter as Play, the spacebar as the middle button, and Escape as Back. Press Enter (Play) to begin play.

3. Wait for the appropriate angle, and press Enter to launch a banana, as shown in Figure 5-21. If you're way off, try holding down the left mouse button and moving to the left or right of the center to guide the banana. The closer the mouse is to the edge of the screen, the more pronounced the adjustment will be. Notice how the banana turns green.

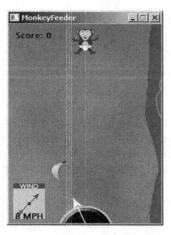

Figure 5-21. *Monkey Feeder in action on the PC*

4. Play constantly. Try to beat your own high score. Try to score 75 consecutive bananas! But wait, we still need to test on the Zune.

5. Stop debugging and open the XNA Game Studio Device Center. Set the plugged-in Zune (assuming you have one) as the default device. Right-click the MonkeyFeeder project (original project for the Zune) and set it as the startup project. Press F5 to deploy and start it.

6. Use the on-screen commands. Use the Play button to fire a banana, as shown in Figure 5-22. Use the touchpad (left or right) to affect the direction of a launched banana. Show it off to your friends.

■**Note** If you are using a first-generation Zune, you won't be able to use the touch features of the program.

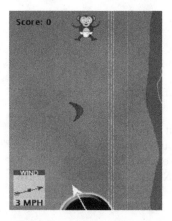

Figure 5-22. *Monkey Feeder on the Zune with touch activated*

Suggested Extensions

There are a few things that were not implemented in this version of Monkey Feeder. You could try implementing the guide to support playing music from the Zune's playlist—after all, how else will your players get through a ten-hour marathon of Monkey Feeder hoping to score Wicked Sick?

You could also support sound effects, difficulty levels with new backgrounds, better animations, and more to expand this simple game. The beauty is that since so much of the game is componentized, you can make several changes without opening a whole can of worms!

Cleaning Up for Deployment

In building Monkey Feeder, you updated the `AssemblyInfo.cs` file to better describe your game. I think it's appropriate to offer some more information on that topic.

When you deploy a game to the Zune without changing any of the assembly information, it shows up in the games list with no description and Microsoft copyrights. The title is the same as the DLL built by Visual Studio, which is usually the same as the solution file. It also usually sports the same default, blue thumbnail image. Here are some tips to make your game appear more professional and take it from development mode to consumer mode.

Making Changes in AssemblyInfo.cs

Any project in the Solution Explorer has a node beneath it called Properties. This node usually contains a file called `AssemblyInfo.cs`. This file contains some general attributes that you can change, as in this snippet from Monkey Feeder's `AssemblyInfo.cs`:

```
// General Information about an assembly is controlled through the following
// set of attributes. Change these attribute values to modify the information
// associated with an assembly.
[assembly: AssemblyTitle("MonkeyFeeder")]
[assembly: AssemblyProduct("MonkeyFeeder")]
[assembly: AssemblyDescription("")]
[assembly: AssemblyCompany("Microsoft")]
[assembly: AssemblyCopyright("Copyright © Microsoft 2008")]
[assembly: AssemblyTrademark("")]
[assembly: AssemblyCulture("")]
```

Simply changing these fields will make a big difference in what players see when your game is on their Zune. For example, adding the space to change "MonkeyFeeder" to "Monkey Feeder" can make your game seem much less "programmery." Changing the empty description to something like "Feed the monkey" adds character and more information about the game. Changing the company, copyright, and trademark can be useful if you are publishing a game and need to include legal terms. Finally, the assembly culture is a way to define a language and region, such as EN-US, EN-UK, EN-CA, FR-CA, and so on.

Changing the Thumbnail

The thumbnail is a user's first impression of your game. If you have a professionally made thumbnail as opposed to the default one, it can make users want to play it (especially if it looks *shiny*).

Even if you don't have a professional artist in your back pocket, it's still a good idea to replace the game thumbnail. Here's all you need to do:

1. Open GameThumbnail.png from your project in your favorite graphics editor.

2. Delete everything in it, leaving a transparent background.

3. Paste in your new icon. Adjust size and colors as necessary.

4. Flatten (if necessary) and save.

The new game icon will now appear in the game list on the Zune.

■**Note** When you change your Zune game's thumbnail, the thumbnail is not automatically set as the application icon for the Windows game. To use the icon for the Windows game, you need to create an .ico version of the icon and set it as the default icon in the Windows game's project properties.

Taking these steps will help to polish a finished game. They are not much work, and they pay off from a user experience perspective!

Check Your Knowledge

Wow, what an action-packed chapter! Test your knowledge with the following quick ten-question quiz.

1. What are unit vectors normally used for?

2. How can you create a vector knowing only an angle?

3. What method of the SpriteFont class allows you to find the width and height of a block of text?

4. What method allows you to check if two bounding boxes collide?

5. What are the main pros and cons of per-pixel collision detection?

6. What kind of data type is simple game state management structured around?

7. What makes a DrawableGameComponent different from a GameComponent? How are they related?

8. How do you make a drawable game component invisible and disabled?

9. Which file can you edit to change the game's externally visible properties, such as its title and description?

10. What is the standard unit of measure for angles in XNA?

Summary

With two real games under your belt—OutBreak and Monkey Feeder—you are well on your way to becoming a Zune game development guru.

In this chapter, you got a crash course in 2D mathematics critical to game development in general. You learned about some fundamental XNA concepts such as game state management, collision detection, and deployment considerations. Finally, you learned how to harness the power of game components to code smarter and more efficiently.

In the next chapter, you'll learn some tips, tricks, and advanced techniques that will help you take your skills to the next level.

CHAPTER 6

■■■

Advanced Techniques

In Chapter 5, you successfully built a Zune game that utilized fairly complex input, vector math, texture scaling, and more. Monkey Feeder, which you built in the final example of Chapter 5, brought together a lot of the concepts addressed thus far in the book.

This chapter introduces some interesting techniques that you can apply in your games. We'll start with a couple of useful things you can do on the Zune, and move onward to solve more complex problems, including rendering in landscape mode, querying battery status, more complicated input, and even creating a visualizer for music.

Device Status

In the course of writing a game, you may come upon situations where you need to know more about the device. Such device properties might include the battery status, whether wireless networking is enabled, and so on.

`PowerStatus` is a static class that gives you access to quite a few properties related to the Zune's power source. You can use this class to determine the current battery level or to see whether the Zune is plugged in.

Note A lot of the device status API is intended for laptops rather than Zunes. However, most of the functionality works the same on the Zune, except where noted.

Checking the Battery Status

`PowerStatus.BatteryChargeStatus` returns a value from the `BatteryChargeStatus` enumeration. The possible values of this property are listed in Table 6-1.

Table 6-1. *Battery Charge Status Values*

Value	Description
BatteryChargeStatus.Charging	The Zune is plugged in and charging.
BatteryChargeStatus.Critical	The battery is at a critically low level.

Continued

Table 6-1. *Continued*

Value	Description
BatteryChargeStatus.High	The battery has a high level of charge.
0 (no assigned enum entry)	The battery's status is neither high nor low; but "normal."
BatteryChargeStatus.Low	The battery's charge is low.
BatteryChargeStatus.NoSystemBattery	This is specific to laptops.
BatteryChargeStatus.Unknown	The battery's condition cannot be determined.

One interesting fact about the BatteryChargeStatus enumeration is that it is set up as a list of flags. The PowerStatus.BatteryChargeStatus can actually have two of these values assigned at once (for example, the battery status can rightfully be both Charging and Low at the same time). This can make things slightly difficult when you are using a switch statement to evaluate the battery state. If the charge status is High & Charging, a switch case that checks for Charging will not execute. This is because numerically, High & Charging is different from just Charging or just High. However, you can use bitwise operators (&, |, ^) on the battery state flags to overcome this problem.

Let's assume you want to build an if statement for just Charging (which can also include High & Charging, Low & Charging, Critical & Charging, or Normal & Charging). In this case, you can strip out the part of the flags you're not interested in by using the & operator, as follows:

```
if (PowerStatus.BatteryChargeStatus & BatteryChargeStatus.Charging ==
    BatteryChargeStatus.Charging)
{
    // TODO: implement code for when the battery is charging
}
```

To avoid confusion, remember that the bitwise AND (&) is different from the Boolean AND (&&). The former looks at each of the possible values assigned to the property. For each of those possible values, if both the operands have it, the result will also have it. Since one of the operands of the bitwise & operation in the preceding code is BatteryChargeStatus.Charging, other operands that have BatteryChargeStatus.Charging assigned as a flag will result in the if statement executing. Table 6-2 shows some examples of the bitwise AND operation using the BatteryChargeStatus values.

Table 6-2. *Some Bitwise AND Operations Using BatteryChargeStatus Values*

Expression	Result
Charging, High & Charging	Charging
Charging, Low & Charging	Charging
Charging, 0 & Charging	Charging
Charging, Critical & Charging	Charging

Expression	Result
High & Charging	0
Low & Charging	0
Critical & Charging	0

Determining Battery Life

Other properties of the PowerStatus class give more granular information about the battery, including the battery's life when on a full charge, current percentage of battery available, and current time remaining. All of these properties are managed directly by the XNA Framework and require no work on your part to implement. Table 6-3 lists the PowerStatus properties related to battery life.

■**Caution** The Zune does not report the BatteryFullLifetime or BatteryLifeRemaining properties. Since these properties are nullable, you can use them, but they will never return a value on the Zune.

Table 6-3. *Battery Life Properties*

Property	Data Type	Description
PowerStatus.BatteryFullLifetime	System.TimeSpan	The amount of time the battery lasts on a full charge. This property is always null on the Zune.
PowerStatus.BatteryLifePercent	float	A percentage, ranging from 0.0f to 1.0f, indicating the current charge.
PowerStatus.BatteryLifeRemaining	System.TimeSpan	The amount of time remaining on the battery's current charge. This property is always null on the Zune.

Determining If the Zune Is Plugged In

When connected via USB (or docked), the Zune automatically charges the battery. You can use the PowerLineStatus property to determine whether the Zune is charging. When this property indicates that the power line is connected, that doesn't necessarily mean the Zune has a data connection; it could be docked or charging via an AC adapter.

You could check the BatteryChargeStatus.Charging property, but the Zune could be plugged in and not charging (at full capacity). Therefore, another property is needed.

The property to access is PowerStatus.PowerLineStatus, and like the battery status properties, it returns a value of an enumeration called PowerLineStatus. The PowerLineStatus enumeration has only three values: Online, Offline, and Unknown.

Determining When the Power Status Changes

The PowerStatus class exposes an event called PowerStatusChanged, to which you can subscribe to receive notification when the power state changes. However, this event does not provide any detailed event arguments, so you can discover only *when* something changes, not what specific value or values have changed.

The Zune can sometimes be a little slow in reacting to changes in its battery/charging status. If you are using the PowerStatusChanged event, be aware that there may be a few-second delay between the power status changing (like unplugging or plugging in the cable) and the reaction of the API to the event happening.

EXERCISE 6-1. A BATTERY MONITOR

In this short example, we'll build a component class that displays information about the battery using the PowerStatus properties. We'll then add that component to a host game class on the Zune to see it in action (see Figure 6-1, at the end of this exercise). The code for this example can be found in the Examples/Chapter 6/ Exercise 1 folder.

1. In Visual Studio, create a new Zune Game project called BatteryMonitor.

2. In the Content folder, create a new folder called Textures.

3. In the Textures folder, create a subfolder called Battery. This folder will hold all of the battery icons. Each of these icons is colored differently (or contains some other indicator) to convey the current battery status in a visual manner.

4. Add the following files from the Examples/Chapter 6/Artwork folder:

   - battery_charging.png

   - battery_critical.png

   - battery_high.png

   - battery_low.png

   - battery_nobattery.png

   - battery_unknown.png

5. In the Content/Textures folder, add the background texture from the Artwork folder, called batterymonbg.png.

6. Add a new sprite font to the Content project. Call it Normal.spritefont. Don't worry about changing the contents of the .spritefont file.

7. To begin creating the battery monitor game component, add a new game component called BatteryStatus.cs to the class. You can add a true game component object if you like, but a class will work just fine. We will be modifying it heavily anyway.

8. Only a few namespaces are needed. The first several lines of BatteryStatus.cs should look like the following code. Pay attention to the namespaces used and the declaration of the BatteryStatus class.

```
using System;
using System.Text;
using Microsoft.Xna.Framework;
using Microsoft.Xna.Framework.Content;
using Microsoft.Xna.Framework.Graphics;

namespace BatteryMonitor
{
    /// <summary>
    /// This is a game component that implements IUpdateable.
    /// </summary>
    public class BatteryStatus : Microsoft.Xna.Framework.DrawableGameComponent
    {
        // ... class implementation here...
    }
```

9. Add a region called `Fields` in the `BatteryStatus` class with the following variables, which hold content references, position vectors, and strings:

```
#region Fields

// Content
SpriteBatch spriteBatch;
SpriteFont normalFont;
Texture2D batteryChargingTex;
Texture2D batteryCriticalTex;
Texture2D batteryHighTex;
Texture2D batteryLowTex;
Texture2D batteryNoneTex;
Texture2D batteryUnknownTex;
Texture2D currentBatteryStatusTex;

// Position
Vector2 batteryStatusTextPosition;
Vector2 batteryStatusIconPosition;
Vector2 batteryStatusTextureOrigin;

// Status Messages
string batteryStatusText = "";

#endregion
```

10. Add a region called `Constructor(s)` to the component and add the following code. This code wires the event to a new event handler method.

```
#region Constructor(s)

public BatteryStatus(Game game)
    : base(game)
```

```
    {
        // Wire up the PowerStatusChanged event.
        PowerStatus.PowerStateChanged +=
            new EventHandler(PowerStatusChangedHandler);
    }

#endregion
```

11. If you used the built-in functionality for generating event handlers, you should have a method called PowerStatusChangedHandler floating around somewhere below the constructor. Copy that method and move it into a new region called Event Handlers. If you don't have that method, just use the one that follows. This code calls a private utility method (which we'll write in the next steps) to update the battery status text and icon.

```
#region Event Handlers

void PowerStatusChangedHandler(object sender, EventArgs e)
{
    ResetBatteryStatusUI();
}

#endregion
```

12. Create a new region called Private Methods. In this region, add a helper method called ResetBatteryStatusUI, which will determine what's on the screen based on the current battery status.

```
#region Private Methods

private void ResetBatteryStatusUI()
{
    // TODO: Implement this method
}

#endregion
```

13. Let's add the first bit of code in the method, which sets the battery status text and determines which icon is currently being shown. The currentBatteryStatusTex object holds a reference to the battery status icon that should be drawn, and this section of code is where that value is modified. Paste this code in place of the // TODO: Implement this method line.

```
StringBuilder sb = new StringBuilder();

// Write the battery's status (Charging, High, etc).
sb.Append("Battery Status: ");

// Check all the battery states
if ((PowerStatus.BatteryChargeStatus & BatteryChargeStatus.Charging)
    == BatteryChargeStatus.Charging)
{
```

```
        sb.AppendLine("Charging");
        currentBatteryStatusTex = batteryChargingTex;
    }
    else
    {
        switch (PowerStatus.BatteryChargeStatus)
        {
            case BatteryChargeStatus.Critical:
                sb.AppendLine("Critical");
                currentBatteryStatusTex = batteryCriticalTex;
                break;
            case BatteryChargeStatus.High:
                sb.AppendLine("High");
                currentBatteryStatusTex = batteryHighTex;
                break;
            case BatteryChargeStatus.Low:
                sb.AppendLine("Low");
                currentBatteryStatusTex = batteryLowTex;
                break;
            case BatteryChargeStatus.NoSystemBattery:
                sb.AppendLine("No Battery");
                currentBatteryStatusTex = batteryNoneTex;
                break;
            case BatteryChargeStatus.Unknown:
                sb.AppendLine("Unknown");
                currentBatteryStatusTex = batteryUnknownTex;
                break;
            case 0:
                sb.AppendLine("Normal");
                currentBatteryStatusTex = batteryHighTex;
                break;
            default:
                sb.AppendLine("?" + PowerStatus.BatteryChargeStatus.ToString());
                currentBatteryStatusTex = batteryUnknownTex;
                break;
        }
    }
```

This code uses the `StringBuilder` class from the `System.Text` namespace to build a string. It's a little cleaner and has a performance advantage over straight string concatenation with the + operator. The code also makes use of the bitwise & operator to decide what to do if the battery is charging. If the battery isn't charging, the code safely checks the other battery charge states without worrying about more than one state assigned at once (such as `High & Charging`).

14. Add the following line to this code, which appends the percentage of battery life remaining to the status string:

```
sb.AppendLine(PowerStatus.BatteryLifePercent + "% remaining");
```

15. Add a `switch` statement to append the power line status to the status string:

```
// Get the power line connection status
switch (PowerStatus.PowerLineStatus)
{
    case PowerLineStatus.Online:
        sb.AppendLine("Connected");
        break;
    case PowerLineStatus.Offline:
        sb.AppendLine("Not Connected");
        break;
    case PowerLineStatus.Unknown:
        sb.AppendLine("Connection Unknown");
        break;
}
```

16. Finally, build the string and assign it to the member variable `batteryStatusText`:

```
// Assign the contents of the stringbuilder to the member variable
batteryStatusText = sb.ToString();
```

That's the end of the `ResetBatteryStatusUI` method, which is really the workhorse of this application.

17. Group any remaining methods into a new region called `Overridden GameComponent Methods`.

18. Locate the `Initialize` method in the game component. If you can't find one, create it by overriding `Initialize`. Add the following code to set up the position vectors:

```
public override void Initialize()
{
    batteryStatusTextPosition = new Vector2(10, 50);
    batteryStatusIconPosition = new Vector2(120, 200);

    base.Initialize();
}
```

19. Locate the `LoadContent` method within the game component. Again, create one if it does not exist by overriding `LoadContent`. Add the following code, which loads assets, calculates an origin, and makes the initial call to `ResetBatteryStatusUI`.

```
protected override void LoadContent()
{
    normalFont = Game.Content.Load<SpriteFont>("Normal");

    batteryChargingTex =
        Game.Content.Load<Texture2D>("Textures/Battery/battery_charging");

    batteryCriticalTex =
        Game.Content.Load<Texture2D>("Textures/Battery/battery_critical");

    batteryHighTex =
        Game.Content.Load<Texture2D>("Textures/Battery/battery_high");
```

```
        batteryLowTex =
            Game.Content.Load<Texture2D>("Textures/Battery/battery_low");

        batteryNoneTex =
            Game.Content.Load<Texture2D>("Textures/Battery/battery_nobattery");

        batteryUnknownTex =
            Game.Content.Load<Texture2D>("Textures/Battery/battery_unknown");

        currentBatteryStatusTex = batteryUnknownTex;

        batteryStatusTextureOrigin =
            new Vector2(currentBatteryStatusTex.Width / 2,
                currentBatteryStatusTex.Height / 2);

        ResetBatteryStatusUI();

        base.LoadContent();
    }
```

20. Locate the Draw method. Add the following code, which gets a sprite batch from the game's Services collection and draws the icon and string to the screen.

```
public override void Draw(GameTime gameTime)
{
    if (spriteBatch == null)
    {
        spriteBatch = (SpriteBatch)Game.Services.GetService(
            typeof(SpriteBatch));
    }

    // Draw the status text in white
    spriteBatch.DrawString(normalFont, batteryStatusText,
        batteryStatusTextPosition, Color.White);

    // Draw the battery icon using the calculated origin
    spriteBatch.Draw(currentBatteryStatusTex, batteryStatusIconPosition, null,
        Color.White, 0.0f, batteryStatusTextureOrigin, 1.0f, SpriteEffects.None,
        0.5f);

    base.Draw(gameTime);
}
```

21. Open Game1.cs. Now we will make some final changes that add the game component, set up the sprite batch, and draw the background. First, add some fields to the Game1 class:

```
GraphicsDeviceManager graphics;
SpriteBatch spriteBatch;
BatteryStatus batteryStatusComponent;
Texture2D gameBackgroundTex;
```

22. In the constructor, initialize and add the batteryStatusComponent to the game's Components collection:

```
// Add components
batteryStatusComponent = new BatteryStatus(this);
Components.Add(batteryStatusComponent);
```

23. In the LoadContent method, create the sprite batch, add it to the game's Services collection, and load the background texture:

```
// Create a new sprite batch, which can be used to draw textures.
spriteBatch = new SpriteBatch(GraphicsDevice);

// Add the sprite batch to the game's services.
Services.AddService(typeof(SpriteBatch), spriteBatch);

// Load the background texture
gameBackgroundTex = Content.Load<Texture2D>("Textures/batterymonbg");
```

24. In the Draw method, clear the screen, begin the sprite batch, draw the background, draw the components, and end the sprite batch:

```
GraphicsDevice.Clear(Color.CornflowerBlue);

spriteBatch.Begin();
spriteBatch.Draw(gameBackgroundTex, Vector2.Zero, Color.White);
base.Draw(gameTime);
spriteBatch.End();
```

25. Deploy the game to the Zune. You should see a screen similar to Figure 6-1. Press the Back button on the Zune to exit.

Figure 6-1. *BatteryMonitor in action*

Advanced Sprite Batch Techniques

On the Zune, all drawing is done via sprite batches. The lack of a dedicated graphics processing unit (GPU) on the Zune rules out the possibility of drawing 3D models or using shaders. And there are no 2D drawing primitives, such as lines, triangles, quads, circles, and so on. So, it's very important and useful to understand how sprite batches work.

How Sprite Batches Work

A sprite batch is a way of grouping several drawing operations into one singular unit. Rather than drawing each individual sprite or string to the graphics device one-by-one, Draw calls to the same sprite batch will be sent as a condensed group to the graphics device.

A sprite batch is started via a call to spriteBatch.Begin(blendMode), where blendMode specifies one of the blend modes discussed in the next section. After the sprite batch has begun, subsequent Draw calls are attached to the SpriteBatch object. It's not until spriteBatch.End() is called that the graphics data is actually sent to be displayed by the device.

Blend Modes

The blend mode determines how colors interact with each other when they overlap. On the Zune, you have only three options for blending: None, AlphaBlend, and Additive. For most purposes, the default blend mode of AlphaBlend is perfectly suitable.

Alpha Blending

SpriteBlendMode.AlphaBlend is the default blend mode. Alpha values are respected, so sprites with transparency will be supported. Using this mode, layered sprites with transparency will expose the texture drawn beneath them (to the degree specified by the texture's alpha value at that pixel).

This blend mode is appropriate for drawing most game objects. It allows the depth of the sprites to become apparent, while permitting varying degrees of transparency. Alpha blending is shown in Figure 6-2 (with translucent gradient textures) and Figure 6-3 (with solid textures on a transparent background).

Note This book is printed in black and white, so the screenshots in this section may not make a lot of sense. However, the Zune game project used to produce these screenshots is provided in the Examples/ Chapter 6/Exercise 2 folder.

Figure 6-2. *Alpha blending with three gradient balls*

Figure 6-3. *Alpha blending with three solid-colored balls with transparent backgrounds*

Notice in Figure 6-3 how the layering of the sprites (determined by draw order) is still apparent, yet the transparency surrounding the balls is gone. This is what alpha blending accomplishes.

SpriteBlendMode.None

The SpriteBlendMode.None blend mode ignores alpha values entirely. All alpha values are converted to 1.0f, so a transparent background will appear black. A partially transparent green will appear to be fully green.

Using this blend mode with a sprite font will result in the text being extremely blocky, since sprite fonts use transparency to create smooth-looking text. This blend mode is not recommended for text (see Figure 6-4).

Figure 6-4. *Using None as the blend mode yields awful results for text (the blocky stuff in the middle).*

There are few rare cases where None is an acceptable blend mode. If all of the sprites have no transparency at all, using this blend mode can marginally improve performance, because alpha blending calculations do not need to occur. However, this small performance gain is reversed if you need to begin a new sprite batch to support alpha blending (if you need to draw a font, for example).

Additive Blending

Additive blending with SpriteBlendMode.Additive means that when two sprites overlap, the colors in the intersecting area are "added" together. Think about your early days of color education when you were taught rules such as "yellow and blue make green."

PRIMARY COLORS AND ADDITIVE BLENDING

Many people will tell you that the primary colors are red, yellow, and blue. When we are taught these things at an early age, we learn them with regard to the pigmentation of objects. However, when referring to light (emitted by displays), the three primary colors are actually red, blue, and green.

The primary colors of pigments are commonly referred to as red, yellow, and blue. This is slightly incorrect. The actual primary colors of pigment are magenta, yellow, and cyan (think CMYK printers). These refer to those colors created by light reflected off a surface. When you see a green piece of clay, you are actually seeing the reflection of light off that clay. Light starts off as pure white, and the clay absorbs ("subtracts") reds and blues. These primary colors of pigment are also called *subtractive primary colors* for that reason.

When working with computer displays, you are working with light, which is why the primary colors in displays, games, graphics editors, and so on are red, green, and blue. This plays directly into additive blending. When you add together the three primary colors of light—red, green, and blue—you get white. Red and green produce yellow, a subtractive primary. Red and blue produce magenta, another subtractive primary. Blue and green produce cyan, the final subtractive primary.

When you choose to use additive blending, be aware that you are working with the additive primary colors, which are the primary colors of light: red, green, and blue.

Additive blending yields very interesting results. Because the colors are "merged" and the layering effect is diminished, additive blending is a great choice for creating glowy effects. Because pixel shaders are nonexistent on the Zune, additive blending is an option for spicing up the appearance of your textures.

Figure 6-5 shows the effect of additive blending on solid-colored circles with transparent backgrounds. The circles themselves are the primary colors: red, green, and blue (unfortunately, not discernible in the black-and-white figure). The intersection of any two colors yields a subtractive primary color (cyan, magenta, or yellow). In the middle, where all colors meet, is the color white. Notice in Figure 6-5 how all of the colors seem to blend together nicely.

Figure 6-5. *Additive blending with three primary color circles*

In Figure 6-6, you can see the effect of additive blending where the three circles are instead filled with radial gradients. Each color blends into the next, and any layering effect is diminished (unlike alpha blending, where layering is preserved). If you look carefully, you can see that the text itself is blended slightly with each of those colors, although it is hard to tell because the text color is already quite light. Additively blending a light color with other colors only makes it lighter.

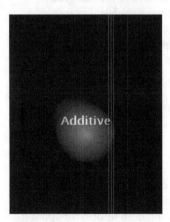

Figure 6-6. *Additive blending with three gradient balls and text*

■**Caution** At the time of this writing, there is a bug in the additive blend mode of sprite batches on the Zune. When a texture is drawn with a tint color that has 100% alpha (such as `Color.White` or `Color.Red`), the sprites will be drawn as if they were alpha blended. To overcome this, draw with a new color that has a fractional alpha value, such as `0.99f`. The unintended side effects of this are very hard (if not impossible) to notice.

EXERCISE 6-2. BLEND MODE EXPLORATION

This is a "see-for-yourself" exercise to better explore the color concepts so poorly illustrated by black-and-white images. You won't need to write any code for this exercise. Just sit back and observe!

1. In Visual Studio, choose File ➤ Open Project. Navigate to the folder `Examples/Chapter 6/Exercise 2/SpriteBlendModes` and open `SpriteBlendModes.csproj`.

2. If you can't find the reference to `Zune Copy of InputHandler`, add it to the solution from `Examples/Chapter 5/Exercise 4/InputState/Zune Copy of InputHandler.csproj`.

3. Connect your Zune and ensure that this device is set as default in the XNA Game Studio Device Center.

4. Press F5 to build, deploy, and debug on the Zune.

5. This example demonstrates multiple blend modes. Press the middle button to change from gradients to solids (solids allow you to see additive blending a little better). Press the Play button to change the blend mode.

6. After observing the blend modes, stop debugging.

Sprite Batches and Game Performance

In previous examples, you have seen multiple game components keep a reference to their own sprite batch and draw them independently of the game. With this approach, the entire concept of the sprite batch is defeated, especially since all of these sprite batches normally use the same blend mode.

If your main game loop manages a sprite batch and you have seven components that manage their own sprite batches, that's a total of eight sprite batches that are created and then resolved to the graphics device every time the game draws.

Truthfully, having just a handful of sprite batches going at any given time will not noticeably impact your performance. Four or five sprite batches versus one is not a terrible performance transgression. This approach, however, is not scalable. Each concurrent sprite batch adds its own amount of memory and processing overhead, both of which are scarce resources on a compact device such as the Zune. You might be surprised in practice to see how quickly multiple sprite batches can contribute to a slower frame rate. Plus, there is a tremendous amount of code duplication involved. Why should each component have its own sprite batch object when it could use a single, shared, smarter object that is centrally managed?

Your management of sprite batches is one of the first places you can turn to for optimization. In order of least to most optimal, here are three common implementations of sprite batch management.

At the component level: Sprite batches are instantiated, begun, and ended on a per-component level. This is the easiest in terms of up-front comprehension. If you understand how to draw to a sprite batch, but don't yet grasp the further implications of using too many of them, this is how you probably write games.

As a global service: A single sprite batch is stored in the main game's Services collection. Each component grabs a reference to this shared object. The sprite batch is begun in the main game loop and ended after the call to base.Draw (which draws all of the game's components). This approach is a little more streamlined. A single, shared sprite batch is used. The downside here is that you are limited to a single blend mode without the addition of special logic. Because the call to SpriteBatch.Begin exists statically in the main game's draw loop, you have only one opportunity to set the sprite batch. If you intend to use only alpha blending, this may be the option that makes the most sense for your games.

As a shared class: A smart wrapper around the SpriteBatch class is created as a singleton (a type of design pattern used to manage singular, global objects). This wrapper class is smart in that it can handle changes of blend modes, and is accessible by all game objects. Creating a shared sprite batch class requires a lot of up-front work, but the payoff is great. You are able to share the sprite batch resource across all of your screens and components, and it smartly decides when a new sprite batch is needed, depending on the blend mode. This approach is most likely necessary if you intend to use additive blending.

Note If you use a shared sprite batch class for additive blending, text should still be drawn with alpha blending, unless you are going for a particular effect. Since you will need to use two blend modes, it's much easier to have a single object manage how it begins and ends the sprite batches, so that it can cram as much into a single sprite batch with the same blend mode as possible.

Let's see how to implement the two approaches to sharing sprite batch resources.

Sharing Objects via Game.Services

Every XNA Framework game class exposes a collection called Services, which you can use to get a reference to frequently used objects. Using a sprite batch as a global service is a perfect example of this.

The Services collection can hold any data type, but it can hold only one of any specific data type. The corresponding object is retrieved by type lookup.

Because game components also hold a reference to the game they are attached to, each individual component can make use of the game's Services property to retrieve specific global objects.

To create a sprite batch and add it as a service in your main Game class, you can use the following code:

```
protected override void LoadContent()
{
    // Other content loading goes here

    spriteBatch = new SpriteBatch(graphics.GraphicsDevice);
    Services.AddService(typeof(SpriteBatch), spriteBatch);

    // More content loading
}
```

In this case, the variable spriteBatch is a member on the main game class. This is the object that's actually referenced when the Services property is queried for a SpriteBatch object.

Remember that sprite batches cannot be created until after the graphics device has been initialized, which is why we place this code in the LoadContent method. As a result, classes that rely on this global object cannot use it until the Draw method is called on those classes. To retrieve a shared sprite batch in a drawable component object, you can use the following code:

```
protected override void Draw(GameTime gameTime)
{
    SpriteBatch spriteBatch = (SpriteBatch)Game.Services.GetService(
        typeof(SpriteBatch));

    // Draw using spriteBatch
}
```

Here, the same sprite batch is retrieved every time into a variable that has the scope of the Draw method. Theoretically, this could decrease performance, although you most likely won't notice it. The operation to retrieve the sprite batch just returns an object by reference, without any fancy instantiation.

The other question that remains is where to place SpriteBatch.Begin and SpriteBatch.End. You could put them in the component's Draw method, but that goes against the principle of sprite batching. You might also run into concurrency issues where SpriteBatch.Begin has already been called somewhere else, causing an exception. The safest option is to put the calls to Begin and End in the main game class's Draw method, with a call to base.Draw in between to draw all of the game components using the same sprite batch. The code in the main game's Draw method would look similar to the following (remember that the spriteBatch member has been added as a service, so all components should use this sprite batch).

```
protected override void Draw(GameTime gameTime)
{
    GraphicsDevice.Clear(Color.Black);

    spriteBatch.Begin();
    // Draw anything that should always be drawn
    // Draw components
    base.Draw(gameTime);
    spriteBatch.End();
}
```

The downside to this approach is that it offers very little flexibility if you need to change the blend mode. If you don't expect to need to use additive blending (and can rely on everything working with alpha blending), this is a high-performance, low-effort approach that consolidates all of your draw calls to the same sprite batch.

Creating a Shared, Smart Sprite Batch Object

My gracious technical editor for this book, Shane DeSeranno, provided me with a singleton class he uses to wrap a SpriteBatch object to make it statically accessible to everything within your game. While many folks are dogmatically opposed to using globals of any kind, this class makes life a lot easier when multiple blend modes are involved. Plus, in the world of game development, you must often make sacrifices of (subjectively defined) elegance in the name of improved performance.

This class can be found in Examples/Chapter 6/Exercise 3. There is a subfolder there called SharedSpriteBatch. This folder contains a project that uses a version of this file that writes out the Begin and End calls to the debugger. We'll explore this project in the next exercise.

SharedSpriteBatch follows the Singleton design pattern, which means it cannot be instantiated. It is decorated with a property called Instance, which returns a singular and centrally managed instance maintained by the SharedSpriteBatch class itself. Because this property is static, you can access it from anywhere in your game as long as you include the namespace where SharedSpriteBatch is located. You don't even need to add this class to the game's Services component to use it!

This class has several overloaded methods for Draw and DrawString, which are modeled precisely after those on the XNA SpriteBatch class. These methods pass those arguments to the underlying sprite batch and handle the rest for you.

The magic of the SharedSpriteBatch class really lies in its Begin method, which smartly determines when a new sprite batch needs to be started. As we discussed, you should invest the resources to start a new sprite batch only when the blend mode changes. If the blend mode has changed, the previous sprite batch needs to be ended. The Begin method looks like this:

```
private void Begin(SpriteBlendMode spriteBlendMode)
{
    if (_mode != spriteBlendMode)
    {
        End();
    }

    if (!_hasBegun)
    {
        _mode = spriteBlendMode;
        _spriteBatch.Begin(_mode);
        _hasBegun = true;
    }
}
```

This method is private, so you never call it directly. The overloads of Draw and DrawString call this method when needed. Just be sure to call SharedSpriteBatch.Instance.End() once in the main game's Draw method to ensure that the sprite batch is always ended, lest you get an exception.

Let's run through a quick exercise to see how this works in practice.

EXERCISE 6-3. A SHARED SPRITE BATCH

This exercise uses the SharedSpriteBatch class described earlier, modified with a few debugger statements so we can see when the underlying sprite batch has been told to begin or end. Don't use this version of the code in production; use the one in the Exercise 3 folder one directory up.

The code draws two groups of three sprites. The first group of sprites uses a different blend mode for each sprite, which should result in three new calls to Begin. The second group of sprites uses the same blend mode (additive), which should result in Begin being called only once. The result looks like Figure 6-7. The first group is at the top of the screen, drawing three cascading circles using different blend modes. The second group starts near the middle, drawing the same three cascading circles using the same blend mode (additive).

Figure 6-7. *Sprites drawn using the shared sprite batch in Exercise 3*

1. In Visual Studio, open the solution located in Examples/Chapter 6/Exercise 3/SharedSprite-Batch/SharedSpriteBatch.csproj.

2. Notice that the default spriteBatch member has been removed completely. Instead, the LoadContent method calls SharedSpriteBatch.Instance.Initialize(this), which initializes the shared sprite batch so that it can create its own local copy using the game's graphics device.

3. Look at the code in the main game's Draw method, which draws the two groups of three sprites. This code clears the screen to a very dark color (so that the effects of the None and Additive blend modes can be better seen). The first group of sprites uses three different blend modes. The second group uses additive blending for all of the sprites. Then the sprite batch is explicitly ended, and the debug version of SharedSpriteBatch is instructed to stop printing debug statements, so that they are not printed infinitely as the game runs.

```
GraphicsDevice.Clear(new Color(0.2f, 0.2f, 0.2f));

// Using multiple blend modes
SharedSpriteBatch.Instance.Draw(SpriteBlendMode.None, red, Vector2.Zero,
    Color.White);
SharedSpriteBatch.Instance.Draw(SpriteBlendMode.Additive, green,
    new Vector2(50, 50), Color.White);
```

```
        SharedSpriteBatch.Instance.Draw(SpriteBlendMode.AlphaBlend, blue,
            new Vector2(100, 100), Color.White);

        // Using the same blend mode (additive)
        SharedSpriteBatch.Instance.Draw(SpriteBlendMode.Additive, red,
            new Vector2(0, 150), Color.White);
        SharedSpriteBatch.Instance.Draw(SpriteBlendMode.Additive, green,
            new Vector2(50, 200), Color.White);
        SharedSpriteBatch.Instance.Draw(SpriteBlendMode.Additive, blue,
            new Vector2(100, 250), Color.White);

        SharedSpriteBatch.Instance.End();
        SharedSpriteBatch.Instance.debug = false; // don't use this in practice
```

4. Press F5 to debug the game (do not run without debugging). Observe the output in the debugger's output window:

```
Begin: None
End
Begin: Additive
End
Begin: AlphaBlend
End
Begin: Additive
End
```

The first three Begin statements in the output correspond to the first three calls to Draw, where the blend modes are different. The final call to Begin corresponds to the three sprites drawn in Additive blend mode. Because these sequential calls use the same blend mode, the sprite batch begins only once, and all three sprites are drawn within that Begin/End block.

5. Stop the debugger.

This approach to using a shared sprite batch has many advantages. The shared sprite batch doesn't care which component is currently drawing; it cares only about the current blend mode and whether it needs to rebegin the sprite batch to support the new blend mode. As long as you always call End on the shared sprite batch instance from your main drawing code (and nowhere else), this code will work like a charm and perform beautifully every time, saving you a lot of work in the process!

Why should you use this approach if you are always using the default blend mode (AlphaBlend)? The class provides overloads of the Draw and DrawString methods that do not take an argument for the blend mode, which will use AlphaBlend automatically. This means that you can modify any code that would ordinarily reference a locally defined sprite batch to use this object instead, and the method signature will look exactly the same. If your game uses the default blend mode everywhere, you can (and should) eliminate any locally defined sprite batches and simply call the appropriate Draw method of the SharedSpriteBatch instance. The SharedSpriteBatch class takes care of all the Begin and End entries for you, meaning you write far less code in the long run.

Games in Landscape Mode

Let's face it: some games are just meant to be played in landscape mode. If you rotate the Zune 90 degrees counterclockwise, it looks more like a traditional widescreen monitor. You have more screen real estate horizontally than vertically. This lends itself well to many different kinds of games where the user interface simply works better in landscape mode.

Challenges with Landscape Mode

The very concept of running in landscape mode presents some important challenges:

- How do I calculate screen coordinates and boundaries?
- How do I handle directional pad input, which is now rotated?
- How do I rotate all of my sprites efficiently?

Let's take a look at each challenge, and then the possible solutions.

Calculating Coordinates and Boundaries

Simply put, writing a game in landscape mode is far more difficult than writing a game in portrait mode. Several conceptual things prevent you from using normal coordinates in your code:

- The origin (0, 0) is now in the lower-left corner of the screen.
- The x coordinate represents up and down, where X = 0 is at the bottom of the screen and moves upward visually as x increases.
- The y coordinate represents left and right, where Y = 0 is at the left of the screen and moves to the right visually as y increases.
- Rectangles don't behave in the same way as they do in portrait mode. Creating a bounding box around a sprite is more involved, because you can't just start at the top-left corner and add the width and height of the sprite.

Handling Rotated Input

The only control really affected by a landscape rotation is the directional pad. If you are considering a game that is rotated 90 degrees counterclockwise, Up on the directional pad is actually Right. Down becomes Left, Right becomes Down, and Left becomes Up. It's slightly confusing to read in text, but place your thumb on any of these areas of the Zune pad while your Zune is in portrait mode, and then rotate the whole mess to see how things change.

Furthermore, if you plan to support touch, the vector returned by the touchpad is also intuitively wrong. Let's say you touch the pad (in portrait mode) at a point that returns a vector ⟨0.5, -0.25⟩, which lies somewhere in the fourth quadrant of the Zune pad. This vector would be incorrect in landscape mode. If you hold your thumb there and rotate it, your thumb is now in the first quadrant of the Zune pad. The correct vector in landscape mode would actually be ⟨0.25, 0.5⟩. What happened there? The y coordinate was negated and moved to the x coordinate. The x coordinate was moved to the y coordinate. The formula for the new coordinates looks like this:

```
rotatedVector.X = -originalVector.Y;
rotatedVector.Y = originalVector.X;
```

What's worse is that the touch vector returned by the pad behaves differently than positional vectors you may be using, because the touch vector is inverted in the y direction (hence the required negation). Therefore, you cannot really write common conversion logic to handle all vectors. Instead, you must write specific code to support the negation of the y coordinate on the touchpad.

Rotating Sprites Efficiently

How do you rotate all of your sprites efficiently? Do you draw every single sprite with a scalar radian value that causes the sprite to be rotated 180 degrees? That's one way to do it, but you need to calculate an origin for the rotation in the portrait coordinate system in order for the rotations to look correct. Plus, sprites that are not in "power-of-two" dimensions will result in poorer aliasing effects. Do you manually rotate all of your sprites in the content creation phase? How would that impact your development process, having to think sideways all the time?

You can also use a render target to predraw your entire sprite batch in a rotated fashion to the back buffer before it is finally rendered to the screen. However, this has been shown to decrease performance drastically. As a general rule of thumb, render targets are avoided, as they are considered major impedances to achieving optimum performance. Unfortunately, render targets also embody the single easiest method of achieving landscape mode.

Possible Solutions for Landscape Mode

The path you choose for writing a game in landscape mode really comes down to what you think is best for the game. If render targets destroy your performance, you will need to do something harder. If you are writing a simple game (such as a card game) that takes no noticeable performance hit from the use of render targets, perhaps they will be an acceptable solution that will help get your game out the door faster.

Approach 1: Landscape from the Get-Go (Not Recommended Unless Crazy)

This is possibly the most performant way to write a game in landscape mode, but it's also the most ridiculously overcomplicated from a programmer sanity perspective. This approach causes you to enter a higher state of conscious known as "landscape brain mode," where you write all of your code under the assumption that these coordinates will be rotated.

In landscape brain mode, you become accustomed to thinking of Vector2.Zero as the bottom-left corner of the screen. Working in this mode means all of your content comes prerotated, with the exception of drawing sprite fonts. This causes you to exit landscape brain mode momentarily to perform a manual calculation of where text should appear when rotated.

You become accustomed to thinking of DPad.Up as DPad.Left. Most of your thoughts begin with a phrase similar to "Okay, so in landscape, this would be . . ."

In this mode, you should be prepared to spend a lot of time with pencil and paper to determine what the actual coordinates of sprites should be at any given time, and how rotated vectors affect them.

When it comes down to implementation, what this really means is that you need to draw all of your source sprites rotated by 90 degrees and then flip the x and y coordinates in your drawing code. The hard work comes in when you are updating world objects and trying to infer these objects' positions, directions, and so on in landscape mode.

If your game is all about high performance, this is an option to consider, but you will probably lose your mind after a while. Other options are far better for your sanity and productivity.

Approach 2: Rotation Matrices in SpriteBatch.Begin

There is an overload for `SpriteBatch.Begin` that takes a `Matrix` object, which you can use to rotate the sprites manually. This is a lot easier than specifying a scalar rotation value in every call to `SpriteBatch.Draw`.

Approach 3: Render Targets (Recommended, Usually)

A render target is a specifically sized area of memory to which you can write before the screen is rendered to the device. Render targets have many useful features, but using them can kill your performance if you have a very large number of sprites and/or effects.

Using render targets allows you to keep your game logic in portrait coordinates, although Zune pad input will still need to be rotated no matter what you do. If you operate in portrait mode, and then rotate the graphics at the very last moment, you don't have to do any crazy flipping of screen coordinates. Render targets provide that exact functionality.

Best Practices and Considerations for Mode Support

It may seem like supporting both portrait and landscape mode would require considerably more work, but as the next example shows, it's quite easy. Plan on supporting both modes to make users happy. Be aware that it will likely require a bit more work on your part.

Using render targets will work fine in most cases, but again, the Zune is a device with limited power. If you choose to use render targets, you should absolutely use a shared sprite batch to minimize the amount drawn to the back buffer in separate calls.

The best approach to take, whether you use render targets or manual rotation, is to keep all of your code in portrait mode and worry about only drawing in landscape. This leaves you with rotating the input yourself, and ensuring that your screen boundaries are flipped (the screen width becomes the height, and the width becomes the height). If you are writing only for the Zune, you could even hard-code (gasp) the screen width to 320 and the screen height to 240.

To make input handling easier, you could expose a property on your `InputState` class to indicate the orientation. Then, in the `DPad` properties, you could perform the extra calculation if the mode is landscape.

Using Render Targets for Landscape Mode

If you plan to create a very complicated game with a lot of sprites and varying blend modes, render targets may not be for you. However, for most applications of landscape mode on the Zune, using render targets is the most generally accepted way of rotating sprites.

The only place you need to worry about render targets is in the `Draw` method of your main game. The render target work flow looks like this (in mostly English):

1. A class-level RenderTarget2D object is declared and initialized with the graphics device in the LoadContent method.

2. In the Draw method, the graphics device is told to draw to your render target object instead of the screen.

3. The screen is cleared, and the sprite batch is started.

4. Sprite batch drawing takes place as usual (as if you were working with portrait coordinates, save for the different screen size). All of your components should be drawn here as well, using base.Draw().

5. The sprite batch is ended. This writes everything in the sprite batch to the render target.

6. The graphics device is told to draw to the screen, by setting the render target to null.

7. A new sprite batch is started. The render target's underlying Texture2D object is accessed and drawn to the screen, rotated 90 degrees (or pi/2 in radians). This draws everything you just drew earlier to the graphics device in one fell swoop.

8. The sprite batch is ended.

When the render target's texture is drawn to the screen, it is drawn at a position of (120, 160) with an origin of (160, 120). These values are used so that the texture appears in perfect alignment with the Zune screen. The coordinate (120, 160) is the center of the Zune screen in portrait mode, which is where the render target texture will be centered when it is drawn. The coordinate (160, 120) represents the center of the render target texture, which defines the point about which the render target texture will be rotated.

In practice, when the final rendering occurs, the render target texture (which is 320 by 240 pixels) is rotated 90 degrees counterclockwise about its center, and then drawn at the center of the screen, which is (120, 160). Figure 6-8 illustrates this process.

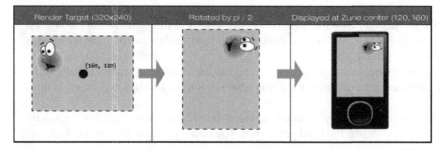

Figure 6-8. *How landscape mode using render targets works*

The code to use a render target requires an extra round of sprite batch drawing, because the graphics device must first be set to draw to the render target buffer, and then to draw that completed buffer to the screen. Some sample code, which would be in a game's Draw method, is shown in Listing 6-1.

Listing 6-1. *A Render Target in Action*

```
protected override void Draw(GameTime gameTime)
{
    // Draw to the render target (backTexture)
    GraphicsDevice.SetRenderTarget(0, backTexture);
    GraphicsDevice.Clear(Color.Black);

    // Draw all textures and components as usual
    spriteBatch.Begin();
    spriteBatch.Draw(ballTex, Vector2.Zero, Color.White);
    base.Draw(gameTime);
    spriteBatch.End();

    // Draw to the screen (no render target)
    GraphicsDevice.SetRenderTarget(0, null);
    GraphicsDevice.Clear(Color.Black);

    // Draw the render target's texture to the screen, rotated and centered
    spriteBatch.Begin();
    spriteBatch.Draw(backTexture.GetTexture(), new Vector2(120, 160), null,
        Color.White, MathHelper.PiOver2, new Vector2(160, 120), 1.0f,
        SpriteEffects.None, 0);
    spriteBatch.End();
}
```

The beauty of using a render target is that all of your original drawing code goes beneath the comment // Draw all textures and components as usual. The graphics device is then set to draw to the screen, and the render target texture is drawn.

If you wish, you can wrap certain blocks of this code in an if statement that checks the current orientation. As long as that orientation is changed only in the Update method, this operation will be safe. An example of this is shown in Exercise 6-4.

EXERCISE 6-4. LANDSCAPE MODE RENDERING

In this short example, you will see how render targets are used to render a game in landscape mode. This example also supports on-the-fly switching of the orientation mode. This game is something of a rehash of one of the earlier examples that sports a ball bouncing around in the visible screen area, so there is nothing truly amazing happening in the game, aside from the support for two orientations.

Rather than coding this example step by step, we'll just use an existing example and look at the parts of the code that matter.

1. In Visual Studio, open the project LandscapeGame.csproj from the folder Examples/Chapter 6/ Exercise 4/LandscapeGame.

2. Notice that the following members are used for the landscape rotation:

```
RenderTarget2D backTexture;
bool isLandscape = false;
```

There are also two properties, ScreenWidth and ScreenHeight, which return a value based on the current orientation (determined by the isLandscape variable).

```
public int ScreenWidth
{
    get
    {
        if (isLandscape)
            return 320;
        else
            return 240;
    }
}

public int ScreenHeight
{
    get
    {
        if (isLandscape)
            return 240;
        else
            return 320;
    }
}
```

3. Next, look at the Update method. It checks input and modifies the orientation when the middle button is pressed.

```
protected override void Update(GameTime gameTime)
{
    if (input.NewBackPress)
        this.Exit();

    if (input.MiddleButtonPressed)
    {
        isLandscape = !isLandscape;

        // Reset ball as it might be out of bounds
        ballPosition = Vector2.Zero;
        ballDirection = initialDirection;
    }

    ballPosition += ballDirection;
    HandleCollisions();

    orientation = isLandscape ? "Orientation: Landscape" :
        "Orientation: Portrait";
```

```
        base.Update(gameTime);
    }
```

4. Review the `HandleCollisions()` method. This method uses the dynamic screen dimension properties, `ScreenWidth` and `ScreenHeight`, to determine if the ball has hit a wall.

```
private void HandleCollisions()
{
    if (ballPosition.X <= 0 ||
        ballPosition.X + ballTex.Width >= ScreenWidth)
    {
        // Flip the vector about X
        ballDirection = Vector2.Reflect(ballDirection, Vector2.UnitX);
    }

    if (ballPosition.Y <= 0 ||
        ballPosition.Y + ballTex.Height >= ScreenHeight)
    {
        // Flip the vector about Y
        ballDirection = Vector2.Reflect(ballDirection, Vector2.UnitY);
    }
}
```

5. Next, take a look at the `Draw` method. It uses the code to draw to a render target, but two sections are wrapped in an `if` statement that checks the orientation. If we are in portrait mode (`isLandscape` is `false`), then there is no need to execute any of the special code for using render targets, so that code won't be executed. Notice that the code that is not wrapped in an `if` statement looks exactly like normal drawing code—the graphics device is cleared, and the textures are drawn at their normal positions. The values 160 and 120 are hard-coded here to represent half the screen height and width, but remember to change that if you plan to port to another platform.

```
protected override void Draw(GameTime gameTime)
{
    if (isLandscape)
    {
        // Set the render target, which draws to the back texture
        GraphicsDevice.SetRenderTarget(0, backTexture);
    }

    // Code to draw the game
    graphics.GraphicsDevice.Clear(Color.Black);

    spriteBatch.Begin();
    spriteBatch.Draw(ballTex, ballPosition, Color.White);
    spriteBatch.DrawString(normal, orientation, Vector2.Zero, Color.White);
    base.Draw(gameTime);
    spriteBatch.End();
```

```
        if (isLandscape)
        {
            // Render the back texture to the screen
            GraphicsDevice.SetRenderTarget(0, null);
            spriteBatch.Begin();
            spriteBatch.Draw(backTexture.GetTexture(), new Vector2(120, 160), null,
                Color.White, MathHelper.PiOver2, new Vector2(160, 120), 1.0f,
                SpriteEffects.None, 0);
            spriteBatch.End();
        }
    }
```

6. Press F5 to run the program. In portrait mode, the game looks like Figure 6-9. In landscape mode, the game looks like Figure 6-10 (rotate this book like you would rotate the Zune). To switch between the two modes, press the middle button. Notice how both the sprite and text are rotated and positioned as you would expect them to be from the supplied code.

Figure 6-9. *The game in portrait orientation*

Figure 6-10. *The game in landscape orientation*

7. Stop the debugger to end the game.

Because the use of a render target requires at least two different sprite batch sessions, you might be wondering how to integrate render targets into a class like SharedSpriteBatch. The way that class is currently organized means that the class itself never really knows when it is finished rendering all of the graphics, since any class anywhere can call it. However, a requirement for using the SharedSpriteBatch class is that you explicitly call End on the object instance from the main game's Draw method. You can use this requirement to draw everything to the render target by default. Then when the new End method is explicitly called, the contents of the back texture are drawn to the screen.

You could take it one step further by modifying the behavior of the class based on some publicly accessible property. You could enable or disable the use of render targets based on the currently selected orientation.

Remember that when using render targets, you can still write all of your game code using normal coordinates. You don't even need to think about landscape, because that step doesn't happen until just before the screen is drawn. The only thing you need to think about is the fact that in landscape, the screen dimensions are different (320 × 240 as opposed to 240 × 320 in portrait).

Componentizing Landscape Mode

Now that we have explored render targets, you may be getting some ideas of how you can incorporate this functionality into a common library all games can use. This library would need to include landscape modifications in three components:

- Graphics (using render targets, or not)
- Input (rotating the directional pad, or not)
- Game logic (flipping the screen width and height depending on the mode, for dynamic positioning)

Ideally, all three of these components would be controlled by a single property setting somewhere. If you plan to build a centralized game state management system based on the sample from the XNA Creators Club, that library would be a great place to build in this functionality.

Game State Management with Screens

As you saw in the previous chapter, the simple method of managing game state can quickly become, well, unmanageable when you add in a few more states. Throw in some more complicated requirements such as transitions and layered windows, and you have quite a tall order to fill. Thankfully, there are many existing samples out there that you can use to get started.

Screen Management Samples

On the Zune, game state is often thought of in terms of *screens*. Most of the existing examples involve a base "screen" class, several concrete screen classes, and a screen manager object that handles the display, removal, layering, and transitions of these screens.

The most comprehensive examples can be found online, at the XNA Creators Club web site. Here are a couple of good source code examples, some with videos and tutorials, that help with advanced game state management:

- http://creators.xna.com/en-US/samples/gamestatemanagement
- http://creators.xna.com/en-US/sample/network_game_state_mgt_sample

The screen management and menu system used in these two examples are widely duplicated in other samples, including community games on Xbox Live Arcade. It is recommended that you familiarize yourself with these samples. Games later in the book will be based on a framework established with these samples.

The first link is a very simple example involving offline game state. The second link shows you how to manage game state in the context of a networked game. Both are very similar, with the second adding network functionality to the basic screen management code.

Most likely, these samples will meet your needs. The game state management sample is extensible enough that you can modify it quickly to suit your needs. You should download the code and examine it to determine if it fits for your specific game. If not, the next section suggests some generic design principles that you can use to build your own screen management system from scratch.

Building a Screen Management System

Several components make up a screen management system. When you are satisfied with your system, you should make it as portable and reusable as possible. You can accomplish this as follows:

- Build your screen manager logic in a separate library.

- Build the project into a separate assembly, which you can reference later (or using the project reference directly in your game projects).

- Make your screen manager and the screens a drawable game component.

There are other components that you can consider including in this general utility library, such as a network state manager, an audio and sound effects manager, and a network state manager. Each of these will be a custom class you write to wrap and expose important logic to any game that can use such logic.

Your screen manager should include a minimum of two main components: a screen manager and a base class for individual screens.

The Base Screen Class

The base class holds everything common to a screen. It implements functionality (or stubs for implementable functionality) such as transitions, input, events, and more.

Depending on the paradigm you choose to manage your sprite batches, you could add a `GameComponentCollection` property to the `BaseScreen` class, which would allow the screen to indirectly add game components to the parent game's `Components` collection. This approach lends itself well to a situation where you want to support each screen having a different sprite batch blend mode.

Another approach would be to implement `virtual` methods for `Draw` and `Update`, which can be overridden by any concrete screen classes that inherit from `BaseScreen`. Here is an example of a `virtual` `Update` method signature:

```
public virtual void Update(GameTime gameTime);
```

You have the option to implement base functionality here, but derived classes can (and should) provide their own implementation of these virtual methods.

Having a base screen class allows you to think broadly about the possible screen implementations. You could include a property to specify whether the screen should be displayed on top of all other screens, similar to a modal dialog. You could implement all of your basic screen input handling logic in this base class, so that all of your concrete screen classes behave similarly with input.

In any case, sit down and think about those properties and operations that are common to all screens in your game. If you use your screen manager as a project reference, you can always go back to encapsulate new functionality as you move from game to game. Just be wary of any side effects your new code may cause.

The Screen Manager Class

The screen manager is responsible for the following:

- Adding new screens to the game
- Removing screens from the game
- Telling individual screens when to begin or end transitions
- Handling the sprite batch implementation of the screens
- Determining the order in which screens are added to the screen list
- Determining which screens are visible
- Determining which screens are updatable
- Providing any shared logic that all screens should have access to, such as transition effects
- Sharing any resources common to all screens, such as fonts, sprite batches, and background textures

Like the base screen class, there are a number of ways to implement this class, based on your individual programming style, as well as the needs of your current and future games.

The screen manager can itself be a drawable game component. If you choose to go this route, however, you must be aware of the resource-sharing issues inherent in doing so. For example, a sprite batch cannot be created without access to the graphics device, so your concrete screens probably won't be able to do anything with the sprite batch until the first time their Draw method is called. Making the screen manager drawable gives you the added benefit of adding this class to the game's component collection once and manipulating that object throughout the game to add new screens. The screen manager would ideally take care of the transitions between screens, displaying topmost screens properly, and sharing resources across all screens. This is good practice in the sense that your main game loop remains uncluttered, and your concrete screen classes are cohesive and independent.

If you plan to use the screen manager to share resources across concrete screens, you need to determine how to access those resources from the base screen class. You can do this by holding a reference to the screen manager in the base screen class, but this tightly couples the screens to the screen manager. You could also use static properties, but this is even less elegant, as it tightly couples the screens to a specific object in a particular game. You could also use the main game's Services collection to get a reference to a sprite batch, but this constrains you to using a single type of blending for all screens.

As a result of this thinking, it's probably best to use the SharedSpriteBatch object discussed earlier in the chapter. This way, all of your screens can use the same sprite batch object, without having to worry about sharing it across components and screens.

Adding New Screens

With the basic functionality in place for a screen manager, you can simply add new classes that inherit from BaseScreen and add those classes directly to the screen manager. The screen manager will take care of the rest. One screen per class file is preferred, because that approach lets you visually associate your screens with files in the solution.

Each screen should implement its own Update and Draw methods that contain logic specific to that screen. The screen manager should take care of the transition effects itself.

Transitioning Between Screens to Manage Game State

When all game functionality is encapsulated per screen, you don't need to worry about game state as much as you would ordinarily. For example, to transition from the start screen to the playing screen, all you would need to do is tell the screen manager to show the playing screen. The playing screen would handle all of its startup and shutdown, and would be shown topmost until something else happens.

If a screen has other screens shown on top of it, that screen should be prevented from updating itself. This can be done through the screen manager, which loops through each screen and calls the Update and Draw methods on those screens. That means each screen should also have a property that determines if it's the topmost screen.

When objects need to be shared between screens, you can either pass them via a method on the new screen, such as Show or AddScreen, share them statically, or share them via the game's Services collection.

Other Components Worth Adding

The screen management system is probably the largest component that you would want to extract into a separate game library. While you're developing that library, you might want to add the other components we've discussed thus far, including the input state handler and support for drawing in landscape mode. This way, all games have the ability to leverage that functionality if needed. This makes the up-front investment in a comprehensive game library a little larger, but the payoff is grand if you plan on making more than one game!

Storage on the Zune

Do you want to save a game's high scores or preferences? The Zune fully supports the XNA storage API. This API is documented fully, with examples, in the XNA documentation. You can read more about the API by going to Help ➤ Contents, and navigating to XNA Game Studio 3.0 ➤ Programming Guide ➤ Storage.

The Zune is allowed access to the device's file system only through the storage API. Once you have obtained a path to the file through the storage subsystem, you can use the regular file input/output (I/O) functionality in the .NET Framework, such as stream readers and writers, to read and write data to files.

The process for managing stored data is as follows:

1. Use the Guide class to show the storage device selector, which returns a StorageDevice object asynchronously.

2. A StorageContainer object is retrieved using the GetContainer method of this StorageDevice object. The container wraps the available storage options for the device.

3. The path to the storage file is obtained using the XNA Framework's `Path.Combine` method (found in `System.IO`), using the container's path and the appropriate file name.

4. The file is opened, created, written to, and so on, using the usual file system operations that you would normally use to access files.

The first step in this process is getting the device storage selector. The code looks like this:

```
Guide.BeginShowStorageDeviceSelector(this.GetStorageDevice, new object());
```

■Note You should call `Guide.BeginShowStorageDeviceSelector` in your `LoadContent` method, as it is asynchronous and can take some time to complete. Calling it early on will assign it and have it available for use immediately. Be aware that this will not behave the same on the Xbox 360, where you want to show the selector before any storage operations.

In this case, `this.GetStorageDevice` is a callback method that the guide will call when the appropriate storage device has been resolved. This method, in turn, calls the companion `Guide.EndShowStorageDeviceSelector`, which returns the `StorageDevice` object you need to continue. `GetStorageDevice` (a private method in your class) has the following implementation:

```
private void GetStorageDevice(IAsyncResult result)
{
    storageDevice = Guide.EndShowStorageDeviceSelector(result);
}
```

Here, the `storageDevice` object is an instance of type `StorageDevice`, which you have declared in the class. The act of retrieving the storage device happens asynchronously; this is the only way to retrieve a storage device in XNA. There is no synchronous, blocking method that will retrieve a storage device immediately. However, on the Zune and PC, the guide never actually shows a selection screen; it will immediately return the first (or only) storage device available on that system. In both cases, the storage device is the hard drive. This eliminates the need to check the guide's visibility before attempting this.

The second step in the process is retrieving a `StorageContainer` object, which can be done with the following code:

```
StorageContainer container = storageDevice.OpenContainer("MyGameTitle");
```

Next, you can concatenate a string that represents the desired file's path:

```
string filename = Path.Combine(container.Path, "highscore.dat");
```

From there on, you can use standard file I/O methods to read from and write to the file. On the Zune, this file path will resolve to a path specific to Zune storage. On the PC, it will resolve to a path similar to `C:\Users\`*YourUsername*`\Documents\Saved Games\`*MyGameTitle*`\AllUsers\highscore.dat`. On the Zune, there is only one player, but if you need to support multiple player data, you can use the overload of the `BeginShowStorageDeviceSelector` that takes a `PlayerIndex` object. The preceding overload just uses the default setting, which writes data for all users.

In the next example, we will modify the Monkey Feeder game to support the storage of high scores.

EXERCISE 6-5. STORAGE SUPPORT FOR MONKEY FEEDER

In this exercise, we will modify the game Monkey Feeder to support storage of high scores. If you have logged a new high score, it will write that high score to the storage device. If your score is not a high score, the high score will be displayed on the game over screen instead. The code can be found in `Examples/Chapter 6/Exercise 5/MonkeyFeederStorage`.

1. Make a copy of the Monkey Feeder game and ensure all of your projects are loaded. You may need to create a new copy of the Monkey Feeder game for Windows. You may also need to add the `InputState` project again, create a copy of that project for Windows or Zune (depending on which you are missing), and add the `InputState` project references to the Zune and Windows versions of the game. Your Solution Explorer window should look like Figure 6-11. I have renamed some of the projects in this screenshot.

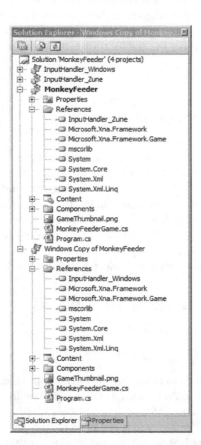

Figure 6-11. *The MonkeyFeederStorage solution*

2. Add the following member variables to MonkeyFeederGame.cs. These variables are used for the text that displays the high score and the storage device.

```
// Storage
private StorageDevice storageDevice;
string finalScoreText;
```

3. Find the SetGameState method in MonkeyFeederGame.cs. Find the case statement for GameState. GameOver. Previously, that block looked like this:

```
case GameState.GameOver:
    enableComponents = false;
    break;
```

4. Modify this code to include user storage. This code gets the storage device and container, and performs read and write operations to a file called highscore.dat.

```
case GameState.GameOver:
    enableComponents = false;

    #region Storage Device

    // Show the storage device and get the filename
    StorageContainer container = storageDevice.OpenContainer("MonkeyFeeder");
    string filename = Path.Combine(container.Path, "highscore.dat");

    // Open a file stream
    FileStream file = File.Open(filename, FileMode.OpenOrCreate,
        FileAccess.ReadWrite);

    int oldScore = -1;
    StreamReader reader = new StreamReader(file);
    if(file.Length > 0)
    {
        // Attempt to read from the file. If there is nothing, oldScore
        // will still be -1.
        oldScore = int.Parse(reader.ReadLine());
    }
    reader.Close();

    if (score > oldScore)
    {
        highScoreText = "\r\nNew High Score: " + score;
        StreamWriter writer = new StreamWriter(file);
        // Erase the contents of the file and write the new score.
        file.SetLength(0);
        writer.WriteLine(score);
        writer.Close();
    }
    else
```

```
        {
            highScoreText = "\r\nHigh Score: " + oldScore;
        }

        // Close the file
        file.Close();

        // Dispose the container to commit the storage changes
        container.Dispose();

        #endregion

        break;
```

5. In the LoadContent method, show the storage device asynchronously with this line of code:

```
Guide.BeginShowStorageDeviceSelector(this.GetStorageDevice, new object());
```

Note that we passed the name of a callback method called GetStorageDevice. Add this method to the Private Utility Methods region:

```
private void GetStorageDevice(IAsyncResult result)
{
    storageDevice = Guide.EndShowStorageDeviceSelector(result);
}
```

6. Locate the Update method of the game. Within this method, find the case statement for GameState. GameOver. Right before the input state is checked for a new button press (and immediately after the finalScoreText string is constructed), append the high score text to the final score text:

```
finalScoreText += highScoreText;
```

7. Run the game by pressing F5. Try it using Windows or the Zune—the results are similar. If you do not set a new high score, you will see the previous high score, as shown in Figure 6-12. If you have beaten the previous high score, you will see your new high score and a congratulatory message, as shown in Figure 6-13. (The screenshots are from the Windows version of the game.)

Figure 6-12. *A new high score was not achieved.*

Figure 6-13. *Your high score was stored as the new high score.*

Using the storage API is quite easy if you have experience using System.IO classes to write and read files. You can also store more advanced data structures by using System.Xml classes to create a new XmlDocument, and serialize the contents of that document (in text) to storage.

■**Caution** The .NET Compact Framework, which runs on Zune and Xbox, does not support binary serialization.

Remember that you can always find more examples of the storage API through the XNA documentation, accessible via Help ➤ Contents ➤ XNA Game Studio 3.0 ➤ Programming Guide ➤ Storage.

Advanced Touch Sensitivity on the Zune

There may come a time where you want game objects to respond to a "flick" or a "nudge" on the Zune pad. A flick has two components:

- The direction in which you move a finger or thumb along the Zune pad.

- The amount of time it took you to move your finger. If you move quickly from one point to another, this should indicate a strong flick. A slow motion indicates a gentle nudge.

To determine these components dynamically, you must maintain a Boolean variable, such as `isTracking`. When this variable is `false`, there is no input on the Zune pad—the vector returned is equal to `Vector2.Zero`. When the game notices that there is input on the Zune pad, the game logs the "start" position and the time at which the Zune pad was touched. The game begins logging the current Zune pad position and waiting for that position to become `Vector2.Zero` again, which means the touchpad was released. When the touchpad is released, tracking stops, and the vector is calculated.

The strength of the vector is stored in a separate variable for speed. This value is determined by the length of the vector divided by the total fractional number of seconds it took for the user to travel that distance.

At the end of a tracking session, you are left with a vector that represents the direction and a value that represents the intensity of the flick. You can append these to the direction of an object in the `Update` method to achieve a realistic, physical effect that is sensitive to the direction and intensity of a flick action.

The next exercise shows you how to implement flick gestures in an XNA game for the Zune.

EXERCISE 6-6. FLICK GESTURES WITH THE ZUNE PAD

This example shows you how to use time spans and tracked positions to derive a vector and an intensity value that, together, represent a "flick" gesture on the Zune pad. In this game, our lovable ball object can be flung around the screen using touch gestures. The ball will also bounce off the walls using simple collision detection. This example also uses a deceleration value, which is subtracted from the ball's velocity with every update so that the ball slows down over time. The code for this example can be found in `Examples/Chapter 6/Exercise 6/TouchThrower`. There are no screenshots for this example, because its focus is on motion and movement only.

1. In Visual Studio, create a new Zune Game project.

2. Add `ball.png` to the `Content` folder from the `Examples/Chapter 6/Artwork` folder.

3. Add the following private fields to your game, leaving the default sprite batch and graphics device intact:

```
// Texture
Texture2D ballTex;

// Tracking variables
bool isTracking = false;
Vector2 touchStartPoint;
Vector2 touchEndPoint;
TimeSpan touchStartTime;
TimeSpan totalTouchTime;

// Speed and deceleration
float velocity;
float deceleration = 0.1f;

// Ball position and direction
Vector2 ballPosition;
Vector2 ballDirection;
```

```
    // Screen width and height
    int screenWidth, screenHeight;
```

4. In the LoadContent method, load the ball texture. Also, set up the screen width, screen height, ball direction, and ball position.

```
protected override void LoadContent()
{
    // Create a new SpriteBatch, which can be used to draw textures.
    spriteBatch = new SpriteBatch(GraphicsDevice);

    ballTex = Content.Load<Texture2D>("ball");
    screenWidth = GraphicsDevice.Viewport.Width;
    screenHeight = GraphicsDevice.Viewport.Height;

    ballPosition = new Vector2(
        screenWidth / 2 - ballTex.Width / 2,
        screenHeight / 2 - ballTex.Height / 2);

    ballDirection = Vector2.Zero;
}
```

5. Add a private method called HandleCollisions. This is a basic collision detection scheme, with no protection for when the ball goes out of bounds and cannot get back (you can implement that yourself if you wish; see the section on collision detection in Chapter 5 for details).

```
private void HandleCollisions()
{
    if (ballPosition.X <= 0 ||
        ballPosition.X + ballTex.Width >= screenWidth)
    {
        ballDirection = Vector2.Reflect(ballDirection, Vector2.UnitX);
    }

    if (ballPosition.Y <= 0 ||
        ballPosition.Y + ballTex.Height >= screenHeight)
    {
        ballDirection = Vector2.Reflect(ballDirection, Vector2.UnitY);
    }
}
```

6. Add a new private method called FlingBall. This method takes three arguments: the time it took to move, the start position, and the end position. This method calculates and applies these values to the ball's direction and velocity.

```
private void FlingBall(TimeSpan touchTime, Vector2 startPoint, Vector2 endPoint)
{
    ballDirection = Vector2.Subtract(endPoint, startPoint);
    // invert Y axis
    ballDirection.Y = -ballDirection.Y;
```

```
        velocity = ballDirection.Length() / (float)touchTime.TotalSeconds;
    }
```

7. Add a new private method called HandleTouchPad. This method is called with every tick of Update, and handles all of the Zune pad tracking. It also calls FlingBall when a fling has been detected.

```
private void HandleTouchPad(GameTime gameTime)
{
    GamePadState state = GamePad.GetState(PlayerIndex.One);
    Vector2 zunePadVector = state.ThumbSticks.Left;

    if (isTracking)
    {
        // If the Zune pad is no longer being touched
        if (zunePadVector == Vector2.Zero)
        {
            // End tracking
            isTracking = false;
            totalTouchTime = gameTime.TotalRealTime.Subtract(touchStartTime);

            // Fling the ball
            FlingBall(totalTouchTime, touchStartPoint, touchEndPoint);
        }
        else
        {
            // Update the current end point
            touchEndPoint = zunePadVector;
        }
    }
    else
    {
        // If the Zune pad has been touched
        if (zunePadVector != Vector2.Zero)
        {
            // Start tracking
            velocity = 0.0f;
            ballDirection = Vector2.Zero;
            touchStartTime = gameTime.TotalRealTime;
            touchStartPoint = zunePadVector;
            isTracking = true;
        }
    }
}
```

8. In the Update method, call HandleCollisions and HandleZunePad. Also, check the velocity to see if it's less than zero. If so, set it back to a flat zero to avoid the ball springing back in the opposite direction when the velocity becomes negative. This method also updates the ball position using the ball's direction multiplied by the velocity.

```
protected override void Update(GameTime gameTime)
{
    // Allows the game to exit
    if (GamePad.GetState(PlayerIndex.One).Buttons.Back == ButtonState.Pressed)
        this.Exit();

    HandleCollisions();

    HandleTouchPad(gameTime);

    // Stop the ball if the velocity becomes negative
    if (velocity > 0)
        velocity = velocity - deceleration;
    else
        velocity = 0f;

    // Update the ball position
    ballPosition += ballDirection * velocity;

    base.Update(gameTime);
}
```

9. In the Draw method, we simply draw the ball texture at its position.

```
protected override void Draw(GameTime gameTime)
{
    GraphicsDevice.Clear(Color.CornflowerBlue);

    spriteBatch.Begin();
    spriteBatch.Draw(ballTex, ballPosition, Color.White);
    spriteBatch.End();

    base.Draw(gameTime);
}
```

10. That's it for this example's code. Ensure that your Zune is connected and set as default in the XNA Game Studio Device Center. Press F5 to run the game. Use your thumb to flick the ball around. Try it with different speeds and see how the game responds. Also, try using "mini-vectors," such as moving your thumb along one side of the Zune pad only. Regardless of where you do the flick motion on the Zune pad, that vector is correctly calculated and applied to the ball's direction.

Graphic Sound Visualizers

One interesting thing about the Zune is that while it does play games, it is first and foremost a music player. When the news broke that the Zune would support XNA games, one of the first things people thought of was creating visualizers that "display" the sound of the currently playing track.

The XNA media API can make this happen. The MediaPlayer class has a static method called GetVisualizerData, which puts data into a VisualizerData object. You can read more about the GetVisualizerData method (and learn more about how this works) in the XNA Game Studio documentation by selecting Help ➤ Contents in Visual Studio and navigating to XNA Game Studio 3.0 ➤ XNA Framework Class Library Reference ➤ Microsoft.XNA. Framework.Media ➤ MediaPlayer class. In that text is a link to the documentation for the GetVisualizerData method, which will be quite useful. Understanding the physics of sound requires a different book entirely, but it is addressed briefly here.

A VisualizationData instance contains two collections of floats: Samples and Frequencies. The Samples collection is essentially an array of length 256 and contains audio sample data over some most recent period of time. Each element ranges from –1.0 to 1.0. The Samples collection can be used to generate the waveform of the sound.

The Frequencies collection, also of length 256, tells you how the sound of the currently playing track is distributed across bands of frequencies (pitches). This is called the frequency power spectrum. According to the documentation, the bands range from 20 Hz to 20 KHz (which is the average audible range of the human ear). These bands are distributed logarithmically across the 256 available slots in the array. The documentation states that as a result of this logarithmic distribution, "elements at the lower end of the spectrum represent a smaller frequency range than those at the upper end of the spectrum" (http://msdn.microsoft.com/en-us/library/microsoft.xna.framework.media.mediaplayer.getvisualizationdata.aspx). In other words, Frequencies[0] represents a very small band (range) of frequencies, and Frequencies[255] represents a very high band of frequencies.

Lower frequencies are the bass frequencies. A bass drum hit usually registers somewhere between 60 and 300 Hz. However, a hi-hat cymbal can register frequencies from 8 to 12 KHz. Harsher sounds can appear above that range as well. Middle A on a keyboard emits a prominent frequency of 440 Hz, although depending on the character of the sound, other frequencies are present as well. That sound range of 20 Hz to 20 KHz is large, and you can expect to find data for each of the 256 logarithmic bands simultaneously at any given moment.

The art of drawing sound using visualization data is pretty subjective, and how you achieve this is up to you. A common approach is to use a 1 × 1 texture as a pixel, positioned so that a sound wave is displayed. You can also scale this 1 × 1 texture to fill the area below it by drawing to a destination rectangle. You can use the sample and visualization data to tint each pixel a certain color to achieve an even cooler effect.

Visualization is a tough nut to crack, however. The truly compelling visualizers use a combination of sample data, frequency data, and special dynamic code that is unique to the visualizer itself to derive a changing pattern on the screen.

In the next exercise, you will learn how to use the frequency and sample data to display the waveform of the sound and the frequency distribution on the screen.

EXERCISE 6-7. A SIMPLE MUSIC VISUALIZER

This exercise covers the use of visualization data to draw information about the currently playing track. All that is used graphically is a background texture and a 1 × 1 white pixel (see Figure 6-15, at the end of this exercise).

Both the sample and frequency data arrays available in the visualization data object have lengths of 256. Because our Zune screen is only 240 pixels wide, we will display the graphic in landscape mode.

If the game updates slowly, the visualizer looks terrible. For this reason, I have opted to avoid using render targets to achieve the rotation, as this would destroy the frame rate. Instead, I have included a previously rotated background object for the waveform. On top of this graphic, the pixels are drawn from the top of the screen to the bottom.

Again, rather than do a step-by-step build of this project, we'll open the one I have built for the book and examine the code. The code can be found in `Examples/Chapter 6/Exercise 7/MusicVisualizer`.

1. In Visual Studio, open `Examples/Chapter 6/Exercise 7/MusicVisualizer/MusicVisualizer.sln`. This loads `MusicVisualizer.csproj` and `InputState_Zune.csproj`. If it does not load automatically, add it from the `Chapter 5/Exercise 4` example (be sure to add the input handler library as a reference).

2. Take a look at the private fields in `Game1.cs`. The requisite texture and position variables are there, with a few added:

```
Vector2 waveformPosition;
Vector2 waveformBoxOrigin;
Vector2 screenCenter;
const int waveformHeight = 50;
bool useFillDisplay = true;

VisualizationData visData;

float frequencyRatio = 0f;
Color tintColor;
```

The waveform height constant determines the amplitude of the waveform. Increase it to make a bigger wave, although the side effect is that it does not appear to be as well connected (since we are using simple pixels without any smart line drawing).

The Boolean variable called `useFillDisplay` will cause the game to draw a filled waveform when `true`, or a single line when `false`.

The `VisualizationData` object is refilled at every call to `Update`. If possible, you could refresh this object in the `Draw` method, where it would reflect the most recent data possible, but we do it in `Update` in this example because the visualization data is required for another calculation.

The frequency ratio is equal to the index of the loudest frequency divided by 255, which gives us a float between 0 and 1. This value, in turn, is used to generate a tint color for the frequency graph.

3. Next, look at the `Initialize` method, which is simple. It enables visualization and instantiates the visualization data object:

```
protected override void Initialize()
{
    MediaPlayer.IsVisualizationEnabled = true;
    visData = new VisualizationData();

    base.Initialize();
}
```

4. Turn your attention to the Update method. This method first checks for some input conditions. It stops the music and exits the game on a Back press. It shows the guide (to allow for a new song to play) when Play is pressed. The middle button causes the waveform display to toggle between the filled graph and the line graph.

```
if (input.NewBackPress)
{
    // Stop the media player if it is playing
    MediaPlayer.Stop();

    // Exit the game
    this.Exit();
}

// Show the guide when Play is pressed
if (input.NewPlayPress)
{
    if (Guide.IsVisible == false)
    {
        Guide.Show();
    }
}

// Change the display when middle is pressed
if (input.MiddleButtonPressed)
{
    useFillDisplay = !useFillDisplay;
}
```

After input is checked, the Update method goes on to refresh the visualization data and calculate the value used for the tint color. This code uses a simple loop to find the index of the frequency array corresponding to the loudest frequency, determines how far along the frequency spectrum that index is, and uses that ratio to linearly interpolate a new color between dark green and white.

```
// Update visualization data
MediaPlayer.GetVisualizationData(visData);

// Determine the band with the maximum frequency
float maxValue = visData.Frequencies[0];
int maxIndex = 0;
for (int i = 1; i < visData.Frequencies.Count; i++)
{
    if (visData.Frequencies[i] > maxValue)
    {
        maxValue = visData.Frequencies[i];
        maxIndex = i;
    }
}
```

```
// Get a ratio of where this index is compared to the rest of the bands
frequencyRatio = (float)maxIndex / (float)visData.Frequencies.Count;

// Use this ratio linearly interpolate between two colors
tintColor = Color.Lerp(Color.DarkGreen, Color.White, frequencyRatio);
```

5. Looking at the Draw method, you can see that it is responsible for the heavy lifting in this application. The calls to spriteBatch.Draw are ugly and multilined—sometimes because the arguments are dynamic; other times because we must use the longer overloads to specify a rotation. First, we check if the media player is playing. If nothing is playing, we display the texture loaded with a graphic that instructs the user to press Play to show the guide menu.

```
if (MediaPlayer.State == MediaState.Stopped)
{
    // Draw the "No current song" background.
    spriteBatch.Draw(noTrackTex, Vector2.Zero, Color.White);
}
```

Otherwise, in an else bracket, we draw various things. Regardless of the display style, we always draw the waveform container box background and the frequency power spectrum.

```
// Draw the waveform background box, rotated at its origin
spriteBatch.Draw(waveformBox, screenCenter, null, Color.White,
    0.0f, waveformBoxOrigin, 1.0f, SpriteEffects.None, 0);
```

Next, we loop through every element in the sample data. We also use this loop to display the frequency power spectrum, which has the same length as the sample data. First, we draw the frequency power spectrum, and then check if the current display style for the waveform should appear filled. This option draws the pixel to a destination rectangle scaled to the value of the sample data at that index. Otherwise, the pixel object is drawn to a dynamically generated Vector2 object.

```
for (int i = 0; i < visData.Samples.Count; i++)
{
    // Draw the frequency bar at the top using rectangles
    spriteBatch.Draw(pixelTex,
        new Rectangle((int)waveformPosition.X + (int)waveformBoxOrigin.X,
            i + (int)waveformPosition.Y,
            (int)(visData.Frequencies[i] * waveformHeight), 1),
        tintColor);

    if (useFillDisplay)
    {
        // Draw samples using rectangles
        spriteBatch.Draw(pixelTex,
            new Rectangle((int)waveformPosition.X,
                i + (int)waveformPosition.Y,
                (int)(visData.Samples[i] * waveformHeight),
                1),
            Color.White);
    }
```

```
        else
        {
            // Draw samples using "pixels"
            spriteBatch.Draw(pixelTex,
                new Vector2(waveformPosition.X + visData.Samples[i] *
                    waveformHeight,
                waveformPosition.Y + i),

            Color.White);
        }
    }
```

6. This code allows for two different display modes to be used. Press F5 to run the game (fix any compilation or reference errors that may occur). Press the Play button to launch the guide, and simply choose Shuffle All to begin playing a song. The default mode is filled mode for the waveform, which results in a screen similar to Figure 6-14.

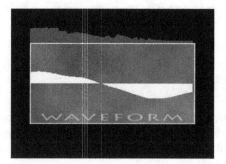

Figure 6-14. *The waveform displayed in filled mode*

7. Toggle the display mode by pressing the middle button. The display will change to a line, which appears connected, as shown in Figure 6-15.

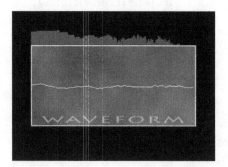

Figure 6-15. *The waveform displayed in line mode*

8. Use the guide menu to find other songs. Try to find a quiet song and a very noisy song, and notice the difference in the waveform. Quieter songs have calmer waveforms; loud, noisy songs produce waveforms that are so violent that it's difficult to even make the wave out. This is due to the fact that the Zune game loop resolves only a certain amount of sample data per update, and "busy" songs pack a lot of information into the sample data. Also notice how the color of the frequency spectrum becomes slightly brighter when higher frequencies are played in the song.

Creating a visualizer can be a lot of fun, but you must think hard about how to produce one that looks good. The key is making an interesting engine that uses the frequency and sample data to output some cool-looking, transformed collection of sprites on the screen that change with time.

Possibly the most important consideration when designing your visualizer is performance. You want the `Draw` method to execute as often as possible, especially if you elect to refresh the visualization data here instead of in `Update`. Your code must be as optimal as possible, using as little memory as possible, and performing the fewest calculations possible per `Draw`.

Check Your Knowledge

By the end of this chapter, you probably feel like there is nothing you *can't* do with the Zune! Test yourself with these ten questions:

1. What `enum` can you use to determine if the Zune is plugged in to its charger?

2. What is the difference between alpha blending and additive blending?

3. Why should you consolidate your sprite batches?

4. How does the game's `Services` collection index its objects?

5. What class did we discuss that you can use to consolidate all of your sprite batch activity globally?

6. What is the preferred method of displaying sprites in landscape mode when performance is not affected?

7. After drawing to a render target, how do you write the contents of that back texture to the screen?

8. When using render targets, should you keep your code in portrait coordinates or manually swap all of the x and y coordinates?

9. How is the storage device obtained on the Zune?

10. How do you retrieve sample data for a currently playing song? What is the data type?

Summary

In this chapter, you have learned about a slew of advanced techniques, including power management, sprite batches, game state management, touch gestures, landscape mode, and visualizers. While you may not use all of these techniques directly, it is crucial that you take your knowledge of shared sprite batches and game state management with you when you begin creating your own games. Even better, retrofit your current games to be smarter with these features!

In the next, final chapter, we will discuss wireless networking between Zunes, and build a popular card game that implements that technology from start to finish.

CHAPTER 7

■ ■ ■

Final Exercise: Multiplayer Crazy Eights

The time has come to put everything together in one final example: a multiplayer card game for the Zune. All Zunes have wireless capability, which allows you to connect and send data to other nearby Zunes in an ad hoc fashion.

The Crazy Eights game incorporates many of the concepts we have covered thus far, including shared sprite batches, game state management, animation, components, game libraries, and sound effects. The final piece of the puzzle is network management, which we will dive into first, before writing this consummate example.

Wireless Networking with the Zune

Because all Zunes have a wireless antenna, you can connect to other nearby Zunes and send/receive data from them. This makes for some very interesting possibilities.

The wireless hardware in the Zune is meant to connect to one other device (to send music) or with a public network (to synchronize your library wirelessly or buy music online). It is theoretically possible to connect up to eight different Zunes in the same multiplayer network session, but you may notice some glitchy behavior when attempting to use more than three (or so) at a time.

Zune multiplayer games are peer-to-peer. This means that any Zune game must be able to act as either the client or the server. There is no centralized game server that serves data. In other words, all Zunes should be capable of acting as a host device and a client device, depending on their role in the game. A single Zune usually plays the role of the server (host), which can unfortunately degrade performance for that Zune if extensive processing is required for the host.

In addition, the work flow for testing multiplayer games is slightly different than with normal games. When you want to test connectivity or connected features, you always need to deploy or run without debugging on at least one device (since you can deploy to only one Zune at a time). Then you must plug in the other Zune, and deploy and run (or debug) the game. If you run one game with debugging on, any breakpoint or exception will cause the debugged device to exit the network session. However, you should still debug at least one device if you are looking for crashes. Just be aware that this Zune will be unable to reenter into the network session. These are just some things to keep in mind when developing multiplayer applications for the Zune.

With that out of the way, let's discuss the elements that compose a multiplayer game.

Elements of a Multiplayer Game

Most multiplayer games include a certain set of elements that make the game playable, and make discovery and synchronization between devices much easier. Zune games, of course, are included under this umbrella.

Think of any multiplayer game you've ever played where the connection scheme is peer-to-peer. The three stages of a peer-to-peer multiplayer game are as follows:

- Create (or join) a game
- Lobby (a holding area for players in the session)
- Playing (where data is being sent and the game is in session)

Much of the matchmaking and lobby functionality is built into the XNA Framework, so you don't need to worry about it. You can leverage this technology in your own game screens to provide a customized experience. You can even retrieve the gamer tag associated with the Zune (if the Zune has a linked gamer tag). When it comes to sending and receiving real data, however, the implementation is solely up to you.

How Data Is Transmitted in Wireless Zune Games

As with many other network games, data is transmitted using a reliable User Datagram Protocol (UDP). You don't need to worry about that, though, because everything is abstracted nicely for you in the XNA Framework.

You have essentially two options for sending data. One is by attaching data to a network gamer's `Tag` object. This is good for attaching some custom information to any given gamer. The `Tag` property is local only, which means that the network session does not take care of synchronizing this information for you (you still need to send it using a packet writer). The other option is to send all data explicitly in the form of packets, which is demonstrated in the next example.

With that in mind, let's explore the XNA network API made available to the Zune.

The Network API and Tags

Nearly everything you need to write network games can be found in the `Microsoft.Xna.Framework.Net` namespace. The `Microsoft.Xna.Framework.GamerServices` namespace provides some functionality that is mostly specific to the Xbox 360 or Games for Windows – LIVE, such as gamer profiles and sign-in related behavior. However, it also provides a `Gamer` class, which is used to hold data about a gamer on the network. You need this information to successfully implement networking between Zunes. At the helm of network games is this `Gamer` object.

`Gamer` is an abstract class, so you are actually dealing with a local gamer (someone playing in the session on the device in front of you) or a remote gamer (someone in the session located somewhere else). Of course, on the Zune, there is only one local gamer per device, but there can be any number of remote gamers, depending on the number of connected devices. These objects contain information about the gamers in the session, such as the gamer tag associated with them. These objects are enumerable in easily accessible collections, so it's quite easy to "loop through" all of the players in the session.

Any local network gamer object also has a property attached to it called Tag, which can be any object. This is different than the gamer tag, which is a string representing the player name. The Tag object can be cast at runtime to any object of your choosing, but be careful not to overload this object with a lot of unnecessary details, as you want to minimize network traffic.

The glue between the network players is the NetworkSession class. This object is responsible for sending and receiving data, as well as discovering and connecting players. This class has asynchronously implemented methods that allow players to create and join their own network sessions. Gamers are always connected using the SystemLink attribute, which is the same session type used to connect multiple Xbox 360 consoles and players on a local area network.

It is generally a good idea to wrap the functionality in the NetworkSession class to make life a little easier for you. You'll see how this works in the next example.

Robot Tag: A Two-Player Game

Before we move into the bulk of the chapter, which covers the creation of a multiplayer Crazy Eights game that supports up to five players, we will start with a simple two-player game that tracks player positions. The important thing to learn from this example is how to send and receive data with the packet writer and packet reader objects.

Robot Tag is a simple game involving two players who chase each other around as robots. If you are chasing, it is your job to hunt down the other player as quickly as possible. If you are being chased, the object is to avoid being caught. The player who evades for the longest time across all rounds is the winner.

As shown in Figure 7-1, Robot Tag is more conceptual, so there are no frills here. It has black backgrounds, a lot of text output at the top-left corner, and so on. Keep in mind that it is but a stepping-stone to more advanced activities later in the chapter.

Figure 7-1. *The Robot Tag game*

■**Note** The foundation of the game is based on the Game State Management sample from the Creators Club web site, so I won't reprint a lot of that code here. The Game State Management sample can be found at http://creators.xna.com/en-US/samples/gamestatemanagement.

Here, I will guide you through the most important parts of this simple game and comment on what makes the network side of things tick. You will see how the game instances interface with one another on different client devices, from discovery and matchmaking to playing the game interactively. All of the networking in this sample uses the built-in functionality from the XNA Framework's `Net` and `GamerServices` namespaces, with the robot position transferred continuously via the gamer's `Tag` object.

Another thing you will notice is that this example doesn't use shared sprite batches or automatic properties, which I recommended in the previous chapter. Again, try not to focus too much on the coding style or implementation in this example. The idea is to understand how to set up a network session and transfer game data using the `Tag` property.

Let's get started checking out Robot Tag for the Zune.

Game Solution Structure

To begin, open `RobotTag.sln` from the `Examples/Chapter 7/Exercise 1/RobotTag` folder. Note the directory structure of the project, as shown in Figure 7-2. We have a game library project called `ZuneScreenManager`, which is only marginally different from what is in the Game State Management sample. It includes some abstract screen classes and menu classes, as well as a new class called `NetworkSessionManager`, which we use to wrap network functionality. Then there is the `RobotTag` Zune game project, which references the `ZuneScreenManager` project and is responsible for running the game.

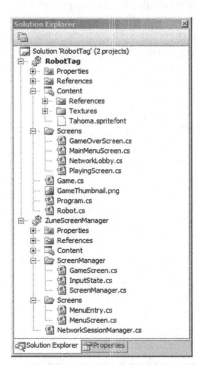

Figure 7-2. *The Solution Explorer view of Robot Tag*

The RobotTag project also includes a concrete class called Robot, which exposes a few properties and has the ability to update and draw itself, similar to a game component. Instances of this Robot class are passed around via the Tag property of the network gamer objects. The RobotTag project also includes some game state screens, textures, and a font, as it is the main project that will handle all the drawing.

Network Session Management

Let's explore how the network session is managed. Open the NetworkSessionManager.cs file from the ZuneScreenManager project. The source code for this file is shown in Listing 7-1.

Listing 7-1. *The NetworkSessionManager Class*

```
using System;
using System.Collections.Generic;
using System.Text;

using Microsoft.Xna.Framework;
using Microsoft.Xna.Framework.Net;

namespace ZuneScreenManager
{
    /// <summary>
    /// This class is responsible for managing network state in a game.
    /// </summary>
    public static class NetworkSessionManager
    {
        #region Fields

        private static NetworkSession networkSession;
        public static PacketReader PacketReader = new PacketReader();
        public static PacketWriter PacketWriter = new PacketWriter();

        #endregion

        #region Public Static Methods

        public static NetworkSession NetworkSession
        {
            get
            {
                return networkSession;
            }
        }

        public static void CreateSession(int maxNetworkPlayers)
        {
            networkSession = NetworkSession.Create(NetworkSessionType.SystemLink,
```

```
                    1, maxNetworkPlayers);
        }

        public static void JoinFirstSession()
        {
            using (AvailableNetworkSessionCollection availableSessions =
                NetworkSession.Find(NetworkSessionType.SystemLink, 1, null))
            {
                if (availableSessions.Count > 0)
                {
                    networkSession = NetworkSession.Join(availableSessions[0]);
                }
            }
        }

        public static void StartGame()
        {
            if (networkSession != null)
                networkSession.StartGame();
        }

        public static void Update()
        {
            if (networkSession != null)
                networkSession.Update();
        }

        #endregion
    }
}
```

First, notice that the NetworkSessionManager class is static. This ensures that there is only one network session in use at any given time. This also gives other classes access to the network session by using the class name only, and allows you to avoid needing to instantiate and track multiple network sessions (which is a bad idea, anyway).

In the Fields region, there is a private, static field called networkSession, which is inaccessible by other classes. This protection defers all network session processing to the manager class. The two other fields are a packet reader and a packet writer, which are used to send and receive data via the underlying protocol.

In the Public Static Methods region, you see a few different methods that are used to handle the connection process. The CreateSession method creates the network session with a session type of SystemLink (the only acceptable session type for Zune games), the maximum local players (one on the Zune), and the maximum total number of network players. This is a blocking call, and if an exception is thrown, it is not caught here. You also see a JoinFirstSession method, which uses the synchronous version of NetworkSession.Find to locate an available session and join it immediately. Later, in the Crazy Eights game example, you will learn how to enumerate network sessions asynchronously.

The Update method is responsible for pumping (forcibly updating) the network session object, which must be done as often as possible to ensure maximum responsiveness. The StartGame method calls StartGame on the underlying session object, which causes the session's state to change to Playing. This also causes the session object to fire an event called GameStarted, which this class could subscribe to. These methods are all you need to get started. They are not necessarily error-proof, but this is a Keep It Simply Simple (KISS) example.

The Robot Object

Next, open Robot.cs from the RobotTag project. The Robot class would probably be better off as a drawable game component, so keep that in mind if you choose to refactor this code. The Robot class exposes two properties: Position and Bounds. These are used to track the robot's on-screen position and the boundary area that limits the robot's movement (so a player cannot move the robot off-screen). The constructor initializes these fields and assigns a tint hue to the robot: red if this Zune is the host; blue otherwise. The constructor code is shown in Listing 7-2.

Listing 7-2. *The Robot Constructor*

```
/// <summary>
/// Creates and initializes a new Robot.
/// </summary>
/// <param name="host">Whether this robot is tied to the Host</param>
/// <param name="width">The screen width</param>
/// <param name="height">The screen height</param>
/// <param name="contentManager">Content Manager to use for loading
/// content</param>
public Robot(bool host, int width, int height, ContentManager contentManager)
{
    // Copy params to fields
    isHost = host;
    content = contentManager;
    screenWidth = width;
    screenHeight = height;

    // Load the robot texture
    texRobot = content.Load<Texture2D>("Textures/robot");

    // Set the movement limiting rectangle
    bounds = new Rectangle(0, 0,
        screenWidth - texRobot.Width, screenHeight - texRobot.Height);

    // Move the robot to its initial position
    ResetPosition();
```

```
    // Set the robot color
    if (isHost)
        robotColor = Color.Red;
    else
        robotColor = Color.Blue;
}
```

The ResetPosition method of the Robot class, shown in Listing 7-3, simply reinitializes the position depending on whether this Zune is the host.

Listing 7-3. *The ResetPosition Method of the Robot Class*

```
/// <summary>
/// Resets the robot position to game starting position
/// </summary>
public void ResetPosition()
{
    int initialX, initialY;

    // Position the robot in the center (x)
    // This is half the screen minus half the robot texture.
    initialX = screenWidth / 2 - texRobot.Width / 2;

    if (isHost)
    {
        // The host will be at the top
        initialY = 0;
    }
    else
    {
        // Other player will be at the bottom
        initialY = screenHeight - texRobot.Height;
    }

    // Set position
    position.X = initialX;
    position.Y = initialY;
}
```

There are two more public methods in the Robot class: Move and Draw. Move takes two integers for X and Y, and updates the position accordingly. Draw just draws the robot texture at its position with the assigned tint hue. See Listing 7-4 for these two methods.

Listing 7-4. *Move and Draw Methods of the Robot Class*

```
public void Move(int x, int y)
{
    position.X += x;
    position.Y += y;
}

public void Draw(SpriteBatch spriteBatch)
{
    spriteBatch.Draw(texRobot, position, robotColor);
}
```

Finally, a public static method on the Robot class determines if one robot collides with another. This method dynamically creates bounding rectangles for the robots and determines if they intersect, as shown in Listing 7-5.

Listing 7-5. *The Static Collision Method of the Robot Class*

```
public static bool Collision(Robot r1, Robot r2)
{
    Rectangle rect1 = new Rectangle((int)r1.position.X, (int)r1.position.Y,
        r1.texRobot.Width, r1.texRobot.Height);
    Rectangle rect2 = new Rectangle((int)r2.position.X, (int)r2.position.Y,
        r2.texRobot.Width, r2.texRobot.Height);

    return rect1.Intersects(rect2);
}
```

That's everything in the Robot class. This is the object that will be passed around in the network session. The Position property is what is sent across the airwaves to update the other peer.

Game Screens

Game.cs has some custom code in it, but all it really does is assign two components to the game: an instance of the screen manager component and an instance of a gamer services component, which is required to grab player information from the network session. The following line of code actually starts the game:

```
screenManager.AddScreen(new MainMenuScreen());
```

This line occurs in the constructor and adds the main menu screen to the screen manager. Now, let's take a look at some of these game screens, beginning with the main menu screen, shown in Figure 7-3.

Figure 7-3. *The main menu screen*

Open `MainMenuScreen.cs` from the `RobotTag` project's `Screens` folder. This class inherits from `MenuScreen`, a base class defined in the game state management project. This particular menu instantiates some menu items and loads a new screen based on what the user selects. The code for the main menu is shown in Listing 7-6.

Listing 7-6. *The Main Menu Screen Code*

```
using System;
using System.Collections.Generic;
using System.Text;

using Microsoft.Xna.Framework;
using Microsoft.Xna.Framework.Graphics;

using ZuneScreenManager;

namespace RobotTag
{
    /// <summary>
    /// Displays the main menu, which only has two menu items.
    /// </summary>
    public class MainMenuScreen : MenuScreen
    {
        #region Constructor(s)

        public MainMenuScreen()
            : base("Zune Tag: Main Menu")
        {
            MenuEntry menuCreate = new MenuEntry("Create Game");
            MenuEntry menuJoin = new MenuEntry("Join Game");
```

```
            // Wire up event handlers for the Menu Item Selected events
            menuCreate.Selected += new
                EventHandler<EventArgs>(MenuCreateHandler);

            menuJoin.Selected += new EventHandler<EventArgs>(MenuJoinHandler);

            // Add the menu entries to the menu
            MenuEntries.Add(menuCreate);
            MenuEntries.Add(menuJoin);
        }

        #endregion

        #region Event Handlers

        void MenuJoinHandler(object sender, EventArgs e)
        {
            ScreenManager.AddScreen(new NetworkLobby(NetworkLobbyType.Join,
                ScreenManager.Game.Content));
        }

        void MenuCreateHandler(object sender, EventArgs e)
        {
            ScreenManager.AddScreen(new NetworkLobby(NetworkLobbyType.Create,
                ScreenManager.Game.Content));
        }

        #endregion
    }
}
```

Look at the event handlers in Listing 7-6. Both cases add a new NetworkLobby screen to the screen manager, although with a different first parameter (NetworkLobbyType.Create or NetworkLobbyType.Join).

The lobby screen, shown in Figure 7-4, is designed to be dual-purpose because it is so simple. From here, a player can create or join a game. The NetworkLobby screen has only three fields: status text, a content manager for loading content, and the lobby type. Note that when a NetworkNotAvailableException is caught, this means that wireless is not enabled on the Zune. These fields are initialized in the constructor, which also creates or joins the network session depending on the lobby type. Then network session events are subscribed to. The constructor and event handlers are shown in Listing 7-7.

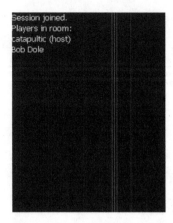

Session joined.
Players in room:
catapultic (host)
Bob Dole

Figure 7-4. *The lobby screen for a joining peer*

Listing 7-7. *The NetworkLobby Screen Constructor*

```
public NetworkLobby(NetworkLobbyType type, ContentManager content)
{
    statusText = "";
    lobbyType = type;
    contentManager = content;

    // Try to create or join the session.
    try
    {
        switch (lobbyType)
        {
            case NetworkLobbyType.Create:
                NetworkSessionManager.CreateSession(2);
                break;
            case NetworkLobbyType.Join:
                NetworkSessionManager.JoinFirstSession();
                break;
        }
    }
    catch (NetworkNotAvailableException)
    {
        statusText = "Error: Wireless is not enabled.";
    }
    catch
    {
        statusText = "An unknown error occurred.";
    }
```

```
    // Wire network session events
    if (NetworkSessionManager.NetworkSession != null)
    {
        NetworkSessionManager.NetworkSession.GamerJoined +=
            new EventHandler<GamerJoinedEventArgs>(GamerJoined);

        NetworkSessionManager.NetworkSession.GameStarted +=
            new EventHandler<GameStartedEventArgs>(GameStarted);
    }
}

void GameStarted(object sender, GameStartedEventArgs e)
{
    ScreenManager.AddScreen(new PlayingScreen());
}

void GamerJoined(object sender, GamerJoinedEventArgs e)
{
    e.Gamer.Tag = new Robot(e.Gamer.IsHost, 240, 320, contentManager);
}
```

In the GamerJoined event handler, we instantiate a new Robot object and assign it to the locally stored gamer object. This is where the robot is first brought to life in a network sense. The GameStarted event handler causes both screens to transition to the playing screen.

The Update method of the lobby screen, shown in Listing 7-8, updates the network session, and also updates the status text with the names of the players in the session and any errors that may have occurred.

Listing 7-8. *The Update Method of the NetworkLobby Screen, Responsible for Updating Status Text*

```
public override void Update(GameTime gameTime, bool otherScreenHasFocus,
    bool coveredByOtherScreen)
{
    // Update the network session
    NetworkSessionManager.Update();

    // Configure display
    switch (lobbyType)
    {
        case NetworkLobbyType.Create: // What the host sees
            statusText = "Session created.\r\nPlayers in room: ";
            statusText += GetGamerListString(
                NetworkSessionManager.NetworkSession.AllGamers);
```

```
                if (NetworkSessionManager.NetworkSession.AllGamers.Count == 2)
                {
                    statusText += "\r\n\r\nPress the middle button to start.";
                }
                break;
            case NetworkLobbyType.Join: // What the other player sees
                if (NetworkSessionManager.NetworkSession == null)
                    statusText = "No sessions found.";
                else
                {
                    statusText = "Session joined.\r\nPlayers in room: ";
                    statusText += GetGamerListString(
                        NetworkSessionManager.NetworkSession.AllGamers);
                }
                break;
        }

    base.Update(gameTime, otherScreenHasFocus, coveredByOtherScreen);
}

private string GetGamerListString(GamerCollection<NetworkGamer> gamers)
{
    string gamerString = "";
    foreach (NetworkGamer gamer in gamers)
    {
        gamerString += "\r\n" + gamer.Gamertag;
        if (gamer.IsHost)
            gamerString += " (host)";
    }
    return gamerString;
}
```

This Update method of NetworkLobby makes use of a private method called
GetGamerListString, which returns a list of all the gamers in the session. The other method
in this class, Draw (not shown), simply draws the status text on the screen at (0, 0).

Next, open the PlayingScreen.cs file from the Screens folder. This screen, shown in
Figure 7-5, is responsible for the game play, text display, texture drawing, and so on. It also
indirectly uses some network functionality. In the constructor, you will see a line that sub-
scribes to the GamerLeft event of the network session:

```
// Subscribe to the GamerLeft event
NetworkSessionManager.NetworkSession.GamerLeft += new
    EventHandler<GamerLeftEventArgs>(PlayerLeft);
```

Figure 7-5. *The playing screen*

The PlayerLeft event handler looks like this:

```
/// <summary>
/// Fired when a gamer leaves. Transitions to the Game Over screen,
/// signaling that the game was prematurely finished.
/// </summary>
/// <param name="sender"></param>
/// <param name="e"></param>
void PlayerLeft(object sender, GamerLeftEventArgs e)
{
    GameOver(true);
}
```

When the other player leaves, the game will automatically transition to the game over screen, passing a value of true to indicate that the game ended prematurely.

Now, let's see how Tag is used further to send and receive position data. Look at the UpdateNetworkSession method in PlayingScreen.cs. This is a private method that handles the sending and receiving of the one parameter we care about (Position) via packet readers and writers. Since this method is called with every update of the screen, the position is constantly being sent out and read. First, we grab the local gamer, cast its tag to a new Robot object, and write its position vector over the wire using an in-order packet delivery scheme. Then we pump the underlying network session to ensure that data gets sent. The following code block handles the "send" portion of the synchronization process; it sends the position of this gamer's robot to all other gamers.

```
private void UpdateNetworkSession()
{
    // Grab a reference to the local gamer
    LocalNetworkGamer localGamer =
        NetworkSessionManager.NetworkSession.LocalGamers[0];
```

```
// Write the local robot position into a network packet and send it
Robot robot = localGamer.Tag as Robot;
NetworkSessionManager.PacketWriter.Write(robot.Position);
localGamer.SendData(NetworkSessionManager.PacketWriter,
    SendDataOptions.InOrder);

// Pump the network session
NetworkSessionManager.Update();
/// Continued below ...
```

Next, we read and process any data sent by other players using the following pattern:

```
// Receive data from the network session
while (localGamer.IsDataAvailable)
{
    NetworkGamer sender;
    localGamer.ReceiveData(NetworkSessionManager.PacketReader, out sender);

    if (sender.IsLocal) // skip local gamers
        continue;

    // Get the sender's robot
    Robot remoteRobot = sender.Tag as Robot;
    remoteRobot.Position = NetworkSessionManager.PacketReader.ReadVector2();
}
}
```

We use a while loop, checking whether data is available for the local gamer on the Zune. We receive the data and skip the processing if the gamer is the local gamer (because the local gamer will also receive any data it sends by default). The ReceiveData method gives us a reference to the network gamer that sent the data, which in turn lets us check to see if that gamer is local and access its Tag object. Then we assign the remote Robot object's Position property to whatever the packet reader reads (a Vector2).

Now let's look at the Update method of the screen, which is responsible for drawing the updated robots on the screen. First, this method calls the UpdateNetworkSession to ensure our robots are most current. The game-play elements (such as round time) are calculated and updated, and then the Robot objects are retrieved using this block of code from the Update method:

```
Robot localRobot, remoteRobot;
localRobot = NetworkSessionManager.NetworkSession.LocalGamers[0].Tag as Robot;
remoteRobot = NetworkSessionManager.NetworkSession.RemoteGamers[0].Tag as Robot;
```

Then the collision detection method is called to determine whether the game state should advance (and in the sample code, some status text is updated):

```
if (Robot.Collision(localRobot, remoteRobot))
{
    // Hang just a sec to account for network latency
    System.Threading.Thread.Sleep(100);
    UpdateWinner(gameTime);
}
```

Notice how we hang for a bit using a Thread.Sleep. This may not be a best practice, but it's not particularly noticeable, and it gives the other device time to arrive at the same conclusion: the two objects are colliding.

The UpdateWinner method just updates the current score and tells each robot to reset its position.

```
private void UpdateWinner(GameTime gameTime)
{
    if (currentRound >= MAX_ROUNDS)
    {
        GameOver(false);
    }
    else
    {
        if (isMyTurn)
        {
            localScore = localScore.Add(roundTime);
        }
        else
        {
            remoteScore = remoteScore.Add(roundTime);
        }

        // New round
        currentRound++;
        roundStartTime = gameTime.TotalGameTime;

        Robot localRobot =
            NetworkSessionManager.NetworkSession.LocalGamers[0].Tag as Robot;
        Robot remoteRobot =
            NetworkSessionManager.NetworkSession.RemoteGamers[0].Tag as Robot;

        localRobot.ResetPosition();
        remoteRobot.ResetPosition();

        isMyTurn = !isMyTurn;
    }
}
```

If all rounds have been played, the game over screen will be shown.

Robot Tag Review

The following are the important points to take away from the Robot Tag game:

- How to create and join network sessions

- How to send and receive data with a packet reader and a packet writer

- How to use the `Tag` property to assign custom data to a local instance of a gamer object

Be sure to open the project for yourself from the `Examples/Chapter 7/Exercise 1/ RobotTag` folder and see how the game works in greater detail.

When you test the game, you will need two Zunes. Add both of them to XNA Game Studio Device Center and deploy each separately. The first deployment must be without debugging, so that you can unplug the Zune and plug in the other one. After plugging the next Zune in, change it to the default device in Device Center and deploy with or without debugging (your choice). Because it is the same game, it will behave the same on both devices, unless one device has a slower processor (as in the first-generation Zunes).

Multiplayer Crazy Eights for the Zune

The remainder of this chapter presents a guided tour of Crazy Eights for the Zune, from the ground up. You will learn how to build every aspect of this multiplayer game to the specifications we define, and we won't skip a single line of code.

The idea of building a game from the ground up naturally includes some game design. Rather than jump directly into code, we'll spend some time up-front on design work. Such work includes definition of the rules, some screen designs, definition of some networking principles, and a basic architecture for the project.

As with any software project that you can't just hack out in a night, it's important to lay the groundwork for successful implementation by gathering thoughts, brainstorming, and getting it all down on paper (or disk). The first step is to understand what Crazy Eights is in the first place.

Rules of Crazy Eights

In Crazy Eights, each player is dealt eight cards. One more card is dealt to start the discard pile, face up, and the remaining stack of cards is drawn from when a player is unable to discard. We will refer to the topmost card on the discard pile as the *active* card.

Play begins arbitrarily and moves in a defined order from player to player. When it is a player's turn, that player must select a card that matches the active card by any of the following criteria:

- The card has the same suit as the active card (clubs, spades, and so on)

- The card has the same face value as the active card (ace, five, jack, and so on)

- The card has a face value of eight (the wildcard)

The player can discard any card fitting these criteria, and the active card becomes the discarded card (so the next player must find a way to match the card discarded by the last player).

Should the player discard an eight, that player must select any suit for the next player to match against. The next player can match any card of this suit.

If the player cannot match any of the cards in their hand to the active card, he must have cards dealt to him until he has a match. After discarding, play moves to the next player in the list.

The object of the game is to run out of cards. The first player to have zero cards is the winner. Should the stack of cards to deal become empty, the current pile of discarded cards is used to deal (though the topmost discarded card remains as the active card).

Game Requirements

Here, we'll explore some high-level requirements (in the software development sense) that will drive our creation of the game.

Core Functional Requirements

In order for our game to function, it must do the following:

- Display cards graphically to the user
- Support up to five network gamers (arbitrarily defined)
- Provide a matchmaking system to create a game session
- Abide by the rules of Crazy Eights
- Cycle through player turns consistently
- Allow players to select a new suit when an eight is played
- Display the local player's hand
- Display the active card
- Notify other players of the new suit when the active suit has changed (when a player plays an eight)
- Display the name of the winner when the game is over

Enhanced Functional Requirements

These requirements add something extra to the game:

- Play a sound effect when a menu selection is changed
- Play a sound effect when a menu item is selected
- Play a sound effect when a card is selected for play by the user
- Display cards in the hand in an organized manner
- Display the selected card in the hand above the other cards to highlight it
- Play a unique sound effect when a player has lost
- Play a unique sound effect when a player has won

- Support a screen management system

- Support player-specified readiness during matchmaking (a session cannot begin until all players are ready)

Nonfunctional Requirements

The following requirements pertain to the style and approach of building the game:

- Send and receive a minimal amount of network data

- Remain synchronized with other peers

- Store only the cards needed to display the player's hand (the game will not keep track of all players' hands)

- Utilize as much local processing as possible, cutting down on network round-trips, requests, and responses

- Allow only the host of the game to manage the deck of cards

These nonfunctional requirements have a direct effect on the architecture. They force us to think about the data we choose to send. When should we send data? How much should we send? Who should process that data, and who should not?

The rule of thumb here is that if a player's Zune can operate locally without needing additional information from the host, it should do so. A good example of this is when a player discards the card she has selected. The only data that should be sent back to the host is the card she discarded. The host doesn't need to know about the new state of the player's cards, because those cards belong to the player. Building in that functionality would give only some marginal benefits—specifically, being able to enumerate every card in every player's hand (which is cheating, by the way).

These nonfunctional requirements allow us to form a clearer picture of which Zunes have certain pieces of data available to them. We can then infer more about how we will operate over the network. We'll explore this piece next.

Network State Design

Here, we lay down some simple rules regarding network data and activity that will shape the construction of the game from a network perspective.

Network Data

The nonfunctional requirements state that we should store and send data only when absolutely necessary. However, the host (the Zune that creates the network session) must contain a superset of that data to maintain consistency across all the peers. For example, if a card is dealt, it should come from the host's collection of cards. If the peer deals its own card, every peer will get a different result, because each peer would need its own deck and that deck is shuffled randomly. You could burden every peer with a full deck of cards consistent with the one the host has, but that would add unnecessary overhead and network activity to the game, so we'll just let the host Zune take care of it.

Remember that this is only one game, not two. As a result, both games will have objects to hold the same piece of data, but on the peer, those objects may be empty. For example, both games contain a player list, but only the host will populate that list. The peer never needs to use it. This emphasizes the duality of peer-to-peer gaming; any instance of the game must be capable of running as the host or as a nonhost peer.

Table 7-1 shows the pieces of data the host and peers should have in their possession during play. Remember that the host is also a player, so the host will contain a superset of the peer data, but only what is necessary to facilitate consistent game play for all peers. This table is derived not from practice, or from some formula, but from sensible thought about what the host and peer require to properly operate.

Table 7-1. *Host and Peer Data for Crazy Eights*

Data	Host	Nonhost Peers
Deck	Yes	No
Discarded cards	Yes	No
Current turn index	Yes	No
Flag indicating whether it is my turn	Yes	Yes
List of players	Yes	No
List of all players' cards	No	No
List of my cards	Yes	Yes
Active card	Yes	Yes
Active suit	Yes	Yes

Implementation of this scheme will result in peers that are "dumb" (not to be disparaging to those peers). Peers will operate under the assumption that the host will send them whatever common data and messages they need, and they will play the game accordingly. For example, a peer will ask to be dealt a card if it cannot play from its hand. The host will send cards back as long as the peer requests a card from the host's deck.

Network Messages

Just as the host and nonhost peers have some different levels of data available to them, the messages sent between the Zunes can differ. There are several messages that only the host should be capable of sending (such as "Deal a card to a player"), and those that all players can send ("I played a card," "Please deal me a new card," and "I am out of cards"). There are also some network messages that require action by only the host and should be ignored by other peers. Again, remember that the host is also a player Zune itself, and it will receive any messages it sends out. The host should also be capable of doing everything the other peers can do, such as playing a card or selecting the suit.

Table 7-2 shows the outbound network messages involved in the game and whether the host and peer should be capable of sending them.

Table 7-2. *Outbound Network Messages for Crazy Eights Host and Peers*

Message	Host	Peer
Send player data	Yes	No
Send a card	Yes	No
Deal active card	Yes	No
Send "Ready to Play"	Yes	No
Set the turn	Yes	No
My hand is complete	Yes	Yes
Play a card	Yes	Yes
Request a card	Yes	Yes
Select a suit	Yes	Yes
Game won (out of cards)	Yes	Yes

When it comes to processing network messages, there are some that only the host should take action on (such as when a player requests a card). Table 7-3 shows whether the host and peer should act on these inbound messages. Again, the host is a player, so it will process a superset of the messages processed by peers. Some of these messages have intended recipients.

Table 7-3. *Inbound Message Processing for Crazy Eights*

Message	Host	Intended Peer	Other Peers
Card dealt	No	Yes	No
All cards dealt	Yes	N/A	Yes
Common card dealt	Yes	N/A	Yes
Turn set	Yes	Yes	No
Player created	Yes	Yes	No
Card played	Yes, with additional processing	N/A	Yes
Card requested	Yes	No	No
Suit chosen	Yes	Yes	Yes
Game won	Yes	Yes	Yes

Things get a bit more complicated here. For example, every peer should act the same when someone plays an eight and chooses a suit, or when someone wins the game. However, some messages have intended recipients. When the host sets the turn, the intended recipient will assume it is his turn, and all other recipients will assume it is not their turn.

In the Robot Tag game we reviewed earlier in the chapter, two Vector2 values were continuously synchronized between two Zunes. Here, you can see from the complexity of the data, outbound network messaging, and processing requirements that we will need to build a slightly more sophisticated system to handle most of this. This realization will affect how we will build the game.

Architectural Options (High Level)

Given that we have a complex network management subsystem, we cannot (sanely) move forward building a game that lives in Game1.cs with the five standard XNA methods. We need to expand and think more broadly to make life a little easier for ourselves in the long run.

The approach we'll use is to build a game state management library that defines some foundational logic for managing screens. This library contains abstract base classes for game screen and menu objects, and also provides a mechanism for sharing resources such as fonts. Any screen that inherits from the base screen can load its own content, update, and draw itself. Screens can also add or remove screens from the screen manager to transition between game states. This allows us to create screens that map to the various game states: main menu, create game, join game, lobby, playing, and game over.

Because we are using this specialized system, traditional game components don't work as well as we might want, because game components are added to the main game's collection of components. We will need to create our own type of component that can be added to a screen object—the screen will handle all of its own components. This gives us one library project so far: the screen manager library.

Because we are striving for a proper object-oriented Zen solution, it makes sense to create a library for all card operations to hold logic common to all card games. This would give us a Card object, a Deck object (that can shuffle, deal, and reset itself), and some helper methods that let us serialize a card for network transmission or compare a card to another card based on its suit and/or value. This project could be used and extended further in other card games.

The final project is the Zune game itself, which references the screen management library and the card game functionality library.

When it comes to the architecture of the Zune game itself, we will use components, screens, and more to tie everything together. Of course, when you build your own games, the object model and architecture are entirely up to you and what you think is prudent.

Screen Design

Are you an "art first" or "functionality first" programmer? Some people can't envision the final product without art in their hands. Others don't want to be constrained by having the art first, as it may cause them to overthink their implementation approach. In any case, having some mockups (at the very least) can help guide you. In the creation of this particular game, I got the foreground of the game (the cards, text, and most of the processing) working before I added pretty backgrounds for the screens.

Here, we will look at the screens used in the game so you can see what you will be up against in terms of implementation. We'll go over these screens in the order in which they would appear during a normal play session. Now, we are beginning to transition out of the "thinking" phase and into the "doing" phase, for you will also learn about the behavior of these screens. This provides more granular requirements-level detail for each screen, much like a functional specification. There are several embedded use cases for each of these screens, but we won't go into too much detail until we start building them.

The Main Menu Screen

The main menu screen, shown in Figure 7-6, is the first one shown in the game. It displays three menu items: Create Game, Join Game, and Quit. The game will transition (or quit) depending on which menu item has been selected. If Create Game is selected, the new game screen will be shown. If Join Game is selected, the join game screen will be shown. If Quit is selected, the game should exit. The currently selected menu item is highlighted. The background color of the screen is green (like a card table), and the text is white. A sound effect is played when you select or choose a menu item.

Figure 7-6. *The main menu screen for Crazy Eights*

The Create Game Screen

The create game screen, shown in Figure 7-7, is responsible for creating the network session and displaying the list of players in the network session. When all players have signaled they are ready, the host can start the game manually. The background is green, and the text is white. This screen does not transition to the lobby screen; it doesn't need to because it already knows who all the players are and whether they are ready.

Figure 7-7. *The create game screen with one other player who is not ready*

The Join Game Screen

The join game screen, shown in Figure 7-8, enumerates all available network sessions and allows you to select from one of them. Joining a game brings you to the lobby screen. The network session has the same name as the Zune that is hosting it.

Figure 7-8. *The join game screen with one available network session*

The Lobby Screen

The lobby screen, shown in Figure 7-9, is where joining players are sent to wait for the host to start the game. It looks similar to the create game screen for the host, but it sits and waits for the game to start, while providing a status message.

Figure 7-9. *The lobby screen*

The Playing Screen

The playing screen, shown in Figure 7-10, is what players see during the game. It's a very simple design, with one card at the top (the active card to match) and the cards in your hand.

This screen allows you to select from available cards, request new cards (when no playable cards are available), and play cards. If an eight is played, the game transitions to the suit selection screen before playing the eight. The actively selected card is shown above all the other cards. Dim (gray) cards cannot be played. If it is not your turn, or if you have no available cards to play, the status text will be different. A sound effect is played when a card is selected in the hand.

Figure 7-10. *The main game play screen when it is your turn*

The Suit Selection Screen

When you play an eight, you will be asked to choose a suit, as shown in Figure 7-11. A sound effect is played when the suit is selected or chosen. When you select the suit, game play will resume at the playing screen.

Figure 7-11. *The suit selection screen*

When another player changes the suit, you will see a graphic indicating that an eight was played and the player's selection for the new suit, as shown in Figure 7-12.

Figure 7-12. *The playing screen with suit changed notification (and no matching cards to play)*

The Game Over Screen

When a player plays his last card, all peers will transition to the game over screen. If the winner's name is the same as your name, you will receive a "You Win" type of message. Otherwise, you will be informed that you have lost, and the name of the winner will be displayed, as shown in Figure 7-13. An appropriate sound effect will also be played.

Figure 7-13. *The game over screen*

Now that you have a good idea what our game will look like, it's time to begin the uphill climb of putting together the code for the game. We will start with the card game library, CardLib.

Building the Card Library

First, we'll build a Zune game library that exposes a Card object and a Deck object. The Card object has a suit and a value, and is comparable to other cards. It can also be serialized into string format for network transmission. The Deck object contains a list of Card objects, and it exposes methods such as Shuffle and Deal to perform basic deck-related operations.

We'll begin by creating the overall solution for our game, and add a new game library to it. We will then add the objects in a bottom-up manner.

1. Create a new Zune Game project called CrazyEights.

2. Add a new Zune Game Library project called CardLib to the solution. Delete any class files that are automatically created.

Adding Suit and Card Value Types

A playing card has a value and a suit. Let's create an enumeration to specify the suit of the card first.

1. In the CardLib project, add a new class called Suit.cs. This file will contain one simple enumeration: Suit.

```csharp
using System;

namespace CardLib
{
    public enum Suit : byte
    {
        Undefined  = 0,
        Clubs      = 1,
        Diamonds   = 2,
        Hearts     = 3,
        Spades     = 4
    }
}
```

At first glance, the ordering and assignment of these enumeration values may seem arbitrary. On further inspection, you notice that they are ordered alphabetically. Furthermore, you will see that the graphical representation of the deck we are using is ordered this way: Clubs, Diamonds, Hearts, and Spades. This is the real driver behind ordering and assigning these enumeration values as such: it makes it far easier to index a card from the image of cards this way. We'll cover this topic in more detail in the "Creating the Player View Component" section later in this chapter. For now, enjoy the fact that the first file we've created has only 13 lines of code—things will become more complex soon enough!

Now that we have the type for a card's suit, we should determine how to store a card's value. For some, a simple integer would do the trick. However, we want to perform some error-checking and provide some further functionality specific to card games. For example, a value of 1 means ace. A king is the same thing as the value 13. You could extend this class to modify the value of the ace to be the highest in a game like poker. This class also overrides the ToString method, which will give us a useful textual description of the card value, such as Ace, Two, Three, Four, Jack, King, and so on.

2. In the CardLib project, add a new class called CardValue.cs. You need only the System namespace here. The empty class definition in the file looks something like the following code. (The comment should be deleted when you start implementing the class in step 3).

```
using System;

namespace CardLib
{
    public class CardValue
    {
        // Implementation to follow...
    }
}
```

3. Add a region for Fields to the CardValue class. The important fields are the numeric value and the string value, both of which are initialized in the constructor.

```
#region Fields

public string ValueText
{
    get;
    private set;
}

public int Value
{
    get;
    private set;
}

#endregion
```

4. Add a region for Constants. These define card values for the ace, jack, queen, and king.

```
#region Constants

public const int ACE = 1;
public const int JACK = 11;
public const int QUEEN = 12;
public const int KING = 13;

#endregion
```

5. Add a region for the Constructor(s). The constructor takes in the value you want to assign, does some domain checking (the card value must be between low ace and high king), and assigns the textual representation of the card value based on the numeric one passed in via a large switch statement.

```csharp
#region Constructor(s)

public CardValue(int value)
{
    // Check the card value's range
    if (value < 1 || value > KING)
    {
        throw new ArgumentException(
            "Card value must be between 1 and 13 inclusive.");
    }
    else
    {
        Value = value;
        switch (Value)
        {
            case ACE:
                ValueText = "Ace";
                break;
            case 2:
                ValueText = "Two";
                break;
            case 3:
                ValueText = "Three";
                break;
            case 4:
                ValueText = "Four";
                break;
            case 5:
                ValueText = "Five";
                break;
            case 6:
                ValueText = "Six";
                break;
            case 7:
                ValueText = "Seven";
                break;
            case 8:
                ValueText = "Eight";
                break;
            case 9:
                ValueText = "Nine";
                break;
            case 10:
                ValueText = "Ten";
                break;
            case JACK:
                ValueText = "Jack";
```

```
                break;
            case QUEEN:
                ValueText = "Queen";
                break;
            case KING:
                ValueText = "King";
                break;
        }
    }
}
```

```
#endregion
```

6. Finally, add the ToString override in a new Overrides region, which just returns the ValueText field. This makes it easier when concatenating strings.

```
#region Overrides
```

```
public override string ToString()
{
    return ValueText;
}
```

```
#endregion
```

Now, we have objects for Suit and CardValue. Next, we'll utilize both of these types in the creation of our Card class.

Creating the Card Class

A Card object is composed of a Suit object and a CardValue object. The Card class also exposes some other useful functionality, such as comparison, serialization, and an overload of ToString to produce a pretty result (such as Ace of Clubs).

Once again, we'll start with a shell of a class called Card and implement it step by step.

1. In the CardLib project, add a new class called Card.cs. Rearrange the code to look like the following stub. Note that the class implements the IComparable interface, allowing us to specify how to compare the card to other cards.

```
using System;
```

```
namespace CardLib
{
    public class Card : IComparable
    {
        // Implementation to follow...
    }
}
```

2. Add a region to contain the four fields: suit, value, a flag specifying whether the card is properly defined, and a flag specifying whether the card is to be shown. The latter field is not used in the Crazy Eights game, but could be used in other card games that require face-down cards.

```
#region Fields

public Suit Suit
{
    get;
    private set;
}

public CardValue CardValue
{
    get;
    private set;
}

public bool IsDefined
{
    get;
    private set;
}

public bool IsShown // Not used in Crazy Eights
{
    get;
    private set;
}

#endregion
```

3. Add a region for constructors. There are three ways to construct a Card object: create a card with a known suit and value, create an undefined card, or identify a card sent over the network. The latter constructor receives an integer index from 1 to 52 and retrieves the card uniquely.

```
#region Constructor(s)

public Card(Suit suit, CardValue value)
{
    Suit = suit;
    CardValue = value;
    IsDefined = true;
    IsShown = false;
}
```

```
public Card()
{
    Suit = Suit.Undefined;
    CardValue = null;
    IsDefined = false;
}

public Card(int value)
{
    if (value < 1 || value > 52)
        throw new ArgumentException("Card value must be between 1 and 52.");

    Suit = (Suit)(value / 13);

    int cardValue = value % 13;
    if (cardValue == 0)
        cardValue = CardValue.KING;

    CardValue = new CardValue(cardValue);

    IsDefined = true;
}

#endregion
```

4. Add a region for public methods. These methods are accessible from any Card object instance. The first method, Serialize, converts the card to an integer from 1 to 52, representing its position in an unshuffled deck. The second method, GetSuitName, gets a proper string value for a suit.

```
#region Public Methods

public int Serialize()
{
    int row = (int)Suit;
    return (row * 13) + (CardValue.Value % 13);
}

public string GetSuitName()
{
    switch (Suit)
    {
        case Suit.Clubs:
            return "Clubs";
        case Suit.Diamonds:
            return "Diamonds";
        case Suit.Hearts:
            return "Hearts";
```

```
        case Suit.Spades:
            return "Spades";
        default:
            return "Undefined";
    }
}
```

```
#endregion
```

5. Add a region for overridden methods and operators. Here, we will define the operators > and <, which we can use to compare two cards by value. We will also define the ToString implementation for the card.

```
#region Overridden Methods and Operators

public override string ToString()
{
    return string.Concat(CardValue.ToString(), " of ", GetSuitName());}

public static bool operator >(Card x, Card y)
{
    return x.CardValue.Value > y.CardValue.Value;
}

public static bool operator <(Card x, Card y)
{
    return x.CardValue.Value < y.CardValue.Value;
}

#endregion
```

6. Add a region called IComparable, which implements the required functionality for the IComparable interface. This allows us to specify how to compare two cards. In this case, we compare by card value only using the operator overloads we defined in step 5.

```
#region IComparable

public int CompareTo(object value)
{
    Card card = value as Card;

    if (card == null)
    {
        throw new ArgumentException(
            "Can only compare Cards to other Cards.");
    }
```

```
        if (this < card)
            return -1;
        else if (this == card)
            return 0;
        else
            return 1;
    }


    #endregion
```

That wraps up our Card class. This class provides some useful methods that will come in handy later. Next, let's wrap this Card object into a manager class of sorts, called Deck.

Creating the Deck Class

The Deck class is very important, because it can instantiate a whole new list of properly valued cards, shuffle them, and deal from that collection. One unique thing about this particular implementation of the card deck is that it includes a separate collection for discarded cards, making this object more of a dealer than a deck. For our purposes, however, this will work well, because Crazy Eights requires that the deck keep track of discarded cards.

1. In the CardLib project, add a new class called Deck.cs with the following stub:

```
using System;
using System.Collections.Generic;

namespace CardLib
{
    public class Deck
    {
        // Implementation to follow...
    }
}
```

2. Add a region for Fields. This region contains the list of cards in the undealt deck, the list of discarded cards, and a private Random object used for shuffling.

```
#region Fields

private Random random;

public List<Card> Cards
{
    get;
    private set;
}
```

```
public List<Card> DiscardedCards
{
    get;
    private set;
}
```

```
#endregion
```

3. Add a Constants region, where we simply define that there are 52 cards in a deck.

```
#region Constants
```

```
public const int CARDS_IN_DECK = 52;
```

```
#endregion
```

4. Add a region for Constructor(s). In the sole constructor, we initialize our fields.

```
#region Constructor(s)
```

```
public Deck()
{
    Cards = new List<Card>(CARDS_IN_DECK);
    DiscardedCards = new List<Card>();
    random = new Random();
}
```

```
#endregion
```

5. Add a region for Private Methods. We have one method here that swaps a card with another card, used by the shuffling algorithm.

```
#region Private Methods
```

```
private void SwapCardsByIndex(int index1, int index2)
{
    // Get the two cards
    Card x, y;
    x = Cards[index1];
    y = Cards[index2];

    // Swap the cards
    Cards[index1] = y;
    Cards[index2] = x;
}
```

```
#endregion
```

6. Add a region for `Public Methods`, and begin it with the `ResetDeck` method. This method creates a properly ordered list of 52 cards and clears the discarded list.

```
public void ResetDeck()
{
    Cards.Clear();

    // For each of the four suits (which are alphabetically ordered
    // from 1 - 4)
    for (int suitIndex = (int)Suit.Clubs;
        suitIndex <= (int)Suit.Spades; suitIndex++)
    {
        // For each possible card index
        for (int cardIndex = 1; cardIndex <= CardValue.KING; cardIndex++)
        {
            // Add the card
            Cards.Add(new Card((Suit)suitIndex, new CardValue(cardIndex)));
        }
    }
}
```

7. Add a method called `ReloadFromDiscarded` to the `Public Methods` region. This method is responsible for copying the cards in the discarded pile to the main deck, while retaining the topmost discarded card in the discard pile. The effect of this method is that all the cards below the topmost discarded card are moved into the main deck, mimicking how you would pick up those cards, turn them over, and start dealing from them again during a Crazy Eights game.

```
public void ReloadFromDiscarded()
{
    if (DiscardedCards.Count == 0)
    {
        throw new Exception("No cards have been discarded; cannot reload.");
    }

    Cards.Clear();
    Cards.AddRange(DiscardedCards);

    // Get the last discarded card
    Card newCard = DiscardedCards[DiscardedCards.Count - 1];

    // Remove that discarded card from the deck
    Cards.Remove(newCard);

    // Clear the discarded card list and re-add the topmost card
    DiscardedCards.Clear();
    DiscardedCards.Add(newCard);
}
```

8. Add a method called Shuffle to the Public Methods region. This method follows the Knuth-Fisher-Yates card-shuffling algorithm, which is one of the most effective shuffling algorithms available. This algorithm randomly swaps every card in the deck with another random card in the deck. You can read more about the card-shuffling algorithm at http://www.codinghorror.com/blog/archives/001015.html.

```
public void Shuffle()
{
    for (int cardIndex = Cards.Count - 1; cardIndex > 0; cardIndex--)
    {
        int randomIndex = random.Next(cardIndex + 1);
        SwapCardsByIndex(cardIndex, randomIndex);
    }
}
```

9. Add a new method called Deal to the Public Methods region. This method attempts to deal a card from the current deck. If there are no cards left in the deck, it will reload the deck with the discarded pile. The topmost card is dealt, removed from the deck, and returned by the method.

```
public Card Deal()
{
    if (Cards.Count <= 0)
        ReloadFromDiscarded();

    Card card = Cards[Cards.Count - 1];
    Cards.Remove(card);
    return card;
}
```

10. Finally, add a method called Discard to the Public Methods region (and close the region). This method adds a card to the discarded pile.

```
public void Discard(Card card)
{
    DiscardedCards.Add(card);
}
```

With that, we have completed the Deck class and the CardLib project. You can compile this project and add unit tests if you wish. One of the major benefits of extracting independent logic to other projects is the high level of testability you get.

Consider doing this for other game objects as well. Complex calculations and logic benefit greatly from automated tests. If you were to write a game like Hold 'em poker, you would most certainly want automated tests in place to ensure that hypothetical methods like IsStraight and IsFlush are working perfectly!

With our CardLib project complete, it is time to address the other project: the screen manager project.

Building the Screen Manager Library

In many cases, you might take the code from the Game State Management sample on the Creators Club web site and port it to a Zune game library for use in your game. This is a perfectly acceptable approach. However, our game will require some customization. First, we want to be able to add components to individual screens, not to the main game object. To accomplish this, we'll need to create our own types of components and allow the screen manager to manage them as well on a per-screen basis.

The screen manager project presents considerable opportunity for us. Because this is an object that will be accessible to all of our game screens, we can embed certain resources here that are intended to be shared, such as a network manager, a shared sprite batch, general sound effects, fonts, menu functionality, and so on. As with the card library, we will build this library from the bottom up (starting with the most granular objects).

Creating the Project and Adding Content

First, we'll create the project and add some content that will be used for any screens that utilize this subsystem.

1. Add a new Zune Game Library project to the solution. Name it GameStateManager.

2. Add two new folders to the Content project of this game library: MenuSounds and Fonts.

3. Right-click the MenuSounds folder you just created and choose Add ➤ Existing Item. Navigate to the Examples/Chapter 7/SoundFX folder and add two of the WAV files there: Selected.wav and SelectChanged.wav. These are the sound effects that will be played as the user cycles through menu options.

4. Right-click the Fonts folder you created. Add two new sprite fonts. The first should be called KootenayLarge.spritefont and should be 13-point Kootenay. The second should be KootenaySmall.spritefont, which is 10-point Kootenay. In both cases, the font will be Kootenay by default, but you can adjust the size of the font by opening the sprite font definition file and changing the Size element manually.

5. Add the input state manager and shared sprite batch class to the project. To do this, right-click the GameStateManager project, choose Add ➤ Existing Item, and navigate to the Examples/Chapter 7/Shared folder. Add InputState.cs and SharedSpriteBatch.cs to the project. The namespaces in these files have already been updated for this project.

Creating Custom Components

Next, let's work on creating our own brand of game components. The types of game components provided by the XNA Framework are always added to the main game's collection, which is not optimal for our case, because we want each screen to manage these components. We also want these components to go away when the associated screen goes out of scope.

We will follow the pattern of the XNA Framework, by having one updatable component type and one drawable component type that can do everything the updatable component can do.

1. In the GameStateManager project, add a new class, called LogicComponent.cs. This is the component that can be updated but not drawn. The stub for this class should look like this:

```
using Microsoft.Xna.Framework;

namespace GameStateManager
{
    public abstract class LogicComponent
    {
        // Implementation to follow...
    }
}
```

2. Add a Fields region to the LogicComponent class. The only field here is a reference back to the screen manager object managing all the screens.

```
#region Fields

public ScreenManager ScreenManager
{
    get;
    private set;
}

#endregion
```

3. Add a region for Constructor(s), and add the simple constructor that sets the screen manager object.

```
#region Constructor(s)

public LogicComponent(ScreenManager screenManager)
{
    ScreenManager = screenManager;
}

#endregion
```

4. Add a region called Overridable Methods. These are methods that any derived LogicComponent should override to specify the logic for that component. This component type can be only initialized and updated, as there is no content to load or draw.

```
#region Overridable Methods

public virtual void Initialize() { }

public virtual void Update(GameTime gameTime) { }

#endregion
```

5. Add a new class to the project called DrawableComponent.cs. This class defines a new type of component that can do everything a LogicComponent can do (thanks to inheritance), and can also load content and draw to the graphics device. The extended functionality is simple and short, as there are only two additional methods, so the entire class is shown in the following snippet.

```
using Microsoft.Xna.Framework;

namespace GameStateManager
{
    public class DrawableComponent : LogicComponent
    {
        public DrawableComponent(ScreenManager screenManager)
            : base(screenManager)
        {

        }

        public virtual void LoadContent() { }

        public virtual void Draw(GameTime gameTime) { }
    }
}
```

In case you were wondering, the reason that both types of components require a reference to the screen manager is so that these components can access the shared resources provided by the screen manager (fonts, network management, and so on). The other classes we build into this project will call the appropriate methods on these components automatically.

We have achieved the same effect as the XNA Framework's game component architecture, but we can attach these components to individual screens, rather than needing to attach them to the overarching Game object.

Next, we'll examine the ScreenManager game component, which manages a collection of BaseScreen objects. This class handles a lot of the plumbing for displaying and updating layered screens. The BaseScreen class is discussed afterward.

Creating the Screen Manager Component

The code for the ScreenManager class is borrowed heavily from the XNA Creators Club Game State Management sample, with a few modifications. You can find the Game State Management sample at http://creators.xna.com/en-US/samples/gamestatemanagement.

1. In the GameStateManager project, add a new class called ScreenManager.cs. Note that this is a true DrawableGameComponent, not one of our custom component types; this is because we want to attach this object to the main game's Components collection.

```
using System.Collections.Generic;
using Microsoft.Xna.Framework;
using Microsoft.Xna.Framework.Graphics;
using Microsoft.Xna.Framework.Content;
```

```
namespace GameStateManager
{
    public class ScreenManager : DrawableGameComponent
    {
        // Implementation to follow...
    }
}
```

2. Add a new region to this class called `Fields`. Add two private collections of `BaseScreen` objects. The first collection contains all the screens managed by the screen manager, and the second contains a list of the screens that need to be updated. Also, add a Boolean variable that will indicate whether the screen manager has been fully initialized.

```
#region Fields

private List<BaseScreen> allScreens = new List<BaseScreen>();
private List<BaseScreen> screensToUpdate = new List<BaseScreen>();

private bool isInitialized;

#endregion
```

3. Add the following fields to the `Fields` region. These objects give all screens access to important shared resources, including the `NetworkManager` object (which we have not added yet).

```
public InputState Input
{
    get;
    private set;
}

public SpriteFont LargeFont
{
    get;
    private set;
}

public SpriteFont SmallFont
{
    get;
    private set;
}

public ContentManager Content
{
    get;
    private set;
}
```

```
public GraphicsDevice Graphics
{
    get;
    private set;
}

public NetworkManager Network
{
    get;
    private set;
}
```

4. Add a region called `Constructor(s)` and add the default constructor, which initializes game components and adds them to the game's `Components` collection.

```
#region Constructor(s)

public ScreenManager(Game game)
    : base(game)
{
    this.Input = new InputState(game);
    this.Network = new NetworkManager(game);

    game.Components.Add(this.Input);
    game.Components.Add(this.Network);
}

#endregion
```

5. Add a region for the overridden methods for the drawable game component, called `GameComponent Overrides`. Add the `Initialize`, `LoadContent`, and `UnloadContent` override methods to this region.

```
#region GameComponent Overrides

public override void Initialize()
{
    base.Initialize();

    isInitialized = true;
}

protected override void LoadContent()
{
    // Load the default fonts
    Content = Game.Content;
    Graphics = Game.GraphicsDevice;
    LargeFont = Content.Load<SpriteFont>("Fonts/KootenayLarge");
    SmallFont = Content.Load<SpriteFont>("Fonts/KootenaySmall");
```

```
        // Tell each of the screens to load their content.
        foreach (BaseScreen screen in allScreens)
        {
            screen.LoadContent();
        }
    }

    protected override void UnloadContent()
    {
        // Tell each of the screens to unload their content.
        foreach (BaseScreen screen in allScreens)
        {
            screen.UnloadContent();
        }
    }

    #endregion
```

6. Add the Update method to the GameComponent Overrides region. This method introduces two new concepts: whether a particular screen is active or covered by another screen. These values are used to determine whether or not to update this screen. Notice that these values are also passed to the BaseScreen object's Update method, which takes these values as parameters in addition to the GameTime.

```
public override void Update(GameTime gameTime)
{
    // Make a copy of the master screen list, to avoid confusion if
    // the process of updating one screen adds or removes others.
    screensToUpdate.Clear();
    screensToUpdate.AddRange(allScreens);

    bool otherScreenHasFocus = !Game.IsActive;
    bool coveredByOtherScreen = false;

    // Loop as long as there are screens waiting to be updated.
    while (screensToUpdate.Count > 0)
    {
        // Pop the topmost screen off the waiting list.
        BaseScreen screen = screensToUpdate[screensToUpdate.Count - 1];
        screensToUpdate.Remove(screen);

        // Update the screen.
        screen.Update(gameTime, otherScreenHasFocus, coveredByOtherScreen);

        if (screen.ScreenState == ScreenState.TransitionOn ||
            screen.ScreenState == ScreenState.Active)
        {
            // If this is the first active screen we came across,
```

```
        // give it a chance to handle input.
        if (!otherScreenHasFocus)
        {
            screen.HandleInput(Input);

            otherScreenHasFocus = true;
        }

        // If this is an active non-popup, inform any subsequent
        // screens that they are covered by it.
        if (!screen.IsPopup)
            coveredByOtherScreen = true;
        }
    }
}
```

7. Add the Draw method to the GameComponent Overrides region. This screen handles the drawing of all the individual screens in the screen manager. Hidden screens are not drawn.

```
public override void Draw(GameTime gameTime)
{
    foreach (BaseScreen screen in allScreens)
    {
        if (screen.ScreenState != ScreenState.Hidden)
            screen.Draw(gameTime);
    }
}
```

8. Add a new region called Public Methods. These methods allow your code to interface with the screen manager by adding, removing, and accessing screens. Add the following three methods to that region. Notice that the AddScreen method also causes the added screen to initialize and load content.

```
#region Public Methods

public void AddScreen(BaseScreen screen)
{
    screen.ScreenManager = this;
    screen.IsExiting = false;

    screen.Initialize();

    // If we have a graphics device, tell the screen to load content.
    if (isInitialized)
    {
        screen.LoadContent();
    }
```

```
        allScreens.Add(screen);
    }

    public void RemoveScreen(BaseScreen screen)
    {
        // If we have a graphics device, tell the screen to unload content.
        if (isInitialized)
        {
            screen.UnloadContent();
        }

        allScreens.Remove(screen);
        screensToUpdate.Remove(screen);
    }

    #endregion
```

That concludes the code for the ScreenManager class. We still have some holes in the project, however. The ScreenManager class uses a class called BaseScreen as well as a NetworkManager class. We will look at BaseScreen next.

Creating the BaseScreen Class

The BaseScreen class is an abstract class that contains all the functionality common to all screens. Real screens inherit from this class and override the behavior defined here. This class also handles the screen-transition logic. As with the ScreenManager class, plenty of the code for BaseScreen is borrowed from the Game State Management sample.

1. In the GameStateManager project, add a new class called BaseScreen.cs. The stub for this file also includes an enumeration for the screen state.

```
using System;
using System.Collections.Generic;
using Microsoft.Xna.Framework;

namespace GameStateManager
{
    public enum ScreenState
    {
        TransitionOn,
        Active,
        TransitionOff,
        Hidden,
    }

    public abstract class BaseScreen
    {
        // Implementation to follow...
    }
}
```

2. Add a region called `Fields` to the `BaseScreen` class definition. Add the list of our custom component type.

```
#region Fields

public List<LogicComponent> Components
{
    get;
    private set;
}


#endregion
```

3. Add the following fields that deal with the screen's transitions to the `Fields` region. The `TransitionAlpha` value can be used to fade between screens or to fade text during transitions (such as in menus).

```
public TimeSpan TransitionOnTime
{
    get;
    protected set;
}

public TimeSpan TransitionOffTime
{
    get;
    protected set;
}

public float TransitionPosition
{
    get;
    protected set;
}

public byte TransitionAlpha
{
    get { return (byte)(255 - TransitionPosition * 255); }
}
```

4. In the `Fields` region, add the following fields, which track various aspects of the screen's status:

```
protected bool otherScreenHasFocus;

public bool IsInitialized
{
    get;
    private set;
}
```

```
public bool IsContentLoaded
{
    get;
    private set;
}

public ScreenState ScreenState
{
    get;
    protected set;
}

public bool IsExiting
{
    get;
    protected internal set;
}

public bool IsPopup
{
    get;
    protected set;
}

public bool IsActive
{
    get
    {
        return !otherScreenHasFocus &&
            (ScreenState == ScreenState.TransitionOn ||
             ScreenState == ScreenState.Active);
    }
}
```

5. In the Fields region, add a final field that will allow the screen to reference the screen manager to which it is attached.

```
public ScreenManager ScreenManager
{
    get;
    internal set;
}
```

6. Create a new region for the constructor called Constructor(s). Add the following constructor to that region. This constructor initializes some fields (including the component collection) and sets the initial screen state to TransitionOn, since any newly added screen should be transitioning on.

```
#region Constructor(s)

public BaseScreen()
{
    Components = new List<LogicComponent>();
    IsInitialized = false;
    IsContentLoaded = false;
    ScreenState = ScreenState.TransitionOn;
}

#endregion
```

7. Add a new region called `Public Virtual Methods`. These methods should be overridden
by concrete screen classes to specify the logic for those screens. Add the `Initialize`
and `LoadContent` methods, which are responsible for explicitly telling all of the screen's
components to initialize and load content (if the component is drawable).

```
#region Public Virtual Methods

public virtual void Initialize()
{
    if (!IsInitialized)
    {
        foreach (LogicComponent component in Components)
        {
            component.Initialize();
        }
        IsInitialized = true;
    }
}

public virtual void LoadContent()
{
    if (!IsContentLoaded)
    {
        // Initialize all components
        foreach (LogicComponent component in Components)
        {

            DrawableComponent drawable = component as DrawableComponent;
            if (drawable != null)
                drawable.LoadContent();
        }
        IsContentLoaded = true;
    }
}

#endregion
```

8. Add virtual stubs for UnloadContent and HandleInput to the Public Virtual Methods region. There is nothing the base class should do here, so the concrete class must override these methods for there to be any effect.

```
public virtual void UnloadContent() { }

public virtual void HandleInput(InputState input) { }
```

9. In the Public Virtual Methods region, add the Update method, which checks and manipulates the various statuses of the screen to update transitions before explicitly updating all of the child components of the screen. This is mostly straight from the Game State Management sample, except that the last block in this function will explicitly update all of the game's child components.

```
public virtual void Update(GameTime gameTime, bool otherScreenHasFocus,
    bool coveredByOtherScreen)
{
    this.otherScreenHasFocus = otherScreenHasFocus;

    if (IsExiting)
    {
        // If the screen is going away to die, it should transition off.
        ScreenState = ScreenState.TransitionOff;

        if (!UpdateTransition(gameTime, TransitionOffTime, 1))
        {
            // When the transition finishes, remove the screen.
            ScreenManager.RemoveScreen(this);
        }
    }
    else if (coveredByOtherScreen)
    {
        // If the screen is covered by another, it should transition off.
        if (UpdateTransition(gameTime, TransitionOffTime, 1))
        {
            // Still busy transitioning.
            ScreenState = ScreenState.TransitionOff;
        }
        else
        {
            // Transition finished!
            ScreenState = ScreenState.Hidden;
        }
    }
    else
    {
        // Otherwise the screen should transition on and become active.
        if (UpdateTransition(gameTime, TransitionOnTime, -1))
        {
```

```
                // Still busy transitioning.
                ScreenState = ScreenState.TransitionOn;
            }
            else
            {
                // Transition finished!
                ScreenState = ScreenState.Active;

                // Update all components
                foreach (LogicComponent component in Components)
                {
                    component.Update(gameTime);
                }
            }
        }
    }
}
```

10. Add the `Draw` method to the `Public Virtual Methods` region. This method causes all
    of the drawable components to be drawn. Calling `base.Draw` from a concrete screen's
    overridden `Draw` method will cause all components to be drawn, mirroring the existing
    pattern for `DrawableGameComponent` in the XNA Framework.

```
public virtual void Draw(GameTime gameTime)
{
    foreach (LogicComponent component in Components)
    {
        DrawableComponent drawable = component as DrawableComponent;
        if (drawable != null)
            drawable.Draw(gameTime);
    }
}
```

11. Add a region called `Public Methods`. This region contains one method to explicitly
    exit the screen. This method utilizes the transition timings to allow a screen to grace-
    fully disappear, rather than instantly disappearing when `RemoveScreen` is called on the
    screen manager.

```
#region Public Methods

public void ExitScreen()
{
    if (TransitionOffTime == TimeSpan.Zero)
    {
        // If the screen has a zero transition time, remove it immediately.
        ScreenManager.RemoveScreen(this);
    }
    else
    {
        // Otherwise flag that it should transition off and then exit.
```

```
            IsExiting = true;
        }
    }
```

```
#endregion
```

12. Finally, add a region called Helper Methods, which contains one method called
    UpdateTransition. This method, included in the Game State Management sample,
    allows the screen to determine where it is in terms of transition.

```
#region Helper Methods

protected bool UpdateTransition(GameTime gameTime, TimeSpan time, ➡
int direction)
{
    // How much should we move by?
    float transitionDelta;

    if (time == TimeSpan.Zero)
        transitionDelta = 1;
    else
        transitionDelta = (float)(gameTime.ElapsedGameTime.TotalMilliseconds /
                            time.TotalMilliseconds);

    // Update the transition position.
    TransitionPosition += transitionDelta * direction;

    // Did we reach the end of the transition?
    if ((TransitionPosition <= 0) || (TransitionPosition >= 1))
    {
        TransitionPosition = MathHelper.Clamp(TransitionPosition, 0, 1);
        return false;
    }

    // Otherwise we are still busy transitioning.
    return true;
}

#endregion
```

That concludes the code for the BaseScreen object. We will utilize most of this functionality, although some of it may go untouched. It's useful to see, however, because you may want it in place when creating your own games.

Next, we'll look at a base menu screen that we can use to create single-selection menus.

Creating the MenuEntry Class

The base menu screen is composed of a list of MenuEntry objects, so we'll look at the MenuEntry class first. This class raises an event when the entry is selected, and updates itself with a pulsating effect when the menu item is active.

1. In the GameStateManager project, add a new class called MenuEntry.cs.

```
using System;
using Microsoft.Xna.Framework;
using Microsoft.Xna.Framework.Graphics;

namespace GameStateManager
{
    public class MenuEntry
    {
        // Implementation to follow...
    }
}
```

2. Add a region called Fields and add the following fields to that region. The font field allows us to specify a unique font per menu item. The selectionFade variable is used internally for the pulsating effect, and the Text property allows us to assign or retrieve the menu text displayed by the menu item.

```
#region Fields

private SpriteFont font;
private float selectionFade;

public string Text
{
    get;
    set;
}

#endregion
```

3. Add a region called Events and Triggers. In this region is an event, Selected, which the menu item fires when OnSelectEntry is called by the concrete menu class.

```
#region Events and Triggers

public event EventHandler<EventArgs> Selected;

protected internal virtual void OnSelectEntry()
{
```

```
    if (Selected != null)
        Selected(this, EventArgs.Empty);
}
```

```
#endregion
```

4. Add a constructor in its own region, which sets the local fields to the arguments.

```
#region Constructor(s)

public MenuEntry(string text, SpriteFont font)
{
    Text = text;
    this.font = font;
}


#endregion
```

5. Add a new region called `Public Virtual Methods`, and start it off with an `Update` method that updates the pulsate effect for the menu item.

```
#region Public Virtual Methods

public virtual void Update(BaseMenuScreen screen, bool isSelected,
                                              GameTime gameTime)
{
    float fadeSpeed = (float)gameTime.ElapsedGameTime.TotalSeconds * 4;

    if (isSelected)
        selectionFade = Math.Min(selectionFade + fadeSpeed, 1);
    else
        selectionFade = Math.Max(selectionFade - fadeSpeed, 0);
}
```

6. Add the virtual `Draw` method to the `Public Virtual Methods` region. This method draws the menu item on screen with its pulsate effect.

```
public virtual void Draw(BaseMenuScreen screen, Vector2 position,
                        bool isSelected, GameTime gameTime)
{
    // Draw the selected entry in yellow, otherwise white.
    Color color = isSelected ? Color.Yellow : Color.White;

    // Pulsate the size of the selected menu entry.
    double time = gameTime.TotalGameTime.TotalSeconds;

    float pulsate = (float)Math.Sin(time * 6) + 1;

    float scale = 1 + pulsate * 0.05f * selectionFade;
```

```
        // Modify the alpha to fade text out during transitions.
        color = new Color(color.R, color.G, color.B, screen.TransitionAlpha);

        // Draw text, centered on the middle of each line.

        Vector2 origin = font.MeasureString(Text) / 2;

        SharedSpriteBatch.Instance.DrawString(font, Text, position, color, 0,
                                origin, scale, SpriteEffects.None, 0);
    }
```

7. Finally, add the virtual `GetHeight` method, which is used to return the height (in pixels) of the menu item. This is used by the `BaseMenuScreen` class to determine how far apart to draw each menu item vertically, and is the same as the line spacing of the font.

```
public virtual int GetHeight(BaseMenuScreen screen)
{
    return font.LineSpacing;
}
```

That concludes the `MenuEntry` class. Next, we'll see how this is used in practice with the `BaseMenuScreen` class.

Creating a Base Class for Menus

The `BaseMenuScreen` class provides a way of delivering menus with a consistent look and feel throughout the game. The menu is very simple and allows us to make a single selection from a list, which is more than enough for our purposes. This screen contains a list of menu entries and handles the input and drawing for the menu.

1. In the `GameStateManager` project, add a new file called `BaseMenuScreen.cs`. Note that we are building on our previous work by making the base menu screen inherit from `BaseScreen`.

```
using System;
using System.Collections.Generic;
using Microsoft.Xna.Framework;
using Microsoft.Xna.Framework.Audio;

namespace GameStateManager
{
    public abstract class BaseMenuScreen : BaseScreen
    {
        // Implementation to follow...
    }
}
```

2. Add a `Fields` region to the class and add the following fields. These fields include sound effects that all menus will play. There is also a read-only collection of menu items exposed.

```
#region Fields

List<MenuEntry> menuEntries = new List<MenuEntry>();
int selectedEntry = 0;
string menuTitle;

// Sound Effects
SoundEffect selectionChangedSound;
SoundEffect selectedSound;

protected IList<MenuEntry> MenuEntries
{
    get;
    private set;
}

#endregion
```

3. Add the constructor, which sets the text and default transition times.

```
#region Constructor(s)

public BaseMenuScreen(string menuTitle)
{
    this.menuTitle = menuTitle;

    TransitionOnTime = TimeSpan.FromSeconds(0.5);
    TransitionOffTime = TimeSpan.FromSeconds(0.5);
}

#endregion
```

4. Add a region called Virtual Methods, which contains OnSelectEntry. This method allows concrete menus to determine what happens when a menu entry is selected.

```
#region Virtual Methods

protected virtual void OnSelectEntry(int entryIndex)
{
    menuEntries[selectedEntry].OnSelectEntry();
}

#endregion
```

5. Add a region called BaseScreen Overrides. This contains the overridden base screen logic which all menus will derive automatically. Add the HandleInput method to this region, which handles which menu item is selected and causes sounds to be played.

```
#region BaseScreen Overrides

public override void HandleInput(InputState input)
{
    // Move to the previous menu entry?
    if (input.MenuUp)
    {
        selectedEntry--;

        if (selectedEntry < 0)
            selectedEntry = menuEntries.Count - 1;
        else
            selectionChangedSound.Play();
    }

    // Move to the next menu entry?
    if (input.MenuDown)
    {
        selectedEntry++;

        if (selectedEntry >= menuEntries.Count)
            selectedEntry = 0;
        else
            selectionChangedSound.Play();
    }

    // Accept or cancel the menu?
    if (input.MenuSelect)
    {
        selectedSound.Play();
        OnSelectEntry(selectedEntry);
    }
}

#endregion
```

6. Add the LoadContent override to the BaseScreen Overrides region. This method loads the sound effects.

```
public override void LoadContent()
{
    selectedSound =
        ScreenManager.Content.Load<SoundEffect>("MenuSounds/SelectChanged");
    selectionChangedSound =
        ScreenManager.Content.Load<SoundEffect>("MenuSounds/Selected");

    base.LoadContent();
}
```

7. Add the Update override to the BaseScreen Overrides region. This method updates each menu item and its status.

```
public override void Update(GameTime gameTime, bool otherScreenHasFocus,
    bool coveredByOtherScreen)
{
    base.Update(gameTime, otherScreenHasFocus, coveredByOtherScreen);

    // Update each nested MenuEntry object.
    for (int i = 0; i < menuEntries.Count; i++)
    {
        bool isSelected = IsActive && (i == selectedEntry);
        menuEntries[i].Update(this, isSelected, gameTime);
    }
}
```

8. Finally, add the Draw method to the BaseScreen Overrides region. This method handles the transition for the screen by sliding the menu items into place and drawing them.

```
public override void Draw(GameTime gameTime)
{
    Vector2 position = new Vector2(120, 110);

    // Make the menu slide into place during transitions, using a
    // power curve to make things look more interesting (this makes
    // the movement slow down as it nears the end).
    float transitionOffset = (float)Math.Pow(TransitionPosition, 2);

    if (ScreenState == ScreenState.TransitionOn)
        position.X -= transitionOffset * 256;
    else
        position.X += transitionOffset * 512;

    // Draw each menu entry in turn.
    for (int i = 0; i < menuEntries.Count; i++)
    {
        MenuEntry menuEntry = menuEntries[i];
        bool isSelected = IsActive && (i == selectedEntry);
        menuEntry.Draw(this, position, isSelected, gameTime);
        position.Y += menuEntry.GetHeight(this);
    }
}
```

Our library is nearly complete! The last shared object we want to expose via this library is a network manager object. You've already seen a lot of this code in the beginning of this chapter, so it should be fairly easy to grasp.

Creating the Network Manager Object

Earlier in the chapter, you saw how to wrap network functionality in a simple class for the Robot Tag game. In that game, the player joined the first available network session. In this game, we are introducing asynchronous network operations (such as querying available sessions) and a much more error-friendly processing environment.

1. In the `GameStateManager` project, add a new class called `NetworkManager.cs`. Notice that it is a normal `GameComponent`, which the screen manager will add to the game's `Components` collection.

```
using System;
using Microsoft.Xna.Framework;
using Microsoft.Xna.Framework.Net;
using Microsoft.Xna.Framework.GamerServices;

namespace GameStateManager
{
    public class NetworkManager : GameComponent
    {
        // Implementation to follow...
    }
}
```

2. Create a region called `Fields` and add the following fields to the region. These fields expose a packet reader and packet writer, a local gamer representing the gamer on this Zune device, and an underlying `NetworkSession` object.

```
#region Fields

public PacketReader PacketReader
{
    get;
    private set;
}

public PacketWriter PacketWriter
{
    get;
    private set;
}

public LocalNetworkGamer Me
{
    get;
    private set;
}
```

```
public NetworkSession Session
{
    get;
    private set;
}
```

```
#endregion
```

3. Add a region called `Events & Delegates`. This region defines events (and corresponding delegates) that are raised at various stages of network processing. This allows game screens to be notified when network events occur.

```
#region Events & Delegates
```

```
public delegate void NetworkSessionsFoundHandler(
    AvailableNetworkSessionCollection availableSessions);
```

```
public delegate void GameJoinedHandler();
public delegate void GameJoinErrorHandler(Exception ex);
```

```
public event NetworkSessionsFoundHandler NetworkSessionsFound;
public event GameJoinedHandler GameJoined;
public event GameJoinErrorHandler GameJoinError;
```

```
#endregion
```

4. Add the constructor. The constructor adds a `GamerServicesComponent` to the game's `Components` collection, which is required for some elements of networking, such as gamer tag acquisition.

```
#region Constructor(s)
```

```
public NetworkManager(Game game)
    : base(game)
{
    game.Components.Add(new GamerServicesComponent(game));
}
```

```
#endregion
```

5. Add a region called `Public Methods`, which will contain several public methods that manipulate the network state. The first such method is called `KillSession`, which completely disposes and resets the network state in the event the game needs to start over or recover from an error.

```
#region Public Methods
```

```
public void KillSession()
{
```

```
        if (Session != null && Session.IsDisposed == false)
            Session.Dispose();

        Session = null;
    }

    #endregion
```

6. In the `Public Methods` region, add a method called `CreateZuneSession`. This method attempts to create a new network session and handles any errors that may arise.

```
public void CreateZuneSession(int maxNetworkPlayers)
{
    KillSession();

    try
    {
        Session = NetworkSession.Create(NetworkSessionType.SystemLink, 1,
            maxNetworkPlayers);

        Me = Session.LocalGamers[0];
    }
    catch (NetworkNotAvailableException)
    {
        throw new NetworkNotAvailableException("Zune wireless is not ➥
enabled.");
    }
    catch (NetworkException ne)
    {
        throw ne;
    }

    if (Session == null)
        throw new NetworkException("The network session could not be ➥
created.");
}
```

7. In the `Public Methods` region, add the following methods, which attempt to join a network session. The first method joins a specific network session asynchronously. The second method specifies a callback method called `GameJoinedCallback`.

```
public void JoinSession(AvailableNetworkSession session)
{
    try
    {
        NetworkSession.BeginJoin(session, new AsyncCallback➥
(GameJoinedCallback),
            null);
    }
```

```
        catch (Exception ex)
        {
            if (GameJoinError != null)
                GameJoinError(ex);
        }
    }

    public void GameJoinedCallback(IAsyncResult result)
    {
        try
        {
            Session = NetworkSession.EndJoin(result);
            Me = Session.LocalGamers[0];

            if (GameJoined != null)
                GameJoined();
        }
        catch (Exception ex)
        {
            GameJoinError(ex);
        }
    }
```

8. In the Public Methods region, add the following methods, which attempt to discover available network sessions. The callback is called asynchronously when sessions are found (or when the operation times out because there are no sessions).

```
public void BeginGetAvailableSessions()
{
    // Destroy any existing connections
    KillSession();

    NetworkSession.BeginFind(NetworkSessionType.SystemLink, 1, null,
        new AsyncCallback(SessionsFoundCallback), null);
}

public void SessionsFoundCallback(IAsyncResult result)
{
    AvailableNetworkSessionCollection availableSessions = null;
    availableSessions = NetworkSession.EndFind(result);

    if (NetworkSessionsFound != null)
        NetworkSessionsFound(availableSessions);
}
```

9. In the Public Methods region, add the StartGame method, which tells the underlying NetworkSession object to start the game if it can.

```
public void StartGame()
{
    if (Session != null && Session.IsDisposed == false)
        Session.StartGame();
}
```

10. Add a new region called GameComponent Overrides. The two methods here will initialize and update the network session in the same fashion that any GameComponent would run these methods.

```
#region GameComponent Overrides

public override void Initialize()
{
    PacketReader = new PacketReader();
    PacketWriter = new PacketWriter();
    Session = null;

    base.Initialize();
}

public override void Update(GameTime gameTime)
{
    if (Session != null && Session.IsDisposed == false)
        Session.Update();

    base.Update(gameTime);
}

#endregion
```

And, voilà! We now have two complete library projects that we will use when building our game. Sure, this is a lot of groundwork. However, these are reusable projects that you can leverage in any other games you decide to build.

Now, it's time to begin work on the Crazy Eights game project. With all of this processing under our belt, it will be fun to begin looking at how the game actually works!

Building Crazy Eights

In your solution, you should already have a Zune Game project called CrazyEights. If you have not done so, go ahead and create this project now. Ensure it is set as the startup project.

In your solution, add references to the two library projects: CardLib and GameStateManager. Right-click the References node under the CrazyEights project and select Add Reference. Move to the Projects tab and Shift-click both projects to add them to the solution.

To prepare the Content project for the files we will be adding, create two new subfolders: Sounds and Textures. Under Textures, add two new subfolders called CardBackgrounds and Screens. We'll be adding files to these directories as we go.

We'll start with the first things first (menu screens and networking) and move on to the game a little later.

Creating the Main Menu Screen

The main menu screen (see Figure 7-6 earlier in the chapter) is a simple screen that launches different screens or exits the game.

The first option, Create Game, will instantiate a new network game. The second option, Join Game, will show a screen that looks for network sessions. The final option, Quit, simply quits the game. The implementation for this screen is strikingly simple. It contains a few MenuEntry instances, some events, and a background.

1. Right-click the Content/Textures/Screens folder and choose Add Existing Item. Navigate to the Examples/Chapter 7/Artwork folder and choose menuBackground.png.

2. In the Screens folder, add a new class called MainMenuScreen.cs. The default namespace will be CrazyEights.Screens. Change the namespace to CrazyEights.

3. The code for this class, shown in Listing 7-9, is self-explanatory. We are loading one texture, adding some menu entries, and wiring up events, and then drawing these elements on the screen. Notice that we are using SharedSpriteBatch to handle the drawing in this screen.

Listing 7-9. *MainMenuScreen.cs*

```
using System;
using Microsoft.Xna.Framework;
using Microsoft.Xna.Framework.Graphics;

using GameStateManager;

namespace CrazyEights
{
    public class MainMenuScreen : BaseMenuScreen
    {
        MenuEntry createGameEntry;
        MenuEntry joinGameEntry;
        MenuEntry quitEntry;

        Texture2D backgroundTex;

        public MainMenuScreen()
            : base("Main Menu")
        {

        }

        public override void LoadContent()
        {
            backgroundTex = ScreenManager.Content.Load<Texture2D>
                ("Textures/Screens/menuBackground");
```

```
        createGameEntry = new MenuEntry("Create Game", ScreenManager.LargeFont);
        joinGameEntry = new MenuEntry("Join Game", ScreenManager.LargeFont);
        quitEntry = new MenuEntry("Quit", ScreenManager.LargeFont);

        createGameEntry.Selected += new EventHandler<EventArgs>(CreateSelected);
        joinGameEntry.Selected += new EventHandler<EventArgs>(JoinSelected);
        quitEntry.Selected += new EventHandler<EventArgs>(QuitSelected);

        MenuEntries.Add(createGameEntry);
        MenuEntries.Add(joinGameEntry);
        MenuEntries.Add(quitEntry);

        base.LoadContent();
    }

    public override void Draw(GameTime gameTime)
    {
        SharedSpriteBatch.Instance.Draw(backgroundTex, Vector2.Zero,
            Color.White);
        base.Draw(gameTime);
    }

    #region Event Handlers

    void QuitSelected(object sender, EventArgs e)
    {
        ScreenManager.Game.Exit();
    }

    void JoinSelected(object sender, EventArgs e)
    {
        ScreenManager.AddScreen(new JoinGameScreen());
    }

    void CreateSelected(object sender, EventArgs e)
    {
        ScreenManager.AddScreen(new CreateGameScreen());
    }

    #endregion
    }
}
```

Take a look at the CreateSelected event handler. Here, we are launching a new screen to create a network game. We haven't created that screen yet (or the join game screen), so the game won't compile. Next, we'll write the CreateGameScreen class.

Building the Create Game Screen

The create game screen (see Figure 7-7 earlier in the chapter) is responsible for creating a new network session and waiting for other players to join it. This screen cannot advance until all players are ready, and the player who initiates this screen will be known as the *host* during play.

The screen has a grid-style layout for outputting player data. Each row will contain the name and status of each player in the session. When all players are ready, the host player can press the middle button to start the game.

1. In the Screens folder, add a new class named CreateGameScreen.cs. Change the namespace to CrazyEights (from CrazyEights.Screens).

2. Add the following file to the Textures/Screens folder: Examples/Chapter 7/Artwork/newGameScreen.png. This graphic serves as the background for the screen.

3. Stub out the class as shown:

```
using System;
using Microsoft.Xna.Framework;
using Microsoft.Xna.Framework.Graphics;
using Microsoft.Xna.Framework.Net;

using GameStateManager;

namespace CrazyEights
{
    public class CreateGameScreen : BaseScreen
    {
    }
}
```

4. Add the following fields to the class. These fields store graphical as well as state elements. For example, the game cannot start until we have at least two ready players, so we have a flag for that. Also add the sole constant, which defines the maximum players at 5 (the maximum number our game can support).

```
#region Fields

private Texture2D backgroundTex;

private string statusText = "";
private Vector2 statusTextOrigin;

private bool createFailed = false;
private bool allPlayersReady = false;
private bool atLeastTwoPlayers = false;

#endregion

#region Constants
```

```
private const int MAX_PLAYERS = 5;

#endregion
```

5. Add a region called `BaseScreen Overrides`. The methods in this region will define how this screen performs as a screen object. First, put the code for the `Initialize` method in place. This method immediately attempts to create a network session and set the local gamer to `Ready`. If an exception is thrown, it is caught and made user-friendly. Also, add the event handler for `GameStarted`, which launches a new `PlayingScreen` (which we have not added yet).

```
public override void Initialize()
{
    try
    {
        ScreenManager.Network.KillSession();
        ScreenManager.Network.CreateZuneSession(MAX_PLAYERS);
        ScreenManager.Network.Session.LocalGamers[0].IsReady = true;

        ScreenManager.Network.Session.GameStarted +=
            new EventHandler<GameStartedEventArgs>(GameStarted);
    }
    catch (NetworkNotAvailableException)
    {
        statusText = "No network available.\r\n" +
            "Enable Wireless on the Zune and try again.";
        createFailed = true;
    }
    catch (NetworkException)
    {
        statusText = "Session could not be created\r\n" +
            "due to network issues.";
        createFailed = true;
    }
    catch (Exception)
    {
        statusText = "An unexpected error occurred.";
        createFailed = true;
    }

    base.Initialize();
}

void GameStarted(object sender, GameStartedEventArgs e)
{
    ScreenManager.RemoveScreen(this);
    ScreenManager.AddScreen(new PlayingScreen(true));
}
```

6. Add the `LoadContent` method to the `BaseScreen Overrides` region. This method uses the screen manager to load the `newGameScreen.png` file, which we added to the project earlier.

```
public override void LoadContent()
{
    backgroundTex = ScreenManager.Content.Load<Texture2D>
        ("Textures/Screens/newGameScreen");

    base.LoadContent();
}
```

7. In the `BaseScreen Overrides` region, add the `Update` method. This method is responsible for determining how many players are ready and if it is okay to start the game. This method also sets and measures the status text.

```
public override void Update(GameTime gameTime, bool otherScreenHasFocus,
    bool coveredByOtherScreen)
{
    // Determine readiness to start the game
    allPlayersReady = true;
    foreach (NetworkGamer gamer in ScreenManager.Network.Session.AllGamers)
    {
        if (gamer.IsReady == false)
        {
            allPlayersReady = false;
            break;
        }
    }

    // Determine the status text
    if (ScreenManager.Network.Session.AllGamers.Count >= 2)
        atLeastTwoPlayers = true;
    else
        atLeastTwoPlayers = false;

    if (allPlayersReady && atLeastTwoPlayers)
        statusText = "READY TO START\r\nPRESS THE MIDDLE BUTTON!";
    else
        statusText = "Waiting for other players...";

    statusTextOrigin =
        ScreenManager.SmallFont.MeasureString(statusText) / 2;


    base.Update(gameTime, otherScreenHasFocus, coveredByOtherScreen);
}
```

8. In the `BaseScreen Overrides` region, override `HandleInput` next. If Back is pressed, the game returns to the main menu screen (since this screen is removed). When the middle button is pressed, the game is started, but only if all players are ready.

```
public override void HandleInput(InputState input)
{
    if (input.NewBackPress)
    {
        ScreenManager.Network.KillSession();
        ScreenManager.RemoveScreen(this);
    }

    if (input.MiddleButtonPressed)
    {
        if (allPlayersReady && atLeastTwoPlayers)
        {
            if (ScreenManager.Network.Session != null)
                ScreenManager.Network.Session.StartGame();
        }
    }
}
```

9. Add the `Draw` method in the `BaseScreen Overrides` region. The `Draw` method draws the background, list of players (if any), and status text.

```
public override void Draw(GameTime gameTime)
{
    SharedSpriteBatch.Instance.Draw(backgroundTex, Vector2.Zero, Color.White);

    if (createFailed == false)
    {
        int playerIndex = 0;
        foreach (NetworkGamer gamer in ScreenManager.Network.Session.➥
AllGamers)
        {
            DrawGamerInfo(playerIndex, gamer.Gamertag, gamer.IsHost, ➥
gamer.IsReady);
            playerIndex++;
        }
    }

    SharedSpriteBatch.Instance.DrawString(ScreenManager.SmallFont, statusText,
        LobbyGameScreenElements.StatusMessagePosition, Color.White,
        0.0f, statusTextOrigin, 1.0f, SpriteEffects.None, 0.5f);

    base.Draw(gameTime);
}
```

10. Add a new region for `Helper Methods` and add the `DrawGamerInfo` method, which takes a gamer and some associated information and draws it on the screen. This method allows the host to take a collection of gamers, iterate through them, and draw each one on the screen such that their information fits in the table in the user interface.

```
private void DrawGamerInfo(int playerIndex, string name, bool isHost, bool
isReady)
{
    Vector2 namePosition = LobbyGameScreenElements.InitialTextListPosition;
    namePosition.Y += LobbyGameScreenElements.PLAYER_VERTICAL_SPACING * ➡
playerIndex;
    Vector2 statusPosition = LobbyGameScreenElements.➡
InitialListStatusPosition;
    statusPosition.Y = namePosition.Y;

    string readyStatus = isReady ? "Ready" : "Not Ready";
    Color readyColor = isReady ? Color.White : Color.LightGray;

    if (isHost)
        name += " (host)";

    SharedSpriteBatch.Instance.DrawString(ScreenManager.SmallFont,
        name, namePosition, readyColor);
    SharedSpriteBatch.Instance.DrawString(ScreenManager.SmallFont,
        readyStatus, statusPosition, readyColor);
}
```

At this point, IntelliSense goes crazy because of the unresolved `LobbyGameScreenElements` class. This is just a static class with some values that help you lay out the create game and lobby screens. We'll add the code for this class next.

11. In the `Screens` folder, add the following new class named `LobbyGameScreenElements.cs`. (I determined the values in this file manually, to produce an attractive screen layout.)

```
using Microsoft.Xna.Framework;

namespace CrazyEights
{
    public static class LobbyGameScreenElements
    {
        public static Vector2 PlayerListPosition;
        public static Vector2 InitialTextListPosition;
        public static Vector2 InitialListStatusPosition;
        public static Vector2 StatusMessagePosition;
        public static Vector2 HighlightInitialPosition;

        public const int PLAYER_VERTICAL_SPACING = 20;
        public const int LIST_OUTLINE_OFFSET = 4;
```

```
        static LobbyGameScreenElements()
        {
            PlayerListPosition = new Vector2(14, 82);
            InitialTextListPosition = new Vector2(16, 82);
            InitialListStatusPosition = new Vector2(155, 82);
            StatusMessagePosition = new Vector2(120, 202);
            HighlightInitialPosition = PlayerListPosition;

            HighlightInitialPosition.X -= LIST_OUTLINE_OFFSET;
            HighlightInitialPosition.Y -= LIST_OUTLINE_OFFSET;
        }
    }
}
```

Now, the create game screen is complete. The next screen to implement is the join game screen, which enumerates all of the available games.

Building the Join Game Screen

The join game screen (shown earlier in Figure 7-8) is responsible for enumerating the available network sessions and allowing the user to pick one.

One caveat with this screen, and network session resolution in general, is that the asynchronous BeginFind method of the NetworkSession class leaves the network session open as it searches. This means that you must wait for the BeginFind method to end (successfully or unsuccessfully) before attempting to close the join game screen or start a new session. This screen handles this simply by preventing exiting until the previous find operation has completed.

1. In the Screens folder, add a new class called JoinGameScreen.cs. Stub it out with the embedded JoinScreenStatus enumeration:

```
using System;
using Microsoft.Xna.Framework;
using Microsoft.Xna.Framework.Graphics;
using Microsoft.Xna.Framework.Net;
using GameStateManager;

namespace CrazyEights
{
    public enum JoinScreenStatus
    {
        Finding,
        Joining,
        Joined,
        Error
    }
```

```
        public class JoinGameScreen : BaseScreen
        {
        }
    }
```

2. Right-click the `Content/Textures/Screens` folder and choose Add Existing Item. Add the file `Examples/Chapter 7/Artwork/joinGameScreen.png`. This is the background for the join game screen, and is identical to the create game screen background, except for some of the text in the graphic.

3. Right-click the `Content/Textures` folder and choose Add Existing Item. Add the file `Examples/Chapter 7/Artwork/listhighlight.png`. This is a rectangular highlight graphic that is drawn under the currently selected session to emphasize the currently selected session.

4. Add a `Fields` region and the following fields to the `JoinGameScreen` class:

```
#region Fields

private Texture2D backgroundTex;
private Texture2D listHighlightTex;

private string statusText;
private int selectedSessionIndex = -1;
private AvailableNetworkSessionCollection availableNetworkSessions = null;
private JoinScreenStatus screenStatus = JoinScreenStatus.Finding;

private Vector2 statusTextOrigin = Vector2.Zero;

#endregion
```

5. Add a region called `BaseScreen Overrides`, which will define this screen's behavior as a game screen. Add the `Initialize` method, which wires up some network events and begins searching for available sessions.

```
#region BaseScreen Overrides

public override void Initialize()
{
    // Wire up events
    ScreenManager.Network.NetworkSessionsFound +=
        new NetworkManager.NetworkSessionsFoundHandler(NetworkSessionsFound);

    ScreenManager.Network.GameJoined +=
        new NetworkManager.GameJoinedHandler(GameJoined);

    ScreenManager.Network.GameJoinError +=
        new NetworkManager.GameJoinErrorHandler(GameJoinError);
```

```
        // Start looking for sessions
        ScreenManager.Network.KillSession();
        ScreenManager.Network.BeginGetAvailableSessions();

        base.Initialize();
    }

    #endregion
```

6. Add a new region called Event Handlers. These methods will handle the network events we subscribed to in the Initialize method. When network sessions are found, we either select the first found session or state that no sessions were found. When the game is successfully joined, we launch a LobbyScreen (which we have not created yet). When an error occurs trying to join a game, we output the error message to the screen.

```
    #region Event Handlers

    void NetworkSessionsFound(AvailableNetworkSessionCollection ⟶
    availableSessions)
    {
        availableNetworkSessions = availableSessions;
        if (availableNetworkSessions == null ||
            availableNetworkSessions.Count < 1)
        {
            selectedSessionIndex = -1;
            screenStatus = JoinScreenStatus.Error;
            statusText = "No sessions were found.\r\n" +
                "Please try again by pressing BACK.";
        }
        else
        {
            if (selectedSessionIndex == -1)
                selectedSessionIndex = 0;
        }
    }

    void GameJoined()
    {
        screenStatus = JoinScreenStatus.Joined;
        statusText = "Game joined.";
        ScreenManager.AddScreen(new LobbyScreen());
        this.ExitScreen();
    }

    void GameJoinError(Exception ex)
    {
        statusText = "An error occurred.\r\nPlease press BACK and try again.";
```

```
            screenStatus = JoinScreenStatus.Error;
        }


    #endregion
```

7. Add the `LoadContent` override method to the `BaseScreen` `Overrides` region. This method loads the required content and sets up the initial status text.

```
public override void LoadContent()
{
    backgroundTex = ScreenManager.Content.Load<Texture2D>
        ("Textures/Screens/joinGameScreen");
    listHighlightTex = ScreenManager.Content.Load<Texture2D>
        ("Textures/listhighlight");

    statusText = "Please wait. Looking for games...";
    statusTextOrigin = ScreenManager.SmallFont.MeasureString(statusText) / 2;

    base.LoadContent();
}
```

8. Add the `Update` override method to the `BaseScreen` `Overrides` region. This method alters the status text and the currently selected network session based on the current screen status.

```
public override void Update(GameTime gameTime, bool otherScreenHasFocus,
    bool coveredByOtherScreen)
{
    switch (screenStatus)
    {
        case JoinScreenStatus.Finding:
            if (availableNetworkSessions == null ||
                availableNetworkSessions.Count <= 0)
            {
                statusText = "Please wait. Looking for games...";
                selectedSessionIndex = -1;
            }
            else
            {
                if (availableNetworkSessions.Count >= 1)
                {
                    statusText = "Press the middle button to join.";
                }
            }
            break;
        case JoinScreenStatus.Joining:
            statusText = "Attempting to join game...";
            break;
        case JoinScreenStatus.Joined:
```

```
                statusText = "Game joined.";
                break;
        }

        statusTextOrigin = ScreenManager.SmallFont.MeasureString(statusText) / 2;

        base.Update(gameTime, otherScreenHasFocus, coveredByOtherScreen);
    }
```

9. Add the `HandleInput` override method to the `BaseScreen Overrides` region. This method will handle four different kinds of input. It will go back to the main menu screen if the network session is not busy looking for games. It will scroll up and down in the list of network sessions if there are available sessions. Finally, it will attempt to join the selected session if it is available when the middle button is pressed.

```
public override void HandleInput(InputState input)
{
    // Kill the session and go back
    if (input.NewBackPress)
    {
        if (availableNetworkSessions != null)
        {
            ScreenManager.Network.KillSession();
            ScreenManager.RemoveScreen(this);
        }
    }

    // Scroll down in the list of sessions
    if (input.NewDownPress)
    {
        if (availableNetworkSessions != null && availableNetworkSessions.➥
Count > 1)
        {
            if (selectedSessionIndex < availableNetworkSessions.Count - 1)
                selectedSessionIndex++;
        }
    }

    // Scroll down in the list of sessions
    if (input.NewUpPress)
    {
        if (selectedSessionIndex > 0)
            selectedSessionIndex--;
    }

    // Attempt to join the selected game
    if (input.MiddleButtonPressed)
    {
```

```
            if (selectedSessionIndex >= 0 && availableNetworkSessions != null
                && availableNetworkSessions.Count > 0)
            {
                screenStatus = JoinScreenStatus.Joining;
                AvailableNetworkSession session =
                    availableNetworkSessions[selectedSessionIndex];

                ScreenManager.Network.JoinSession(session);
            }
        }
    }
```

10. Add the Draw override method to the BaseScreen Overrides region. This method will
    draw all of the session information and status text on screen. It also utilizes a private
    method called DrawSessionInfo to draw the session information with highlights.

```
public override void Draw(GameTime gameTime)
{
    // Draw the background
    SharedSpriteBatch.Instance.Draw(backgroundTex, Vector2.Zero, Color.White);

    // Draw the network sessions
    if (availableNetworkSessions != null)
    {
        for (int sIndex = 0; sIndex < availableNetworkSessions.Count; ➥
sIndex++)
        {
            AvailableNetworkSession session = availableNetworkSessions➥
[sIndex];

            DrawSessionInfo(sIndex, session.CurrentGamerCount,
                session.HostGamertag);
        }
    }

    // Draw the status text
    SharedSpriteBatch.Instance.DrawString(ScreenManager.SmallFont, statusText,
        LobbyGameScreenElements.StatusMessagePosition, Color.White, 0.0f,
        statusTextOrigin, 1.0f, SpriteEffects.None, 0.5f);
}
```

11. Finally, create a new region called Private Methods and add the GetHighlightPosition
    and DrawSessionInfo methods to that region. GetHighlightPosition determines
    where to draw the highlight graphic given a specific index into the list of sessions.
    DrawSessionInfo uses GetHighlightPosition and the currently drawn network session
    to draw the text above the highlight. Notice how this screen also makes use of the val-
    ues in LobbyGameScreenElements.cs.

```
#region Private Methods

private Vector2 GetHighlightPosition(int positionIndex)
{
    Vector2 position = LobbyGameScreenElements.HighlightInitialPosition;
    position.Y += positionIndex * LobbyGameScreenElements.PLAYER_VERTICAL_➡
SPACING;
    return position;
}

private void DrawSessionInfo(int sessionIndex, int numGamers, string ➡
hostGamertag)
{
    Vector2 namePosition = LobbyGameScreenElements.InitialTextListPosition;
    namePosition.Y +=
        LobbyGameScreenElements.PLAYER_VERTICAL_SPACING * sessionIndex;

    Vector2 statusPosition = LobbyGameScreenElements.InitialListStatus➡
Position;
    statusPosition.Y = namePosition.Y;

    string sessionStatus = numGamers.ToString() + " player";
    sessionStatus += numGamers == 1 ? "" : "s";

    // Determine the text color for the session
    Color sessionColor = sessionIndex ==
        selectedSessionIndex ? Color.White : Color.Black;

    // Draw the highlight
    if (sessionIndex == selectedSessionIndex)
    {
        // Draw the highlight before the text
        SharedSpriteBatch.Instance.Draw(listHighlightTex,
            GetHighlightPosition(sessionIndex), Color.White);
    }

    // Draw the host gamer tag
    SharedSpriteBatch.Instance.DrawString(ScreenManager.SmallFont,
        hostGamertag, namePosition, sessionColor);

    // Draw the session status
    SharedSpriteBatch.Instance.DrawString(ScreenManager.SmallFont,
        sessionStatus, statusPosition, sessionColor);
}

#endregion
```

We are nearly at a point where we can compile and test the game safely. There are two screens we still need to implement. The first is LobbyScreen.cs, which is where a joining user is taken after joining a network session. The second is PlayingScreen.cs, where most of the game logic occurs. Let's look at LobbyScreen.cs first.

Building the Lobby Screen

The lobby screen (shown earlier in Figure 7-9) allows joining players to declare their readiness to begin. This screen also shows the names of other network players in the session. When the host starts the game, this screen disappears, and all players are transitioned to the playing screen.

1. In the Screens folder, add a new class called LobbyScreen.cs. Stub it out as follows:

```
using System;
using Microsoft.Xna.Framework;
using Microsoft.Xna.Framework.Graphics;
using Microsoft.Xna.Framework.Net;

using GameStateManager;

namespace CrazyEights
{
    public class LobbyScreen : BaseScreen
    {
    }
}
```

2. Right-click the Content/Textures/Screens folder and choose Add Existing Item. Browse to the file Examples/Chapter 7/Artwork/lobbyScreen.png and add it. This graphic is also based on the create game screen background, with a grid that will show the players in the session.

3. Add a Fields region and the following three fields to the class:

```
#region Fields

private Texture2D backgroundTex;
private string statusText;
private Vector2 statusTextOrigin = Vector2.Zero;

#endregion
```

4. Add a region called BaseScreen Overrides and add the Initialize method, which wires up network events to local handlers. Add the event handlers as well.

```
#region BaseScreen Overrides

public override void Initialize()
{
    // Wire up events
```

```
        ScreenManager.Network.Session.GameStarted +=
            new EventHandler<GameStartedEventArgs>(GameStarted);

        ScreenManager.Network.Session.SessionEnded +=
            new EventHandler<NetworkSessionEndedEventArgs>(SessionEnded);

        base.Initialize();
    }

    #endregion
    #region Event Handlers

    void GameStarted(object sender, GameStartedEventArgs e)
    {
        ScreenManager.RemoveScreen(this);
        ScreenManager.AddScreen(new PlayingScreen(false));
    }

    void SessionEnded(object sender, NetworkSessionEndedEventArgs e)
    {
        ScreenManager.RemoveScreen(this);
    }

    #endregion
```

5. Add the `LoadContent` override method to the `BaseScreen Overrides` region. This method loads the background texture and initializes status text.

```
    public override void LoadContent()
    {
        backgroundTex = ScreenManager.Content.Load<Texture2D>
            ("Textures/Screens/lobbyScreen");

        statusText = "When you're ready,\r\npress the MIDDLE button.";
        statusTextOrigin = ScreenManager.SmallFont.MeasureString(statusText) / 2;

        base.LoadContent();
    }
```

6. In the `BaseScreen Overrides` region, add the `HandleInput` override method, which will attempt to set the player as `Ready` (or exit the screen).

```
    public override void HandleInput(InputState input)
    {
        if (input.NewBackPress)
        {
            ScreenManager.Network.KillSession();
            ScreenManager.RemoveScreen(this);
        }
```

```
            if (input.MiddleButtonPressed)
            {
                if (ScreenManager.Network.Session != null)
                {
                    try
                    {
                        ScreenManager.Network.Session.LocalGamers[0].IsReady = true;
                        statusText = "Waiting for the host to start.";
                    }
                    catch
                    {
                        this.ExitScreen();
                    }
                }
            }
        }
```

7. Add the Draw method to the BaseScreen Overrides region. This method loops through all the players in the session and draws them with the private DrawGamerInfo method (shown in step 8).

```
public override void Draw(GameTime gameTime)
{
    // Draw background
    SharedSpriteBatch.Instance.Draw(backgroundTex, Vector2.Zero, Color.White);

    // Draw players in session
    int playerIndex = 0;
    foreach (NetworkGamer gamer in ScreenManager.Network.Session.AllGamers)
    {
        DrawGamerInfo(playerIndex, gamer.Gamertag, gamer.IsHost, ➥
gamer.IsReady);
        playerIndex++;
    }

    // Draw status text
    SharedSpriteBatch.Instance.DrawString(ScreenManager.SmallFont, statusText,
        LobbyGameScreenElements.StatusMessagePosition, Color.White,
        0.0f, statusTextOrigin, 1.0f, SpriteEffects.None, 0.5f);

    base.Draw(gameTime);
}
```

8. Finally, add a new region called Private Methods, and add the DrawGamerInfo method. This method draws information for a specific network gamer in a list on the screen.

```
#region Private Methods

private void DrawGamerInfo(int playerIndex, string name, bool isHost, bool
isReady)
{
    Vector2 namePosition = LobbyGameScreenElements.InitialTextListPosition;
    namePosition.Y += LobbyGameScreenElements.PLAYER_VERTICAL_SPACING * ➥
playerIndex;
    Vector2 statusPosition = LobbyGameScreenElements.➥
InitialListStatusPosition;
    statusPosition.Y = namePosition.Y;

    string readyStatus = isReady || isHost ? "Ready" : "Not Ready";
    Color readyColor = isReady || isHost ? Color.White : Color.LightGray;

    if (isHost)
        name += " (host)";

    SharedSpriteBatch.Instance.DrawString(ScreenManager.SmallFont,
        name, namePosition, readyColor);

    SharedSpriteBatch.Instance.DrawString(ScreenManager.SmallFont,
        readyStatus, statusPosition, readyColor);
}

#endregion
```

All of our matchmaking screens are complete! We can now stub out PlayingScreen.cs and
do a quick build.

Adding the Playing Screen, Compile and Deploy Check

Now we will get the playing screen started, but we won't fully implement it. This is the last
piece of this phase's puzzle. After doing this, you should be able to create and join network
sessions between two wireless-enabled Zune devices.

1. In the Screens folder, add a new class called PlayingScreen.cs. The following stub
   will match the constructor signatures called from the create game and lobby screens.
   When called from the create game screen, the playing screen is constructed with
   host = true. When called from the lobby screen, the playing screen is instantiated
   with host = false.

```
using Microsoft.Xna.Framework;
using GameStateManager;
using CardLib;
```

```
namespace CrazyEights
{
    public class PlayingScreen : BaseScreen
    {
        private bool isHost;

        public PlayingScreen(bool host)
        {
            isHost = host;
        }
    }
}
```

2. Compile the game at this time. Correct any typos or other errors (consult the provided source code if necessary).

3. Run without debugging to one Zune. Once the game is running on that Zune, swap out with a different Zune. Set this new Zune as the default and deploy with debugging on. (In both cases, wait until the wireless icon shows up in the Zune user interface before connecting.) You should be able to create and join network sessions between the two Zunes without any trouble.

We will come back to the playing screen in a little while. First, we need to write some more complex helper classes that will manage the display and game flow.

Three classes play a central role in the management of the game. The first is called the Crazy Eights game manager component, which handles the turn system, game rules, and top-level network calls. Next is the player view component, which is a drawable component shown on the screen with a collection of cards. This component is drawn directly into the player screen and is the main point of interaction between user and game. The playing screen instantiates, adds, and handles the communication between these two components. The playing screen also handles some game logic, but to a far lesser extent than the other two classes. The outbound network messaging is handled by a static class called NetworkMessenger, which you will see shortly. The game manager component handles receipt of network traffic.

Before building these more complex classes, let's create the CrazyEightsPlayer object, which brings together some useful fields that our more complex logic classes can use.

Creating the CrazyEightsPlayer Class

The CrazyEightsPlayer class is used to represent a player in the game with a bit more detail than, say, the NetworkGamer class does.

Every peer will keep a list of CrazyEightsPlayer objects. A CrazyEightsPlayer object has a few obvious properties attached to it: a list of cards, a name, whether it is this player's turn, and whether this player is the host. To avoid having every peer stay up-to-date with every player's hand, only the host will maintain a list of each player's cards.

1. Right-click the CrazyEights game project and add a new class to it, called CrazyEightsPlayer.cs. Stub it out like so:

```
using System.Collections.Generic;
using CardLib;

namespace CrazyEights
{
    public class CrazyEightsPlayer
    {
        // Implementation to follow...
    }
}
```

2. Add the Name, Cards, IsHost, and IsMyTurn fields to the class:

```
#region Fields

public string Name
{
    get;
    private set;
}

public List<Card> Cards
{
    get;
    private set;
}

public bool IsHost
{
    get;
    private set;
}

public bool IsMyTurn
{
    get;
    set;
}

#endregion
```

3. Add the constructor, which initializes the fields. We will set the turn to `false` by default, since the host will determine when to set this value to `true` via a network message. We will also instantiate the cards to a new array of cards. This means we need to know only the player name and whether that player is the host.

```
#region Constructor(s)

public CrazyEightsPlayer(string name, bool isHost)
{
    Name = name;
    IsHost = isHost;
    IsMyTurn = false;
    Cards = new List<Card>();
}

#endregion
```

4. Add a public method called `DealCard`. This is an abstraction of the dealer actually dealing the card to a player. It just adds the specified card to this player's list of cards. This method is called when cards are initially dealt at the beginning of the network session.

```
#region Public Methods

public void DealCard(Card card)
{
    Cards.Add(card);
}

#endregion
```

5. Finally, override the `Equals` method. This will allow us to check, by player name, whether two player objects correspond to the same gamer. This will be useful when we want to receive only network messages intended for us, and in other situations where we need to determine whether two player objects are the same.

```
#region Overriden Methods

public override bool Equals(object obj)
{
    CrazyEightsPlayer player = obj as CrazyEightsPlayer;
    if (player == null)
        return false;

    return player.Name == this.Name;
}

#endregion
```

Next, you will see the game take shape from the network side of things with the NetworkMessenger class.

Creating the NetworkMessenger Class

The `NetworkMessenger` class is responsible for sending outbound network messages to all peers in the session. Whenever the host or peer needs to synchronize a piece of information with the other gamers on the network (or even one gamer in particular), a method of this class is called.

The network messaging infrastructure works on the basic premise that we will first send a single byte indicating what the following data is to be used for, and then send the data atomically (piece by piece). If you were to build a huge game with many different message types that needed to be easily extended, there would probably be a better approach. For our situation, we will define an enumeration (of type `byte`) that sets up nine different network messages. The `NetworkMessenger` class will expose static methods that send the data for each of these messages.

1. In the `CrazyEights` game project, add a new class called `NetworkMessenger.cs`. Stub it out as follows:

```
using System;
using Microsoft.Xna.Framework.Net;
using GameStateManager;
using CardLib;

namespace CrazyEights
{
    public enum NetworkMessageType : byte
    {

    }

    public static class NetworkMessenger
    {

    }
}
```

Here, we have a public enumeration called `NetworkMessageType` that inherits from `byte`. This means that we can easily cast members of this enumeration back to a `byte` for sending or receiving, and that helps to minimize network traffic. Also, in our game, `byte` is not used for any other purpose, so it helps you mentally mark these values as message types.

2. Add the following values to the `NetworkMessageType` enumeration. Each value is described in Table 7-4, and they map very closely to the messages discussed in the "Network State Design" section earlier in the chapter.

```
public enum NetworkMessageType : byte
{
    HostSendPlayer,
    HostDealCard,
    HostAllCardsDealt,
    HostDiscard,
```

```
        HostSetTurn,
        PlayCard,
        RequestCard,
        SuitChosen,
        GameWon
    }
```

Table 7-4. *Network Message Types*

Message	Sent by	Processed by	Description
HostSendPlayer	Host	All players	Sends a new CrazyEightsPlayer to all other players.
HostDealCard	Host	Intended player	Deals a card to a player.
HostAllCardsDealt	Host	All players	Message sent when all cards have been dealt, indicating that play may start.
HostDiscard	Host	All players	Sent when the first card is discarded from the deck.
HostSetTurn	Host	Intended player	Sets the player's turn to True if it is the intended player; False otherwise.
PlayCard	Player	All players	Adds the played card to the discard pile.
RequestCard	Player	Host	Sent when a player needs to draw a card. Answered with HostDealCard.
SuitChosen	Player	All players	Sets the currently active suit to the one chosen by the player who played the eight.
GameWon	Player	All players	Sent when a player wins the game by running out of cards.

3. Now that we have the network message types in place, it's time to determine what the structure of the data will look like when it is sent. First, we must have a reference in this class to the screen manager, which contains a NetworkManager object. We must also ensure that this value has been set before attempting to use it. Add the following two fields to the NetworkMessenger class:

```
public static class NetworkMessenger
{
    private static ScreenManager screenManager;
    private static bool isInitialized = false;
}
```

4. We will also need a static method on this class that sends all of the available data in the packet writer in one go. We use a foreach loop for two reasons. One is that if the game is ever ported to a device where there can be more than one local player (such as the Xbox 360), this code will still work. The other reason is that, in all cases, we will always have a local gamer object to work with, which the foreach loop provides. Implement the SendData method as follows, along with the Initialize method that sets the screen manager object.

```
public static void Initialize(ScreenManager manager)
{
    screenManager = manager;
    isInitialized = true;
}

private static void SendData()
{
    if (isInitialized == false)
        throw new Exception("This object must be initialized first.");

    foreach (LocalNetworkGamer gamer in screenManager.Network.Session.➥
LocalGamers)
        gamer.SendData(screenManager.Network.PacketWriter,
            SendDataOptions.ReliableInOrder);
}
```

Notice that the send data options specify reliable in-order messaging. This requires the most network bandwidth, but because our game sends a comparably small amount of data infrequently, it's better to choose robustness over performance.

5. Implement the static `Host_SendPlayer` method, which sends a player and indicates whether that player is the host. This method maps to the `HostSendPlayer` message type.

```
public static void Host_SendPlayer(NetworkGamer gamer)
{
    screenManager.Network.PacketWriter.Write(
        (byte)NetworkMessageType.HostSendPlayer);

    screenManager.Network.PacketWriter.Write(gamer.Gamertag);
    screenManager.Network.PacketWriter.Write(gamer.IsHost);
    SendData();
}
```

6. Implement the static `Host_DealCard` method, which sends a card to a player. It sends the card in its serialized string form. This method maps to the `HostDealCard` message type.

```
public static void Host_DealCard(Card card, CrazyEightsPlayer player)
{
    screenManager.Network.PacketWriter.Write((byte)NetworkMessageType.➥
HostDealCard);
    screenManager.Network.PacketWriter.Write(player.Name);
    screenManager.Network.PacketWriter.Write(card.Serialize());
    SendData();
}
```

7. Implement the static `Host_Discard` method, which informs the players of the newly discarded card. It sends the card in its serialized string form. This method maps to the `HostDiscard` message type.

```
public static void Host_Discard(Card card)
{
    screenManager.Network.PacketWriter.Write((byte)NetworkMessageType.➡
HostDiscard);
    screenManager.Network.PacketWriter.Write(card.Serialize());
    SendData();
}
```

8. Implement the static Host_ReadyToPlay method, which informs the players
   that all players have their cards and play can begin. This method maps to the
   HostAllCardsDealt message type.

```
public static void Host_ReadyToPlay()
{
    screenManager.Network.PacketWriter.Write(
        (byte)NetworkMessageType.HostAllCardsDealt);

    SendData();
}
```

9. Implement the static Host_SetTurn method, which tells the players to set the current
   turn index. This method maps to the HostSetTurn message type.

```
public static void Host_SetTurn(int turn)
{
    screenManager.Network.PacketWriter.Write((byte)NetworkMessageType.➡
HostSetTurn);
    screenManager.Network.PacketWriter.Write(turn);
    SendData();
}
```

10. Implement the static PlayCard method, which informs the other players that this player
    has played a card. This method maps to the PlayCard message type.

```
public static void PlayCard(Card card)
{
    screenManager.Network.PacketWriter.Write((byte)NetworkMessageType.➡
PlayCard);
    screenManager.Network.PacketWriter.Write(card.Serialize());
    SendData();
}
```

11. Implement the static RequestCard method, which informs the host that this player
    needs a card dealt. This method maps to the RequestCard message type.

```
public static void RequestCard(CrazyEightsPlayer player)
{
    screenManager.Network.PacketWriter.Write((byte)NetworkMessageType.➡
RequestCard);
    screenManager.Network.PacketWriter.Write(player.Name);
    SendData();
}
```

12. Implement the static SendChosenSuit method, which informs the other players that this player has chosen a suit (sent as an integer). This method maps to the SuitChosen message type.

```
public static void SendChosenSuit(Suit suit)
{
    screenManager.Network.PacketWriter.Write((byte)NetworkMessageType.➡
SuitChosen);
    screenManager.Network.PacketWriter.Write((byte)suit);
    SendData();
}
```

13. Finally, implement the static GameWon method, which informs all gamers that the gamer with the specified name has won the game. This does not cross-check with the host's game status. Whenever a player runs out of cards, that player sends this message. When players receive this message, they transition to the game over screen. This method maps to the GameWon message type.

```
public static void GameWon(string winner)
{
    screenManager.Network.PacketWriter.Write((byte)NetworkMessageType.➡
GameWon);
    screenManager.Network.PacketWriter.Write(winner);
    SendData();
}
```

We've finished all of the network message plumbing we need to send appropriate messages between Zunes. The important thing to remember here is the order in which data is sent. For example, the Host_DealCard method deals the player's name, followed by the card. Therefore, the data must be received in that same order (player then card).

Next, we'll build the player view component, which is responsible for displaying the player's "heads-up display," so to speak.

Creating the Player View Component

The player view component runs as a child of the playing screen and is more of a display component than anything else. However, this component is one of the most crucial to the user experience. It handles all of the bells and whistles that allow a player to visualize what is happening in the game.

Each Zune will have a player view component running in the playing screen during game play. This component is responsible for displaying runtime data to the player, including the following:

- All the cards in the player's hand

- A graphical notification overlay when the active suit has changed (after another player plays an eight and selects a suit)

- The current card to play against

- Any status text

It also allows the player to select from playable cards, while dimming others. See Figure 7-10, earlier in this chapter, for an example of this.

This screen is also derived from our custom DrawableComponent class, so that it may adopt the life span of its parent screen (PlayingScreen). As such, we could choose to handle input within this component, but instead we will handle input in the playing screen, because input events such as PlayCard will require access to the CrazyEightsGameManager component (built next) as well to propagate those changes to other Zunes.

We'll approach the implementation sequence differently for this component. You need to understand how a card graphic is drawn, as we have not covered that yet.

In the player view component, we'll add the deck.png image shown in Figure 7-14. I mentioned earlier that many elements of the card library are built around the arrangement of this card deck.

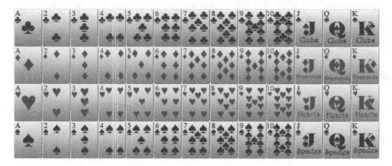

Figure 7-14. *The layout of the card deck*

If you look at the values of our Suit enumeration, you'll see Clubs = 1, Diamonds = 2, Hearts = 3, Spades = 4. This is alphabetical, yes, but you can see in Figure 7-14 that the cards go from values of 1 to 13 from left to right, and repeat in this order of suits going downward. This allows us to "index" into this image, given the suit and value, in much the same way that you would access an element in a matrix or a two-dimensional array. The method that accomplishes this specific piece of logic is called GetSourceRect, which we'll add at the beginning of the PlayerViewComponent class. GetSourceRect takes a Card object and returns a Rectangle that we can use as the source rectangle. Then we can simply draw the entire Deck texture, specifying this source rectangle, and we will receive a the graphic that represents the card that was input. "Genius," you say? It's actually a very common practice in game development.

Now, let's build the player view component.

1. In the CrazyEights game project, add a new class called PlayerViewComponent.cs. Stub it out as shown:

```
using System;
using Microsoft.Xna.Framework;
using Microsoft.Xna.Framework.Graphics;
using Microsoft.Xna.Framework.Audio;
using CardLib;
using GameStateManager;
```

```
namespace CrazyEights
{
    public class PlayerViewComponent : DrawableComponent
    {
    }
}
```

2. Right-click the Content/Textures folder and add deck.png from Examples/Chapter 7/
Artwork. This image is shown in Figure 7-14.

3. Right-click the Content/Sounds folder and add CardSelect.wav from Examples/
Chapter 7/SoundFX.

4. Add a region for Private Utility Methods to the PlayerViewComponent class and add
the GetSourceRect method to it, as follows. This method makes use of card size constants, which we haven't defined just yet, so don't be worried if IntelliSense nags
at you.

```
#region Private Utility Methods

private Rectangle GetSourceRect(Card card)
{
    // Only draw defined cards.
    if (!card.IsDefined)
        throw new ArgumentException("Undefined cards cannot be drawn.");

    // Define the value (subtract 1 because arrays are zero-based)
    int cardColumn = card.CardValue.Value - 1;

    // Define the suit (subtract 1 because are enum has
    // the first defined suit starting at 1, not zero)
    int cardRow = (int)card.Suit - 1;

    // Calculate the X position, in pixels.
    int x = cardColumn * CARD_WIDTH;

    // Calculate the Y position, in pixels.
    int y = cardRow * CARD_HEIGHT;

    // Create the rectangle and return it.
    return new Rectangle(x, y, CARD_WIDTH, CARD_HEIGHT);
}

#endregion
```

With that piece of code, we get a source rectangle for any card we want! This means
that we can draw deck.png with the specified source rectangle, and we'll just get the
card we requested. Now, we can resume implementing this class from the top.

5. Add a region called Fields to the class. This region will hold all the values that this component should expose, such as the currently selected card, the player this component represents, and whether or not the player currently has a move.

```
#region Fields

public CrazyEightsPlayer Player
{
    get;
    set;
}

public Card SelectedCard
{
    get
    {
        return Player.Cards[selectedIndex];
    }
}

public bool HasMove
{
    get;
    private set;
}

#endregion
```

6. Add a region called Private Variables to the class and the following variables. These are privately used values that contribute to the effect of the screen, and do not need to be exposed. Note the values for card animation. These will be used in a SmoothStep function to "slide" the selected card up from the group.

```
#region Private Variables

// Status text
private string statusText = "";

// Positioning and measurement
private Vector2 screenCenter;
private Vector2 currentCardPosition;
private Vector2 statusTextPosition;
private Vector2 statusTextOrigin;
private int screenWidth;

// Currently selected card index
private int selectedIndex = 0;
```

```
// Content
private SoundEffect cardSelectedSound;
private Texture2D deckTexture;
private Texture2D backgroundTex;

// "Suit changed" overlay textures
private Texture2D clubTex, diamondTex, heartTex, spadeTex;

private Color overlayTintColor;

// For card animation
private bool animatingSelected = false;
private float animateDistance = 0.0f;
private float stepValue = 0.0f;

#endregion
```

7. Add the following constants. The first two specify the size of a single card, in pixels. The last specifies the maximum width of the card viewer control; the player's cards will always be shown together in a horizontal area 220 pixels wide or less.

```
#region Constants

private const int CARD_WIDTH = 44;
private const int CARD_HEIGHT = 60;
private const int MAX_WIDTH = 220;

#endregion
```

8. Add the constructor for this component. It initializes the currentCardPosition (the card to play against) and the tint color for the overlay graphics (the ones that say "Suit Changed"). It also initializes this component with the necessary ScreenManager reference.

```
#region Constructor(s)

public PlayerViewComponent(ScreenManager screenManager)
    : base(screenManager)
{
    currentCardPosition = new Vector2(98, 48);
    overlayTintColor = new Color(1.0f, 1.0f, 1.0f, 0.8f);
}

#endregion
```

9. Add the method `SelectCard` to the `Private Methods` region. This method is called internally by the component by public methods. This method will attempt to select a playable card, play a sound effect, and set the currently selected card. If the player has a move, this card will animate itself; otherwise, the first card will be selected internally. This way, when the next turn comes up, the search for playable cards will begin from the far left side (index 0). This method also makes use of the `Player` field, which is set externally.

```
#region Private Methods

private void SelectCard(int index)
{
    StopAnimating();

    if (HasMove)
    {
        if (Player.IsMyTurn)
            cardSelectedSound.Play();
        selectedIndex = index;
        animatingSelected = true;
    }
    else
        selectedIndex = 0;
}
```

10. Add the method `SelectLastCard` to the `Private Methods` region. This method is used to select the last card in the list.

```
private void SelectLastCard()
{
    selectedIndex = Player.Cards.Count - 1;
}
```

11. In the `Private Methods` region, add the `StopAnimating` method, which resets animation of the cards. This is the last private method, so add the `#endregion` marker.

```
private void StopAnimating()
{
    stepValue = 0.0f;
    animateDistance = 0.0f;
    animatingSelected = false;
}

#endregion
```

These are the internal card selection methods. We need to expose some public methods that attempt to select cards based on user input, for example.

12. The first method we'll write is called SelectFirstPlayableCard. This method starts at the leftmost card and tries to find a playable card. If no cards are found, HasMove is set to false and the last card is selected internally. This method makes use of the static method CrazyEightsGameManager.CanPlayCard (which we haven't added yet), which checks to see if the selected card can be played. Add a region called Public Methods and add the SelectFirstPlayableCard method:

```
#region Public Methods

public void SelectFirstPlayableCard()
{
    StopAnimating();

    Card card;
    bool foundCard = false;
    for (int i = 0; i < Player.Cards.Count; i++)
    {
        card = Player.Cards[i];
        if (CrazyEightsGameManager.CanPlayCard(card))
        {
            foundCard = true;
            HasMove = true;
            SelectCard(i);
            break;
        }
    }

    if (foundCard == false)
    {
        HasMove = false; // No playable card found
        SelectLastCard();
    }
}

#endregion
```

13. In the Public Methods region, add a method called SelectNextCard, which is called when the user clicks the Right button of the Zune to select the next card to the right. This method starts at the currently selected card and moves toward the right of the deck. If no playable cards are found after looping over once, HasMove is set to false. If HasMove is already false (there are no playable cards), this method has no effect.

```
public void SelectNextCard()
{
    if (HasMove)
    {
        int startIndex = selectedIndex;
        selectedIndex++;
```

```
            // Search for playable cards
            while (selectedIndex != startIndex)
            {
                if (selectedIndex > Player.Cards.Count - 1) // loop over
                    selectedIndex = 0;

                if (CrazyEightsGameManager.CanPlayCard(Player.➥
Cards[selectedIndex]))
                    {
                        SelectCard(selectedIndex);
                        HasMove = true;
                        break;
                    }

                selectedIndex++;
            }

            // No playable card found
            if (selectedIndex == startIndex &&
                CrazyEightsGameManager.CanPlayCard(
                    Player.Cards[selectedIndex]) == false)

                HasMove = false;
        }
    }
```

14. Add a method called SelectPreviousCard to the Public Methods region. This method is
    basically the inverse of the SelectNextCard method. It moves to the left instead of the
    right, but otherwise does the same thing.

```
public void SelectPreviousCard()
{
    if (HasMove)
    {
        int startIndex = selectedIndex;
        selectedIndex--;

        while (selectedIndex != startIndex)
        {
            if (selectedIndex < 0) // Loop over
                selectedIndex = Player.Cards.Count - 1;

            if (CrazyEightsGameManager.CanPlayCard(Player.Cards➥
[selectedIndex]))
                {
                    SelectCard(selectedIndex);
                    HasMove = true;
                    break;
                }
```

```
                    selectedIndex--;
                }

            // No playable card found
            if (selectedIndex == startIndex &&
                CrazyEightsGameManager.CanPlayCard(
                    Player.Cards[selectedIndex]) == false)

                HasMove = false;
        }
    }
```

Next, we'll begin implementing the LoadContent, Update, and Draw methods. First, we need to load some textures to use. (We already added deck.png.)

15. Right-click the Content/Textures/Screens folder and choose Add Existing Item. Add playingBackground.png from Examples/Chapter 7/Artwork.

16. Right-click the Content/Textures/CardBackgrounds folder and choose Add Existing Item. Add the following four files from Examples/Chapter 7/Artwork: clubBackground. png, diamondBackground.png, heartBackground.png, and spadeBackground.png. These images will be overlaid on the screen when the suit is changed.

17. Add a new region called DrawableComponent Overrides. Override the LoadContent method as follows. This method takes some screen measurements and loads content (textures and a sound).

```
public override void LoadContent()
{
    // Get screen dimensions
    Viewport viewport = ScreenManager.Graphics.Viewport;
    screenCenter = new Vector2(viewport.Width / 2, viewport.Height / 2);
    screenWidth = viewport.Width;

    // Load sprite batch and textures
    spriteBatch = new SpriteBatch(ScreenManager.Graphics);
    deckTexture = ScreenManager.Content.Load<Texture2D>("Textures/deck");
    backgroundTex = ScreenManager.Content.Load<Texture2D>(
        "Textures/Screens/playingBackground");

    // Load in the card backgrounds for when an eight is played
    clubTex = ScreenManager.Content.Load<Texture2D>(
        "Textures/CardBackgrounds/clubBackground");
    diamondTex = ScreenManager.Content.Load<Texture2D>(
        "Textures/CardBackgrounds/diamondBackground");
    heartTex = ScreenManager.Content.Load<Texture2D>(
        "Textures/CardBackgrounds/heartBackground");
    spadeTex = ScreenManager.Content.Load<Texture2D>(
        "Textures/CardBackgrounds/spadeBackground");
```

```
    // Initialize text positions
    statusTextPosition = new Vector2(120, 155);
    statusTextOrigin = ScreenManager.SmallFont.MeasureString(statusText) / 2;

    cardSelectedSound = ScreenManager.Content.Load<SoundEffect>(
        "Sounds/CardSelect");

    base.LoadContent();
}
```

18. Override the Update method. Based on what you've seen already in this screen, you might be worried that this is a complicated method. Actually, the Update method is very simple. It handles the animation of the selected card, and modifies the status text based on whose turn it is and whether you have a playable card. Most of the nasty code is in the Draw method.

```
public override void Update(GameTime gameTime)
{
    if (animatingSelected)
    {
        stepValue += (float)gameTime.ElapsedGameTime.TotalSeconds / 0.2f;
        animateDistance = MathHelper.SmoothStep(0.0f, 20.0f, stepValue);
        if (stepValue >= 1.0f)
        {
            animatingSelected = false;
            stepValue = 0.0f;
        }
    }

    // Update status text
    if (Player != null)
    {
        if (Player.IsMyTurn)
        {
            if (HasMove == false)
            {
                statusText = "You have no playable cards.\r\n" +
                    "Press MIDDLE to draw a card.";
            }
            else
                statusText = "Select a card to play.";
        }
        else
            statusText = "Waiting for other players...";
    }

    statusTextOrigin = ScreenManager.SmallFont.MeasureString(statusText) / 2;
```

```
    base.Update(gameTime);
}
```

In this method, we first check to see if we are animating the selected card. If so, we add a slice of time to the step value. Then we calculate the distance away from the rest of the cards using a SmoothStep function with a minimum of 0 and a maximum of 20. This will cause the card to gradually move 20 pixels higher than the other cards when it is selected, highlighting it, in effect. Then the status text is modified to tell the player what to do based on the game status. If the player has no move, he is told to draw a card. If the player has a move, he is told to select a card to play. Otherwise, he is told that another player is busy.

19. We are left with the Draw method, which is admittedly rather complicated. Part of what makes this method so complex is the requirement to draw the cards with a stacked appearance, but the selected card must always appear on top. We will analyze this method in chunks so you can get a better feel for it. Go ahead and stub out the Draw method as follows:

```
public override void Draw(GameTime gameTime)
{

}
```

Add the following code to draw the background:

```
SharedSpriteBatch.Instance.Draw(backgroundTex, Vector2.Zero, Color.White);
```

The whole component should be drawn only if the player actually exists, so we need to wrap everything that follows in an if statement:

```
if (Player != null)
{
```

The next bit of code defines the width of the display area for the cards and the position where the cards will start being drawn. When there are more than five cards in view, the list of cards will show up in the full 220 pixels of space. Otherwise, the cards will be displayed in a smaller area, so that when two or three cards are available, they appear closer together instead of spaced really far apart. A spacing variable is also initialized. This variable indicates how much space (in pixels) exists between each of the cards, given the area they are confined to when distributed evenly across that area. If the cards end up overlapping, spacing will be negative. This code sets up those variables.

```
int width;
int startPosition;

if (Player.Cards.Count > 5)
{
    width = MAX_WIDTH;
    startPosition = 10;
}
```

```
    else
    {
        width = 150;
        startPosition = 45;
    }

    float spacing = (float)(width - (CARD_WIDTH * Player.Cards.Count)) /
        (Player.Cards.Count - 1);
```

Next, we set up four temporary variables. These store data needed for drawing each card: the depth to draw at, the destination vector (or point), the card to draw, and the tint color for the card (which will be gray if the card cannot be played).

```
float depth = 0.0f;
Vector2 destination = new Vector2();
Card card;
Color tintColor;
```

Now, we loop through all of the cards and draw them. The destination vector starts off with a Y component of 200, which is modified if the selected card is animating. The X component of this vector (startPosition) is added to as the loop proceeds. The tint color for the card is determined by whether the card can be played. If it's the current player's turn, the selected card is animated and drawn at the highest depth of 1.0f. Otherwise, all the cards are drawn with increasing depth values. The start position is then incremented by the spacing value times the card width. Draw calls with a depth value closer to 1.0f are drawn at the top, and those with depth values closer to 0 are drawn nearer the back. To accomplish the depth effect, we use the SharedSpriteBatch's Draw method that allows us to specify the sort mode, to which we supply FrontToBack.

```
for (int i = 0; i < Player.Cards.Count; i++)
{
    card = Player.Cards[i];
    destination.X = startPosition;
    destination.Y = 200;

    tintColor = CrazyEightsGameManager.CanPlayCard(card) ? Color.White : ➥
Color.Gray;

    if (i == selectedIndex && Player.IsMyTurn)
    {
        destination.Y = 200 - animateDistance;

        SharedSpriteBatch.Instance.Draw(SpriteSortMode.FrontToBack, ➥
deckTexture,
            destination, GetSourceRect(card), tintColor, 0.0f, Vector2.Zero,➥
1.0f,
            SpriteEffects.None, 1.0f);
    }
    else
```

```
    {
        depth += 0.001f;

        SharedSpriteBatch.Instance.Draw(SpriteSortMode.FrontToBack, ➥
deckTexture,
            destination, GetSourceRect(card), tintColor, 0.0f, Vector2.Zero,➥
1.0f,
            SpriteEffects.None, depth);
    }

    startPosition += CARD_WIDTH + (int)spacing;
}
```

We can then close the top-level if statement in which this for loop sits.

Regardless of whether we have a player assigned to this component yet, it should still draw the current play card, suit overlay (if any), and the status text. The current play card (or the card to be played against) is determined from the Crazy Eights game manager component as a static property, as are the SuitChanged and ActiveSuit properties. We'll implement those in the next section. The final blocks of code draw those three common components on the screen.

```
// Draw the discarded card
if (CrazyEightsGameManager.CurrentPlayCard != null)
{
    SharedSpriteBatch.Instance.Draw(deckTexture, currentCardPosition,
        GetSourceRect(CrazyEightsGameManager.CurrentPlayCard), Color.White,
        0.0f, Vector2.Zero, 1.0f, SpriteEffects.None, 1.0f);
}

// Draw the overlay if the suit has changed
if (CrazyEightsGameManager.SuitChanged)
{
    switch (CrazyEightsGameManager.ActiveSuit)
    {
        case Suit.Clubs:
            SharedSpriteBatch.Instance.Draw(
                clubTex, Vector2.Zero, overlayTintColor);
            break;
        case Suit.Diamonds:
            SharedSpriteBatch.Instance.Draw(
                diamondTex, Vector2.Zero, overlayTintColor);
            break;
        case Suit.Hearts:
            SharedSpriteBatch.Instance.Draw(
                heartTex, Vector2.Zero, overlayTintColor);
            break;
        case Suit.Spades:
            SharedSpriteBatch.Instance.Draw(
```

```
                spadeTex, Vector2.Zero, overlayTintColor);
            break;
    }
}

// Draw the status text, if any
SharedSpriteBatch.Instance.DrawString(ScreenManager.SmallFont,
    statusText, statusTextPosition, Color.White, 0.0f, statusTextOrigin, 1.0f,
    SpriteEffects.None, 0f);

base.Draw(gameTime);
```

That concludes the (rather hairy!) Draw method. Don't forget to check your curly braces!

Thankfully, this also concludes the player view component code. We have only a few things left to cover! One is the Crazy Eights game manager component, which you have heard a lot about. The time has come to finally implement this class and see what all the fuss is about.

Creating the Crazy Eights Game Manager Component

The LogicComponent class is responsible for handling all the rules and sending all the network messages for the Crazy Eights game. It abstracts away all of the game logic, so that the game play screen can just focus on being a screen. I'm not necessarily happy with the need to have some properties exposed as static, but for now, that's acceptable—it just works!

This component exists to run background logic only; it doesn't draw or load any kind of content. It's the engine behind our game; the glue in the woodwork; the . . . well, you get the picture.

1. In the CrazyEights project, add a new class called CrazyEightsGameManager.cs. Stub it out as shown:

```
using System;
using System.Collections.Generic;
using Microsoft.Xna.Framework.Net;
using GameStateManager;
using CardLib;

namespace CrazyEights
{
    public class CrazyEightsGameManager : LogicComponent
    {

    }
}
```

2. Add the following fields to the class in a region marked `Fields`. Some are marked `static` because other components and classes need to access these values. For example, there can only be one current card and active suit. This class also manages the deck, list of players, and so on. Some of these fields are only populated on the host side, however.

```
#region Fields

public CrazyEightsPlayer Me
{
    get;
    private set;
}

public Deck Deck
{
    get;
    private set;
}

public int TurnIndex
{
    get;
    private set;
}

public static Card CurrentPlayCard
{
    get;
    private set;
}

public List<CrazyEightsPlayer> Players
{
    get;
    private set;
}

public static bool SuitChanged
{
    get;
    private set;
}

// This field is marked private
private static Suit chosenSuit;
```

```
public static Suit ActiveSuit
{
    get
    {
        if (SuitChanged)
            return chosenSuit;
        else
            return CurrentPlayCard.Suit;
    }
}
```

```
#endregion
```

3. This engine also makes extensive use of events to notify other game elements when certain things happen. Specifically, there are events for when all players have joined, all cards have been dealt, players cards need to be updated, and when the game is won. Add a region for Events and Delegates and add this code:

```
#region Events and Delegates

public delegate void AllPlayersJoinedHandler();
public delegate void AllCardsDealtHandler();
public delegate void CardsUpdatedHandler();
public delegate void GameWonHandler(string playerName);

public event AllPlayersJoinedHandler AllPlayersJoined;
public event AllCardsDealtHandler AllCardsDealt;
public event CardsUpdatedHandler CardsUpdated;
public event GameWonHandler GameWon;

#endregion
```

4. Add a region for the constructor, which initializes these values and sets the current turn to a dummy index of -1.

```
#region Constructor(s)

public CrazyEightsGameManager(ScreenManager screenManager)
    : base(screenManager)
{
    Players = new List<CrazyEightsPlayer>();
    Deck = new Deck();
    TurnIndex = -1;
}

#endregion
```

5. Add a region called LogicComponent Overrides and add the Initialize method. This initializes the NetworkMessenger with the current ScreenManager (remember that we must initialize that class) and resets/shuffles the deck (which matters only on the host, as the deck is not used on the peers).

```
#region LogicComponent Overrides

public override void Initialize()
{
    NetworkMessenger.Initialize(ScreenManager);

    Deck.ResetDeck();
    Deck.Shuffle();
}

#endregion
```

6. Add a region called Public Static Methods. This contains the CanPlayCard method, which returns a Boolean value indicating whether the specified card is valid against the current play card. According to the rules, you can play a card if it matches the suit or value, or if it is an eight.

```
#region Public Static Methods

public static bool CanPlayCard(Card chosenCard)
{
    if (CurrentPlayCard == null)
        return false;

    if (chosenCard.Suit == ActiveSuit)
        return true;
    if (chosenCard.CardValue.Value == CurrentPlayCard.CardValue.Value)
        return true;
    if (chosenCard.CardValue.Value == 8)
        return true;

    return false;
}

#endregion
```

7. Add a Private Methods region and a private method to advance the current turn:

```
#region Private Methods

private void AdvanceTurn()
{
    TurnIndex++;
```

```
        // This will reset TurnIndex to zero when the turn
        // is equal to Players.Count and needs to reset.
        TurnIndex = TurnIndex % Players.Count;

        NetworkMessenger.Host_SetTurn(TurnIndex);
    }

    #endregion
```

8. Add a region called `Public Methods`. We will add two methods here. One will retrieve a player object by name, and the other will discard a specified card and set the current play card.

```
    #region Public Methods

    public CrazyEightsPlayer GetPlayerByName(string name)
    {
        foreach (CrazyEightsPlayer player in Players)
        {
            if (player.Name == name)
                return player;
        }

        throw new Exception("Player '" + name + "' not found.");
    }

    public void Discard(Card card)
    {
        Deck.Discard(card);
        CurrentPlayCard = Deck.DiscardedCards[Deck.DiscardedCards.Count - 1];
    }

    #endregion
```

9. Create a region called `Host-side Networking Methods`. These methods are responsible for initiating a message from the host (or receiving data when the host is the intended recipient). The networking methods utilize the static methods we wrote in the `NetworkMessenger` class. In the `Host_NewRound` method, we load all the players, deal all their cards, discard the first play card, and send the "Ready to Play" message. The `Host_SendPlayers` method is used to send out player data. The `Host_CardRequested` method is used to respond to a player asking for a card to be dealt.

```
    #region Host-side Networking Methods

    public void Host_NewRound()
    {
        Deck.ResetDeck();
        Deck.Shuffle();
```

```
        foreach (CrazyEightsPlayer player in Players)
        {
            for (int i = 0; i < 8; i++)
            {
                NetworkMessenger.Host_DealCard(Deck.Deal(), player);
            }
        }

        NetworkMessenger.Host_Discard(Deck.Deal());
        NetworkMessenger.Host_ReadyToPlay();

        AdvanceTurn();
    }

    public void Host_SendPlayers()
    {
        foreach (NetworkGamer gamer in ScreenManager.Network.Session.AllGamers)
        {
            NetworkMessenger.Host_SendPlayer(gamer);
        }
    }

    public void Host_CardRequested(string playerName)
    {
        Card dealtCard = Deck.Deal();
        NetworkMessenger.Host_DealCard(dealtCard, GetPlayerByName(playerName));
    }

    #endregion
```

10. Add a Peer Networking Methods region. This is for methods that any peer can invoke: PlayCard, RequestCard, and ChooseSuit.

```
    #region Peer Networking Methods

    public void PlayCard(Card card)
    {
        Me.Cards.Remove(card);
        if (Me.Cards.Count <= 0)
            NetworkMessenger.GameWon(Me.Name);
        else
            NetworkMessenger.PlayCard(card);
    }

    public void RequestCard()
    {
        NetworkMessenger.RequestCard(Me);
    }
```

```
public void ChooseSuit(Suit suit)
{
    NetworkMessenger.SendChosenSuit(suit);
}
```

```
#endregion
```

11. Finally, add a region called Receive Data, with a similarly named method. This method contains a big switch statement that checks for all of the available network messages. Remember that both the host and the peers will receive the same data they send, but this block of code is where you determine how to process the received messages. Let's start off by stubbing out this region and method:

```
#region Receive Data

public void ReceiveNetworkData()
{

}

#endregion
```

We are now working within the ReceiveNetworkData method. Add two string variables. The player name and serialized card value are used frequently, so we just moved them up here.

```
int card = -1;
string name = "";
```

Now we begin the "big read." This is a loop that checks for available data, then pops off the message type and decides what to do with it. Remember that we always send the network message type first, followed by the actual data. Also remember that every network message has a type, and that type is always sent first, so it is safe to pop that off before entering the switch statement.

```
foreach (LocalNetworkGamer gamer in ScreenManager.Network.Session.LocalGamers)
{
    while (gamer.IsDataAvailable)
    {
        NetworkGamer sender;
        gamer.ReceiveData(ScreenManager.Network.PacketReader, out sender);

        // Interpret the message type
        NetworkMessageType message =
            (NetworkMessageType)ScreenManager.Network.PacketReader.ReadByte();

        switch (message)
        {
            // Implementation following...
```

```
        }
    }
}
```

We are now working within the `switch` statement, where we determine what to do with received data. All of these cases should go in place of the `// Implementation follow-ing...` comment. I will describe what happens (in a declarative style) in each of these situations, case by case, so that you can see how we finally wrap around to the game logic. The first case occurs when the host deals someone a card. "If I am the intended recipient, I will add this card to my list and declare that my cards have changed."

```
case NetworkMessageType.HostDealCard:
    name = ScreenManager.Network.PacketReader.ReadString();
    card = ScreenManager.Network.PacketReader.ReadInt32();

    CrazyEightsPlayer player = GetPlayerByName(name);
    if (player.Equals(Me) || Me.IsHost)
    {
        player.DealCard(new Card(card));
        if (CardsUpdated != null)
            CardsUpdated();
    }
    break;
```

Next, "If the host says it has dealt all the cards, I will notify my components that play may begin by firing the appropriate event."

```
case NetworkMessageType.HostAllCardsDealt:
    if (AllCardsDealt != null)
        AllCardsDealt();
    break;
```

"When the host discards the initial card, I will make note of it and notify my components that cards have changed."

```
case NetworkMessageType.HostDiscard:
    card = ScreenManager.Network.PacketReader.ReadInt32();
    Discard(new Card(card));

    if (CardsUpdated != null)
        CardsUpdated();

    break;
```

"When the host sets the turn, I will set my turn flag accordingly (`true` if it is my turn; `false` otherwise). I will then update the cards."

```
case NetworkMessageType.HostSetTurn:
    int turn = ScreenManager.Network.PacketReader.ReadInt32();
    TurnIndex = turn;
```

```
    if (Players[turn].Equals(Me))
    {
        Me.IsMyTurn = true;
    }
    else
        Me.IsMyTurn = false;

    if (CardsUpdated != null)
        CardsUpdated();

    break;
```

"When the host sends player data, I will copy that player to my list. If that player is me, I will make note of which one is me. If the host has sent all the players, I will fire the appropriate event."

```
case NetworkMessageType.HostSendPlayer:
    name = ScreenManager.Network.PacketReader.ReadString();
    bool isHost = ScreenManager.Network.PacketReader.ReadBoolean();

    CrazyEightsPlayer newPlayer = new CrazyEightsPlayer(name, isHost);
    Players.Add(newPlayer);
    if (newPlayer.Name == ScreenManager.Network.Me.Gamertag)
    {
        this.Me = newPlayer;
    }

    if (Players.Count == ScreenManager.Network.Session.AllGamers.Count)
    {
        if (AllPlayersJoined != null)
            AllPlayersJoined();
    }
    break;
```

"When someone plays a card, I will make note of the card played (and whether it was an eight). If I am the host, I will discard this card into my deck, and then I will advance the turn."

```
case NetworkMessageType.PlayCard:
    card = ScreenManager.Network.PacketReader.ReadInt32();

    CurrentPlayCard = new Card(card);
    if (CurrentPlayCard.CardValue.Value != 8)
        SuitChanged = false;

    if (CardsUpdated != null)
        CardsUpdated();

    if (Me.IsHost)
```

```
    {
        Deck.Discard(CurrentPlayCard);
    }

    AdvanceTurn();

    break;
```

"If I am the host and someone requests a card, I will deal that player a new card."

```
case NetworkMessageType.RequestCard:
    name = ScreenManager.Network.PacketReader.ReadString();
    if (Me.IsHost)
        Host_CardRequested(name);
    break;
```

"If someone has chosen a suit after playing an eight, I will set the current suit to the one chosen."

```
case NetworkMessageType.SuitChosen:
    Suit suit = (Suit)ScreenManager.Network.PacketReader.ReadByte();
    SuitChanged = true;
    chosenSuit = suit;
    if (CardsUpdated != null)
        CardsUpdated();
    break;
```

"If someone has won the game, I will fire the appropriate event, so my screen knows to move to the game over screen."

```
case NetworkMessageType.GameWon:
    name = ScreenManager.Network.PacketReader.ReadString();
    if (GameWon != null)
        GameWon(name);
    break;
```

That concludes the method that receives network messages. You can see how each case responds differently. Some cases will process the sent data only if the machine running this code is the host. Others will be processed regardless of who the player is.

Now, we have all of the central components built and ready to go. We have three remaining pieces, and they are all super easy (they are short screens!). Let's start by building the suit selection screen, a simple menu that allows you to select a suit.

Creating the Suit Selection Menu

This suit select screen (shown earlier in Figure 7-11) is responsible for displaying a menu with four choices: Clubs, Diamonds, Hearts, and Spades. When the user clicks a menu item, an event is fired that indicates which suit was chosen via the event arguments.

1. Right-click the Screens folder in the CrazyEights game project and add a new class
   called SuitSelectionMenu.cs. This class will also contain a new kind of event argument,
   which exposes a value of type Suit. We'll start off the stub with this event argument
   type included:

```
using System;
using Microsoft.Xna.Framework;
using Microsoft.Xna.Framework.Graphics;

using CardLib;
using GameStateManager;

namespace CrazyEights
{
    public class SuitSelectionEventArgs : EventArgs
    {
        public Suit Suit
        {
            get;
            private set;
        }

        public SuitSelectionEventArgs(Suit suit)
            : base()
        {
            Suit = suit;
        }
    }

    public class SuitSelectionMenu : BaseMenuScreen
    {
        // Implementation to follow...
    }
}
```

2. In the SuitSelectionMenu class, add a Fields and Events region with the following
   fields and events:

```
#region Fields and Events

MenuEntry clubsEntry;
MenuEntry diamondsEntry;
MenuEntry heartsEntry;
MenuEntry spadesEntry;

Texture2D menuBackground;
```

```
public delegate void SuitSelectedHandler(SuitSelectionEventArgs e);
public event SuitSelectedHandler SuitSelected;

#endregion
```

3. Add the constructor, which sets the title:

```
#region Constructor(s)

public SuitSelectionMenu()
    : base("Select Suit")
{

}

#endregion
```

4. Right-click the Content/Textures/Screens folder and choose Add Existing Item. Add the file Examples/Chapter 7/Artwork/suitSelectBackground.png.

5. Add a region called Overrides. Override the LoadContent method, which loads the background for the screen.

```
public override void LoadContent()
{
    menuBackground = ScreenManager.Content.Load<Texture2D>(
        "Textures/Screens/suitSelectBackground");
    base.LoadContent();
}
```

6. Override the Initialize method, which creates menu items and wires up the appropriate event handlers. We will add the event handlers in step 8.

```
public override void Initialize()
{
    MenuEntries.Clear();

    clubsEntry = new MenuEntry("Clubs", ScreenManager.LargeFont);
    diamondsEntry = new MenuEntry("Diamonds", ScreenManager.LargeFont);
    heartsEntry = new MenuEntry("Hearts", ScreenManager.LargeFont);
    spadesEntry = new MenuEntry("Spades", ScreenManager.LargeFont);

    clubsEntry.Selected += new EventHandler<EventArgs>(ClubsSelected);
    diamondsEntry.Selected += new EventHandler<EventArgs>(DiamondsSelected);
    heartsEntry.Selected += new EventHandler<EventArgs>(HeartsSelected);
    spadesEntry.Selected += new EventHandler<EventArgs>(SpadesSelected);

    MenuEntries.Add(clubsEntry);
    MenuEntries.Add(diamondsEntry);
    MenuEntries.Add(heartsEntry);
    MenuEntries.Add(spadesEntry);
```

```
        base.Initialize();
    }
```

7. Override the Draw method and draw the background texture using the shared sprite batch.

```
public override void Draw(GameTime gameTime)
{
    SharedSpriteBatch.Instance.Draw(menuBackground, Vector2.Zero, Color.➥
White);
    base.Draw(gameTime);
}
```

8. Finally, add a region for Event Handlers and add the four special event handlers to the region. These event handlers instantiate new SuitSelectionEventArgs objects with the chosen suit. This way, subscribers will know which suit was selected.

```
#region Event Handlers

void ClubsSelected(object sender, EventArgs e)
{
    if (SuitSelected != null)
        SuitSelected(new SuitSelectionEventArgs(Suit.Clubs));
}

void DiamondsSelected(object sender, EventArgs e)
{
    if (SuitSelected != null)
        SuitSelected(new SuitSelectionEventArgs(Suit.Diamonds));
}

void HeartsSelected(object sender, EventArgs e)
{
    if (SuitSelected != null)
        SuitSelected(new SuitSelectionEventArgs(Suit.Hearts));
}

void SpadesSelected(object sender, EventArgs e)
{
    if (SuitSelected != null)
        SuitSelected(new SuitSelectionEventArgs(Suit.Spades));
}

#endregion
```

Ah, what a breath of fresh air it is to see a screen that's not very complex. Even with all the events, this screen is still very compact. The game over screen is even simpler. Both of these screens are used directly by the playing screen, which we will finalize after building the game over screen.

Building the Game Over Screen

The game over screen (shown earlier in Figure 7-13) is arguably the simplest in the entire game. It takes in the name of the winner, draws a background, and displays a message. When the user clicks the middle button, the game ends.

1. Right-click the `CrazyEights/Screens` folder and add a new class called `GameOverScreen.cs`. Stub it out as shown:

```
using Microsoft.Xna.Framework;
using Microsoft.Xna.Framework.Graphics;
using Microsoft.Xna.Framework.Audio;

using GameStateManager;

namespace CrazyEights
{
    public class GameOverScreen : BaseScreen
    {
        // Implementation to follow...
    }
}
```

2. Add the screen background texture to the `Content/Textures/Screens` folder. This is the file `Examples/Chapter 7/Artwork/gameOverScreen.png`.

3. Load the two sound effects. Right-click the `Content/Sounds` folder and choose Add Existing Item. Add the `Lose.wav` and `Win.wav` files from `Examples/Chapter 7/SoundFX`.

4. Add the following private fields to the `GameOverScreen` class:

```
#region Private Fields

// Text
private string text;
private Vector2 textOrigin, textPosition;

// Content
private Texture2D backgroundTex;
private SoundEffect sound;

// Flag
private bool isWinner;

#endregion
```

5. Add the constructor, which sets the text displayed.

```
#region Constructor(s)

public GameOverScreen(string winnerName, string myName)
    : base()
```

```
    {
        if (winnerName == myName)
        {
            isWinner = true;
            text = "You won!\r\n";
        }
        else
        {
            isWinner = false;
            text = "You lost.\r\n";
        }

        text += winnerName + " wins!";
    }

    #endregion
```

6. Add a region called BaseScreen Overrides. Override Draw (which draws the background and the status text) and HandleInput (which quits the game on a middle button press).

```
public override void Draw(GameTime gameTime)
{
    SharedSpriteBatch.Instance.Draw(backgroundTex, Vector2.Zero, Color.White);
    SharedSpriteBatch.Instance.DrawString(ScreenManager.SmallFont, text,
        textPosition, Color.White, 0.0f, textOrigin, 1.0f,
        SpriteEffects.None, 0.0f);
    base.Draw(gameTime);
}

public override void HandleInput(InputState input)
{
    if (input.MiddleButtonPressed)
        ScreenManager.Game.Exit();
}
```

7. Finally, override LoadContent, which loads the background texture and the appropriate sound (the lose or win sound). When the sound is loaded, it is played immediately.

```
public override void LoadContent()
{
    backgroundTex = ScreenManager.Content.Load<Texture2D>(
        "Textures/Screens/gameOverScreen");

    textPosition = new Vector2(120, 160);
    textOrigin = ScreenManager.SmallFont.MeasureString(text) / 2;

    if (isWinner)
        sound = ScreenManager.Content.Load<SoundEffect>("Sounds/Win");
```

```
    else
        sound = ScreenManager.Content.Load<SoundEffect>("Sounds/Lose");

    sound.Play();

    base.LoadContent();
}
```

That concludes the game over screen. The last main chunk of work we have to do is to complete the playing screen.

Wrapping Up the Playing Screen

The playing screen, PlayingScreen.cs, will bring together the game manager and the player view components to handle messaging between the two, and will respond to events that cause the game to change states.

1. Open PlayingScreen.cs, which we created earlier. It should look like this:

```
using Microsoft.Xna.Framework;
using GameStateManager;
using CardLib;

namespace CrazyEights
{
    public class PlayingScreen : BaseScreen
    {
        private bool isHost;

        public PlayingScreen(bool host)
        {
            isHost = host;
        }
    }
}
```

We will continue without having to remove any of this code.

2. Add the following three private fields to the PlayingScreen class (two components and one screen):

```
PlayerViewComponent playerView;
CrazyEightsGameManager gameManager;
SuitSelectionMenu suitMenu;
```

3. Create a region called BaseScreen Overrides. Here, we will start with the Initialize method. This method creates and adds the components, wires up event handlers, and starts the game if this is the host. It also listens for suits to be selected when appropriate.

```
#region BaseScreen Overrides

public override void Initialize()
{
    playerView = new PlayerViewComponent(ScreenManager);
    gameManager = new CrazyEightsGameManager(ScreenManager);
    Components.Add(gameManager);
    Components.Add(playerView);

    suitMenu = new SuitSelectionMenu();
    suitMenu.SuitSelected +=
        new SuitSelectionMenu.SuitSelectedHandler(SuitSelected);

    base.Initialize();

    gameManager.AllPlayersJoined +=
        new CrazyEightsGameManager.AllPlayersJoinedHandler(AllPlayersJoined);
    gameManager.AllCardsDealt +=
        new CrazyEightsGameManager.AllCardsDealtHandler(AllCardsDealt);
    gameManager.CardsUpdated +=
        new CrazyEightsGameManager.CardsUpdatedHandler(CardsUpdated);
    gameManager.GameWon +=
        new CrazyEightsGameManager.GameWonHandler(GameWon);

    if (isHost)
    {
        gameManager.Host_SendPlayers();
    }
}

#endregion
```

4. Override the `HandleInput` method. Left and Right will cycle through the player's cards if the player has a move. Back will remove the screen and return to the main menu. The middle button is multipurpose. If it's your turn, pressing the middle button will play the selected card (or draw cards until one is playable). If the card you played is an eight, it will allow you to select a suit.

```
public override void HandleInput(InputState input)
{
    if (input.NewRightPress)
    {
        if (playerView.HasMove)
            playerView.SelectNextCard();
    }

    if (input.NewLeftPress)
    {
```

```
            if (playerView.HasMove)
                playerView.SelectPreviousCard();
    }

    if (input.NewBackPress)
    {
        if (ScreenManager.Network.Session != null)
            ScreenManager.RemoveScreen(this);
    }

    if (input.MiddleButtonPressed && gameManager.Me.IsMyTurn)
    {
        if (playerView.HasMove)
        {
            Card selected = playerView.SelectedCard;
            if (selected.CardValue.Value == 8)
            {
                ScreenManager.AddScreen(suitMenu);
            }
            else
                gameManager.PlayCard(selected);
        }
        else
        {
            gameManager.RequestCard();
        }
    }

    base.HandleInput(input);
}
```

5. Override the Update method, which causes the game manager to receive network data.

```
public override void Update(GameTime gameTime, bool otherScreenHasFocus,
    bool coveredByOtherScreen)
{
    gameManager.ReceiveNetworkData();
    base.Update(gameTime, otherScreenHasFocus, coveredByOtherScreen);
}
```

6. Finally, add all of the event handler methods, which respond to events on the game manager and suit-selection menu objects:

```
#region Event Handlers

void GameWon(string playerName)
{
    ScreenManager.RemoveScreen(this);
```

```
        ScreenManager.AddScreen(new GameOverScreen(playerName, ➥
    gameManager.Me.Name));
    }

    void CardsUpdated()
    {
        playerView.SelectFirstPlayableCard();
    }

    void AllCardsDealt()
    {
        playerView.SelectFirstPlayableCard();
    }

    void AllPlayersJoined()
    {
        playerView.Player = gameManager.Me;

        if (isHost)
        {
            gameManager.Host_NewRound();
        }
    }

    void SuitSelected(SuitSelectionEventArgs e)
    {
        gameManager.ChooseSuit(e.Suit);
        ScreenManager.RemoveScreen(suitMenu);

        gameManager.PlayCard(playerView.SelectedCard);
    }

    #endregion
```

Notice that we are not actually drawing anything in this screen. That's because the player view component is already drawing everything automatically by virtue of being added to this screen. Another way to architect this would have been to have everything in the player view component exist in the playing screen instead. However, the player view component started as a way to display the cards in that stacked order, and it simply became easier to include all of the drawing in that component.

We have but one file left to modify, and then we will be finished!

Coding the Entry Point (Game.cs)

Now, we just need to make some modifications to the main game class. We are working with generated code here, so read carefully.

1. If you haven't already done so, rename the default `Game.cs` to `CrazyEightsGame.cs`.

2. Add the appropriate `using` directives:

```
using System;
using Microsoft.Xna.Framework;
using Microsoft.Xna.Framework.Graphics;

using CardLib;
using GameStateManager;
```

3. The only two fields you need on this class are the graphics device and the screen manager (you can remove the default sprite batch that is created for you):

```
public class CrazyEightsGame : Microsoft.Xna.Framework.Game
{
    GraphicsDeviceManager graphics;
    ScreenManager screenManager;
    // ... rest of class below ...
}
```

You can delete the entire `Initialize`, `Update`, and `UnloadContent` methods. We don't need them with all of the work our screen manager component does for us.

4. In the constructor, along with the generated code, create a new screen manager component, add it to the components collection, and add a main menu screen to it.

```
public CrazyEightsGame()
{
    graphics = new GraphicsDeviceManager(this);
    Content.RootDirectory = "Content";

    // Frame rate is 30 fps by default for Zune.
    TargetElapsedTime = TimeSpan.FromSeconds(1 / 30.0);

    screenManager = new ScreenManager(this);
    Components.Add(screenManager);

    // Start the game with the main menu screen.
    screenManager.AddScreen(new MainMenuScreen());
}
```

5. All you need in `LoadContent` is the initialization of the shared sprite batch object:

```
protected override void LoadContent()
{
    SharedSpriteBatch.Instance.Initialize(this);
}
```

6. All you need in the Draw method is the graphics device clear, the call to draw all components, and the explicit End for the shared sprite batch:

```
protected override void Draw(GameTime gameTime)
{
    GraphicsDevice.Clear(Color.DarkGreen);
    base.Draw(gameTime);
    SharedSpriteBatch.Instance.End();
}
```

It's Play Time!

The game is complete. Remember that if you can't get your version of the game to work, you can find the working version in the Examples/Chapter 7/CrazyEights folder.

Ensure both Zunes have wireless enabled, and deploy without debugging to both of them. On one Zune, create a new game. On the other Zune, choose Join Game and join the available session. Indicate you are ready by pressing the middle button. On the host Zune, press the middle button to start the game. Game play will begin, and the first person to run out of cards is the winner.

Summary

This book has taken you on a journey from the most basic XNA fundamentals to the more advanced concepts involved in creating a fully networked Zune game. You have learned about the media player, visualizers, landscape mode, and Zune pad input. You have learned good architecture techniques, such as sprite batch sharing and optimizing network usage.

Most of these concepts come into play regardless of the type of game you want to write. Moreover, the techniques and principles you learned in this book can be quickly applied to other XNA-capable platforms, such as the PC and Xbox 360.

A whole world of game development awaits you. Be sure to check out the samples at the Creators Club web site, http://creators.xna.com, to expand your knowledge even further. Please see the appendices for further reading and a quick reference for Zune development.

APPENDIX A

■■■

Recommended Resources

On the Web, you can find a wealth of information that will help you jump-start, complement, and expand your knowledge of XNA game development. Here, I have compiled a short list of online resources you can check out at your leisure.

Blogs

These bloggers have written about many XNA development topics:

Game Theory, Dan Waters (`http://www.danwaters.com`): As an academic evangelist, I travel the United States, showing Microsoft technology to students and faculty. My blog often covers gaming-related topics. You can find screencasts, source code, and more.

XNA Team Blog (`http://blogs.msdn.com/xna/`): The XNA team blog is run by the XNA community evangelist, currently Kathleen Sanders, formerly of 1UP.com fame. This is the place to check for all the official announcements regarding the XNA Framework.

Shawn Hargreaves Blog (`http://blogs.msdn.com/shawnhar/`): Shawn is a software development engineer on the XNA team. His blog focuses on XNA game development, and it is an excellent resource for some of the more challenging technical topics you may find yourself entrenched in during XNA development.

The ZBuffer, The ZMan (`http://www.thezbuffer.com/`): The ZMan (or, as I call him, Andy) is an XNA MVP whose blog details his exploits with Managed DirectX and XNA games. His blog also has plenty of XNA tutorials.

Nick on Tech, Nick Gravelyn (`http://www.nickontech.com/`): Nick and his brother develop games together for the Xbox, Zune, iPhone, and other popular platforms. Nick is well respected in the XNA community, and his blog ranges from the philosophical to the concrete.

Blue Rose Games, Bill Reiss (`http://www.bluerosegames.com/brg/`): Bill is a good friend of mine from the Florida .NET community. He has been an XNA and a Silverlight MVP, and is currently involved in creating games for the Web, the Zune, the Xbox, and more. Bill is a knowledgeable game developer and presents many tutorials on his web site for all to share.

Microsoft Resources

If you need official information, you can always check out what Microsoft offers online:

XNA Game Studio Documentation (http://msdn.microsoft.com/en-us/library/bb200104.aspx): This link will take you to the official XNA Game Studio 3.0 documentation. It can be very helpful if you need to know more about a class, method, or property, or how to accomplish certain tasks. There are also plentiful examples in the documentation.

XNA Creators Club (http://creators.xna.com/): The Creators Club is your one-stop shop for education, resources, samples, and more. As you take your knowledge to the next level, the Creators Club will prove to be a tremendously valuable resource.

XNA Developer Center (http://msdn.microsoft.com/en-us/xna/default.aspx): The XNA Developer Center is a portal site that aggregates many popular XNA RSS feeds and communities, along with updated news, samples, downloads, and more.

Creators Club Samples

There are seemingly limitless samples at the Creators Club. In particular, you should check out these:

Education catalog (http://creators.xna.com/en-US/education/catalog/): This is the link for the main list of all education resources available on the Creators Club web site.

Redistributable Font Pack (http://creators.xna.com/en-US/contentpack/fontpack): You can embed various fonts in your game, but many of them require special rights to redistribute. The fonts included in this sample are free and licensed by Microsoft for you to redistribute in your games.

Game State Management (http://creators.xna.com/samples/gamestatemanagement): Referenced heavily throughout this book, the Game State Management sample provides you with a great starting point for any game.

Network Game State Management (http://creators.xna.com/en-US/sample/network_game_state_mgt_sample): The same as the Game State Management sample, with the added benefit of including network support.

Marblets (http://creators.xna.com/starterkit/marblets): This starter kit shows you how to build a puzzle game using XNA. It currently works on the PC and Xbox 360.

Platformer Starter Kit (included with XNA Game Studio 3.0): This starter kit shows you how to build a platformer game, similar to Mario Bros. or Sonic on the XNA platform. It currently runs on the PC and Xbox 360.

■ ■ ■

Zune Development Quick Reference Guide

This appendix shows you how to accomplish many different effects outside the context of more detailed examples.

Animation

To animate a sprite, load a sprite sheet and change the source rectangle over time using a method to calculate the source rectangle.

```
private void UpdateSourceRect()
{
    int width = _texture.Width / _numFrames;
    int height = _texture.Height;
    int frameOffset = _currentFrameIndex * width;

    _sourceRect.X = frameOffset;
    _sourceRect.Y = 0;
    _sourceRect.Width = width;
    _sourceRect.Height = height;
}
```

Sprite animation is covered in Chapter 3.

Input Handling

Input handling is made much easier through the use of an input state component. You can find such a component in the downloadable code that accompanies this book (available from this book's details page at http://www.apress.com), within the Examples/Chapter 7/Shared folder. This component allows you to check for input in this fashion:

```
if (input.NewLeftPress)
{
    ProcessLeftPress();
}
```

Input handling is covered in Chapter 4.

Gesture Support

If you want to support gestures such as "flicking," you must track the start and end time of the touch on the touchpad and the direction tracked. This excerpt from Chapter 6 illustrates such code:

```
private void HandleTouchPad(GameTime gameTime)
{
    GamePadState state = GamePad.GetState(PlayerIndex.One);
    Vector2 zunePadVector = state.ThumbSticks.Left;

    if (isTracking)
    {
        // If the Zune pad is no longer being touched
        if (zunePadVector == Vector2.Zero)
        {
            // End tracking
            isTracking = false;
            totalTouchTime = gameTime.TotalRealTime.Subtract(touchStartTime);

            // Fling the ball
            FlingBall(totalTouchTime, touchStartPoint, touchEndPoint);
        }
        else
        {
            // Update the current end point
            touchEndPoint = zunePadVector;
        }
    }
    else
    {
        // If the Zune pad has been touched
        if (zunePadVector != Vector2.Zero)
        {
            // Start tracking
            velocity = 0.0f;
            ballDirection = Vector2.Zero;
            touchStartTime = gameTime.TotalRealTime;
            touchStartPoint = zunePadVector;
            isTracking = true;
        }
    }
}
```

Gesture support is covered in Chapter 6.

Forcing Screen Dimensions on Windows

If you make a copy of your Zune game for Windows, it may not appear the same size. To force the screen dimensions, add the following code in your game's Initialize method:

```
graphics.PreferredBackBufferHeight = 320;
graphics.PreferredBackBufferWidth = 240;
graphics.ApplyChanges();
```

Forcing screen dimensions is covered in Chapter 4.

Playing Music

You can play a specific Song object with the following line of code:

```
MediaPlayer.Play(song);
```

Alternatively, you can show the guide menu on the Zune, which will allow users to select their own background music.

```
#if ZUNE
Guide.Show();
#endif
```

Playing music is covered in Chapter 4.

Collision Detection

The simplest form of collision detection involves checking the intersection of two bounding rectangles:

```
private bool CollisionDetected(Vector2 aPosition, Texture2D aTexture, Vector2
    bPosition, Texture2D bTexture)
{
    Rectangle boundingBoxA = new Rectangle(aPosition.X, aPosition.Y, aTexture.Width,
        aTexture.Height);

    Rectangle boundingBoxB = new Rectangle(bPosition.X, bPosition.Y, bTexture.Width,
        bTexture.Height);

    return boundingBoxA.Intersects(boundingBoxB);
}
```

More detailed collision detection can be achieved using per-pixel collision detection, as in the following example. However, for performance reasons, it is better to first check for simple collision detection, as in the preceding snippet, before testing for per-pixel collision.

```
private bool CheckPerPixelCollision()
{
    // Get bounding rectangles for each object
```

```
        Rectangle greenBoundingBox = new Rectangle((int)greenBallPos.X,
            (int)greenBallPos.Y, greenBallTex.Width, greenBallTex.Height);

        Rectangle otherBoundingBox = new Rectangle((int)otherBallPos.X,
            (int)otherBallPos.Y, otherBallTex.Width, otherBallTex.Height);

        // Determine the rectangle of intersection and
        // dereference its properties for performance.
        Rectangle collisionRegion = Rectangle.Intersect(greenBoundingBox,
            otherBoundingBox);

        int left = collisionRegion.Left;
        int right = collisionRegion.Right;
        int top = collisionRegion.Top;
        int bottom = collisionRegion.Bottom;

        Color greenBallCurrentColor, otherBallCurrentColor;
        int greenBallColorIndex, otherBallColorIndex;

        // Loop horizontally through the collision region.
        for (int row = top; row < bottom; row++)
        {
            for (int column = left; column < right; column++)
            {
                greenBallColorIndex = GetColorIndex(greenBoundingBox, row, column);
                otherBallColorIndex = GetColorIndex(otherBoundingBox, row, column);

                greenBallCurrentColor = greenBallColorData[greenBallColorIndex];
                otherBallCurrentColor = otherBallColorData[otherBallColorIndex];

                if (greenBallCurrentColor.A != 0 && otherBallCurrentColor.A != 0)
                    return true;
            }
        }

        return false;
}
```

Collision detection is covered in Chapters 4 and 5.

Changing Game Properties

You can change the name, description, author, and other fields describing your game either by editing the contents of AssemblyInfo.cs or by right-clicking the game's Properties node and choosing Open (which effectively does the same thing). For the Crazy Eights game (built in Chapter 7), the values are as follows:

```
[assembly: AssemblyTitle("Crazy Eights")]
[assembly: AssemblyProduct("Crazy Eights")]
[assembly: AssemblyDescription("Crazy Eights on the Zune")]
[assembly: AssemblyCompany("")]
[assembly: AssemblyCopyright("Copyright © Dan Waters")]
[assembly: AssemblyTrademark("")]
[assembly: AssemblyCulture("")]
```

Avoid changing the GUID, also shown in `AssemblyInfo.cs`.
Changing game properties is covered in Chapter 5.

Changing the Thumbnail

You can change the game's thumbnail by right-clicking the game project in Visual Studio, choosing Properties, and clicking the Application tab. You can then browse to a new PNG file or specify one that already exists in the project.

Changing the game thumbnail is covered in Chapter 5.

Checking Battery Status

You can check the battery status of the Zune using properties of the `PowerStatus` class, as shown in this snippet:

```
StringBuilder sb = new StringBuilder();

// Write the battery's status (Charging, High, etc).
sb.Append("Battery Status: ");

// Check all the battery states
if ((PowerStatus.BatteryChargeStatus & BatteryChargeStatus.Charging)
    == BatteryChargeStatus.Charging)
{
    sb.AppendLine("Charging");
}
else
{
    switch (PowerStatus.BatteryChargeStatus)
    {
        case BatteryChargeStatus.Critical;
            // Do stuff
            break;
        // etc.
    }
}
```

Checking the battery status is covered in Chapter 6.

Drawing in Landscape Mode

Drawing in landscape mode (rotated clockwise 90 degrees) is accomplished through render targets. This Draw method uses a render target for the Zune, rotated 90 degrees counterclockwise:

```
protected override void Draw(GameTime gameTime)
{
    // Draw to the render target (backTexture)
    GraphicsDevice.SetRenderTarget(0, backTexture);
    GraphicsDevice.Clear(Color.Black);

    // Draw all textures and components as usual
    spriteBatch.Begin();
    spriteBatch.Draw(ballTex, Vector2.Zero, Color.White);
    base.Draw(gameTime);
    spriteBatch.End();

    // Draw to the screen (no render target)
    GraphicsDevice.SetRenderTarget(0, null);
    GraphicsDevice.Clear(Color.Black);

    // Draw the render target's texture to the screen, rotated and centered
    spriteBatch.Begin();
    spriteBatch.Draw(backTexture.GetTexture(), new Vector2(120, 160), null,
        Color.White, MathHelper.PiOver2, new Vector2(160, 120), 1.0f,
        SpriteEffects.None, 0);
    spriteBatch.End();
}
```

Landscape mode is covered in Chapter 6.

Using Storage

The Zune provides limited access to the file system through the XNA Framework's storage API. This snippet from Chapter 6 illustrates how a storage container is obtained and then read from and written to:

```
// Show the storage device and get the filename
Guide.BeginShowStorageDeviceSelector(this.GetStorageDevice, new object());
StorageContainer container = storageDevice.OpenContainer("MonkeyFeeder");
string filename = Path.Combine(container.Path, "highscore.dat");

// Open a file stream
FileStream file = File.Open(filename, FileMode.OpenOrCreate,
    FileAccess.ReadWrite);
```

```
int oldScore = -1;
StreamReader reader = new StreamReader(file);
try
{
    // Attempt to read from the file. If there is nothing, oldScore
    // will still be -1.
    oldScore = Convert.ToInt32(reader.ReadLine());
}
catch { }

if (score > oldScore)
{
    highScoreText = "\r\nNew High Score: " + score;
    StreamWriter writer = new StreamWriter(file);
    // Erase the contents of the file and write the new score.
    file.SetLength(0);
    writer.WriteLine(score);
    writer.Close();
}
else
{
    highScoreText = "\r\nHigh Score: " + oldScore;
}

// Close the file
file.Close();

// Dispose the container to commit the storage changes
container.Dispose();
```

Using Zune storage is covered in Chapter 6.

Creating Visualizers

You can visualize the currently playing track using the MediaPlayer's GetVisualizationData method. This method returns a collection of samples and a collection of frequencies that represent the distribution of each at that instant in time. You can then write your own special algorithm to visualize that information however you choose. The exercise in Chapter 6 uses the following snippet:

```
for (int i = 0; i < visData.Samples.Count; i++)
{
    // Draw the frequency bar at the top using rectangles
    spriteBatch.Draw(pixelTex,
        new Rectangle((int)waveformPosition.X + (int)waveformBoxOrigin.X,
            i + (int)waveformPosition.Y,
            (int)(visData.Frequencies[i] * waveformHeight), 1),
            tintColor);
```

```
    if (useFillDisplay)
    {
        // Draw samples using rectangles
        spriteBatch.Draw(pixelTex,
            new Rectangle((int)waveformPosition.X,
                i + (int)waveformPosition.Y,
                (int)(visData.Samples[i] * waveformHeight),
                1),
                Color.White);
    }
    else
    {
        // Draw samples using "pixels"
        spriteBatch.Draw(pixelTex,
            new Vector2(waveformPosition.X + visData.Samples[i] *
                waveformHeight,
            waveformPosition.Y + i),

        Color.White);
    }
}
```

Creating visualizers is covered in Chapter 6.

APPENDIX C

■ ■ ■

Check Your Knowledge Answers

This appendix contains the answers to the questions in the "Check Your Knowledge" sections of Chapters 2 through 6.

Chapter 2

1. The SpriteBatch object is used to draw textures to the screen.

2. The Initialize method is where you set the initial state and values of objects and fields unrelated to content.

3. You change the background color of the game by modifying the color specified in the Draw method at graphics.GraphicsDevice.Clear(Color.CornflowerBlue).

4. The Update method is used to change the state of your game on an ongoing basis.

5. The game runs in a default scenario of a fixed-step time loop. That means that every 1/60 second, the rotation variable will be incremented by 0.02. Since the rotation variable is incremented at a regular interval rather than a variable one, it will always be smooth.

6. False. A local copy is always made so that the file can be easily built and loaded by the game.

7. The gameTime variable, passed to the Update method by the XNA framework's game loop, is used to retrieve all aspects of current game time.

8. The Texture2D object represents a drawable 2D texture.

9. You must call spriteBatch.Begin() to start drawing to a SpriteBatch object, and consequently you must call spriteBatch.End() after you are finished drawing.

10. You use the LoadContent method to initialize objects that hold references to content.

Chapter 3

1. PNG is the most practical file type for textures that make use of alpha blending.

2. The 3D asset types are not supported on the Zune because it does not have any hardware acceleration capabilities.

3. A `.spritefont` file contains an XML-formatted description of a font that exists on the development computer.

4. False. The `SoundEffect` class can play only WAV files.

5. The content loader of the content pipeline transforms a compiled asset to a managed object at runtime.

6. The Zune's screen resolution is 240 pixels wide by 320 pixels high.

7. The Zune display's color depth is 16-bit color with an 8-bit alpha channel.

8. The Content DOM provides a model for commonly used asset types.

9. The XML content type can be used for configuration or special text-based data.

10. You must omit the file extension of an asset when loading it at runtime because assets are compiled to the XNB format and no longer exist in their original format at runtime.

Chapter 4

1. To access XNA Game Studio Device Center, from Visual Studio, choose Tools ➤ Launch XNA Game Studio Device Center.

2. Take a screenshot of a game running on the Zune by right-clicking the device in XNA Game Studio Device Center and choosing Take Screen Capture.

3. Running with debugging can increase overhead, so run without debugging when you want an accurate approximation of how your game will really run when it is deployed.

4. Textures that are optimal for the Zune are those whose width and height are powers of 2 (for example. 2, 4, 8, 16, 128).

5. The Zune pad maps to the left thumbstick.

6. To ensure that Zune-specific code is not compiled into the Windows version of the game assembly, use conditional preprocessor directives like `#if ZUNE`.

7. To force a Windows game to match the preferred back buffer width and height, call the `ApplyChanges` method of the graphics object after setting the preferred back buffer width and height.

8. The `MediaPlayer` class is used to play, pause, and stop music and control the volume.

9. An alternative to writing your own music browser and player is to use the built-in Zune guide interface, which you can display by calling `Guide.Show()`.

10. `GetAlbumArt` returns a `Texture2D` object ready for your use.

Chapter 5

1. Unit vectors normally indicate direction, because they have a length of 1.

2. Set the x component of the vector to the sine of the angle and the y component to the cosine of the angle. Negate the y component to make it work correctly in the XNA coordinate system, which is vertically flipped.

3. The `MeasureString` method measures text and returns a `Vector2` object indicating the width and height.

4. The `Rectangle.Intersects` method allows you to check for intersection with another `Rectangle` object.

5. A pro is that per-pixel collision detection is far more accurate than simple collision detection. A con is that per-pixel collision detection is extremely costly, especially on the Zune, and will likely cause significant slowdowns.

6. Simple game state management uses an enumeration with a list of the possible game states in it.

7. While `DrawableGameComponent` inherits from `GameComponent`, it is different in that it has the added benefit of knowing how to draw itself, as well as a `Visible` property to show and hide it.

8. Set the game component's `.Enabled` property to `false` to stop it from updating. Set its `.Visible` property to `false` to stop it from being drawn.

9. These properties are found in the `AssemblyInfo.cs` file.

10. Angles in XNA are measured in radians, not degrees. The `MathHelper` class provides constants for different measures of pi to help you convert if necessary.

Chapter 6

1. You can use `PowerLineStatus` to determine if the Zune is plugged in to its charger.

2. Alpha blending shows the object drawn below it. Additive blending blends the colors together using an additive algorithm.

3. Each new sprite batch created, and each call to `Begin()`, has associated overhead. Consolidating sprite batches is the correct thing to do. It fulfills the objective of writing sprite data as a batch rather than individually.

4. The `Services` collection indexes the objects added to it by the object's type.

5. You can use the `SharedSpriteBatch` class to consolidate all of your sprite batch activity globally.

6. Render targets are preferred when performance is not an issue. When performance degrades, try rotating with matrices or by using draw overloads that take a rotation argument.

7. After drawing to a render target, write the contents of that back texture to the screen as follows:

```
GraphicsDevice.SetRenderTarget(0, null);
```

8. When using render targets, keep all code in portrait coordinates. The screen is not rotated until immediately before it was drawn. Keep yourself sane.

9. The storage device is obtained on the Zune by calling `Guide.BeginShowStorageDevice-Selector`, which asynchronously calls a callback method, where you can call `Guide.EndShowStorageDeviceSelector`, which returns a `StorageDevice` object.

10. Use the `MediaPlayer.GetVisualizationData(visData)` to fill a `VisualizationData` object. Use this object's `Samples` collection, which is an enumerable collection of 256 floats.

Index

You Need the Companion eBook

Your purchase of this book entitles you to buy the companion PDF-version eBook for only $10. Take the weightless companion with you anywhere.

We believe this Apress title will prove so indispensable that you'll want to carry it with you everywhere, which is why we are offering the companion eBook (in PDF format) for $10 to customers who purchase this book now. Convenient and fully searchable, the PDF version of any content-rich, page-heavy Apress book makes a valuable addition to your programming library. You can easily find and copy code—or perform examples by quickly toggling between instructions and the application. Even simultaneously tackling a donut, diet soda, and complex code becomes simplified with hands-free eBooks!

Once you purchase your book, getting the $10 companion eBook is simple:

❶ Visit **www.apress.com/promo/tendollars/**.

❷ Complete a basic registration form to receive a randomly generated question about this title.

❸ Answer the question correctly in 60 seconds, and you will receive a promotional code to redeem for the $10.00 eBook.